# TimeOut

# Shanghai

**timeout.com/shanghai**

Mom - LV purse
Dad - Terracotta Warrior
Mike -
Joe - Terracotta Warrior
J & A - chopsticks
J & K - paper cutout
C & R - bracelet & tee shirt
Kate - bracelet
Auntie B -
Evan -
Daisy / Priscilla

**Published by Time Out Guides Ltd,** a wholly owned subsidiary of Time Out Group Ltd.
Time Out and the Time Out logo are trademarks of Time Out Group Ltd.

© **Time Out Group Ltd 2006**
Previous edition 2004

10 9 8 7 6 5 4 3 2 1

**This edition first published in Great Britain in 2006 by Ebury Publishing**
Ebury Publishing is a division of The Random House Group Ltd,
20 Vauxhall Bridge Road, London SW1V 2SA

**Random House Australia Pty Limited** 20 Alfred Street, Milsons Point, Sydney, New South Wales 2061, Australia
**Random House New Zealand Limited** 18 Poland Road, Glenfield, Auckland 10, New Zealand
**Random House South Africa (Pty) Limited** Isle of Houghton, Corner Boundary
Road & Carse O'Gowrie, Houghton 2198, South Africa

Random House UK Limited Reg. No. 954009

**Distributed in USA by Publishers Group West**
1700 Fourth Street, Berkeley, California 94710

**Distributed in Canada by Publishers Group Canada**
250A Carlton Street, Toronto, Ontario M5A 2L1

For further distribution details, see www.timeout.com

To 31 December 2006: ISBN 1-904978-67-3
From 1 January 2007: ISBN 9781904978671

A CIP catalogue record for this book is available from the British Library

Colour reprographics by Wyndeham Icon, 3 & 4 Maverton Road, London E3 2JE

Printed and bound in Germany by Appl

Papers used by Ebury Publishing are natural, recyclable products made from wood grown in sustainable forests

**Time Out Guides Limited**
**Universal House**
**251 Tottenham Court Road**
**London W1T 7AB**
**Tel  + 44 (0)20 7813 3000**
**Fax + 44 (0)20 7813 6001**
**Email guides@timeout.com**
**www.timeout.com**

## Editorial

**Editor** Ismay Atkins
**Consultant Editor** Rebecca Catching
**Deputy Editor** Simon Coppock
**Copy editing** Natalie Whittle
**Listings Checkers** Claire Lee, Spencer Dodington,
   Shen Yong
**Proofreader** Tamsin Shelton
**Indexer** Holly Pick

**Editorial/Managing Director** Peter Fiennes
**Series Editor** Ruth Jarvis
**Deputy Series Editor** Lesley McCave
**Business Manager** Gareth Garner
**Guides Co-ordinator** Holly Pick
**Accountant** Kemi Olufuwa

## Design

**Art Director** Scott Moore
**Art Editor** Pinelope Kourmouzoglou
**Senior Designer** Josephine Spencer
**Graphic Designer** Henry Elphick
**Digital Imaging** Dan Conway
**Ad Make-up** Jenni Prichard

## Picture Desk

**Picture Editor** Jael Marschner
**Deputy Picture Editor** Tracey Kerrigan
**Picture Researcher** Helen McFarland

## Advertising

**Sales Director** Mark Phillips
**International Sales Manager** Ross Canadé
**International Sales Executive** Simon Davies
**Advertising Sales** (Shanghai) Nicole Qian
**Advertising Assistant** Kate Staddon

## Marketing

**Group Marketing Director** John Luck
**Marketing Manager** Yvonne Poon
**Marketing & Publicity Manager, US** Rosella Albanese

## Production

**Group Production Director** Mark Lamond
**Production Manager** Brendan McKeown
**Production Coordinator** Caroline Bradford

## Time Out Group

**Chairman** Tony Elliott
**Managing Director** Mike Hardwick
**Financial Director** Richard Waterlow
**TO Magazine Ltd MD** David Pepper
**Group General Manager/Director** Nichola Coulthard
**TO Communications Ltd MD** David Pepper
**Group Art Director** John Oakey
**Group IT Director** Simon Chappell

## Contributors

**Introduction** Ismay Atkins. **History** Andrew Humphreys. **Shanghai Today** JFK Miller (*The new rich* Lisa Movius). **Megalopolis Now** Andrew Humphreys. **Where to Stay** Amy Fabris-Shi (*Peace at the Cathay* Peter Hibbard). **Sightseeing Introduction** Andrew Humphreys. **The Bund** Andrew Humphreys. **People's Square & Nanjing Donglu** Spencer Dodington (*Shanghai Museum in a day* Simon Ostheimer). **Jingan** Mark Kitto (*Walk on* Peter Hibbard). **The Old City** Spencer Dodington (*Totally Lupu-y* Andrew Humphreys; *Walk on* Simon Ostheimer). **Xintiandi** Spencer Dodington. **French Concession** Andrew Humphreys. **Xujiahui, Hongqiao & Gubei** Rebecca Catching. **Pudong** Sophie Loras (*Pearl of the East* Phil Boyle). **Hongkou** Spencer Dodington. **Restaurants & Cafés** Andrew Humphreys, Jarrett Wrisley (*Shanghai dumplings* Jarrett Wrisley; *Hairy crabs* Mary Helen Trent). **Pubs & Bars** Andrew Humphreys, Jarrett Wrisley. **Shops & Services** Miriam Rayman. **Festivals & Events** Rebecca Catching. **Children** Kristin Baird Rattini. **Film** Andrew Humphreys (*The goddess of Shanghai* JFK Miller). **Galleries** Rebecca Catching. **Gay & Lesbian** James Lewis. **Mind & Body** Amy Fabris-Shi. **Music** Lisa Movius (*Hip hop hopes* Miriam Rayman). **Nightlife** Paul Emmerson. **Performing Arts** Rebecca Catching (*Turning tricks* Sophie Loras). **Sport & Fitness** Miriam Rayman. **Getting Started** Lim Hui Sin. **The Canal Towns** Lim Hui Sin. **Hangzhou & Moganshan** Lisa Movius, Mark Kitto. **Suzhou** Lim Hui Sin. **Putuoshan** Lim Hui Sin. **Directory** Spencer Dodington.

The Editor would like to thank Chen Hangfeng, Tim Hoerle, Andrew Humphreys and all contributors to previous editions of *Time Out Shanghai*, whose work forms the basis for parts of this book.

The Editor flew to Shanghai with Virgin Atlantic (www.virgin-atlantic.com; direct flights daily from Heathrow).

**Maps** JS Graphics (john@jsgraphics.co.uk); maps are based on material supplied by Netmaps.

**Photography** by Mark Parren Taylor, except: page 10 Roger Viollet/Getty Images; pages 13, 16 Bettmann/Corbis; page 17 Taylor Gallery, London/The Bridgeman Art Library; pages 82,139 (bottom image) Jonathan Perugia; page 143 Insh; page 155 Getty Images; page 161 Imagenet; page 164 CPA Media; page 165 Ji Wenyu; page 170 Uniphoto/AAA Collection; page 180 Mathias Guillin; page 191 John Gollings; pages 208, 212 Giles Robberts/Alamy.

The following images were provided by the featured establishments/artists: pages  36, 71, 129, 152, 174, 177, 188.

# Contents

# Introduction

The 21st century, economists say, belongs to China – and we've no reason to doubt them. The breakneck speed at which the country's economy has developed over the course of just a few decades has left the rest of the world looking on in disbelief, slack-jawed and blinking their eyes. China is in the middle of a boom of staggering proportions, and nowhere is this more palpable than in Shanghai – China's largest and most dynamic city, its designated modern, no… postmodern… *beyond* modern showpiece.

A grey industrial port town only 25 years ago, Shanghai is now big, bright and brazen. It contains over 17 million people, 4,000 skyscrapers (with another 1,000 in the pipeline) and 100,000 taxis; it has video screens so huge they fill entire buildings, neon-lit elevated highways, and buildings shaped like rockets and spaceships. Beijing may have the grand historical edifices and the cultural edge, but Shanghai most certainly has the glitz. Everyone wants a piece of the action. It's the new darling of the jet set and the main topic of conversation for big-bucks investors – Shanghai attracted more direct foreign investment in 2004 than Mexico and Indonesia put together, according to US journalist Ted Fishman in his dramatically titled book *China, Inc.: How the Rise of the Next Superpower Challenges America and the World.* Politicians in the US and Europe are keeping a very close eye on their new competitor, while thousands of East Asian movers and shakers have simply upped and moved in.

For the savvy tourist (and visitor numbers have more than doubled since 2003), rampant capitalism and a rash of shiny new malls won't mean all that much. Instead they will find themselves sucked in by the tangible energy of a city in the throes of major change, overwhelmed by the heady feeling – gazing across the Huangpu River at the stupefying sci-fi skyline of Pudong – that they're in the front row for an exclusive preview of the future.

This is precisely the effect the city planners crave, as they bulldoze historical areas to make way for the polished and the futuristic. But it's a mistake to overlook the lure of Shanghai's captivating past. In its ritzy 1930s heyday, when the city was divided up into foreign concessions, Shanghai was the most powerful business centre in Asia. It had the architecture, ballrooms and glamorous restaurants to prove it – not to mention brothels, opium dens and gangsters. The colonial period lives on in the shape of splashy buildings along the riverside Bund, revivified by a sprinkling of world-class bars and restaurants; on civilised tree-lined streets of the former French Concession where there's now buzzing nightlife; and, among the fast-disappearing – but still just about visible – remnants of traditional *shikumen* housing.

Nothing and no one, however, is allowed to get in the way of the city planners' drive for development and profit – not heritage buildings, not the dispersal of working-class communities, not even environmental concerns. The result is a city that is simultaneously exhilarating and alarming – but one that has become a compelling and vital spectacle.

It's full-on, it's frantic and, with the world's largest Ferris wheel on the way in time for World Expo 2010, it's time to climb aboard and enjoy the ride.

## ABOUT TIME OUT CITY GUIDES

This is the second edition of *Time Out Shanghai* one of an expanding series of Time Out guides produced by the people behind the successful listings magazines in London, New York and Chicago. Our guides are all written by resident experts who have striven to provide you with all the most up-to-date information you'll need to explore the city or read up on its background, whether you're a local or a first-time visitor.

## THE LOWDOWN ON THE LISTINGS

We have tried to make this book as easy to use as possible. Addresses, phone numbers, metro information, opening times and admission

prices are all included in the listings. However, businesses can change their arrangements at any time. Before you go out of your way, we'd strongly advise you to phone ahead to check opening times and other particulars. While every effort and care has been made to ensure the accuracy of the information contained in this guide, the publishers cannot accept responsibility for any errors it may contain.

## THE LIE OF THE LAND

Shanghai is massive, but the areas of interest covered by this book are restricted to a manageable few square kilometres of the city centre, either side of the banks of the Huangpu

metro is partially signed in English so we've included metro details with each listing. For more information on getting around and the various transport options, *see pp216-218.*

## ESSENTIAL INFORMATION

For all the practical information you might need for visiting the area – including visa and customs information, details of local transport, a listing of emergency numbers, information on local weather and a selection of useful websites – turn to the Directory at the back of this guide. It begins on page 216.

## PRICES AND PAYMENT

We have noted where venues such as shops, hotels and restaurants accept the following credit cards: American Express (**AmEx**), Diners Club (**DC**), MasterCard (**MC**) and Visa (**V**). Many shops, restaurants and attractions will also accept other cards, including JCB, as well as travellers' cheques issued by a major financial institution (such as American Express).

Prices in this book are given in Chinese *reminbi* (RMB). At the time of going to press exchange rates were around RMB 8 to the US dollar or RMB 15 to the pound sterling.

The prices we've supplied should be treated as guidelines, not gospel. If prices vary wildly from those we've quoted, please write and let us know. We aim to give the best and most up-to-date advice, so we always want to know if you've been badly treated or overcharged.

## TELEPHONE NUMBERS

The international dialling code for China is 86 and the code for Shanghai is 021 (drop the zero if calling from overseas). Follow with the eight-figure number as given in this guide.

## MAPS

The map section at the back of this guide includes a useful overview map of the city, as well as tiled street maps. Map references throughout this guide indicate the page number and square for every venue. The street maps start on page 242, and now pinpoint specific locations of hotels (**❶**), restaurants and cafés (**❶**) and bars (**❶**).

## LET US KNOW WHAT YOU THINK

We hope you enjoy the *Time Out Shanghai Guide*, and we'd like to know what you think of it. We welcome tips for places that you consider we should include in future editions and take note of your criticism of our choices. You can email us at guides@timeout.com.

River. This central district is easy to fathom, and small enough to explore on foot. For further details of the city's geography, *see p46.*

Street signs are in both English and Chinese. Because many streets are so long they are often prefixed by 'north', 'south', 'east', 'west' or 'central'. So the main highway Yanan Lu progresses from Yanan Xi Lu (West Yanan Road) to Yanan Zhong Lu (Central Yanan Road) to Yanan Dong Lu (East Yanan Road). Maoming Lu is either Maoming Nan Lu (South Maoming Lu) or Maoming Bei Lu (North Maoming Lu)

Travelling around on public transport is made difficult by the language barrier, but the

There is an online version of this book, along with guides to over 100 international cities, at **www.timeout.com**.

# timeout.com

Over 50 of the world's greatest
cities reviewed in one site.

# In Context

The **French Concession** in 1895.

# History

From muddy port town to towering metropolis in just a few centuries – Shanghai has always taken the fast lane.

Throughout its history Shanghai has been shaped by lucrative trade, cheap and plentiful labour and relative calm compared with the rest of China. While wars and unrest plagued interior China for most of the late 19th and early 20th centuries, Shanghai was largely safeguarded by business-motivated Chinese-Western coalitions. This gave the city's residents an aloof feeling that they were impervious to the ills of the rest of China. Indeed, were they part of China at all?

## OPIUM OPENS THE GATES

Prior to 1842 Shanghai was a prosperous but slightly isolated Chinese town. Its position on the Yangtze River delta with a safe harbour on the tributary Huangpu River guaranteed its importance as a trading port.

Rice, cotton and other crops were brought to Shanghai to be carried on barges and sampans up the Yangtze and its tributaries or to be shipped down the coast and thence inland again along China's extensive canal network.

Shanghai at this time was apparently a pleasant sight: a bustling, modestly sized centre of commerce encircled by a wall three and a half miles (5.6 kilometres) in circumference. Local leaders had built the city walls in the 16th century to protect themselves from Japanese coastal raiders. On the flat marshy delta that stretched around were numerous fishing and farming villages, but otherwise, the landscape was featureless.

Unlike most cities built upon trade, Shanghai, along with China's other ports, remained exclusively Chinese. It had long been the desire of the ruling Qing Dynasty (1644-1912) to keep its borders sealed from the outside world. Opinion at the Beijing court was that foreigners were uncivilised, thus there could be no reason to interact with them.

This did not mean that there was no contact at all. Since the early 19th century the British East India Company and others had exported Chinese tea, silks and porcelain to Britain. However, they never had anything of equal value to sell to China. To redress this situation the enterprising, if unprincipled, British decided to capitalise on the Chinese penchant for opium smoking. They introduced an Indian-grown product that was more refined than the Chinese version. In a short spell of time, the balance of trade was reversed.

Unable to curb the increasingly widespread opium addiction among its populace, the Qing court instead concentrated on shutting down the drug industry. Britain responded by sending gunboats under the premise of protecting free trade in an action that came to be known as the First Opium War. The expected results were swift: a few skirmishes on the coast were followed by Chinese acquiescence to all British demands at the 1842 Treaty of Nanking. Among those demands was that China cede Hong Kong to Britain and the British right to trade and reside in five mainland Chinese cities: Ningbo, Amoy (Xiamen), Fuzhou, Guangzhou and Shanghai. In 1843 the first British traders arrived in Shanghai and were allotted 0.2 square mile (0.6 square kilometre) of muddy riverbank, just north of the walled city.

### HARDSHIP CITY

The British called their land the British Settlement, reflecting the fact that it was neither a leased territory nor a government-controlled colony. They named their stretch of riverfront the Bund, a Hindi word meaning 'embankment' that the traders brought with them from India. These early traders governed themselves under the laws of their own country, a right called extraterritoriality. The US and France jealously claimed the same concessions from the beleaguered Qing court. The Americans settled north of Suzhou Creek while the French were sandwiched in between the British Settlement and the Chinese walled city to the south.

As late as 1848, there were fewer than 100 resident foreigners in Shanghai. Their mudflat settlements resembled the colonial bungalow style favoured in South-east Asia and India, with wide verandas to shade the buildings from the heat of summer. The city at this time was considered a 'hardship post' on account of the bitter winters and stiflingly hot summers, regular flooding, pestilent mosquitoes and foul stenches. 'As regards the people who live in this region,' wrote an early arrival, quoted in Pat Barr's *To China With Love: the Lives and Times of Protestant Missionaries in China*,

'the dampness moistens them, the saltiness stiffens them, the wind shrivels them and the stagnant waters poison them.' There was also an almost complete absence of European females. Foreign men found sexual solace in service professionals from China, the Philippines and elsewhere. Otherwise, leisure conformed to the traditional British Empire pursuits of horses and shooting. Early expatriates constructed Shanghai's first racetrack just inland from the Bund (later to be superseded by a larger track on what is now People's Square).

Small and underpopulated, the foreign settlements found themselves at risk from the rising tide of the Taiping Rebellion. In 1837 a village schoolmaster near Canton took the teaching of a Methodist missionary from America to heart and declared himself 'God's Chinese Son', or Tien Wang, the Celestial King. His religious preaching quickly turned into propaganda of rebellion against the ruling Qings. His movement to create Taiping, the 'reign of eternal peace', spread to become effectively a civil war in which 20 to 30 million people are believed to have died.

> ### 'Shanghai's first fortunes were amassed by an emerging elite of property barons.'

In 1860 and 1862 Taiping forces menaced Shanghai, but were repulsed by British and French expeditionary forces led by a 30-year-old general, Charles George Gordon, who would later go on to be immortalised as the imperial Victorian hero Gordon of Khartoum.

### CONSOLIDATION OF FOREIGN POWER

The rebellion irrevocably altered Shanghai. Before the insurrection, the foreign-controlled part of Shanghai had been dwarfed by the larger Chinese city. By the end of hostilities the reverse was true. Foreign militias had proven their overwhelming strength and ability to protect property and civilians. Not so in the Chinese city where gangsters known as the 'Small Swords', as well as militant factions allied to either Qing or Taiping, were destroying property and terrorising residents. The foreign settlements took pity on the Chinese and offered shelter – but at a price. Driven by Chinese demand, the cost of an acre of land soared from £50 in 1850 to £20,000 in 1862. Shanghai's first fortunes were amassed by an emerging elite of property barons, of whom some of the most successful were three family dynasties of Baghdadi Jews (*see p12* **The Jewish dynasties**).

# The Jewish dynasties

David, Elias and Victor. Or rather, Sassoon, Sassoon and Sassoon. Three men, one family business and, between them, a huge pot of cash. The Sassoons were the first of several Iraqi-Jewish families to arrive in Shanghai, all of which left an indelible impression.

The Sassoon wealth was not of the quick-buck or gold-rush variety. When Victor began to load up his portfolio with lucrative Shanghai real estate in the 1930s, he was continuing a tradition of enterprise that had been upheld by previous generations. The family was from Baghdad, but had outposts all over the world, trading in – among other things – cotton and opium. The founder of the business, David Sassoon, had set up a trade axis between Bombay and China. His son Elias improved the business in Shanghai, before handing the baton to Victor.

Already a man of some repute due to his extravagant approach to business in Bombay, Victor arrived in the city to great excitement. Shanghai at this time was in cash-rich party mode and Victor upped the ante on the social scene by building the Cathay Hotel (now the Peace Hotel, see p33 **Peace at the Cathay**) and using its eighth-floor ballroom for a series of legendary soirées. But when World War II struck and the Japanese seized the city, Victor moved elsewhere. The Sassoon fortune eventually passed to Victor's wife, an American who had nursed and wed him in his dotage.

Two other Iraqi-Jewish families synonymous with Shanghai wealth, the Hardoons and Kadoories, both began on the bottom rung of the Sassoon ladder. Silas Hardoon started as a rent collector for Sassoon & Sons. The job gave him a taste for real estate and, after a few false starts, he set up his own highly successful business. Hardoon won seats on the Municipal Councils of the French Concession and the International Settlement, but remained fascinated by Chinese culture. This aspect of his personality baffled the British and he was perceived as deeply eccentric when he married a Eurasian and took to Buddhism.

The head of the Kadoorie dynasty, Elly, was born in Baghdad and also started his career in Bombay working for Sassoon & Sons. He was transferred to Shanghai, where he became rich through merchant banking, real-estate deals and rubber manufacturing. The Kadoorie family now lives in Hong Kong, using its wealth for good causes. Their most ostentatious legacy in Shanghai is a residence that was once known as the Marble Hall – it survives today as the **Children's Palace** in Jingan (see p69).

At this time Shanghai's foreign settlements now housed some 300,000. In 1863, alarmed by the Taiping episode, the Americans had joined with the British to form one International Settlement. The new unified Settlement governed itself through the auspices of the Shanghai Municipal Council, which was made up of a small number of representatives of British and American landowners. Leaders of the French Concession declined to join the English-speakers, instead formalising their governing body as an extension of the French colonial government in Hanoi. Both the International Settlement and the French Concession took advantage of their superior military strength in the face of Qing weakness to expand their respective territories into the surrounding Chinese countryside. By the early 20th century the two territories occupied no less than 12 square miles (31 square kilometres).

Throughout the second half of the 19th century the International Settlement and French Concession prospered. Increasingly settled and self-confident, residents built ever more handsome structures backed by an impressive infrastructure. Shanghai boasted not only China's best roads and hotels, but also its first gaslights (1865), telephones (1881), electric power (1882), running water (1884), cars (1901) and trams (1908).

Shanghai's next great change came in the aftermath of the Sino-Japanese war of 1895. Acceding to victorious Japan's terms, the Qing court granted Japan similar rights to those it had allowed the Western powers earlier in the century. Japan, however, asked for one other concession: the right to open factories in Shanghai. The Western powers valued the city for its market and raw materials; the Japanese saw greater potential in its cheap and pliable labour. Other countries copied, taking the line that a concession to one was a concession to all.

The city's Chinese population was employed to spin silk, mill grain, roll cigarettes… Workers' conditions were grim and wages pitiful – so much so that already in 1905 there were the first stirrings of organised unrest. This moment can be seen as the beginning of modern

Shanghai – even modern China. On the one hand were the rich foreign capitalists, on the other the masses of uneducated but increasingly organised labourers.

In 1912 the feeble Qing Dynasty gave way to a fledgling republic headed by the revolutionary figure of Sun Yatsen. In short order Sun and his followers were ousted from Beijing by a power-hungry rival and, forming a new Nationalist Party, or Kuomintang, they relocated to the southern city of Canton. Attracted by the safety of the Settlements, Sun also kept a house in Shanghai's French Concession (*see p80*), which he shared with his bride Soong Qingling (*see p87* **Gone for a Soong**).

## COMMUNIST THREATS AND A BRUTAL RESPONSE

In 1917 events that were happening far beyond China's borders were soon to have a major impact on Shanghai. Communist victory in the Russian Revolution resulted in the flight of the defeated 'White Russians'. Over 40,000 made their way overland across Siberia to Vladivostok, which was only a few days' sail from Shanghai. As many as could afford the passage made the Chinese city their new home.

The Russians influenced Shanghai life in many ways. They introduced a new cosmopolitanism with their music, food and fashion. Parts of the French Concession, in particular around the central expanse of avenue Joffre (now Huaihai Zhonglu), took on a Slavic

air with bakeries, dance and music studios, and Muscovite cafés. However, many came bereft of belongings and funds and were forced to take the most menial or unsavoury work to survive.

High-born women eked out an existence selling their jewellery and family heirlooms, or working as nightclub hostesses and prostitutes. Such is the fate of the Countess Sofia Belinskya as played by Natasha Richardson in 2005's Merchant Ivory movie *The White Countess*. Many in the city's long-term foreign resident community resented the Russians for destroying the myth of the omnipotent foreigner: for the first time the Chinese could see Caucasians performing the same sort of demeaning tasks that up until then had been exclusively the lot of Asiatics.

Shanghai was also buffeted by one other significant repercussion of the war in Europe. Under the terms of the concluding Treaty of Versailles, the Chinese territories belonging to defeated Germany were to be handed back not to China but to Imperial Japan.

Chinese student leaders led anti-Japanese and anti-Western strikes accompanied by boycotts of foreign goods. This was part of a general wave of protest that came to be known as the 4 May Movement. Leftist-leaning leaders of the Movement formed links with international Communism and in 1922 Mao Zedong and others held the first meeting of the Chinese Communist Party in a small lane house in the French Concession (*see p80*).

**Communist army** soldiers in 1949, the year they took Shanghai. *See p17.*

# Shanghaied

Order in Shanghai was increasingly difficult to maintain for its foreign rulers. They counterattacked with anti-Communist propaganda and the main English-language newspaper the *North China Daily News* carried instructions on 'How to Spot Communists at Moving Picture Shows and Other Public Gatherings'. Strikes were becoming more disruptive. In 1925 a Japanese foreman shot a striking Chinese worker in a Shanghai textile mill, triggering mass protests on the streets. On 30 May a mob surrounded the headquarters of the Municipal Police hoping to free students held inside; police shot directly into the crowd instantly creating 11 martyrs.

Anti-foreign sentiment was channelled into mass support for the Kuomintang under its new leader Chiang Kaishek, who had succeeded Sun Yatsen on his death in 1925. On a mission to unite China and rid the country of imperialists the Kuomintang marched north out of Canton. In 1927 the 'Northern Expedition' reached Shanghai where the Communists, in alliance with the Kuomintang, had organised a city-wide strike. But what the Communists didn't know was that Chiang had struck a deal with arch-capitalist-cum-gangster Du Yuesheng (*see p16* **City of sin**) and together the two parties had agreed to do the dirty work of the beleaguered Shanghai Municipal Council and rid the city of its disruptive Communist elements.

On 12 April 1927 Green Gang thugs and Nationalist soldiers rounded up thousands of suspected Communists and strike leaders and executed the lot, decapitation by sword, often in full public view. Chiang's motive for partaking in the massacre was to win the support of the wealthy bankers, traders, property barons and industrialists of Shanghai. Job done, the Kuomintang retreated to headquarters in Nanjing where money from Shanghai poured into Nationalist coffers.

## THE SHANG-HIGH LIFE

With the political uncertainties and labour unrest of the 1920s out of the way, the Shanghailanders (the name given to the city's long-term foreign residents) and Shanghainese could concentrate on what they did best: making money. The average man in the street was untroubled by the collusion of Shanghai municipal leadership, Chinese military power and Shanghai organised crime. All they knew was that the city was booming. Over the next decade, despite unprecedented aggression from Japan just outside Shanghai's borders, cultural and business life within the city was at its apex. In pursuit of profit, Shanghai became the most international metropolis ever seen.

An article published in US magazine *Fortune* in 1935 describes Shanghai as 'the fifth city of the earth, the megalopolis of continental Asia, inheritor of ancient Baghdad, of pre-War Constantinople, of nineteenth-century London, of twentieth-century Manhattan.' It ascribes to Shanghai the tallest buildings outside the American continent, 50,000 junks at the city's wharves and the 'greatest concentrated silver hoard on earth'. This vast wealth is 'justly claimed', according to *Fortune*, by 'just a few thousand white men,' which, broken down by nation, included 9,331 British, 3,614 Americans, 1,776 French and 1,592 Germans.

Life for Shanghai's foreign business elite (known as taipans) revolved around the club, the most exclusive of which was the great, gloomy Shanghai Club with its Long Bar. Noël Coward, laying his cheek on the bar, said he could see the curvature of the earth. Then there were the races, dinners, fancy-dress balls and nightclubs, particularly the Chinese dance palaces with their 'taxi dancers' – slim girls clad in *qipaos* slit to the hip whose company on the dancefloor was bought with a ticket. Though not exactly prostitutes, the girls would become concubines to the men with money to pay for them.

During the 1920s and '30s the city became a legend. It was the city of money, gangsters, drugs, warlords, brothels and spy rings but, above all, also of opportunity. In addition to

Coward, other famous figures flocked to see for themselves this so-called 'whore of the Orient', including Christopher Isherwood and WH Auden (whose socialist leanings the city offended), George Bernard Shaw and Charlie Chaplin. It was during this time that the Bund, the ultimate account of Shanghai's foreign-dominated wealth, took its familiar shape; 1923 saw the completion of the grandiose domed Hongkong & Shanghai Bank building, while the imposing brown-stone cliff-face of the Cathay Hotel (now the Peace Hotel) was added in 1929 (*see p33* **Peace at the Cathay**).

Even as the rest of the world suffered in the lead-up to World War II, Shanghai experienced its greatest exuberance. Its citizens must have thought that the magic that had so far blessed their city would shield it forever. Japan, however, had other ideas.

### SCORCHED BY THE RISING SUN

China's political weakness – as proved by its inability to form a strong national government since the fall of the Qing Dynasty – was an irresistible temptation to natural resource-poor Japan. It had already seized Manchuria from China in 1931 by creating its puppet 'Last Emperor' regime. From there it menaced Beijing and Tianjin. In 1932 Japanese troops had invaded the Chinese-run parts of Shanghai following anti-Japanese rioting. International condemnation, however, had forced them to relinquish their gains. Events were to prove more dangerous a second time around.

By 1937 Japanese forces had conquered much of northern China. As they menaced Shanghai, Chiang Kaishek mobilised his forces in the Chinese quarters of Shanghai. The ensuing fighting brought heavy casualties to both sides and almost total destruction to Chinese Shanghai (these events form the backdrop to Kazuo Ishiguro's haunting novel *When We Were Orphans*). Death also came to the International Settlement when Chinese pilots mistakenly dropped bombs on the Bund's Palace Hotel and on entertainment complex Great World, where Chinese refugees fleeing the Japanese had taken shelter – over 1,000 were killed and another 1,000 wounded in the largest ever death toll from a single bomb until Hiroshima.

The Japanese were victorious and this time no amount of international pressure could get them to relinquish their territorial gains. With control over a large part of the International Settlement, Japanese leaders pressured the Municipal Council for a greater role in city politics. The more prescient could see that swallowing only part of Shanghai would not sate Japanese hunger. Many civilians left the

# The king's Shanghai squeeze

On 22 November 1924 29-year-old Mrs Wallis Simpson, née Bessie Wallis Warfield of Baltimore, disembarked on to the Bund. She and travelling companion Mary Sadler checked into the fashionable Astor House Hotel. Mrs Simpson was in China in an attempt to patch things up with first husband Earl Winfield Spencer, a US naval intelligence officer. The attempts at reconciliation failed, but the estranged wife wasn't one to stay home and cry.

Her alternative course of action is revealed in a document known as the 'China Dossier', said to have been prepared by MI6 in 1935, when Wallis Simpson was on the verge of becoming the Queen of England thanks to her position as the consort of King Edward VIII. However, two husbands previously, back in Shanghai, it is alleged that Wallis Simpson spied for the Soviets using her then-husband's naval contacts. She peddled drugs and had a succession of rich lovers, who would have benefited from the techniques she acquired when frequenting the 'purple mansions' (high-class brothels) of Hong Kong. The future Duchess of Windsor was said to have mastered the 'Shanghai squeeze', described as the ability to make a 'matchstick feel like a Havana cigar' through the manipulation of the vaginal muscles.

She was also rumoured to have featured in a series of raunchy postcards that were doing the rounds of Shanghai – in them, she was said to be wearing nothing but a lifebuoy. All of which reduces the annus horribilis suffered by the present Queen Elizabeth when her royal offspring were going through their marital difficulties to the level of a tea spill on the tablecloth.

All the above is detailed with relish in Charles Higham's *Wallis: Secret Lives of the Duchess of Windsor* (1988), a work treated with scorn by rival biographer Greg King, author of *The Duchess of Windsor: the Uncommon Life of Wallis Simpson* (1999).

# City of sin

In addition to being the wealthiest, most sophisticated and most cosmopolitan city in all Asia, 1920s Shanghai was naturally the most vice-ridden and dangerous too. Opportunity was there for all: not just the upper-crust British financiers, Jewish property tycoons, Japanese industrialists and Chinese revolutionaries, but also Chinese gangsters, Filipino musicians and Russian thugs, as well as cardsharps, pickpockets, murderers for hire and, of course, prostitutes of all nationalities.

At one time the International Settlement alone boasted almost 700 brothels and one in every 13 women in the city was reckoned to be a prostitute. At the same time, more illegal drugs were seized in Shanghai each year than in the whole of the United States. Kidnapping, extortion and violence were a constant threat, as reflected in the city's lexicography by Blood Alley (rue Chu Pao-san) in the French Concession, so named for the frequency of brawls there. Shanghai, wrote a Chinese journalist, is a 'city of forty-eight-storey skyscrapers built upon twenty-four levels of hell'. He was, of course, being slightly melodramatic – the highest skyscraper at the time was only 22 floors high.

Although Shanghai was policed, the division of the city into three separate jurisdictions created the conditions for rampant criminality. A wanted man looking to escape justice in one part of the city could just hop over into a neighbouring section, since co-operation between the French, international and Chinese police forces was minimal. Bernard Wasserstein, in his book *Secret War in Shanghai* (1999), describes some of the foreign rogues of the Shanghai underworld who benefited from neighbourhood-hopping. There was the American gun-runner 'Pegleg' Kearney, who was only 90 centimetres tall, having had both his legs amputated. He travelled everywhere by rickshaw. Captain Pick was a White Russian opera singer and theatrical impresario who also moonlighted as an extortionist, blackmailer and murderer, while the Austrian Dr Albert von Miorini was a gynaecologist who peddled dope, ran a brothel and gambling den, and was implicated in a murder by lethal injection.

Such characters, colourful as they are, were small fry compared to Du Yuesheng, also known as Big-Eared Du. His not-so-secret triad, the Green Gang, controlled every organised labour group, from beggars to stevedores and on up, including the Chinese municipal employees.

Du also ran a handful of respectable businesses, notably the Chung Wai Bank, one of the largest Chinese financial concerns of the day, but his real power lay in the money he made from his monopoly on the opium trade. He also had a nice line in kidnapping, organising the snatches then offering his services as a mediator, taking 50 per cent of the ransom. The French Concession authorities were in his pocket, as were several prominent members of the Municipal Council. Even future Nationalist leader Chiang Kaishek was a good friend.

Du's power lasted as long as capitalistic ambition was respectable in Shanghai. When the Communists won the battle for control of the mainland in 1949, the crimelord (like most of the city's underworld) fled to Hong Kong to escape China's new leadership, who would have remembered his complicity in the 1927 slaughter of their brethren (*see p14*). He lingered in Hong Kong in ill health for another two years, but lavish spending and drug habits meant that he died poor.

The Shanghai riverfront in the early 19th century – now the **Bund**.

city and ominously Britain and America began to scale back their military presence, citing the overwhelming Japanese numerical superiority.

On the morning of 8 December 1941, almost the same time as Japanese bombers were destroying Pearl Harbor, Japanese forces attacked the two remaining gunships of the Anglo-Saxon powers, which were moored off the Bund (an event powerfully described in the opening chapters of JG Ballard's *Empire of the Sun*). They then invaded the International Settlement and in early 1942 interned Allied nationals in detention centres around the city, where they remained for the next three years, until the Japanese surrendered to the Americans on 15 August 1945.

**LIBERATION: THE FUN STOPS HERE**
The US navy moved to occupy Japan in late 1945, also taking the reins in Shanghai. During the war both the International Settlement and the French Concession had ceased to exist, thus the Americans filled a power vacuum in the first-ever united Shanghai. They held control of the city for only a year before handing over to Chiang Kaishek.

From the end of 1945 until 1948 Shanghai attempted to rebuild its former glory. Returning industrialists invested in new factories and built new homes. However, it was to be something of a last hurrah, as by late 1948 Chiang's government was on its last legs, having lost countless military campaigns to the Communists. The Nationalists started to plan for an evacuation to Taiwan, the capitalists

headed for Hong Kong. Believers in the 'New China' stayed put. On 25 May 1949, in an event known as the 'Liberation', the Communists marched silently into a Shanghai that had already been abandoned by the Nationalist leadership and its army. The peasant conquerors, who still carried emergency rations of crushed locusts strapped to their backs, must have gazed in wonder at the towering buildings and the department store windows filled with imported luxury items.

### 'After 1953 all Shanghai companies were henceforth to be "owned by the people".'

Most Shanghainese accepted the new state of affairs with their usual pragmatic stoicism. The middle classes – still donning their business suits and hats for another day in the office on the day of Liberation – presumed that nothing much would change. At first what change did occur took place slowly. Those foreign and Chinese industrialists who had chosen not to abandon their businesses found themselves gradually pressed with crippling demands, as comparatively prosperous Shanghai was milked to finance schemes in the rest of China. Then in 1953 the Communists announced that all Shanghai companies were henceforth to be 'owned by the people'. The last group of Westerners left. Surviving dance halls and privately owned villas were converted into 'cultural palaces' and the stylish apparel that

The world-beating **Maglev** train.

the peacocks of the former 'Paris of the East' were known for was traded in for grey unisex tunics and caps.

In 1966 Mao launched his Cultural Revolution aimed at consolidating his own power by exposing those leaders and Party members who did not follow the Maoist line. Shanghai was the headquarters for a group later termed the 'Gang of Four' – Zhang Chunqiao, Yao Wenyuan, Wang Hongwen and Mao's wife, Jiang Qing. They were fervent supporters of Mao's policies and exerted great control over the activities of the new revolutionary, militant Red Guards, whose job it was to rid the country of the 'Four Olds': old culture, old customs, old habits and old ways of thinking. There was no exact definition of 'old' and it was left to the Red Guards to decide – in other words it was a licence to create chaos. Shanghai's streets were renamed, buildings were destroyed (notably Jingan Temple, while Xujiahui Cathedral had its spires lopped off) and large numbers of Shanghainese – who the average Chinese viewed as tainted by Western decadent ways – were forced into demeaning public self-criticism sessions before being locked up.

By the early 1970s, when President Nixon visited Shanghai for his historic meeting with Zhou Enlai, the city that had enjoyed the first electricity and cars in China was completely dark at nightfall. Shops stood empty. The city's residents were cowed and had to watch what they said in case someone overheard and reported them. The vibrant, decadent capitalist paradise of the 1930s had been put to death.

### THE LIGHTS COME BACK ON

The start of the rebirth came in 1976 with the death of Mao. A more moderate Communist Party leadership arrested the reviled Gang of Four. A shell-shocked Shanghai reopened its

schools and factories. In 1978 Deng Xiaoping became China's new leader and launched a new era of reform. The benefits were slow to come to Shanghai. The city's industries were still harnessed for the greater good of greater China and over 80 per cent of all revenues were still directed to Beijing. With no investment the city was stagnant. In 1988 the tallest building in town remained the Park Hotel built in 1934. But there was one event with irrefutable impact: this was the Anglo-Chinese Joint Declaration in 1984 agreeing the handover of the British colony of Hong Kong. Now there would be a city in China that was even more foreign and tainted than Shanghai.

In 1990 the government in Beijing decreed that Shanghai was to become the country's new economic powerhouse. The city government was allowed to use fiscal revenues to develop long-neglected infrastructure. Pudong was set up as an investment-friendly Special Economic Zone and furnished with a first skyscraper, the Oriental Pearl TV Tower (*see p94* **Pearl of the East**). While South-east Asia experienced crisis and new-returnee Hong Kong stumbled, the 1990s were a boom time for Shanghai. The skyline changed beyond recognition as the city attempted to make up for the 40 years that it had lost under Communism.

On the surface, Shanghai at the beginning of the 21st century appears very much like the modern city it would like to be. Its German-built Maglev train is the fastest in the world. The thriving designer heritage mall Xintiandi and the Rolls-Royce dealership at the Westin hotel seem to uphold the rosy statistics touting the city's rediscovered economic might. But such rapid growth doesn't come without pain, and the average citizen is paying for his or her modernity. The rich are most certainly getting richer but at the foot of shining skyscrapers elderly beggars rummage through garbage bins – a city in which everyone once cycled to work in identical blue overalls now has a society that almost rivals Brazil's as the most unequal on earth. While the speed of growth is exhilarating, such rapid urban development comes at the expense of the city's rich architectural heritage as the government seems hell bent on demolishing all pre-war structures to replace them with skyscrapers and urban parkland. Increased wealth is attracting ever-increasing numbers of migrants from the hinterland who need to be provided with ever more housing, which, in turn, sends the city sprawling outwards with more roads, more congestion, more pollution. The positive aspect here,

though, is that most ordinary citizens are aware of the changes and express open concern at the cost of their city's race to wealth.

In such a climate of hyper capitalism and open discussion, it's easy to forget that all of this is being overseen by a Communist state. Clues remain, however, in a fondness for sloganeering and finger-wagging. The red banners have gone but they've been replaced with enamelled plaques warning against the 'Seven no-nos'. These range from SARS-sensible 'No spitting' to the prissy 'No foul language'. According to the government this is necessary to bring Chinese behaviour in line with that of 'global citizens'. Which is in some ways ironic: Shanghai, after all, is the place that began the concept of the modern global city.

# Key events

**1684** Following Emperor Kangxi's green light to maritime trade, Shanghai flourishes as a nexus of trade along the Yangtze River.
**1839** British and Chinese forces clash in the First Opium War.
**1842** The embattled Qing court signs the Treaty of Nanjing, giving Britain the right to trade and settle in Shanghai.
**1843** A British settlement is established on a muddy patch of ground near the Huangpu River and Suzhou Creek. The Brits name it the Bund.
**1849** The French negotiate the same rights as the British, and set up the French Concession.
**1853** Taiping Rebellion forces capture Nanjing and begin a campaign of violence against Shanghai. Settlement troops defend the city.
**1863** The British and American settlements combine forces to form the International Settlement.
**1895** The Qing court is defeated in the Sino-Japanese war. The Japanese win the right to trade, settle and open factories in Shanghai.
**1905** First organised labour protest.
**1911** The weak Qing Dynasty concedes power to early Republican forces.
**1917** An international decree makes opium illegal; Shanghai is filled with smugglers.
**1919** The Treaty of Versailles awards Germany's Chinese territories to Japan. Chinese students protest, sparking labour unrest.
**1922** The first meeting of the Chinese Communist Party takes place in a small lane house in the French Concession.
**1927** Gangster Du Yuesheng strikes a deal with Nationalist leaders to kill off the

Communist faction in Shanghai. The coalition is a success and fosters economic prosperity.
**1937** Japanese troops take increasing control of China, including Shanghai.
**1941** On the same morning they bomb Pearl Harbor, the Japanese seize the International Settlement. The French Concession is already captured by default of the Vichy Government.
**1945** American forces occupy Shanghai following Japan's surrender.
**1946** Chiang Kaishek's Nationalist government is reinstalled in Nanjing.
**1949** The Communist People's Liberation Army marches into Shanghai. Mao forms the People's Republic of China.
**1966** The Gang of Four, which includes Mao's wife, instigates the bloody Cultural Revolution.
**1976** Mao dies and the Gang of Four is arrested and tried.
**1978** Deng Xiaoping pledges to reform and open up the Chinese economy.
**1989** The Tiananmen Square anti-government protests leave Shanghai largely unaffected.
**1990** Shanghai is earmarked by the government as the economic hope for China. Pudong is declared a Special Economic Zone.
**1993** The Oriental Pearl Tower goes up and becomes an icon of the new Shanghai.
**2002** The city makes a successful bid to host the 2010 World Expo.
**2003** The Maglev, the world's fastest train, goes into service running between Pudong International Airport and the city.
**2006** Shanghai hosts the sixth summit of the Shanghai Cooperation Organisation (SCO), watched keenly by international diplomats.

# Shanghai Today

## A city on the edge of tomorrow.

Shanghai has always been a city of purpose and ambition. The allure of opportunity and the heady whiff of easy wealth that lured immigrants, both foreign and domestic, to Shanghai during its colonial heyday is heavy in the air again. The riverfront **Bund** (*see p49*), once the showpiece of East Asia, is back in the frame, its dignity restored through a healthy injection of private capital and a reimagining as a fine dining and fashion spot. The former **French Concession** (*see p80*) is again alight with prestige bars and restaurants, and more new openings than there are dates in the diary.

Entrepreneurs have been decamping from Hong Kong, Singapore and Taiwan, and heavy investors from the US and Europe are calling the place home. Word of what's happening is out and everyone wants a bit of the Shanghai glam: Tom Cruise co-opts the Pudong skyline to add dazzle to his *Mission: Impossible III*; Richard Branson arrives to promote Shanghai–London air links (there are now more direct international flights to Shanghai than to Beijing); and dedicated photo-opportunist Victoria Beckham stalks over just to see what the fuss is about – 'I'm very excited to get an inside look at the world's most happening city,' says she.

The boomtown exuberance of Shanghai today has a sense of impatience and adventure similar to that which characterised the emergence of some of the world's other great cities during their zenith. Think of New York in the 1950s or Hong Kong in the 1980s. But far from being content to play catch-up, Shanghai is instead looking to offer the world a glimpse of the future.

## 'Shanghai is not so much emulating other world cities as creating its own blueprint.'

Prime exhibit 'A' is, of course, **Pudong**, the district on the east bank of the Huangpu River that has been transformed, in just 16 years, from bleak wetland to a science-fiction cityscape unlike any in the world. Perhaps, in fact, it's not New York or Hong Kong that we should be comparing Shanghai to, but Florence in the time of the Medicis – Shanghai is not so much emulating other world cities as creating its own blueprint.

## CHANGES AT STREET LEVEL

As Shanghai's skyline changes beyond recognition, so inevitably does the way of life of its residents. Until the 1990s the majority of Shanghainese lived in a type of terraced dwelling both unique and quintessential to the city, the *shikumen* or lane house (*see p79* **Changing lanes**). In the decade that followed approximately 25 square kilometres of land (nearly ten square miles), including vast tracts of these traditional residences, were razed to make way for modern high-rises, underground parking garages and shiny shopping malls. The razing shows no sign of slowing down: in 2005 alone, another 8.5 square kilometres (more than three square miles) were demolished.

> **'Along with the old bricks and mortar has gone the extraordinarily rich street life that once typified Shanghainese culture.'**

Along with the old bricks and mortar has gone the extraordinarily rich street life that once typified Shanghainese culture. Where locals might once have gathered in the communal alleyway to talk or play mah-jong, they now convene in the air-conditioned comfort of a private apartment. You can still find vignettes of Shanghainese life – laundry hanging from bamboo poles, locals going about their business in pyjamas or taking a nap in a rattan chair – but, with 4,000 high-rises within the city already and a further 1,000 on the drawing board, such scenes are becoming ever less common. The ubiquitous piledriver is a more fitting symbol of Shanghai today. It should be noted, though, that not everybody bemoans the demise of the *shikumen*. Those Shanghainese who are old enough to remember the coal stoves, *ma tong* (bucket toilets) and cramped living quarters that sometimes accommodated several families in a single house have reason to welcome their new homes with indoor plumbing.

In the government's ideal model of urban planning, every piece of land would be given a specific function. Pudong's Lujiazui district is the most obvious example of a newly invented zone, with officials concentrating on developing it into the city's new financial centre with wide, curving streets that make it unfriendly to pedestrians. In other parts of Pudong, former parcels of farmland have been zoned into 'high-tech parks' with clusters of software and biotech campuses. Meanwhile, in the centre of the city, certain streets have been designated 'art streets' while others are promoted as 'bar streets', where pubs blare out Top 40 hits and young women wear dresses that double as beer advertisements (or at least they do until some government official buys a house in the neighbourhood, decides it's too noisy and indulges in a little rezoning).

## IMAGE-CONSCIOUS OFFICIALS

Nothing, it seems, will impede Shanghai's grand plan to create the perfect modern city. Nor will anything be allowed to get in the way of Shanghai's image, which local officials go to great lengths to burnish. The notorious Xiangyang Market, which once specialised in cheap counterfeits of famous brands, is now closed for good, the victim of a crackdown by authorities on the rampant piracy that had tarnished China's international image. In addition, local censors recently delayed the release in China of *Mission: Impossible III*, which was partly filmed in Shanghai, because they were unhappy about scenes in the movie showing laundry hanging on bamboo poles and a slow response by police to a high-speed chase.

For the June 2006 Shanghai Co-operation Organisation (SCO) meeting, held in Pudong, the authorities greened expressways with tens of thousands of potted plants and closed offices and schools for the days of the summit so the streets wouldn't appear crowded. While some private companies decided voluntarily to close

Bamboo laundry racks.

during the high-profile five-day summit, others were visited by local police and told they had no choice in the matter. Some residents living close to summit venues weren't allowed to open windows or hang laundry outside. One foreigner was asked to vacate his apartment at set times on two consecutive days of the summit; it was suggested that he instead 'enjoy the free coffee and soft drinks' on the Club Floor of his apartment block.

## 'For the most part, the Shanghainese remain startlingly apolitical, choosing to concentrate on making money.'

Given Shanghai's inclination to show its polished side to outsiders – and also its tendency to measure its achievements in speed, height and distance – you'd be forgiven for thinking that the city had some sort of an inferiority complex. The city could be content with simply having the fastest train in the world, the German-built Maglev. Its top speed is 430kmh (266mph), easily surpassing the Japanese bullet train. But that's seemingly not enough and other records are being chased. Plans to build the world's largest Ferris wheel to the north of the Bund are taking shape; the super-sized fairground ride will rise some 200 metres (656 feet) in time for the Shanghai World Expo in 2010. Shanghai also now boasts Lupu Bridge, the world's longest arched bridge, spanning 35 kilometres (21 miles) (see p71 **Totally Lupu-y**). But most impressive of all is the construction in Pudong of what will be – if perhaps only temporarily – the tallest skyscraper in the world, the **Shanghai World Financial Centre**. The building, which was originally planned to be 94 storeys and 460 metres (1,510 feet) tall, was revised so that it will top out at 101 storeys and 472 metres (1,548 feet).

### SHANGHAI ON THE WORLD STAGE
The Shanghai Co-operation Organisation emphasises the growing importance of Shanghai on the world stage – and few could disagree. When it formed five years ago, the SCO – which groups China, Russia, Uzbekistan, Tajikistan, Kyrgyzstan and Kazakhstan – was an obscure regional organisation with a nondescript name. Now it is regarded as a rival to NATO, and nations, including Iran, are lining up to be a part of it; US and European diplomats watched carefully in 2006 as Iranian president Mahmoud Ahmadinejad sat in on the

summit. India and Pakistan are also set to join, increasing the likelihood that the organisation will become a counterweight to America's influence in Asia.

For the most part, though, the Shanghainese remain startlingly apolitical, choosing to concentrate on making money. Foreigners in the 1930s came for trade and that's still what makes the city tick. It's easier to make business partners here than friends. Practically every lunch is a business lunch, complete with the trading of business cards. Old retired men check their stocks at local trading centres that look like the off-track betting parlours in America. At bookstores, the hottest selling books fly off the business and management shelves with translated titles such as *Rich Father, Poor Father* or *Who Moved My Cheese?* Show a Shanghainese person something you bought and the typical response is 'Where'd you buy that? I can get it cheaper.'

### ENVIRONMENTAL CONCERNS
Being at the cutting edge of China's economic miracle does have its entries in the debit column. For one, it has taken a heavy toll on the environment, particularly in terms of water and air pollution. Shanghai's own environmental protection bureau estimates that 70 per cent of the city's one million cars do not even reach the oldest European emission standards. And rising pollution levels from industrial waste in the Huangpu River, a major source of drinking water for Shanghai, remain an urgent problem. Inspection by the Shanghai environmental supervision department indicated that water quality in 84 per cent of Shanghai's main watercourses was below the worst grade.

There is, however, a development taking shape on the outskirts of Shanghai that could provide a model for a cleaner way forward. Dongtan, on the nearby island of Chongming, is set to become the world's first 'eco-city', a fully self-sustaining urban environment. It is already the largest single development anywhere in the world and is expected to support an initial 'demonstrator' population of 50,000 by 2010, a number set to rise to half a million by 2040.

If all goes to plan, Dongtan will be a genuine fusion of environmental responsibility and economic development. Priority projects include the process of capturing and purifying water in the landscape to support life in the city. The first phase is planned to be completed by 2010 to coincide with the World Expo, which Shanghai will host under the theme 'Better City, Better Life'. With the number of visitors expected to top 50 million, Shanghai will be able to showcase this marvel of sustainable development to the world.

## AFTER THE GOLD RUSH

Old Shanghai, typified by the Bund and the former Concessions, was a testament to Western achievement. The Shanghai being built today is being shaped by Chinese hands, hearts and minds, and this renaissance could even surpass the boom of the colonial era.

In fact, in yet another comparison, the city's current flush might be likened to the California Gold Rush of the mid 19th century. But will the bubble burst? It's anybody's guess. Shanghai's fortunes will rise so long as China remains in the world's spotlight. And, given the growth rate of its GDP, which hovers at around eight per cent a year; its immense impact on the global economy (rumoured to be on course to overtake the US); and the country's increasing cultural engagement with the rest of the world, that looks like being a very long time indeed.

# The new rich

In late August 2006 Shanghai played host to the Asian debut of the much-hyped Millionaires' Fair. No millionaires were for sale, perhaps to the disappointment of Shanghai's single women, but on show instead was a roster of pricey toys, including yachts, mansions, cars, diamond-studded watches and couture brands. Gawkers and daydreamers there were aplenty, but actual buyers for the exploding luxury sector in China are still as rare as a limited edition Cartier watch.

International marketeers view China's nouveaux riches as the Holy Grail – and they can be just as elusive. Experts concur that their numbers and wealth are swelling, fuelled by the overheating Chinese economy, but they disagree on statistics and definition. After all, in a country that remains relatively poor, the bar for qualifying as rich could be quite low. While China's National Bureau of Statistics claims that 22 per cent of urban households earn at least a comfortable RMB 200,000 (£13,600) per year, Morgan Stanley estimates that only one per cent of the overall Chinese population can afford luxury goods.

Urban China – especially rapidly gentrifying Shanghai – is worlds apart from the country's rural majority. Yet even in Shanghai the visibility of the nouveaux riches far outstrips their actual numbers and spending. Magazines such as *Shanghai Tatler* report breathlessly on the activities and wardrobes of the city's diamond-encrusted few, mostly living on fortunes made almost overnight from the real-estate bubble. Posh bars and restaurants make a big splash on opening night in the hope of roping in wealthy locals out to impress a date or a client. Virtually every new housing development, no matter how dubious its quality, claims to offer 'luxury villas' – which are priced accordingly. Every other woman on Shanghai's pavements seems to be carrying the same new Louis Vuitton bag, and you can barely spit in Shanghai without hitting a construction site for a new luxury mall, yet no one can say how many of those bags are authentic and even the existing malls have few shoppers. Indeed, even Shanghainese who *are* able to afford luxury goods are savvy enough to buy them in Hong Kong, where they are 15 to 20 per cent cheaper.

The real drivers of consumption in Shanghai aren't the high-profile rich but what economists call the 'aspirational middle classes', the middle managers and young entrepreneurs. They are already very comfortable by Chinese standards but yearn to make more and, ultimately, to have it all: the Beemer, the European-themed villa, the authentic Louis Vuitton. It is these people who are really transforming Shanghai, simply by their eagerness and willingness to always and unquestioningly buy up.

# Megalopolis Now

## Shanghai's love of skyscrapers brings on that sinking feeling.

It's a measure of how seriously the city government takes such things that Shanghai has a public exhibition hall devoted solely to urban planning. Not only that, but the Meccano-like building is one of a quartet of grand cultural institutions (City Hall, the Shanghai Museum and the Shanghai Grand Theatre) – some pretty exalted company – on central People's Square. With its position at Shanghai's cultural and administrative ground zero, the message is clear: urban planning is right up there, along with Tang Dynasty porcelain and annual revisits by the Bolshoi Ballet. The centrepiece of the **Urban Planning Centre** (*see p61*) is a vast, tennis court-sized 1:2,000-scale model of downtown Shanghai circa 2010. This is not fantasy, nor even science fiction. This is Shanghai as it will be just a few years from now.

For anyone viewing the model today, the impact is slightly dulled from when it was first exhibited in 2000. At that time the difference between the orderly domino rows of dinky little wooden blocks and the brick-and-stone reality was immense. That is no longer the case. And it isn't the model that has changed.

Since the early 1990s, when Chinese premier Deng Xiaoping declared Pudong a special economic development zone, Shanghai has been growing faster and higher than any other city in the world. Back in 1991 there were exactly six buildings over 100 metres (330 feet) tall. Fifteen years later there are 4,000, of which 2,000 are skyscrapers (defined as habitable buildings higher than 125 metres/410 feet) – more, incredibly, than the total on the entire west coast of America. At one point in the mid 1990s, one quarter of the world's construction cranes were at work in Shanghai. In short, it makes the skyscraper boom of New York in the 1930s and '40s look like a dozy kid in a sandpit. To fuel this building boom, China (Shanghai is, of course, not the only Chinese city rocketing skywards) currently consumes 40 per cent of the world's concrete and 90 per cent of its steel. Building projects elsewhere in the world are on hold because there's not enough steel to go round.

## 'The process of urbanisation, which in Europe took 200 years, will take just 20 years in China.'

The construction statistics are mind-boggling, but they are possibly not mind-boggling enough. They lag behind the numbers attached to the flash-flood of rural dwellers into China's cities. At present 38 per cent of the national population lives in cities, but experts predict that this number could double by 2020. As eminent British architect Sir Norman Foster, visiting Beijing in 2005, noted in a speech to young architects and planners, the process of urbanisation – the movement of people to the

cities – which in Europe took 200 years, will take just 20 years in China. This means that Shanghai, with its current population of 20 million (up from three million little more than half a century ago), could be looking at 40 to 60 million inhabitants in less than 15 years from now. And this in what is already one of the world's most densely populated cities; Shanghai's urban planning administration bureau ventures to claim that it is *the* most densely populated city in the world.

In the race to solve pressing social issues, you get the sense that aesthetics have had to be jettisoned as excess baggage. Already, the term 'Shanghai skyline' is turning up in international journalism as a synonym for 'dog's dinner'. There is a nice story connected to one of the more extravagant old villas in the French Concession (the Hengshan Moller Villa, *see p38*) that has it being designed by the 12-year-old daughter of its millionaire owner; the story is no doubt untrue, but small children with crayons would provide a convincing explanation for the designs of many of the city's recent high-rises, topped variously by crowns, flying saucers and a giant ball and pincer arrangement. But not everything is gaudy. Norman Foster & Partners created a graceful curving 40-storey tower on the South

Bund as the headquarters of the **Jiushi Corporation** and – of course – there's the soaring **Jinmao Tower** (*see p92*), a gorgeous 88-storey fusion of oriental pagoda and art deco. In 2007 the Jinmao will be joined by what will be the tallest building in the world, the 101-storey **World Financial Centre**. It is a stunning design by New York-based Kohn Pederson Fox Associates of a twisting prism with a giant hole punched out of the tapering top to relieve wind pressure. The hole was originally to be cylindrical but apparently the effect looked too much like a Japanese flag, so it will now be rectangular.

It is not just aesthetics that have suffered. The rapid redevelopment of Shanghai has come at great social cost, with entire quarters of the city having been bulldozed to make way for the gleaming skyscrapers. The demolished blocks were largely home to the city's poor, but the authorities and their private partners have made forced acquisitions of property without proper compensation and a contempt for fairness. Tenants in poorer areas whose buildings are under threat of demolition are regularly offered derisory sums of money that are completely insufficient to allow them to buy into the new development; instead they are offered alternative accommodation far from the centre. In wealthier areas, the compensation is greater. There's no appeal to the law or the police, and those who make a stand are frequently intimidated and physically attacked. Shanghai's rapid modernisation is made possible only by the contempt in which the new China seems to hold its ordinary citizens.

### 'The frantic drive upwards is proving more than the earth can bear.'

The World Financial Centre, however, may be where the skyward race stops. In 2005 the Shanghai government went on skyscraper alert. The forest of high-rises has created a grid of street-level canyons prone to mini whirlwinds and dangerous gusts that can suck glass panels out of curtain walls with potentially fatal results. More alarming still is the fact that the ground can't take it either. Shanghai is slowly sinking. The city is built on marshy ground, with a rock bed too deep to be of any use and a high water-table that keeps things soggy. As far back as the early 20th century, the grand monuments on the Bund were having to be underpinned by rafted foundations to prevent subsidence. The frantic drive upwards of the last 15 years is proving to be more than the earth can bear.

The **Jinmao Tower**.

One answer is to build outwards rather than upwards. The plan is that by 2020 Shanghai will no longer be a traditional metropolis with one centre, but a megalopolis with several parallel centres. On the outskirts of Shanghai seven new cities, each of one million people and each with seven satellite towns of 200,000 people, are being built. Just a couple of years ago, Anting – a hamlet west of Shanghai – was growing spinach. Now, out of farmers' fields, an entire German-style town has sprouted, its multicoloured gingerbread homes modelled on those of Weimar in Germany (and designed by Albert Speer Jr, son of the house architect of Hitler's Third Reich). Also in Anting is a huge Volkswagen plant, a General Motors

factory and Shanghai's multibillion dollar Formula One racetrack. Anting has become, in the words of its publicists, the 'Detroit of Asia'.

If that wasn't sufficiently bizarre, Pujiang, another Shanghai suburb, is in the process of being transformed into an Italian dreamscape complete with canals, while Fencheng will duplicate the Ramblas shopping arcade in Barcelona. None, however, is as ambitious as Songjiang, where realtors are already selling living space in ye olde England of Thames Town. In late 2005 banners advertising Thames Town were strung all along Shanghai's shopping street Huaihai Lu, backed by an ad campaign advising anyone who is fond of Premier League football and the Beatles to sign up right away. Thames Town has half-timbered Tudor-style buildings at its centre, a waterfront of Victorian red-brick warehouses, hedges and verdant lawns, pubs serving 'real ales', an unconsecrated church (for registry weddings only) and a hall where planners envision screening a James Bond film festival.

But rather than a bucolic waterside Henley, what the planners have in mind is something more like Cambridge or Oxford: nine universities, encompassing 100,000 students and staff, are to be relocated to this site. There's a train link that will cover the 30-kilometre (20-mile) journey into central Shanghai in 15 minutes and a giant terminal building that will house what is claimed to be the biggest shopping mall in China.

It has struck more than a few commentators as ironic that in looking for a way forward, Shanghai is mimicking the French, British, Americans and others who, in the late 19th century, carved up the city into a clutch of valuable foreign-controlled concessions. One urban planning official announced in a 2002 press circular that 'foreign visitors will not be able to tell where Europe ends and China begins', which is exactly what they used to say a century back. Granted, some of the developments have taken pains to garnish their EuroDisney themes with Chinese characteristics. In Pujiang, for instance, the Italianate dwellings have their windows placed for maximum feng shui and extra master bedrooms for parents who often live with newly-weds. But as more of Old Shanghai is knocked down to be replaced with shiny, plastic towers, as the poor are left stranded while the middle classes move into their new village green residences, in the end Shanghai's concession to an international future may prove as politically unpopular as its foreign concessions of the past.

# Where to Stay

**Astor House Hotel**. *See p31*.

# Where to Stay

There's blow-the-budget corporate luxury and ageing classics aplenty – but fresh-faced mid-range beds are lacking.

Join the premier league at **JW Marriott**. *See p35.*

Shanghai's hotel scene is booming. You can tell by the 90 per cent year-round occupancy rates, the heady room prices and the ambitious renovation plans. And you can hear it echoing around the city's construction sites as the world's top hotels dig into this prosperous city in the lead-up to hosting the 2010 World Expo. The next few years will see several established brands – the Ritz-Carlton, Westin, Shangri-La, St Regis – opening second or third hotels on either side of the Huangpu River, and the rise of leisure-focused second movers like W Hotels, Le Meridien, Conrad, Park Hyatt and Peninsula.

For now at least, hotels in Shanghai remain emphatically geared towards the business traveller. There are a handful of revamped golden oldies, notably the **Peace Hotel** (*see p32*) and the **Metropole** (*see p32*), but standards of service fail to live up to the august surrounds and the rooms are showing their age. Mid-range and budget travellers are poorly catered for, although additions such as cheap but cheerful motel chain **Motel 168** (*see p44*) are helping to close the gap. Most of the hotels in these lower price brackets are Chinese-run and they are often unattractive by Western standards; in the following pages we list the best of what's available.

Part of the problem is that the idea of small, independent establishments has been slow to catch on here. Fortunately, this looks set to change as a number of boutique brands invest in plots of desirable real estate – an historic home here, an old warehouse there – with plans to offer China's affluent international and domestic travellers the lifestyle experience that has been sorely missing in Shanghai. In a city of millions, producing a sense of individuality and personal attention is sure to make for very hot property.

Much of Shanghai's accommodation is in the area of the Bund or in the leafier neighbourhood of the French Concession. The former is convenient for the Old City, People's Square and the business district of Pudong, just across the water; the latter is good for dining and nightlife. Be warned: grinding traffic can make a room in the wrong part of town a real frustration.

## CHAIN HOTELS

Shanghai's booming economy has attracted the global chains in numbers. In addition to the places reviewed in the main text and below, other internationals who have set up shop include Accor, Hilton, Holiday Inn, Howard Johnson, Novotel, Ramada, Sheraton, Sofitel and St Regis; check the group websites for details. Don't expect a great deal of character, but you'll get the same standards of service and comfort as you last found at the same chain's outlet in Dallas, Kuala Lumpur, Zurich…

## BOOKING INFORMATION

Given the high occupancy rates, booking a room in advance is highly recommended. Hotels in the budget category – and even some of the mid-range places – may not have a competent English-speaking reservation line. The best bet is to email where possible, or to fax with a request that the hotel acknowledges receipt. Alternatively, for ease of booking and some genuinely good accommodation rates, try www.english.ctrip.com.

In this guide the listings are divided into the following categories: **Expensive** upwards of RMB 1,660 ($200) for a standard double room; **moderate** RMB 500-1,660 ($60-$200); and **budget** under RMB 500 ($60). We give rates in RMB, as that is how your bill will appear, but payment can usually be made in RMB, dollars or any other hard currency. Prices, of course, fluctuate; we contact every hotel listed for their current tariff, but do check before you travel. For most hotels in the moderate and expensive categories, room rates are subject to a 15 per cent surcharge.

## The Bund

### Expensive

#### Westin

*Bund Centre, 88 Henan Zhong Lu, by Guangdong Lu (6335 1888/fax 6335 2888/www.westin.com/ shanghai). Metro Henan Zhong Lu.* **Rates** RMB 3,245 single/double; RMB 4,095 suite. **Credit** AmEx, DC, MC, V. **Map** p244 L5 ❶

Part of the Bund Centre complex (dominated by a 50-storey, tiara-topped tower that sparkles on the skyline), the Westin's 331 guestrooms and suites will be bumped up to 570 with the opening of a slick new Executive Tower in September 2006, replacing the long-stay residences. The stylish end of corporate, this well-placed five-star carries off the business of bed and board with panache. The dramatic main

atrium turns on the razzle-dazzle with petrified palms and a Vegas-style cantilevered glass staircase with programmed lighting – an OTT look that won't be to everyone's taste. Rooms are done out in cherrywood and come with Westin's signature Heavenly Beds and huge bathrooms with rainforest showerheads. Italian restaurant Prego does a good line in pizzas, Eest serves excellent Chinese, Japanese and Thai, while the Stage hosts one of the most popular brunch buffets in town. Also on the premises is the Banyan Tree spa (*see p176*). A popular, central choice.

*Bars (1). Concierge. Disabled-adapted rooms (3). Gym. Internet (high-speed). No-smoking floors. Parking (RMB 10/hour). Pools (1 indoor). Restaurants (4). Room service (24-hour). Spa. TV.*

## Moderate

### Astor House Hotel

*15 Huangpu Lu, by Wusong Lu (6324 6388/fax 6324 3179/www.pujianghotel.com). Metro Henan Zhong Lu.* **Rates** RMB 580-1,080 double; RMB 1,888-3,800 suite. **Credit** MC, V. **Map** p245 N3 ❷

## The best Hotels

### For waking up on top of the world

Experience an 88-storey high at the **Grand Hyatt** (*see p44*), the tallest hotel in the world.

### For corporate chic

Plush Pudong digs by the river's edge are the order of the day at the new-look **Pudong Shangri-La** (*see p44*), home to high-profile drinking and dining spot Jade on 36.

### For boutique-style B&B

Adorable antique furnishings and gourmet meals are on the menu at the **Old House Inn** (*see p41*), in a heritage-listed lane house.

### For the pocket

Prolific budget chain **Motel 168** (*see p44*) may skimp on price but not on rain showerheads.

### For location, location, location

In the heart of the city, at People's Square, inner-city living doesn't come much better than at the luxury **JW Marriott** (*see p35*).

### For that 1930s Shanghai feel

The tatty **Astor House Hotel** (*see above*) is a terrific backpacker haunt with a sumptuous lineage – enjoy it while you can still afford to.

> ► ❶ Green numbers given in this chapter correspond to the location of each hotel as marked on the street maps. *See pp240-249.*

This budget favourite was once the haunt of the champagne set, who gathered for decadent dances in the Peacock Hall. The city's first electric lights and telephone made their debut here. Today the building retains a magically musty vibe, as well as much of the original Victorian detailing. Hanging in the lobby are black and white pictures of distinguished former guests (Charlie Chaplin and Albert Einstein reputedly stayed here), and staff are knowledgeable on local history. Recent decades of guests are more likely to have been Dirk from Copenhagen on a six-month trip round the world and Shaz looking for work teaching English to fund the coming winter in Chiang Mai, but that looks set to change, with gradually rising rates and whispers that the hotel will be returned to its former five-star splendour.
*Bars (2). Business centre. Concierge. Disabled-adapted rooms (2). Internet (high-speed). No-smoking floors. Parking (free). Restaurants (3). Room service (24-hour). TV.*

## Metropole Hotel

*180 Jiangxi Zhong Lu, by Fuzhou Lu (6321 3030/ fax 6329 8662/www.metropolehotel-sh.com). Metro Henan Zhong Lu.* **Rates** RMB 650-850 single/double; RMB 1,200 suite. **Credit** MC, V. **Map** p245 M5 ❸

While not as famous as its sibling, the nearby Peace *(see p32)*, this 1930 art deco hotel lords it over one of Shanghai's most charismatic intersections, just two blocks inland from the Bund. It boasts a strikingly angular exterior, fit for Fritz Lang's *Metropolis*. Unfortunately, the lobby is both poky and chintzy. The rooms are on the small side and have been renovated into blandness, but they're nevertheless comfortable. The cellar bar, with its heavy wooden tables and dim lighting, still looks every bit the old colonial den, and it is sometimes used as a film set – hotel guests (mainly Chinese) are occasionally invited to ham it up as extras. Though the infamous Cellar Bar remained closed as we went to press, it's a short stroll through the historic backstreets to some of bars and clubs of the Bund.
*Bars (1). Business centre. Disabled-adapted rooms (1). Internet (high-speed). Restaurants (1). Room service. TV (pay movies).*

## Panorama Hotel

*53 Huangpu Lu, by Wuchang Lu (5393 0008/www. accorhotels-asia.com).* **Rates** RMB 1,200 double; RMB 1,400 suite. **Credit** AmEx, DC, MC, V. **Map** p245 N3 ❹

A modern four-star, affiliated with the Accor group, the Panorama is aptly named: its riverside site affords some excellent views over the water toward Pudong and of the Bund. These tend to be monopolised by the suites, which come decked out with Persian-style carpets, comfortable sofas, and raised jacuzzi tubs on white marble bases. The hotel also has serviced apartment suites. It's a swish, well-designed place with a complete range of services and offers good value for money – the only drawback is the location, north of Suzhou Creek and close to nowhere except the cruise ship terminal.

*Bars (1). Business centre. Concierge. Gym. Internet (high-speed). Parking (free). Restaurants (1). Room service (24-hour). TV.*

## Peace Hotel

*20 Nanjing Xi Lu, by Zhongshan Dong Yi Lu (6321 6888//fax 6329 0300/www.shanghaipeacehotel.com). Metro Henan Zhong Lu.* **Rates** RMB 730 single; RMB 880 double; RMB 2,210 suite. **Credit** MC, V. **Map** p245 M4 ❺

Shanghai's most famous hotel claims an illustrious history of decadence and debauchery *(see p33* **Peace at the Cathay)**, but these days the state-run Peace is well past its prime. Rooms overlooking the river are OK, but many others face the internal courtyard with its pollution-darkened walls and wind-whipped trash. While the lobby remains elegant, the top-floor ballroom has suffered a disastrous revamp. The house restaurants should also be given a miss – there are much better options in the neighbourhood. For history enthusiasts, a small museum with memorabilia collected from the former Cathay and Palace Hotel next door (now the south building) can be viewed (by appointment only; call extension 6030). Persistent rumours link the Peace with a takeover from one of the top international chains, but until then we recommend popping in for a drink on the sprawling rooftop terrace or catching the jazz band (which proudly proclaims the average age of its musicians is 75) at the hotel bar, then departing to a less hyped and more hospitable bed elsewhere.
*Bars (2). Business centre. Concierge. Disabled-adapted rooms (2). Gym. Internet (high-speed). No-smoking rooms. Parking (RMB 7/hour). Restaurants (2). Room service (24-hour). TV.*

## Seagull Hotel

*60 Huangpu Lu, by Wuchang Lu (6325 1500/ www.seagull-hotel.com).* **Rates** RMB 1,200-1,760 single/double; RMB 2,000 suite. **Credit** AmEx, DC, MC, V. **Map** p245 N3 ❻

At the confluence of the Huangpu River and Suzhou Creek, just east of the Waibaidu Bridge, the Seagull's rooms boast excellent views of the river and its traffic, as well as Pudong and the Bund skyline. So who cares if the hotel's public spaces are decked out in a rather naff 1970s-style white marble and gold? Since becoming a WORLDHOTELS First Class Collection member in mid 2005, the 130 guest rooms have been refashioned with endearingly kitsch faux-Victorian furnishings, velvet drapes and plasma TVs. Business suites come with PCs, printers and fax machines. Like the Panorama *(see above)* across the road, it's a bit of a schlep to the action, but the enormous neon Epson sign on the roof is a useful beacon when you're trying to find your way home.
*Bars (1). Concierge. Disabled-adapted rooms (1). Gym. Internet (high-speed). Parking (free). Pool (1 indoor). Restaurants (2). Room service (24-hour). TV.*

## Shanghai Mansions

*20 Suzhou Bei Lu, by Wusong Lu (6324 6260/ fax 6306 5147/www.broadwaymansions.com).*

# Peace at the Cathay

Much as the landmark Oriental Pearl Tower heralded the awakening of new ambitions for Shanghai in the early 1990s, the Cathay Hotel epitomised 1930s modernity and symbolised the increasing prosperity and importance of Asia's number one metropolis.

The building was the personal vision of Sir Victor Sassoon who, having moved the opium-enriched family fortune from Bombay, set out to transform Shanghai into a modern cosmopolitan city with a spectacular new skyline. The hotel was designed by the British architect 'Tug' Wilson and opened in 1929.

Almost from its sensational opening night the Cathay became Shanghai's premier rendezvous – the 'Claridge's of the Far East'. Then, as now, the eighth floor was the main public area, in particular the extravagant Chinese grillroom. For many tourists the grillroom provided their only taste of China. Since the mid 1920s world cruising had been in fashion for a predominantly rich American clientele. As visitors gingerly alighted from their tenders, the European buildings of the Bund would confound those anxiously looking for the prescribed (and fictional) opium-smoking, pigtailed Chinaman. They were more likely to bump into a fellow American, wishing to catch up with news from home. Conversely, the Cathay's grillroom (added in 1933), with its dragon-motif ceiling fashioned after door panels from the former imperial palace in Beijing, contained all the treasures they expected to see in China.

The eighth floor also housed the main dining room and ballroom. Rose-tinted curtains and carpets splashed with gold, dull silver and gold walls, white birch furniture, a white maple dancefloor and a liberal show of Lalique lighting fused together to create one of the most beautiful dining rooms in the world. It also provided the setting for Sir Victor's legendary fancy-dress parties, which were customarily perverse in nature. He could be seen wielding a whip or cane at his circus or school parties, while respectable local figures, half-clad, ran amok through the hotel. The ballroom routinely received celebrated callers such as Douglas Fairbanks, Ronald Coleman, Charlie Chaplin and, possibly, Noël Coward, although he may have been too busy penning *Private Lives* (written in his Cathay suite).

Unfortunately, the heyday of the Cathay was short-lived. Commencing with the bombing incident of August 1937 that became known as 'Bloody Saturday', the hotel's fortunes fell with those of the city. The parties continued, however, right up to the Japanese occupation of Shanghai in 1941. After the war, the hotel played host to the American and British military, only to be usurped by the Nationalists and made redundant by the Communists. The building resumed its former duty when it was paired with the neighbouring Palace Hotel to become the **Peace Hotel** in 1956.

As the Peace it hosted 'friendship groups' and official delegations, largely from the Soviet bloc. The hotel remained open during the Cultural Revolution when, although guests were thin on the ground, staff numbers climbed to over 300. Rolled through political and technical education, they spent endless hours cleaning and recleaning the hotel.

The hotel became commercial again under the aegis of the Jinjiang Group Holding Company following the opening of China to tourists in 1978. While the hotel had not suffered at the hands of the Red Guards (staff even put a plain false ceiling below the dragon designs on the eighth floor), there has been some ungracious modernisation since. The greatest indignity being the despoliation of Sassoon's personal suite in 1995. The hotel remains a popular tourist haunt (*see p53*), but it is a shadow of its former self.

**Ruijin Hotel.**
*See p41.*

**Rates** RMB 1,090-1,690 double; RMB 2,900-8,000 suite. **Credit** AmEx, DC, MC, V. **Map** p245 N3 ⑦
Unlike other historic Shanghai buildings (for the colourful life and times of this former mansion block, *see p56*), this one has not yet been overwhelmed by taller skyscrapers. Even sandwiched between the raised highway of Wusong Lu and the girder frame of the Waibaidu Bridge it remains an imposingly solid affair. Sadly, as is often the case, the interior has been stripped of dignity – the most recently renovated floors seem to have come straight out of an IKEA catalogue. If you do stay here (again, it's a fringe location), insist on a Bund view; rear rooms overlook nothing more than asphalt and concrete.
*Bars (1). Business centre. Concierge. Disabled-adapted rooms (1). Internet (high-speed). No-smoking floors. Parking (free). Restaurants (3). Room service (24-hour). TV.*

### Xinxietong International Hotel

*398 Beijing Dong Lu, by Shandong Nan Lu (6352 2888/6351 6200/www.xxt-hotel.com). Metro Henan Zhong Lu.* **Rates** RMB 1,300 single/double; RMB 1,500 suite. **Credit** AmEx, DC, MC, V.
**Map** p244 L3 ⑧
A modern and comfortable Chinese-managed hotel close to the Bund and Suzhou Creek. Rooms are spacious, tastefully decorated and well looked after, with large windows overlooking the Creek. It's an interesting neighbourhood too, of small ageless streets lined with lots of small shops specialising in a cornucopia of the curious and unfathomable. Some of the architecture in the backstreets behind the Bund, though faded, is quite striking. Hotel staff speak limited English, but there is usually someone around who can help with translation problems.
*Bars (1). Business centre. Concierge. Internet (high-speed). No-smoking floors. Parking (free). Restaurants (1). Room service (24-hour). TV (pay movies).*

## Budget

### Captain Hostel

*37 Fuzhou Lu, by Sichuan Zhong Lu (6323 5053/fax 6321 9331/www.captainhostel.com.cn). Metro Henan Zhong Lu.* **Rates** RMB 60 dormitory; RMB 450-550 double; RMB 1,200 suite. **Credit** (doubles & suites only) DC, MC, V. **Map** p245 M5 ⑨
This is just about the only proper backpackers' in town. While there are a handful of cheapo flophouses, this is the only place where the words 'Lonely Planet' elicit a glimmer of recognition. The hostel is simple but clean, the rooms basic but smart. The dormitories each have several sets of bunk beds and share bathroom facilities (which include hot showers), while doubles are equivalent to those found in most other mid-range hotels, with en suites, air-con and other conveniences. The location is grand, an attractive 1920s block just a sailor's hornpipe from the Bund and not much further to the Old City, Nanjing Lu or People's Square. There are internet stations in the lobby, bikes available for rent and top-floor bar

Captain Bar (*see p124*), with a great riverside deck. A second hostel has recently opened in Pudong, behind the Jinmao Tower (527 Laoshan Dong Lu, by Zhangyang Lu, 5836 5966, fax 5836 5956).
*Bars (1). Business centre. Internet (shared terminals). Room service (24-hour). TV.*

### Jinjiang Inn

*33 Fujian Nan Lu, by Jingling Zhong Lu (6326 0505/fax 6311 4542/www.jj-inn.com). Metro Henan Zhong Lu.* **Rates** RMB 199 single; RMB 239 double; RMB 319 suite. **Credit** MC, V.
**Map** p244 L6 ⑩
Economy hotel chain Jinjiang Inn has multiple outposts around town, but we favour this one for its strategic location between the Bund and the Yu Gardens. With a slogan in the lobby announcing the chain's intention to 'create a VIP experience for the masses', the JJ is pitching to the budget-conscious Chinese business traveller. Stopping short of red-carpet treatment, it does stretch to clean, well-managed establishments. Decor is functional, amenities simple and the beds are hard by Western standards, but the price and location are crowd-pleasing. It is predicted that by 2010 there will be 600-plus Jinjiang Inns across the country.
*Business centre. Internet (high-speed). TV.*
**Other locations**: 873 Tianyaoqiao Lu, by Zhongshan Nan Er Lu, Shanghai Stadium (5116 3355); 718 Xi Jiangwan Lu, by Dalian Xi Lu, Hongkou (6516 3286); No.5, Lane 1600, Changning Lu, by Zunyi Lu, Changning (5273 1538).

## People's Square

### Expensive

### JW Marriott

*Tomorrow Square, 399 Nanjing Xi Lu (5359 4969/fax 6375 5988/www.marriotthotels.com/ shajw). Metro People's Square.* **Rates** RMB 2,400 single/double; RMB 3,760-3,920 suite. **Credit** AmEx, DC, MC, V. **Map** p244 H5 ⑪
Opened in 2003, the Marriott occupies the upper part of the 60-storey rocket ship that is the Tomorrow Square development on the north-west corner of People's Square (a location convenient for just about everywhere). The airy lobby and check-in are on the 38th floor with two floors of restaurants and bars above and, above them, 342 guestrooms. These are a cut above the five-star norm ('JW' is the Marriott's premier-league brand), with plenty of space, impeccable service, comfy beds and power massage jets in the showers. Best of all are the simply fantastic views over the city, made the most of by the massive picture windows – the sight of the city at night, lit up in multicoloured, dancing neon, makes a stay here truly memorable. The JW boasts a small library on the uppermost floor, reached by a winding staircase; a branch of the renowned Mandara Spa (*see p177*); several high-end restaurants; a swimming pool; a vast gym with views over the city; and a swanky bar. Highly recommended. **Photos** *p30*.

The **Regent Shanghai**: contemporary, cutting-edge *and* comfy. *See p43.*

*Bars (1). Business centre. Concierge. Disabled-adapted rooms (3). Gym. Internet (high-speed). No-smoking floors. Parking (RMB 10/hour). Pools (1 indoor, 1 outdoor). Restaurants (3). Room service (24-hour). Spa. TV.*

## Radisson Hotel Shanghai New World

*88 Nanjing Xi Lu, by Xizang Zhong Lu (6359 9999/fax 6358 9705/www.radisson.com). Metro People's Square.* **Rates** *RMB 2,250 single/double; RMB 3,500 suite.* **Credit** *MC. V.* **Map** *p244 J4* ⑫

The Nanjing Lu skyscraper that looks as if a spaceship landed on top of it stood empty for years before the Radisson took it over in June 2005. Now the ship is flashing and whirling (there is a revolving restaurant on the 45th floor) and things are really starting to take off. The interiors are exuberant and – in the spirit of the eastern end of this infamous strip – slightly tacky and inexplicably popular. Rooms and public spaces are decorated with an excess of gilt gold, a riot of bold patterns and faux-Versace furnishings. However, the spacious family suites (replete with eight-seater dining table, lounge area and two bedrooms, each with double bed and huge en suite) are a good option for those travelling as a group. The undeniable advantages of the Radisson are its relatively affordable rates, complimentary broadband internet access in each of the 520 rooms and a super-central location (at Exit 7 of People's Square station). There's also a swimming pool, virtual golf and an adjoining shopping centre, cinema, ice-skating rink and Madame Tussauds. It was good enough for the crew of *Mission: Impossible III* during filming in Shanghai in 2006.

*Bars (1). Business centre. Concierge. Disabled-adapted rooms (4). Gym. Internet (high-speed). No-smoking floors. Pool (1 indoor). Restaurants (3). Room service (24-hour). Spa. TV.*

## Moderate

### Park Hotel

*170 Nanjing Xi Lu, by Huanghe Lu (6327 5225/fax 6327 6958/www.parkhotel.com.cn). Metro People's Square.* **Rates** *RMB 1,466 single; RMB 1,466-1,566 double; RMB 1,900 suite.* **Credit** *MC, V.* **Map** *p244 H5* ⑬

Today it is dwarfed by its skyscraping neighbours, but when it opened in 1934 this was the tallest building in Asia (*see p82* **Building a reputation**). In those days it overlooked a racecourse; now it addresses the park and cultural institutions of People's Square – which remains a good location, convenient for sightseeing and the shops of Nanjing Lu. Although the exterior is still imposing, don't expect great shakes from the interior: modernisations in 1998 stripped away much of the original art deco character. The lobby retains some art deco detailing and fabulous black and white photographs documenting the hotel's glory days – a far cry from the pokey rooms, which are furnished in identikit fashion with bland furniture, basic amenities and tired bathrooms. The hotel hosts lots of delegations and other groups.

*Bars (1). Business centre. Concierge. Disabled-adapted rooms (1). Gym. Internet (high-speed/wireless). No-smoking floors. Parking (RMB 30/day). Restaurants (3). Room service (24-hour). TV.*

### Yangtze Hotel

*740 Hankou Lu, by Yunnan Zhong Lu (6351 7880/fax 6351 6012/www.e-yangtze.com). Metro People's Square.* **Rates** *RMB 980-1,280 superior; RMB 1,180 deluxe; RMB 1,280-1,980 executive.* **Credit** *MC, V.* **Map** *p244 J5* ⑭

Dating from the same year (1934) as the nearby Park Hotel (*see p36*), the Yangtze is of comparable size but is less architecturally distinguished. It has a similarly good location, one block east of People's

Square, just behind the popular shopping and cinema complex of Raffles City (see p134) and close to the museums, the Bund and the Old City. Like the Park, it underwent extensive renovation in the late 1990s, re-emerging as what the management claims was the first internet and e-commerce hotel in Shanghai. Deluxe rooms on the fifth and sixth floors come with computers, flat-screen TVs and mini wrought-iron balconies over the street, but we recommend the well-preserved Executive floors with gracefully worn wood panelling, yellowed wallpaper and antique lamps. Bag one overlooking the bell-tower of the Ladislaus Hudec-designed Moore Memorial Church (see p63).
*Business centre. Concierge. Disabled-adapted rooms (2). Internet (high-speed). No-smoking floors. Restaurants (2). Room service. TV.*

## Budget

### Shanghai YMCA hotel

*123 Xizang Nan Lu, by Yanan Dong Lu (6326 1040/ fax 6320 1957/www.ymcahotel.com). Metro People's Square.* **Rates** RMB 100 dormitory; RMB 400 single; RMB 460 double; RMB 800 suite. **Credit** AmEx, DC, MC, V. **Map** p244 K6 🚇
The location couldn't be better: on the edge of the Old City and French Concession, and just five minutes' walk from both People's Square and Xintiandi. The hotel itself is a 1929, 11-storey, Chinese-style building with a startling variety of rooms (165 of them), ranging from backpacker dorms to deluxe suites. Facilities are slightly run-down, but the view from the rooms has improved greatly since the municipality built a park across the road. The fitness facility often schedules classes in traditional Chinese exercise.
*Business centre. Concierge. Internet (high-speed). Restaurants (2). Room service. TV (TV room).*

## Jingan

### Expensive

### Four Seasons

*500 Weihai Lu, by Shimen Yi Lu, Jingan (6256 8888/fax 6287 1004/www.fourseasons.com). Metro Shimen Yi Lu.* **Rates** RMB 3,300 single/double; RMB 4,800 suite. **Credit** AmEx, DC, MC, V. **Map** p243 F5 🚇
Fans of the particular brand of elegance and sophistication usually associated with the name Four Seasons may find themselves a little non-plussed by the chain's Shanghai property, a purpose-built 37-storey twin-spired tower. The cavernous lobby and adjacent atrium café are pleasant enough, as are the large rooms, but they lack that extra oomph that usually sets the Four Seasons apart. Neither is the location too great: although the hotel is within walking distance of most places, the immediate surroundings are distinctly lacking in glamour.

Bars (1). Business centre. Concierge. Disabled-adapted rooms (2). Gym. Internet (high-speed). No-smoking floors. Parking (RMB 10/hour). Pool (1 indoor). Restaurants (3). Room service (24-hour). Spa. TV.

### Portman Ritz-Carlton

*Shanghai Centre, 1376 Nanjing Xi Lu, by Xikang Lu, Jingan (6279 8888/fax 6279 8800/www.ritzcarlton.com). Metro Jingan Temple.* **Rates** RMB 3,150 single; RMB 3,320 double; RMB 4,700-39,840 suite. **Credit** AmEx, DC, MC, V. **Map** p243 E5 🚇
As part of the Shanghai Centre, the Portman is at the heart of expat life; ranged around the forecourt are various consulates and airline offices, the excellent City Supermarket, café/delis Element Fresh (see p105) and Cheese & Fizz (see p114), a California Pizza Kitchen and the Long Bar (see p127). The hotel itself, entered across a bridge over a fish-filled water feature, offers 598 classy rooms over 50 floors. Rooms are being renovated in phases with rich rosewood, Italian marble and LCD TVs, and the style throughout is one of sober luxury. Bonuses include on-call 'technology butlers', one of the city's top Italian restaurants (Palladio; see p107), a sizeable health club and a 24-hour Club Lounge serving a variety of (complimentary) food and drink for guests in 'Club' rooms. Service throughout is exemplary, although what really wins favour is the fact that, despite opening way back on 1 January 1998, the Portman still feels like one of the most vibrant and essential places to stay in town.
*Bars (1). Business centre. Concierge. Disabled-adapted rooms (2). Gym. Internet (high-speed). No-smoking floors. Parking (free). Pool (1 indoor, 1 outdoor). Restaurants (4). Room service (24-hour). Spa. TV (widescreen/DVD/TV room).*

## Old City

## Budget

### Shanghai Classical Hotel

*242 Fuyou Lu, by Liushi Lu, Jingan (6311 1777/ fax 6355 6284/www.laofandian.com).* **Rates** RMB 400 single/double; RMB 800 suite. **Credit** MC, V. **Map** p245 M6 🚇
With its yellow walls, curved tiled roofs, red lanterns and ornate Chinese windows, this Qing Dynasty-styled hotel offers affordable boarding. It's right beside the Yu Gardens, which makes it very convenient for exploring the Old City but a little far from the nightlife action of the French Concession. It has 66 comfortable and modern guest rooms, and a restaurant that dates back to 1875 and serves Shanghainese cuisine. The rooftop bar has fine views of the gardens below, which look especially pretty during the annual Lantern Festival (see 153).
*Business centre. Concierge. Disabled-adapted rooms (2). Internet (high-speed). Restaurants (1). Room service. TV.*

# Xintiandi

## Expensive

### 88 Xintiandi

*380 Huangpi Nan Lu, by Taicang Lu (5383 8833/ fax 5383 8877/www.88xintiandi.com). Metro Huangpi Nan Lu.* **Rates** RMB 2,300 single/double; RMB 3,330-5,740 suite. **Credit** AmEx, DC, MC, V. **Map** p248 H7 ⑲

Aesthetically speaking, Shanghai could do with many more ventures like 88 Xintiandi, a boutique hotel that looks exquisite with its updated Chinese art deco. Part of the massive Xintiandi shopping and nightlife complex, 88 is aimed primarily at the wealthy business traveller, and the high-spec rooms come with all the requisite creature and technological comforts, including a kitchenette and complimentary broadband. The best of the 53 rooms overlook the artificial lake; the others address a busy shopping plaza. Given the beautiful rooms, we were disappointed to have our latest stay marred by noise from the nightclubs on the plaza below (be sure to request a quiet room if you're a light sleeper) and rather indifferent service. Guests have access to both the private clubhouse across the street and the Alexander fitness club within the shopping complex, and there is an indoor pool on site.
*Concierge. Internet (high-speed). No-smoking floors. Pool (1 indoor). Room service. TV.*

# French Concession

The **Radisson Plaza Hotel** (78 Xingguo Lu, by Huashan Lu, 6212 9998, www.radisson.com, RMB 1,330 single/double) is set in six hectares (15 acres) of beautiful gardens. Relatively small, the hotel has a boutique feel. The Clark Hatch fitness group manages the pool, gym, bowling alley and squash courts.

## Expensive

### City Hotel

*5-7 Shanxi Nan Lu, by Yanan Zhong Lu (6255 1133/fax 6255 0211/www.cityhotelshanghai.com). Metro Shanxi Nan Lu.* **Rates** RMB 1,300-1,800 single/double; RMB 2,700-3,000 suite. **Credit** AmEx, DC, MC, V. **Map** p243 F6 ⑳

A standard four-star that's now a little elderly (it's more than 20 years old) and lacking in character, the City Hotel has ample compensation in the form of a fine location (midway between the French Concession's restaurants and nightlife and those of Jingan) and some very competitive rates. The guest rooms and suites (of which there are 274 over about 30 floors) are on the small side, but modern-looking and well maintained. Request one facing south to catch the sun and views down bicycle-thronged Shanxi Nan Lu.

*Bars (1). Business centre. Concierge. Disabled-adapted rooms (1). Gym. Internet (high-speed). No-smoking floors. Parking (RMB 10/hour). Pool (1 indoor). Restaurants (3). Room service (24-hour). Spa. TV.*

### Hengshan Moller Villa

*30 Shanxi Nan Lu, by Yanan Zhong Lu (6247 8881/fax 6289 1020/www.mollervilla.com). Metro Shanxi Nan Lu.* **Rates** RMB 2,500-4,200 double; RMB 7,500 suite; RMB 850 new building. **Credit** AmEx, DC, MC, V. **Map** p243 E6 ㉑

Popular mythology has it that this dreamy villa was built to a design drawn by the 12-year-old daughter of a wealthy Jewish businessman. It seems a plausible explanation for the steeples, spires, pointy red gables and patterned brickwork that give the place the look of a gaudy Gothic castle. The fun continues inside, with all-out high camp rooms with chandeliers, faux Louis XIV furniture and extravagant drapes. No wonder the villa and manicured gardens are a popular photo-op for Chinese newly-weds. When booking, specify that you want to stay in the house itself (with 15 unique guestrooms), and not the markedly cheaper but personality-free concrete box next door – a later addition aimed at the Japanese market. **Photo** *p39.*
*Bars (1). Business centre. Concierge. Internet (high-speed). No-smoking floors. Parking (free). Restaurants (2). Room service (24-hour). TV.*

### Okura Garden Hotel

*58 Maoming Nan Lu, by Changle Lu (6415 1111/fax 6415 8866/www.gardenhotelshanghai.com). Metro Shanxi Nan Lu.* **Rates** RMB 1,500 single; RMB 1,700 double; RMB 4,400-120,000 suite. **Credit** AmEx, DC, MC, V. **Map** p247 F7 ㉒

The Okura Garden looks a bit like a miniature White House, complete with lawn, with a great 33-storey concrete monstrosity behind it. The beautiful baroque building is what remains of the old Cercle Sportif French Club. The hotel later became a favoured retreat of Chairman Mao; no surprise, given its two grand lobbies, sweeping staircases, art deco detailing and original 1926 oval ballroom with stained-glass dome ceiling. The new block contains the accommodation – 500 guestrooms that are comfortable if undistinguished. Part of the Okura group, the hotel is geared to travellers from Japan: staff speak Japanese, the rooms have kimono-style robes, slippers and green tea, and there are a fine Japanese restaurant, Yamazato, and a top-floor teppanyaki bar. Stop for a coffee in the lobby lounge, Oasis, and soak in the live classical music and elegant colonial vibe.
*Bars (3). Business centre. Concierge. Disabled-adapted rooms (1). Gym. Internet (high-speed). No-smoking floors. Parking (free). Pool (1 indoor). Restaurants (5). Room service (24-hour). Spa. TV.*

## Moderate

### Donghu Hotel

*70 Donghu Lu, by Huaihai Zhong Lu (6415 8158/ fax 6415 7759/www.donghuhotel.com). Metro Changshu Lu or Shanxi Nan Lu.* **Rates** RMB 718

Hengshan Moller Villa.
See p38.

Airline flights are one of the biggest producers of the global warming gas $CO_2$. But with **The CarbonNeutral Company** you can make your travel a little greener.

Go to **www.carbonneutral.com** to calculate your flight emissions then 'neutralise' them through international projects which save exactly the same amount of carbon dioxide.

Contact us at **shop@carbonneutral.com** or call into the office on **0870 199 99 88** for more details.

**CarbonNeutral**®flights

single; RMB 878-1,102 double; RMB 1,440-6,400 suite. **Credit** AmEx, DC, MC, V. **Map** p246 D7 ㉓

The Donghu – WORLDHOTEL's latest First Class Collection member – is a collection of mansion blocks in walled grounds, dating from the 1920s and '30s, and formerly home to infamous gangster Du Yuesheng (see p16) and his sundry mistresses. In their current demobbed incarnation the assorted buildings offer 310 large but characterless guestrooms, including seven residential villas, which come equipped with all the usual amenities. Recreational facilities include a good Korean barbecue restaurant (and many more fabulous restaurants a short walk away along Huaihai Lu), a gym, tennis court, billiards room, sauna and a cigar bar. The real draw, though, is the garden setting, lush with trees and flowers and with a large swimming pool.
*Bars (3). Business centre. Concierge. Disabled-adapted rooms (1). Gym. Internet (high-speed). No-smoking floors. Parking (free). Pool (1 indoor). Restaurants (1). Room service (24-hour). TV (pay movies).*

## Jingan Hotel

*370 Huashan Lu, by Changshu Lu (6248 1888/fax 6248 2657/www.jcbus.co.jp/jingan/index_e.htm). Metro Jingan Temple.* **Rates** RB 530-800 single; RMB 900-1,100 double; RMB 1,200-4,900 suite. **Credit** MC, V. **Map** p242 C6 ㉔

These days the four-star Jingan is hidden behind the bulk of the Hilton, but when it was built in 1934 its Spanish styling (curved arches, whitewashed adobe walls and tiled roof) must have made quite an impact. Popular with a middle-aged European clientele, the guestrooms are basic with a somewhat faded charm, but the function rooms still have that wow factor, particularly the ninth-floor restaurant with its ornate pillars, wall carvings and glitzy chandeliers. When booking, avoid the budget three-star wing, added in 1985 to cater for Japanese tourists.
*Bars (1). Business centre. Disabled-adapted rooms (4). Concierge. Gym. Internet. No-smoking floors. Parking (RMB 10/hour). Restaurants (1). Room service. TV.*

## Jinjiang Hotel

*59 Maoming Nan Lu, by Changle Lu (6258 2582/ fax 6472 5588/www.jinjianghotels.com). Metro Shanxi Nan Lu.* **Rates** RMB 958 single; RMB 1,058 double; RMB 1,788 suite. **Credit** AmEx, DC, MC, V. **Map** p247 F7 ㉕

Constructed in 1931 as plush residences for the French, the Jinjiang Hotel, a courtyard complex made up of five heritage buildings, is now a three-star, state-run facility with ambitions to recapture some of that golden-era flair. Topped by an imposing red turban, the Sikh doorman harks back to the days when Indians were just one of the multitude of nationalities that found plentiful employment in boomtown Shanghai. Careful management has retained choice elements of the buildings' original interiors, such as the moulded fireplaces, and all guestrooms in the main Cathay Building and

conference facilities in the Grand Hall are undergoing a massive refurb, set to be completed in 2007. Across the lawn is the 'Jinjiang Gourmet Street' and Yin (see p117), one of the city's best MSG-free Chinese restaurants.
*Business centre. Concierge. Disabled-adapted rooms (1). Internet (high-speed). No-smoking floors. Parking (free). Pool (1 indoor). Restaurants (4). Room service (24-hour). TV.*

## The Nine

*9 Jianguo Xi Lu, by Taiyuan Lu (6471 9950/fax 6433 2123). Metro Hengshan Lu.* **Rates** RMB 700 single/double; RMB 1,000-1,300 suite. **No credit cards. Map** p246 D10 ㉖

This beautiful art deco B&B is run in laid-back (albeit slightly exclusive) style, shunning press and soliciting most of its reservations by word of mouth alone. Entering through large wooden gates, the lucky few (there are only five rooms) immediately get a sense that this is more private residence than hotel. Exquisite antique furniture and Buddhist sculptures engender an air of taste and tranquillity, as do the peaceful garden and secluded balconies. The guestrooms – all with en suite – have their own unique ambience and objects d'art. Upstairs rooms are brightest and, although the Penthouse comes with a kitchen and large terrace, we love the Junior Suite with its own private library.
*Internet (high-speed). Room service. TV (TV room).*

## Old House Inn

*No.16, Lane 351, Huashan Lu, by Changshu Lu (6248 6118/fax 6249 6869/www.oldhouse.cn). Metro Changshu Lu.* **Rates** RMB 470-520 single; RMB 720-1,030 double. **Credit** MC, V. **Map** p242 C7 ㉗

The first of its kind in Shanghai, Old House is a small, independently run B&B set down a typical residential alley. The 70-year-old lane house was converted by Shanghainese architect-owner Wu Haiqing. A dozen elegant guestrooms – king, queen, doubles and singles – with wooden floors, elegant Ming Dynasty-style furniture and stylish bathrooms are connected by creaking stairs and rickety corridors. Breakfast is served in the hip ground-floor restaurant and bar, A Future Perfect (see p117), which spills out into a leafy courtyard garden. Old House Inn is the kind of highly individual place that Shanghai needs more of; we can't recommend it highly enough. **Photo** p42.
*Internet (high-speed). No-smoking floors. Room service (24-hour). TV.*

## Ruijin Hotel

*118 Ruijin Er Lu, by Fuxing Zhong Lu (6472 5222/ fax 6473 2277/http://china.showhotel.com/shanghai/ ruijing). Metro Shanxi Nan Lu.* **Rates** RMB 800 single; RMB 1,320 double; RMB 3,500 suite. **Credit** MC, V. **Map** p247 F8 ㉘

What's now a guesthouse used to be the Morriss Estate, home to an eccentric newspaper tycoon and his pack of racing hounds. In its current form the place is composed of five old villas surrounded by lawns and wooded gardens with a small lake. Opt

**Old House Inn.**
*See p41.*

for Building 2, the original 1920s family home, with larger rooms and art deco details. What could be an amazing boutique property remains slightly underwhelming due in large part to mismanagement and poor service. Still, the setting can't be beat, especially given that one of Shanghai's best bars (Face Bar, *see p129*), with accompanying upstairs Thai restaurant (Lan Na Thai, *see p120*) and Indian restaurant Hazara are within the stunning grounds. **Photo** *p43.*
*Bars (4). Business centre. Concierge. Gym. Internet (high-speed). Parking (RMB 100/day). Pool (1 indoor). Restaurants (4). Room service. Spa. TV.*

### Taiyuan Villa

*160 Taiyuan Lu, by Yongjia Lu (6471 6688/fax 6472 2618). Metro Hengshan Lu.* **Rates** RMB 500 single; RMB 1,200 double; RMB 2,400 suite. **Credit** MC, V. **Map** p246 D9 ㉙
This state-owned mansion, built in 1928 by a French nobleman, is best known as the former digs of General George Marshall, who was chief mediator between Nationalist Chinese leader Chiang Kaishek and Communist leader Mao Zedong. After the Communist victory, it became Madame Mao's favourite pied à terre in Shanghai. Decked out in Chinese furniture, it has a nostalgic atmosphere. The history, architecture and lovely garden go a long way to making up for a lack of facilities – though guests can use the gym and business centre in the serviced apartments next door. Broadband is to be installed – apparently by the end of 2006 –

throughout the villa. Note that government delegations often book the whole villa for weeks on end.
*Business centre. Concierge. No-smoking floors. Parking (free). Pool (1 indoor). Restaurants (2). Room service. TV.*

## Hongqiao & Changning

Just eight minutes from Hongqiao airport, the well-equipped **Marriott Hongqiao** (2270 Hongqiao Lu, by Jianhe Lu, 6237 6000, www.marriott.com) is a low-rise that welcomes guests with bronze statues and petrified palm trees. Its Champions sports bar is a hangout for expats. Excellent fitness facilities include a 24-hour health club, indoor swimming pool and tennis courts. The only drawback is the location, which is right on the edge of town.

### Expensive

### Cypress Hotel

*2419 Hongqiao Lu, by Huqingping Lu (6268 8868/ fax 6268 1878/www.cypresshotel.com).* **Rates** RMB 1,280 single; RMB 1,920 double; RMB 3,200 suite. **Credit** AmEx, DC, MC, V. **Map** p240 A4 ㉚
Situated in the grounds of the former estate of Shanghai tycoon Sir Victor Sassoon, this is more country lodge than hotel. The residences are surrounded by extensive lawns and wooded gardens

landscaped with ponds, streams, pavilions and bridges. The guest rooms are fairly unexceptional visually, though supremely comfortable; executive rooms have separate office areas. Although some distance from the city centre, the hotel is close to Hongqiao (domestic) airport and to the zoo.

*Bars (1). Business centre. Concierge. Gym. Internet (high-speed). No-smoking floors. Parking (free). Pool (1 indoor). Restaurants (3). Room service (24-hour). TV.*

### Regent Shanghai

*1116 Yanan Xi Lu, by Panyu Lu (6115 9988/fax 6115 9977/www.regenthotels.com). Metro Jiangsu Lu.* **Rates** from RMB 2,500 single/double. **Credit** AmEx, DC, MC, V. **Map** p240 C4 ㉛

This is a relative newcomer to the Shanghai hotel scene, which could account for its rather odd location, squeezed up against the Yanan elevated highway. Hardly the most tourist-friendly locale, but it is right next to the growing business district of Zhongshan Park and just a short drive to both Hongqiao Airport and Nanjing Lu – besides, it's the kind of luxury outpost it's worth going out of your way for. The Regent Shanghai moves away from the stately ambience for which the brand is known, and throws itself wholeheartedly at a more contemporary look (trendy white pod chairs in the lobby, for example), in keeping with the cutting-edge building in which it's housed: a distinctively shaped 53-storey tower marked by a neon-blue lightening bolt. All rooms feature 42-inch plasma TVs and many of the bathrooms have retractable glass walls or floor-to-ceiling windows looking out over the city. Other highlights include the L'Institut de Guerlain spa (*see p177*), a high-tech gym with 30m (100ft) infinity pool, and a great Italian restaurant called Amici. **Photo** *p36*.

*Bars (1). Business centre. Concierge. Disabled-adapted rooms (2). Gym. Internet (high-speed). No-smoking floors. Parking (free). Pool (1 indoor). Restaurants (3). Room service (24-hour). Spa. TV (widescreen).*

## Moderate

### Manpo Boutique Hotel

*660 Xinhua Lu, by Dingxi Lu (6280 1000/ fax 6280 6606).* **Rates** RMB 1,370 single/double; RMB 1,640-2,100 suite. **Credit** AmEx, DC, MC, V. **Map** p240 C4 ㉜

Don't be misled by the name: this isn't really a boutique hotel, although, with just 76 guestrooms, it is considered small for Shanghai. Rather it is a modern four-star, situated in an exclusive area along a tree-lined road that leads to the state guesthouse where visiting dignitaries stay when in town. It's a brutal looking thing from the outside, but inside is reasonably grand, with lavish use of marble. It has a good clutch of extras – suites come

**Ruijin Hotel.**
*See p41.*

equipped with kitchenettes and there is a small gym and billiards room. The hotel also has two restaurants, one of which specialises in shark-fin dishes. The proximity to Hongqiao (domestic) airport and the Shanghai Mart and Intex expo/conference centres may make this a useful option for business travellers.

*Business centre. Concierge. Gym. Internet (high-speed). No-smoking floors. Parking (free). Restaurants (2). Room service (24-hour). TV.*

## Budget

### Motel 168

*1119 Yanan Xi Lu, by Zhaohua Lu (5117 7777/fax 5117 7778/www.motel168.com). Metro Jiangsu Lu.* **Rates** RMB 238-298 single; RMB 348 double; RMB 358-428 suite. **Map** p242 A7 ㉝

Started in 2004 by the local Merrilyn group, China's first 'motel' chain already has 20 properties in Shanghai and is rapidly expanding across the country. Offering simple, serviceable accommodation and great value for money, these cheap and cheerful places are extremely popular with Chinese budget travellers, so be sure to call the Shanghai reservation hotline (6316 8168) a few days in advance. Rooms come equipped with basic amenities and free broadband, striving for some style with feature pebbles, sculptures and a bold colour scheme. We like the Yanan Lu motel, right across from the Regent (*see p43*), with a 24-hour cafeteria and branch of the popular Merrilyn restaurant serving Shanghai, Jiangsu and Zhejiang cuisine. For an extra RMB 100 or so, Motel 268 next door offers a more upscale experience, with trendy contemporary apartments and use of a very pleasant communal kitchen and laundry. Other central locations include Jingan (715 Aomen Lu, by Xikang Lu, 5115 6000), Xujiahui (400 Wanping Nan Lu, by Xietu Lu, 5157 7788) and Lujiazui (365 Shangcheng Lu, by Pucheng Lu, 5115 6111).

**Pudong Shangri-la.**

*Internet (high-speed). Parking (free). Restaurants (2). Room service (24-hour). TV (pay movies).* **Other locations**: throughout the city.

## Pudong

## Expensive

### Grand Hyatt

*88 Shiji Dadao, by Yincheng Lu (5049 1234/fax 5049 1111/www.shanghai.hyatt.com). Metro Lujiazui.* **Rates** RMB 3,800 single/double; RMB 5,700 suite. **Credit** AmEx, DC, MC, V. **Map** p245 O5 ㉞

Shanghai's one true destination hotel, the Grand Hyatt occupies the top 34 floors of the cloud-piercing 88-storey Jinmao Tower, thus claiming the title of the world's highest hotel. As if that wasn't enough, the design is stunning. The central atrium, which soars 33 floors from the hotel lobby, is a sci-fi spectacular of seemingly infinite circular galleries. The 555 guestrooms and suites are some of the most spacious in town, with floor-to-ceiling windows to make the most of the incredible views; those facing the river on the 40th to 50th floors offer the finest panoramas. The hotel also boasts a clutch of fine restaurants (including Cucina, *see p122*, with inventive modern Italian cooking), a dream of a bar in the appropriately named Cloud 9 (*see p131*) and a health centre, pool and gymnasium with – you guessed it – spectacular views.

*Bars (5). Business centre. Concierge. Disabled-adapted rooms (2). Gym. Internet (high-speed). No-smoking floors. Parking (free). Pool (1 indoor). Restaurants (5). Room service. Spa. TV.*

### Pudong Shangri-La

*33 Fucheng Lu, by Yincheng Dong Lu (6882 8888/fax 6882 6688/www.shangri-la.com). Metro Lujiazui.* **Rates** RMB 2,150 single; RMB 2,320 double; RMB 4,500 suite. **Credit** AmEx, DC, MC, V. **Map** p245 O5 ㉟

The opening of its $138 million second tower in late 2005 made Pudong Shangri-La the biggest five-star hotel in Shanghai – and one of the very best. The new glass tower looks like a hip younger sibling of the more flamboyant original building. This sleek contemporary-design aesthetic continues in the 375 spacious new rooms and suites, which have 32-inch LCD TVs, DVDs and floor-to-ceiling windows giving views across the river to the Bund (rooms that end in 60, 61 and 62 are best). At 54sq m (581sq ft) the Premier Rooms are said to be the biggest in town. There's also the heavenly day spa CHI (*see p176*) and 12 excellent new drinking and dining destinations. The jewel in the crown – Jade on 36 restaurant and bar (*see p122*) – boasts dazzling views of the Bund, French chef Paul Pairet's deliciously quirky cuisine and fabulously eccentric design elements.

*Bars (3). Business centre. Concierge. Gym. Internet (high-speed). No-smoking floors. Parking (free). Pool (1 indoor). Restaurants (5). Room service (24-hour). Spa. TV (widescreen/DVD).*

# Sightseeing

MOCA Shanghai. *See p60.*

# Introduction

Forget dusty museums and grand monuments – Shanghai is where to get stuck into the right now.

Street life in the **French Concession**.

For imperial palaces, dynastic tombs, ancient city walls and creaking grand old museums the place to head in Shanghai is the airport. You'll find all of those things in Beijing and countless other Chinese cities. But not in Shanghai. While there are a few incense-fogged temples and a pretty ornamental garden with a zigzag bridge, this is a city that doesn't thumb its nose at tradition so much as jump in its bulldozer and flatten it. Which isn't to say there is nothing to see and do here – far from it –

▶ On pages 252 to 255 of this guide we list the key streets and sights of each major central area of Shanghai written in **Chinese script**.

it's just that the quintessential Shanghai experiences differ from those of other cities.

Our list of highlights starts with eating. We can't conceive of a finer introduction to the city than an evening at **Bao Luo** (*see p112*), **1221** (*see p107*) or **Yin** (*see p117*), gorging on dish after dish of local specialities (snake, eel and jelly fish, optional), bombarded by the cacophonous jabbering of groups of fellow diners. Our critics' choice box (*see p101*) gives further suggestions of places to eat.

The next essential experience is to shop. It doesn't matter if the activity is normally anathema to you, in Shanghai it's a whole different ball game – actually, it's not a ball game at all, it's a blood sport. Don't believe us? Then try haggling at **Yu Bazaar** (*see p70*) for a proper fan, which the vendor swears is worth RMB 500. Yet, by the end of the day, you will walk out sheepishly with a new suitcase, bought to transport the hoards of Chinese kitsch that you just couldn't resist. After all, it was just so cheap!

After that, nights should be spent in orgies of old colonial indulgence, sipping Gin Slings on the veranda of a villa that once belonged to a 1920s opium lord, or high-flying on some rooftop terrace nibbling canapés while looking across at the Vegas-style show that is the city's skyline after dark. Novelties in any other city, but Shanghai has an excess of such places.

## SHANGHAI GEOGRAPHY

Shanghai is divided into a multitude of local municipalities but these are not very helpful to the visitor, so we've instead divided the city up into our own, more easily digestible geographical areas. Thumbnail sketches of these areas might read:

● **The Bund & around** – the heart of colonial Shanghai with a grand waterfront promenade.

● **People's Square & Nanjing Dong Lu** – museums and a busy Chinese shopping street.

● **Jingan** – the central business district with top-end malls and two plastic temples.

● **The Old City** – the original Chinese bit with beautiful gardens, a temple and a bazaar.

● **Xintiandi** – a modern redevelopment of an old quarter, now a top spot for shopping, dining and entertainment.

● **French Concession** – low-rise, tree-lined and pretty... little to see but lots of shopping, dining and drinking.

● **Xujiahui, Hongqiao & Gubei** – far-flung south-western suburbs with a real temple, gardens and a bloody history.

● **Pudong** – east of the river financial district with rapidly sprouting skyscrapers.

● **Hongkou** – largely residential area but with sites of cultural and Jewish significance.

Shanghai operates on an east–west axis. Its two main streets are **Nanjing Lu** and **Huaihai Lu**. The first connects Jingan with People's Square and the Bund, the other the French Concession with Xintiandi and the Old City. Both are pedestrian-friendly and many of the city's sights are located on or just off one or the other. Running parallel to and between the two is **Yanan Lu**, an elevated highway for fast-moving traffic. At night this expressway is lit in red and blue neon – trust Shanghai to make a feature of a flyover.

## GETTING AROUND

Despite the immense size of the greater city, the districts that will most interest visitors are closely grouped and manageable in size. Getting around on foot is easy. There's also

# Essential Shanghai

### ...in one day

Everyone should start by seeing **the Bund**, where the architectural glories of the past face off against the architectural glories of the future over the water in Pudong. Cross under the river in the Tourist Tunnel for a coffee at one of a string of **riverside cafés**. Cross back over to the Bund, perhaps by **ferry**, for a lunch with a view. Afterwards, stroll west down pedestrianised **Nanjing Lu** to experience full-on Chinese commercialism. Exit into People's Square for some culture at the **Shanghai Museum** and/or see the city's future at the **Urban Planning Centre**.

Flag down a taxi for **Ruijin Er Lu** and a sundowner on the terrace of Face bar. You are now in the heart of the **French Concession**, with at least a dozen excellent restaurants within easy walking distance including standouts Bao Luo, Shintori, South Beauty and Yin. Whichever of these you choose, there is an equally outstanding bar just a few minutes away.

### ...in two days

Day one, as above; start day two with breakfast in the **French Concession**, which is a beautiful place to wander, working your way east along Huaihai Lu or Fuxing Lu and aiming to end up in ye olde Shanghai precincts of **Xintiandi** for lunch. Continue east to **Dongtai Antiques Market** to stock up on souvenirs of Mao and then follow Fangbang Zhong Lu to the Old City and the gorgeous **Yu Gardens**.

By this time, it should be early evening, the perfect time to take a short taxi ride north back to the **Bund** for an evening cocktail at one of the rooftop bars, from which you can watch Pudong twinkle into life. Given the culinary talent concentrated on this riverfront strip, it would be churlish not to stay around for dinner. Wrap up with late drinks at Barbarossa (party atmosphere) or Kathleen's 5 (romantic and yet more jaw-dropping views), both nearby on **People's Square**.

Cruising the **Huangpu River**.

a good, modern metro system, although it can be crowded and what English-language signage there is isn't easy to spot. We recommend that you make use of taxis, which are both plentiful and cheap. For more information on navigating the city, *see pp216-218*.

## TOURS AND CRUISES

**Jinjiang Tour Buses** (6426 5559) offer a one-day bus tour of the city for RMB 50 per person (RMB 145 including admission to sights), departing from the Shanghai Stadium (666 Tianyaoqiao Lu; *see p192*) at 9.05am daily. The route takes in the Bund, the Yu Gardens, Xintiandi, People's Square and the Shanghai Museum. The tour finishes at 4.30pm.

It's also worth checking the website of the **Chinese Culture Club** (www.chinese cultureclub.org). This is an organisation dedicated to introducing China and its culture to foreigners through talks, courses and also regular tours around specific parts of the city or its environs.

The **Huangpu River Cruise** (239 Zhongshan Dong Yi Lu/the Bund, 6374 4461) company offers a one-hour river cruise up to the Yangpu Bridge (RMB 35 for the day and RMB 50 overnight) or a much better three-and-a-half-hour, 60-kilometre (37-mile) round trip up to the Yangtze River. Tickets cost RMB 90-120; the more expensive tickets include refreshments. Departure times vary but there's usually one in the afternoon at 2pm. The times are posted at the Jinling Pier, just south of the Meteorological Signal Tower; this is also where the boats depart.

# Shang-high

It's getting so that you can spend whole days at a time in Shanghai, dining, drinking, sleeping, working out, never coming down below cloud-level except to scoot from one elevator lobby to another. The number of rooftop bars and restaurants and high-altitude hotel rooms is mind-boggling, and it's only set to grow as the city continues to rise. Here's our pick of the city views.

● **New Heights/Bar Rouge** – beautiful bars with beautiful views across the river to the Pudong skyline. *See p123 & p125.*
● **JW Marriott** – as a non-guest you can enjoy Shanghai from reception on the 38th floor, or at one of numerous bars and restaurants. But if you've the money you can have it all to yourself from your room up on floor 60. *See p35.*

● **CJW** – a restaurant and bar housed in the twinkling crown that tops the 50-storey Bund Centre. *See p105.*
● **Kathleen's 5** – not very high at all as these things go, but still a lovely view over neighbouring Renmin Park. *See p105.*
● **Grand Hyatt** – you check in at floor 54 and then it's just up, up and away at the world's highest hotel. Non-guests can drink and dine on floor 87. *See p44.*
● **Oriental Pearl Tower** – its three high-altitude observation decks seem piffling compared to the nearby Grand Hyatt, but they still give us the willies. *See p93.*
● **Sky Dome Bar** – a bar in the flying saucer grounded atop the 45-storey Radisson on the corner of People's Square. *See p127.*

# The Bund & Around

The architectural showpiece of the colonial era shines once more as Shanghai's ritziest strip.

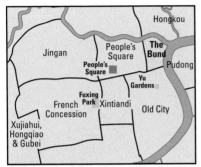

Hongkou

Jingan
People's Square
**The Bund**
Pudong

People's Square

Yu Gardens

Fuxing Park
French Concession
Xintiandi
Old City

Xujiahui, Hongqiao & Gubei

**Maps p51 & p245**

The Bund (or Waitan to the Chinese) is Shanghai's most famous landmark, its skyline the city's historical signature. Developed largely in the early years of the 20th century, it is a kilometre-long waterfront sweep of the most magnificently pompous buildings, many of them the former headquarters of Western-owned banks and institutions. Christopher Isherwood, visiting in May 1938, viewed the rampant capitalism set in stone with distaste: 'The biggest animals have pushed their way down to the brink of the water.' Just over a decade later the Communists wholeheartedly shared his sentiments and drove everybody out. The halls and corridors of these great buildings were largely dormant for 50 years. Upkeep was poor but the Communists, to their credit, destroyed nothing. Now the grand old dame is stirring back to life and is again the most prestigious bit of real estate in all China.

The word 'Bund', often mistaken for a German expression, derives from Hindustani and means an embankment or an artificial causeway. The area was given its name by the British, even though it was little more than a muddy towpath when they first arrived in the 1840s. That changed in the 1880s, when the Shanghai Municipal Council decided to create an esplanade along the entire waterfront. The Bund was further widened in the early 1920s, assuming its present state in the mid 1990s.

Apart from their diverse architectural styles, which range from neo-Grecian to Italian Renaissance and art deco, the buildings are impressive in terms of scale and height – a number of them have at some point claimed (and quickly conceded) the title of tallest building in Asia. Amazingly, the bulk of the materials used for their construction and decoration were imported, including tons of rare Italian marble, granite from Japan and just about everything from toilets to pre-moulded ceilings from England. The buildings have seen little outward change over the last half-century, apart from some despoliation during the Cultural Revolution, although many of their grand interiors have been lost. Each has been designated a heritage structure by the Shanghai Municipal Government.

The revival started in 1999 with **M on the Bund** restaurant (*see p103*). Then in 2002 a law that had nominally zoned the Bund for finance and shipping was dropped, opening the floodgates for countless ambitious developers. Since then, some of the world's most famous retail and hospitality brands have been vying to get a piece of what they believe will be the

The **Bund** promenade.

Sightseeing

On the **Bund** rush hour is any hour.

Madison Avenue of China. At the time of writing, all but building Nos.1, 2 and 27 had been snapped up. The buildings are leased whole, which puts them out of reach of all but the wealthiest of investors, who then need to attract the sort of super-rich tenants that aren't fazed by stratospheric ground rents. So **Three on the Bund** has Armani, Evian Spa and a clutch of high-profile international, celeb chef-driven restaurants, while **Bund 18** boasts Cartier, Aquascutum, Boucheron and Ermenegildo Zegna, plus more celebrity chefs. **Six on the Bund**, set to open in late 2006, will offer more of the same. As eye-popping as these developments are, this is almost certainly just the beginning.

For key sights and streets around the Bund written in **Chinese script**, *see pp252-255.*

## Along the Bund

Most visitors arrive on the Bund beside the Peace Hotel, having walked down Nanjing Dong Lu; this means you start about two-thirds of the way up its length. A better way of doing it is to get a taxi to take you to Three on the Bund (an address most taxi drivers know), so that you can then walk two blocks south and start at No.1 the Bund.

● **No.1 McBain Building (1916)** A grand eight-storey, neo-classical monolith built by the McBains, a wealthy British trading family. It was unoccupied as we went to press.

● **No.2 Shanghai Club (1911)** A one-time bastion of British old boy snobbery, the Club was the place for toast and marmalade and freshly ironed newspapers at breakfast, pink gins before lunch and martinis at the famed Long Bar at six. It was strictly members only, no women and no Chinese. Noel Barber, in his *The Fall of Shanghai*, tells of how a young banker was caught in the crossfire between Japanese and Chinese soldiers skirmishing on the Bund. He ran for the nearest cover, which happened to be the Shanghai Club, and was promptly ordered off the premises because he wasn't a member. The building later housed the Seaman's Club, with Mao's portrait replacing that of King George VI. For a short spell it was the Dongfeng backpacker hotel. It was unoccupied as we went to press.

● **No.3 Three on the Bund (1915)** Originally built for the Union Assurance Company of Guangdong. In 2002 the House of Three (a Hong Kong investment holding company) became the first private company to own a Bund structure. It pumped in some $70 million and employed the services of star

American architect Michael Graves to create a magnificent postmodern interior. Occupying the main floor is an Armani flagship store, while the six floors above contain more retail, an Evian Spa (see p176), the Shanghai Gallery of Art (see p168), and restaurants Laris (see p103), Whampoa Club, Jean-Georges (for both, see p102) and New Heights (see p103). It's all very exclusive and terribly expensive, but it costs nothing to ride the lift up to the seventh floor and walk through the New Heights bar-restaurant and to the rooftop terrace to enjoy what is arguably the finest view in Shanghai.

● **No.5 Huaxia Bank/M on the Bund (1921)** The former HQ of a Japanese shipping line is where the trend for the regeneration of the Bund began, when in 1999 the M on the Bund restaurant (see p103) became the first high-profile venture to stake a claim to Shanghai's 'best address' (although the entrance is actually round the corner on Guangdong Lu). It has since been joined by basement jazz bar Five (see p124). Most of the rest of the building is now occupied by the Huaxia Bank: stick your head in the front door to admire the lovely marble main hall.

● **No.6 Bund Six (1897)** Currently under wraps, the four-storey mock-Gothic building that was once the Commerical Bank of China will reopen in late 2006 as yet another top-end purveyor of luxury chic.

● **No.7 Bangkok Bank (1908)** An attractive four-storey neo-classical manse built for the Great Northern Telegraph Company, which had introduced the telephone to Shanghai as early as 1881 (Britain had to wait until 1884). It's not open to the public.

● **No.9 China Merchants Group Bank (1901)** Off-limits to the public, although parts of the ground floor house a few boutiques.

● **No.12 Hongkong & Shanghai Bank (1923)** Architects Palmer & Turner were given the simple instruction 'Dominate the Bund' and, when completed in 1923, the resulting bit of stone boastfulness was considered the 'finest building east of Suez'. It was the first major Asian building with central air-conditioning and offered desk space for some 600 employees. It is now occupied by the Pudong Development Bank, which keeps it open to the public (although note the sign that warns there's no entry for those wearing 'slippery dress'). The building is distinguished by – among other things – two bronze lions flanking the entrance (see p53 **Pride of Shanghai**) and original interior fittings. There are also some fine mosaic ceilings (discovered by accident after they had been plastered over), including one adorning a rotunda that depicts Shanghai alongside New York, London and

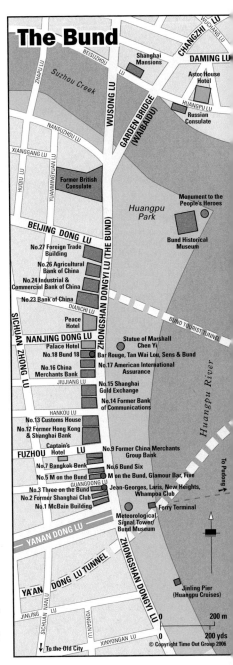

The Bund

Hongkong & Shanghai Bank. *See p51.*

Tokyo – which gives you an idea of the city's one-time historic importance as a world financial hub. The grand banking hall is magnificent. The Bonomi Café on the second floor, with a terrace overlooking the bank's quadrangle, is a fine spot for a breather.

● **No.13 Customs House (1927)** Also designed by Palmer & Turner, the Customs House is capped by a huge clocktower that once housed a bell that chimed in the fashion of Big Ben, hence its nickname 'Big Ching'. The bell was dismantled during the Cultural Revolution and replaced by loud speakers playing a taped version of 'The East is Red', the anthem of the People's Republic. Since 1986 the tower has once again reverted to the Big Ben melody. The building remains a customs house, so entry is denied to the public, but you can take a peek at

# On the river

The Bund waterfront was once lined by jetties, from which masses of coolies hauled crates into the trading houses. Those scenes are long gone, although Shanghai is still China's biggest port and river traffic remains heavy.

A **ferry** across to Pudong is one way of getting out on the river; these leave from a terminal just south of the Meteorological Signal Tower. They depart every 15 minutes throughout the day and the fare is RMB 8 eastbound, free westbound. There are also regular **river cruises** departing from the Jinling Pier, which is just a couple of hundred metres south of the ferry terminal; for further details, *see p48.*

the entrance vestibule with its faded mosaics depicting Eastern shipping and commerce. The portico wall is splashed with some revolutionary zeal in the form of a sculpture commemorating the Communist seizure of the city in 1949.

● **No.14 General Union Building (1947)** A rare late addition to the Bund, built as the Bank of Communications and executed in striking art deco style. Closed to the public.

● **No.15 Shanghai Gold Exchange (1902)** Built as the Russo-Asiatic Bank in Italian Renaissance style. Closed to the public.

● **No.16 China Merchants Bank (1927)** Another Palmer & Turner building, this one in neo-Grecian style, which was originally commissioned as the Bank of Taiwan. Visitors can take a look at the striking main banking hall, done out in black and white marble.

● **No.17 American International Assurance (1923)** The AIA has reclaimed a property it originally occupied in 1927 – it was one of the first of the Bund's former tenants, who left en masse in 1949, to return. Back then it shared its tall, narrow premises with the offices and printing presses of the *North China Daily News*, aka 'the Old Lady of the Bund', which ran from 1864 to 1951 and was the mouthpiece of the Shanghai Municipality. Over the ground-floor windows is a series of three fine Italian marble panels and the chiselled motto of the old newspaper: 'Journalism, Art, Science, Litterature [*sic*], Commerce, Truth, Printing'.

● **No.18 Bund 18 (1923)** The building was originally the Chartered Bank of India and Australia. It still has magnificent Italian marble columns and facings on the ground floor, which are looking better than ever after $15 million's worth of renovation carried out by Venetian architects prior to launching in 2005 as a glamorous multi-level complex for dining and shopping. There's a gallery, a Who's Who of exclusive retail outlets, and top-end restaurants **Sens & Bund** (*see p102*) and **Tan Wai Lou** (*see p102*), all crowned by one of the city's best roof terraces at **Bar Rouge** (*see p123*), which is where Tom Cruise gave his press conference when in town filming *Mission: Impossible III*.

● **No.19 Palace Hotel (1906)** The building on the south side of Nanjing Dong Lu at the Bund began life as the Palace (it's now an annexe of the neighbouring Peace). It is the oldest surviving hotel building in Shanghai – though, despite a keystone displaying the date as 1906, it didn't fully open until 1908. The building was scheduled to be demolished in 1939, but was saved by the advent of World War II. In JG Ballard's *Empire of the Sun*, it is from a river-facing room in the hotel that the 12-year-old Jim witnesses the Japanese gunboat attack on the HMS *Petrel* (December 1941) that signalled the beginning of the end of International-era Shanghai. Despite its gaudy redecoration, the ground-floor Chinese restaurant retains many of the features that made it the place to hang out in 1930s Shanghai.

● **No.20 Peace Hotel (1929)** Formerly Sassoon House, incorporating the Cathay Hotel (*see p33* **Peace at the Cathay**). The foyer is still splendid, as is the small mezzanine bar, which is next to the bookshop, reached by two small staircases off the foyer. It's also worth going up to the roof garden for the views of the river and beyond, although a hefty cover charge is demanded whether you take a drink or not.

● **No.23 Bank of China (1939)** The other moderne structure on the Bund, the Bank of China stands a few metres lower than the neighbouring Peace. Original plans for a twin-towered building climbing over 20 metres (66 feet) higher than the hotel had to be scrapped as Sir Victor Sassoon wouldn't tolerate anything outdoing his triumphal showpiece.

● **No.24 Industrial & Commercial Bank of China (1924)** Successfully blending neo-Grecian with Eastern designs, the former Yokohama Specie Bank building is liberally adorned with granite sculptures and bronze work featuring Japanese warriors; only two defaced sculptures have survived above the ground-floor windows.

● **No.26 Agricultural Bank of China (1916)** Originally built as the Yangtze Insurance Association.

● **No.27 Foreign Trade Building (1992)** Opened as the EWO Building, HQ for trading company Jardine Matheson, one of the most influential British companies in Asia. The company was presided over by two pillars of

# Pride of Shanghai

It's one of the most familiar banks on the UK high street, but not all of HSBC's customers will know that the initials stand for the **Hongkong & Shanghai Banking Corporation** (*see p51*). The company was established in 1865, with offices in the two named cities, to finance trade between China and Europe. Expansion meant a grand new office in Shanghai in 1923, which was fronted by two guardian lions made of bronze. One looks cross, the other one snarls; the snarler (the left-hand one of the pair) used to be known as Stephen, after the Hong Kong branch's general manager AG Stephen, and the cross lion was called Stitt, after the general manager of the Shanghai branch. Despite their fearsome countenances, these lions are considered by the Chinese to be symbols of good fortune and pedestrians touch their paws in the hope that some of the lions' power (and some of the bank's wealth) will rub off. But authentically shiny as the statues' paws are from the thousands of hands that have rubbed them, these two are

not the originals. The originals disappeared during the Japanese occupation and it long was assumed they'd been melted down for scrap – until they turned up in the 1980s in the basement of the Shanghai Museum, which is where they remain (*see p60*). In addition to the two pairs in Shanghai, there are also two larger, but otherwise identical, felines in Hong Kong (but also cast in Shanghai), which sit outside that city's high-tech, Norman Foster-designed HSBC HQ, as well as a fourth pair kept at the HSBC building in London.

The HSBC had to abandon its Bund premises – and lions – soon after the Communists took control of the city. Then in 1995, with Shanghai earmarked as China's new economic powerhouse, the company sought to return to its old home, only to baulk at the sum requested by the Chinese authorities. Instead, the bank is now located in its own HSBC Tower across the river in Pudong and the current residents of No.12 the Bund, the Pudong Development Bank, have been left looking after the cats.

British society, the Keswick brothers. Tony Keswick acted as chairman of the Shanghai Municipal Council and was chief of underground operations in the Far East during World War II.

● **North of Beijing Dong Lu** The northernmost stretch of the Bund includes the former buildings of the Glen Line shipping company (1922), the Banque de l'Indochine (1914) and the plain façade of the NYK shipping company (1926). All of these buildings have been totally gutted and none are currently accessible to the public. The grassed compound at the end of the Bund is the former British Consulate. All of this area is scheduled for major redevelopment in the near future – watch this space.

## Huangpu Park

The area between the Bund and the river was originally created as the Public Gardens in 1868, although 'public' excluded people of Chinese origin. (The infamous and frequently mentioned sign that supposedly read 'No Dogs or Chinese Allowed' never actually existed, however.) The Chinese were finally allowed to enter the park in 1928. Council records reporting this change in regulation are to be found in the underground **Bund Historical Museum** (*see below*), which is located at the base of the **Monument to the People's Heroes**, an ugly concrete monolith designed by a local university professor.

The northern perimeter of the park is bounded by **Suzhou Creek**, which is crossed by way of the **Garden Bridge** (Waibaidu Qiao), built by the British in 1907 and originally paved with wooden blocks and traversed by tramlines. At the southern end of the park is an underpass and access to the psychedelic **Bund Tourist Tunnel** (*see p91*), which takes visitors across to Pudong.

There's another museum further south, opposite No.1 on the Bund, the extremely modest **Bund Museum** (*see below*). It is housed in the old (1907) Meteorological Signal Tower. More worthwhile than the museum is the terrace café located on the upper level, which has great views of the Bund.

### Bund Historical Museum

*1 Zhongshan Dong Yi Lu, Huangpu Park (5308 8987). Metro Henan Zhong Lu.* **Open** 9am-4pm daily. **Admission** free. **Map** p245 N4.
A small, subterranean museum with a reasonably interesting collection of historical photographs. As we went to press it was closed for renovation; call to check it's open before visiting.

### Bund Museum

*Meteorological Signal Tower, Zhongshan Dong Yi Lu, by Yanan Dong Lu (3313 0871). Metro Henan Zhong Lu.* **Open** 9am-noon, 1-5pm daily. **Admission** free. **Map** p245 M5.

# Raising the stakes

Architecturally the Bund is a joy but ergonomically it's a nightmare. Pedestrians have no place on it at all. It was bad enough back in the old days when the street was crammed with rickshaws and trams, and an army of coolies zipped between them ferrying bundles from the wharves on one side of the road to the warehouses on the other. It's far worse now, with the Bund resembling the first straight on a Formula 1 circuit – except the race never ends. Crossing the ten lanes of traffic is only possible at one spot, which is the pedestrian tunnel by the Peace Hotel.

This being Shanghai, there is, of course, a man with a very radical plan to improve things. Raymond Shaw, a Beijing-born American who runs the China office of an engineering multinational, suggests raising the 30 buildings on the Bund by seven metres (23 feet). That way a people-friendly canopy can be built over the road that separates the buildings from the riverfront park, and

the Bund will look exactly the same only taller. A more rational mind might think to suggest burying the road in a tunnel, except the land beside the river is marshy and unstable – and a tunnel wouldn't create the 200,000 square metres (2,100,000 square feet) of luxury retail space Shaw's plan does.

Shaw already has solid credentials in the removals field. When the city's first elevated highway threatened to shake apart a 1930s concert hall (now known as the Shanghai Concert Hall, *see p187*), his company lifted the building and dragged it 60 metres (197 feet) south. He told the *Financial Times* that the Bund project is 'less challenging' and a snip at RMB 3 billion (£213 million). In a city that has to have the fastest train in the world, even if there's nowhere for it to go, and the tallest building in the world, even though the city is already sinking under the weight of its 4,000 high-rises, you wouldn't bet against it engineering the world's tallest six-storey buildings either.

Across the river: the unmistakeable skyscrapers of **Pudong**.

Housed in a 49m-high (161ft) tower that once delivered typhoon warnings to local shipping, the Bund Museum has little more than a small collection of old prints and a replica 1855 map of the area.

## Inland of the Bund

At the southern end of the Bund, the elevated highway Yanan Dong Lu delineates what was once the boundary between the French Concession and the International Settlement. Three blocks inland, shaken by the traffic thundering by at first-floor level, is the musty **Natural History Museum** (*see p56*). A range of tourist souvenirs and sundry inessentials are peddled at the neighbouring **Shanghai Friendship Store** (*see p133*).

One block north is the **Bund Centre**, a hulking office complex whose distinctive crown dominates the skyline. Its restaurant and bar, **CJW** (*see p105*), is 50 floors up and has some of the best views in town. A block north again, the intersection of Fuzhou Lu and Jiangxi Zhong Lu is dominated by the Bund Centre of its day, an early 20th-century grouping of imposing corner buildings. The two matching 19-storey art deco monoliths on the west side were built by Sir Victor Sassoon as the **Metropole Hotel** and **Hamilton**

**House** in 1932. The former remains a hotel (*see p32*), while the latter houses various offices, as was originally intended. The squat building on the north-west corner (built 1922) is now occupied by government offices, but prior to 1949 it housed the American Consulate General and the US Court for China.

One block north again, on the south side of Hankou Lu, the three-storey building with the portico that extends over the pavement used to be the headquarters of the Shanghai Municipal Council. Formed in 1854 to administer the affairs of the British and American settlements, the handful of men who made up the Council – predominantly British – to all intents and purposes ran the city, operating an international court, police force and, at one point, an international army brigade. Across the street, the red-brick former **Holy Trinity Cathedral**, built in the late 1860s, would look very much the part as an English city cathedral (although to the Chinese, it's the Hong Miao, or 'Red Temple'). Its Gothic-inspired architecture was based on the designs of Sir George Gilbert Scott, one of England's most celebrated Victorian architects, responsible for London's Albert memorial and the St Pancras railway station. The cathedral is set to reopen for worship at the end of 2007.

Jiulong Lu.

North of Nanjing Dong Lu are more examples of fine Concession-era architecture, including a sleek deco building on the corner of Nansuzhou Lu that was built in 1928 as the Capitol Theatre; it housed the Far Eastern headquarters of all the big American film companies. Neighbouring Huqiu Lu was formerly known as Museum Road because of the foreign-run Shanghai Museum at No.20, housed in the Royal Asiatic Society building; the museum has long been closed, but you can still see traces of the 'RAS' sign up on its crown.

### Natural History Museum

*260 Yanan Dong Lu, by Henan Zhong Lu (6321 3548). Metro Henan Zhong Lu.* **Open** 9am-4.50pm Tue-Sun. **Admission** RMB 5. **No credit cards**. **Map** p244 L5.

This magnificent 1920s building began life as the Cotton Goods Exchange. Converted to its current use in 1950, the structure exhibits the same signs of age as its poorly displayed stuffed exhibits. The main atrium hall, which is where the cotton trading took place, has an impressive display of dinosaur skeletons, but the principal story told here isn't about prehistory so much as a far more recent fall from grandeur – witness the badly neglected state of the old mosaic floors, woodwork and stained-glass windows. An extensive display of invertebrates,

fish, birds and mammals fills the upper two levels, while a pair of locally discovered Ming Dynasty mummies rests on the ground floor.

## North of Suzhou Creek

The northern side of Suzhou Creek, which used to be known as the Broadway, is dominated by the mighty art deco **Shanghai Mansions** (*see p32*), which used to be Broadway Mansions. When completed in 1933, the 19-storey block was the highest building in Asia. Its British owners made a fortune with its opportune sale to a Japanese government company in 1939. After the war it was a popular residence for foreign correspondents – they had the best spot in the city from which to observe the triumphant Communist troops parading along the Bund in 1949. It now functions as a very average hotel.

A block east is another hostelry, the **Astor House Hotel** (*see p31*), which now largely caters for budget travellers. The first hotel on the site opened in 1858 but the present building, in English Renaissance style, opened in 1911. Once one of the best hotels in Asia, it's still worth a visit for a glimpse of the old lobby and newly restored ballroom, which accommodated post-reform China's first securities exchange until its move to Pudong in 1998.

In front of the hotel, where its gardens once unfolded, is one of the few surviving German-designed buildings in the city. The **Russian Consulate** was built in 1917 and is still in use in its intended role. East of here many further remnants of the early 20th century survive in the form of shabby but charming wooden-framed houses and warehouses. **Jiulong Lu**, in particular, is a fine time warp of a street. However, the whole area, known as 'North Bund', is set to be transformed into a waterfront showpiece with hotels, a world trade plaza, an international terminal for cruise ships and a 'cultural street' featuring a 200-metre-high (656-foot) Ferris wheel – as a comparison, the London Eye only reaches the paltry height of 135 metres (443 feet).

Along the creek west of Shanghai Mansions, the building with a clocktower is the **Chinese Post Office**, built in 1924 and still functioning as the city's main postal depot. It is also home to the new **Shanghai Post Museum** (250 Suzhou Bei Lu, 6362 9898, closed Mon, Tue, Fri), an interesting museum with a stunning atrium and a rooftop garden. A little further down the creek the elongated ten-storey art deco apartment block known as **Embankment House** was the largest of its time when it opened in 1932. A few years later it was used as a processing centre for Jews escaping the Nazi regime. It's now a fashionable address for expats.

# People's Square
# & Nanjing Dong Lu

Tangled transport system meets cultural aspirations on the site of a high-society racecourse.

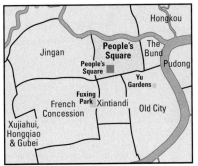

**Map p244**

All roads, buses and metro lines lead to People's Square (Renmin Guangchang), Shanghai's transportation hub – its point zero. Never planned to accommodate human herds of this size, the bus and metro lines cross in a haphazard fashion that adds significant time to your journey. Just regard it as an adventure as a temporary member of China's proletariat. While you jostle for position amid a sea of heads and wonder if the Shanghainese are meant to pass each other on the left or right, take time to gaze up at the staggering number, variety and scale of the man-made structures around you.

Never imperial, regal or grand, People's Square is a great formless space – part park, part concrete plaza, barely hemmed in by a fringe of buildings and a stretch of elevated highway – and seemingly always under construction. In recent years it has gained a clutch of grand cultural edifices. These represent the largest manifestation of the city leaders' unabashed ambition to bring Shanghai international recognition as a cultural centre, each of them strikingly modern symbols of the city's grand cultural aspirations.

The square's perimeters are loosely defined by two of the city's main east–west arteries, **Nanjing Dong Lu** (Shanghai's Oxford Street) and **Yanan Dong Lu** (the elevated road that traces the old border between the International

Settlement and the French Concession); in a bureaucratic fit of copying in triplicate, there are bus stations at the north-eastern, south-eastern and south-western corners of the square. But keep your eyes on the prize: people visit this part of town to see four of the city's best museums, including the superb **Shanghai Museum** (*see p60*), as well as enjoying the relative tranquillity of its small green spaces.

For key sights and streets in the French Concession in **Chinese script**, *see pp252-255*.

## RACEY BEGINNINGS

People's Square started life as the Shanghai racetrack. It was built by the British in 1862 and races were held in the spring and autumn of each year right up until the Japanese occupation in 1941. In the off-season the ground was used for training, riding and games of polo. The city gentry raced short-nosed Mongolian ponies and laid bets (ladies wagered fans, gloves and bonnets). It was the Far Eastern equivalent of Ascot, a gathering of power and wealth, a weekly high-society spectacle. It was a fine source of gossip, intrigue and outrage, including the occasion when a Japanese general with a bee in his bonnet about the lack of Nipponese representation on the Municipal Council shot the city's leading British citizen, Sir William Keswick, during post-race celebrations at the clubhouse.

In 1941, when the Japanese seized Shanghai, the racecourse became a holding pen for enemy nationals – Jim, the young protagonist of JG Ballard's *Empire of the Sun*, is briefly interned here. Following the 1949 Communist takeover, the racecourse was ploughed out of existence and during the Cultural Revolution it became a venue for pro-government propagandising. The Red Guard used the open area for enforced self-criticism sessions by notorious 'criminals'. It is only in recent years that the joint square and park has been given a more attractive face. The turning point was perhaps in the mid 1990s, when the municipal government moved to its new home here, abandoning the former Hongkong & Shanghai Bank on the Bund.

**Museum of Contemporary Art Shanghai**, known as the MOCA. *See p60.*

## Museums & parks

The races, horses and stables are gone, but the clubhouse survives at the corner of Nanjing Xi Lu and Huangpi Bei Lu. Built in 1934, it's distinguished by a grand **clocktower**. The rooftop is now occupied by bar-restaurant Kathleen's 5 (*see p125*); on the way up note the insignia of the SRC (Shanghai Race Club) above the main door, the brass plaque on the first floor honouring club members who died in the Great War and the cast-iron horses' heads worked into the design of the balustrade. Back outside, there's a lovely sculptural grouping of loafing locals, a nod to the building's largest current tenant, the **Shanghai Art Museum** (*see p60*). Imposing in its time, the clubhouse is now dwarfed by neighbouring developments like Tomorrow Square, with its signature angular glass tower, crowned with four pincers grasping at the sky. It's the tallest building this side of the river and should be home to a Bond villain, but instead houses the swanky **JW Marriott** (*see p35*). Although the management won't thank us for mentioning it, you can take the lift up to the 38th floor reception for some fantastic views over the square.

Equally emblematic of the new Shanghai is the striking industrial-orientalism of the **Shanghai Grand Theatre**, which takes the form of a plinth with a rocker on top. It was designed by French architect Jean-Marie Charpentier, who explains his creation thus: 'the layout is a geometrical square, the perfect shape in Chinese which symbolises Earth. The curved roof is a segment of a circle representing Sky'. It is undeniably gorgeous at night thanks to some very effective lighting. The soaring foyer is also quite magnificent and generally open to the public. The three auditoriums can be visited as part of daily guided tours – or you could attend a performance (*see p187*).

Beside the theatre is the yawning avenue **Renmin Dadao**, of a width tailored to mighty parades of massed armies and rocket-carrying trucks, although such parades don't happen any more. On the north side is **City Hall** (closed to the public) and the space module that is the **Urban Planning Centre** (open to the public and well worth a visit, *see p61*). To the south is the centrepiece of People's Square, the world-class **Shanghai Museum** (*see p60*), with its highly distinctive profile inspired by the *ding*, an ancient bronze cooking vessel. For decades visitors to China were denied access to its exhibits of ceramics, calligraphy, bronzes and other antiquities; now it's open to all. The most recent addition to the list of must-dos in the square is **MOCA Shanghai** (*see p60*), the first contemporary art museum in the city and also the city's first to be privately financed yet not-for-profit.

For less culture and more relaxation, visit the **walled garden** with ponds in the north-west corner of the square, beside Nanjing Xi Lu. Early morning it fills with folk practising tai chi. The open plazas around City Hall and the

Shanghai Museum are softened with manicured gardens and flowerbeds, as well as a musical fountain. They are constantly busy with strollers, bench-sitters and kite flyers (flying kites is banned in most parts of the city). Between City Hall and the Grand Theatre is what's known as **English Corner**, where eager citizens gather to practise their spoken language on acquiescent Westerners. Those who want to practise Japanese – the second most common foreign language studied in Shanghai – gather in the walled garden. Those interested in developing a closer relationship with China should head straight to the **lotus pond** in front of Barbarossa (see p125), which has become Shanghai's unofficial matchmaking market. Calculating mothers and fathers comb the grounds looking for the perfect match for their child. Parents carry photos of their children that bear their child's age, occupation

# Shanghai Museum in a day

When you arrive in People's Square, you can't miss the impressive form of the **Shanghai Museum** (see p60), with its round top in the shape of an ancient Chinese cooking vessel. The building also embodies the ancient Chinese notion of the square earth under a round sky. Its immense collection carries over 120,000 pieces presented in 11 galleries – which is why you may want to take our whistle-stop tour.

Start at the **North Entrance**. Hand over the very reasonable RMB 20 entry fee and pick up some free colour-coded gallery information sheets from the atrium helpdesk. Then head straight up the escalators, not stopping until you reach the fourth floor.

Your first stop, the **Chinese Minority Gallery**, showcases the dress and handicrafts of China's 55 ethnic minorities. Check out the ingenious salmon-skin jacket, worn by the Hezhen people from Heilongjiang, then the terrifying Tibetan skull masks, formerly used in sacrificial rituals. Another highlight is a life-sized boat from the Gaoshan people of Taiwan, which bears a startling resemblance to a Native American canoe. Skip the Coin Gallery, unless you've a particular interest in old money, but do stroll through the **Jade Gallery**, with its elegant exhibits, ancient symbols of wealth and power; and eye up the refined pieces in the **Ming and Qing Furniture Galleries**, housing several mock Chinese residences of the era.

One floor down is the **Painting Gallery**. In a masterstroke of conservation and presentation, the museum authorities have installed motion-sensitive lighting that only illuminates each painting when you stand before it. This dramatic effect works best with the must-see collection of ancient landscapes, especially the vivid *Thatched Houses and a Mill Wheel* by Wang Jian (1668). Skip the Calligraphy Gallery next door – unless you can read Chinese, the endless rolls of scrolls rapidly become boring – and likewise the Chinese Seals – another one for enthusiasts only.

Instead, ride an escalator down to the second-floor **Ceramics Gallery**. The words at the entrance read 'Pottery belongs to all mankind, but porcelain is China's invention', an impressive claim, and one the fierce-looking Tang Dynasty Heavenly Guardians on display would no doubt give their glazed right arm to protect. Indeed, each statue is already happily squashing a troll-like figure beneath its feet. As a counterweight to their polychrome gaudiness, you should also see *Western Man on Camel*, also from the Tang Dynasty (AD 618-907). Try not to be offended by the fact that the *laowai* ('foreigner') somewhat resembles a gnome.

Now muster your remaining reserves of energy and hustle down to the first floor. First, drop by the **Bronze Gallery** for its world-renowned collection of ancient (now oxidised) ritual bronzes, the oldest of which have been around since the 21st century BC; have a peek at the ox-shaped wine vessels (11th-13th century BC) and the three-legged *ding* (food vessels). Your final destination, the **Ancient Chinese Sculpture Gallery**, is where you can meditate on the extraordinary Buddhist carvings. This study in devotion is best encapsulated by the *Thousand Buddha Stele* (Northern Zhou period, AD 557-581), a slab of stone impressively covered in mini carvings of Buddha.

Round off your trip with a quick drink or bite to eat at the second-floor teahouse or head down to the first floor, beyond the ticket check, where you'll find the mediocre restaurant and a gift shop (there are less impressive kiosks on every floor). When you're ready, leave by the **South Exit**. People's Square sometimes seems like it has been occupied by half the population of China (especially on weekends and public holidays); the quickest way to escape the madding crowd is to bear left and into the nearest metro entrance or taxi.

**Sightseeing**

and salary expectations (of the prospective spouse, that is). It's a fascinating glimpse into the Chinese obsession with marriage and the meddlesome nature of Chinese parents.

Not all activity is above ground. Below the square is the Hong Kong Shopping Centre or **D Mall** (*see p134*), which fills a vast former air-raid shelter burrowed out in the 1960s in the wake of the Sino-Soviet split. With low ceilings, low prices and narrow corridors, it's a hectic kind of shopping experience, a place that buzzes with giddy teenagers perusing the bargain-basement beauty parlours, cheap accessories stalls and gaming arcades.

## Museum of Contemporary Art Shanghai (MOCA Shanghai)

*Gate 7, People's Park, 231 Nanjing Xi Lu (6327 9900/www.mocashanghai.org). Metro People's Park or Square.* **Open** 10am-6pm Mon, Tue, Thur-Sun; 10am-10pm Wed. **Admission** rates vary according to exhibition. **No credit cards. Map** p244 H5.

Fronted by Taiwanese diva/curator Victoria Lu and billed as a 'platform for the most exciting art from China and the world', MOCA is by far Shanghai's funkiest museum. The art, though often trend-conscious, is also accessible and interesting. There is no permanent collection, instead there is a series of temporary shows, which have recently included photography duo Pierre & Gilles; Swiss Design Now!; Fiction@Love, an exhibition of works all influenced by anime and manga; and the 'Age of Metamorphosis: European Art from the Pecci Collection'. Exhibits make the most of all the open

space and light. As you walk up the spiral ramp of this all-glass cocoon, past the wacky installations, you're presented with a terrific city panorama. The restaurant at the top serves less-than-impressive food, but is worth a visit for its spectacular veranda, surrounded by treetops and concrete spires, where you can enjoy a glass of Prosecco and a snack after viewing the exhibits.

## Shanghai Art Museum

*325 Nanjing Xi Lu, People's Square (6327 4030/ www.cnarts.net/shanghaiart). Metro People's Park or Square.* **Open** 9am-4.45pm daily (last entrance 4pm). **Admission** RMB 20; RMB 5 under-16s, students. **No credit cards. Map** p244 H5.

This museum houses traditional Chinese artworks and a collection of contemporary art that predominates in the exhibition areas. The Romantic landscapes are a little dull, but the patriotic daubings are a hoot, particularly the image of Bush and other world leaders in Chinese tunics at the APEC meeting in Shanghai in 2001. Permanent collections are supplemented by hangings of international artists and the building hosts the prestigious Shanghai Biennale (*see p155*). Unfortunately, there are few explanations in English and, despite the signs advertising it, no audio tour exists. The museum has a good gift shop (*see p137*).

## Shanghai Museum

*201 Renmin Dadao, People's Square (6372 3500/www.shanghaimuseum.net). Metro People's Square.* **Open** 9am-5pm daily (last entrance 4pm). **Admission** RMB 20; RMB 5 under-16s. **No credit cards. Map** p244 J6.

**Shanghai Museum.**

People's Park

The Shanghai Museum was established in 1952 and originally operated in an old bank building down near the Bund. This distinctive new building, which opened in 1996 at a cost of around $50 million, was designed by esteemed Shanghai architect Xing Tonghe. Six stone lions and a pair of mythical beasts guard the entrance to the place, and the granite walls are decorated with designs that were inspired by those found on ancient Chinese bronze-ware. The 120,000 or so pieces on show span Chinese history from the Neolithic Age right up to the present day. Superb collections of sculpture, calligraphy, coins, furniture, ceramics, jade-ware, minority ethnic handicrafts and particularly ancient bronzes are shown in state-of-the-art displays.

All the museum's major displays are annotated in English and a good Acoustiguide commentary is available for RMB 40 (plus your passport or RMB 500 as deposit), as are free double-page guides to each of the museum's collections. In addition, the museum hosts top-quality international touring exhibitions, such as the astounding display of Louis XIV's artefacts exhibited in 2006. The museum shop has a fine range of replicas from the various collections and is the city's best source of books on Shanghai and Chinese arts and culture.

To get the best out of this vast museum, *see p59* **Shanghai Museum in a day**.

### Urban Planning Centre

*100 Renmin Dadao, at Xizang Zhong Lu, People's Square (6318 4477). Metro People's Park or Square.* **Open** 9am-5pm Mon-Thur; 9am-6pm Fri-Sun. **Admission** RMB 25; RMB 5 under-16s. **Credit** AmEx, DC, MC, V. **Map** p244 J5.

A showcase of the city's ongoing architectural development, the centre evokes past, present and future through models, dioramas and multimedia displays. A countdown clock, displaying the days left until Shanghai hosts the 2010 World Expo, hammers home the message that this is a city with definite goals and ambitions. These are set out in what's billed as the largest of its kind in the world – a huge model of how the central part of the city should look come 2020. It can be viewed at eye-level on the third floor or from above on the fourth. The fourth floor also highlights a series of key projects for future growth, including 11 spectacularly massive new town projects in the suburban districts. The basement exit area contains a little-frequented and rather tepid mock-up of a 1930s street – better to go to the Shanghai History Museum in Pudong (*see p93*) for that sort of thing. The hall has a number of good bookstores and an audio tour is available. For more details on the development of Shanghai, *see pp25-28* **Megalopolis now**.

## Around People's Square

High-rise hotels and shopping complexes surround the square – which is just as it has always been. Today the JW Marriott dominates; not so long ago it was the Park Hotel. Built by Ladislaus Hudec (*see p82* **Building a reputation**) in 1934 and rising 22 storeys, the **Park Hotel** was the tallest building in Shanghai until as recently as 1988. Because of this distinction, the centre point of Shanghai is still regarded as being its main entrance. The rust-coloured tiled exterior remains a

Nanjing Dong Lu.

monument to vertical art deco design, but the top-floor dance club with retractable roof is sadly now defunct.

Running north from the Park is **Huanghe Lu**, which looks exactly like everyone's idea of 'Chinatown': a narrow street crowded with tall neon signs, washtubs of writhing things on the pavement and tables of people eating cooked formerly writhing things in myriad tiny restaurants. It's colourful, exotic and fun: go with an appetite.

What is now the Shanghai Athletics Association building, next to the Park Hotel, was the interrogation centre for enemies of the state during the Cultural Revolution. It was here that the daughter of author Nien Cheng (*Life and Death in Shanghai*) was beaten to death by overzealous Red Guards.

At the north-east corner of People's Square twin spires mark another Ladislaus Hudec design, the red-brick **Moore Memorial Church**, built in the late 1920s and named after Texan Arthur J Moore, who donated funds for its construction. Then as now it serves a large community of Chinese Christians.

## Nanjing Dong Lu

Nanjing Dong Lu has traditionally been regarded as 'China's number one shopping street'. While the Bund symbolised British imperial might, Da Ma Lu (literally, the 'big road') was always far more egalitarian. Throughout the 20th century shoppers of every nationality and class have thronged to its department stores, where, in addition to the finest and most expansive selection of foreign and domestic goods, the retailers competed for attention with rooftop garden terraces and restaurants, in-store cinemas, amusement halls, radio studios where shoppers could watch local singing sensations and even, in one case, an in-store hotel.

Today the road holds little of the cachet it once did and Shanghai's best shopping is most definitely elsewhere. However, as a spectacle of the crowded, gaudy, neon-lit China of coffee-table photo books it is unbeatable. Evening strollers can expect to be approached with offers of massage and other services from 'Chinese ladies', as well as hash and money (rent) boys. If you don't fancy walking, there's a silly little electric 'train' that runs up and down the street, plastered with ads for McDonald's.

Look out for the **Shanghai No.1 Department Store** (800 Nanjing Dong Lu), which for many years was the largest in China and boasted the country's first escalators. Next door, across Guizhou Lu, is the unmissable **Shanghai No.1 Foodstore** (*see p146*). The

corner of Guizhou Lu and Nanjing Dong Lu is the site of the 30 May Massacre, where in 1925 British policemen killed 11 Chinese anti-Japan protestors (*see p14*). At **No.635**, on the corner of Zhejiang Zhong Lu, is the former Wing On, a department store that once boasted two whole floors of entertainments, while **No.429** used to be Sincere, so named because it was the first store to feature fixed prices. It was also the first department store on Nanjing Dong Lu, opened in 1917. Ahead of you now is the Bund, but it's also worth exploring the streets to the south.

## South of Nanjing Dong Lu

Once known for its brothels and bars, **Fuzhou Lu** is Shanghai's emporium of books and artist supplies. These range from the tiny suppliers of stationery and paper to the mighty state-owned booksellers. For English-language titles try **Shanghai's City of Books** or the **Foreign Languages Bookstore** (for both, *see p138*). One block south, Guangdong Lu specialises in small shops selling beauty supplies. Come here for anything from Chinese opera make-up to a new camphor-wood comb.

The building tiered like a wedding cake at the corner of Xizang Zhong Lu and Yanan Dong Lu was, prior to 1949, the hub of Shanghai nightlife. Billing itself as **Great World**, it was an adult amusement palace and, in the words of city biographer Stella Dong, 'No one establishment said more about Shanghai during the last decades of semicolonialism than this hodgepodge of the most déclassé elements of East and West'. Quite innocuous when it was opened in 1916 by a local pharmacist who'd made his fortune with a cure-all tonic, the place become notorious after its takeover by arch-gangster 'Pockmarked' Huang in 1931. Its six storeys offered sing-song girls (whose clothing got more revealing with each successive floor), whores, cabaret and gambling. The rooftop reputedly lacked a safety rail, offering a quick way out of debt for chronic losers. Josef von Sternberg visited in the early 1930s while scouting locations for *Shanghai Express*, a movie that, as Stella Dong writes, 'had film audiences all over the world – except perhaps in Shanghai – wondering what Marlene Dietrich really meant when she said, "It took more than one man to change my name to Shanghai Lily".' During the Communist years the building survived as a wholesome 'youth palace'; it is currently closed, awaiting redevelopment.

Immediately west is the transplanted **Shanghai Concert Hall** (*see p187*), while running down the east side of Great World is aromatic **Yunnan Nan Lu**, one of Shanghai's few good areas for street eats.

# Jingan

Traffic, temples and Tiffany's.

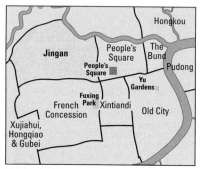

Map p242 & p243

Jingan – named after the Jingan Temple
(or Jingan Si), a local Buddhist landmark –
translates approximately as 'peace and quiet'.
In reality, the area is anything but peaceful
these days. The main thoroughfare, Nanjing
Xi Lu, starts as a part-pedestrianised street
near the Bund – and becomes a four-lane,
traffic-jammed high street as it enters Jingan.
A fifth lane appears as soon as space allows,
and the din of car horns will serenade you
as you stroll through the string of sparkling
luxury shopping arcades. At odds with its
Buddhist history, this area was the launch
pad of China's now-burgeoning luxury goods
market, and all the big-name designers are now
here: Burberry, Louis Vuitton, Gucci, Prada
and Shanghai's first Tiffany & Co.

Despite the intense redevelopment, among
all the mirrored glass and polished terrazzo,
pockets of a far older Shanghai remain. Jingan
was absorbed into the International Settlement
in 1899 and retains some evocative reminders
of its colonial-era heritage (*see p66* **Walk on:
Cars, clubs and couture**).

**BUBBLING WELL ROAD**

Long ago, the Jingan section of Nanjing
Xi Lu was quaintly named Bubbling Well
Road and was the main artery that facilitated
the International Settlement's expansion into
the countryside. Unfortunately, the fields
surrounding the new suburbia were a major
depot for the city's nightsoil, once collected at
dawn from doorsteps in every urban centre in
China and carted to the outskirts for 'recycling'.
Early editions of the *North China Daily News*,

the English-language paper established in
1850, frequently published letters and articles
complaining of the stink. Those long-gone fields
are now covered by perfume and cosmetic
emporiums – and the sweet smell of progress.

Bubbling Well Road ran from the Shanghai
racetrack – today's People's Square – to the
western end of the International Settlement,
marked by the Jingan Temple. When it was
first laid, the road passed through the centre of
the racetrack, which was gated. Non-members
of the Jockey Club paid a small toll to use that
particular stretch.

By the 1930s the area around Bubbling
Well Road was no longer suburban; it had
been swallowed up by the expanding city. The
population density sent land prices sky-high,
with the result that many owners sold or razed
their mansions and erected exclusive clubs,
dance halls and residential tower blocks
along Bubbling Well Road and other nearby
thoroughfares. Some of Shanghai's most
celebrated clubs of the era – including DD's
and the Majestic – indulged in their particular
brand of hedonism just up the road from where
the Portman Ritz-Carlton (*see p37*) now stands.

For key sights and streets in Jingan written
in **Chinese script**, *see p252-255*.

## Nanjing Xi Lu

Walking from People's Square, after passing
under the north–south Chengdu Bei Lu flyover,
you'll come across a garden centre-style façade
on the north side of Nanjing Xi Lu that contains
the **Antiques, Bird and Plant Market**.
While not a large market, it does have plenty
of atmosphere. The two central courtyards are
surrounded by shops specialising in old light
fittings, vases and furniture, and just north of
the antiques section is a small area devoted to
seasonal plants and songbirds. The best time to
visit is Friday afternoon, when the courtyards
fill with upcountry folk who spread their
meagre wares on mats for inspection.

Across the road from the market, a small
side street slips down the south side of Nanjing
Lu and follows it west, curving back to rejoin
it after a couple of blocks. This was formerly
Love Lane, which was full of dance halls before
the Liberation. Today it is **Wujiang Lu**, one of
Shanghai's busiest centres for street food. At

midday and during the early evening the tiny eateries and holes in the wall are packed and long queues form outside. This shambolic little street seems to be the one allowance the authorities have made for the Shanghainese love of *renao* (loosely translated as a hot and noisy atmosphere, a gently chaotic disorder) – or local 'colour' – in their quest to turn downtown Shanghai into a pristine, modern city. Try the fried dumplings (*shengjian*), which are sold at several joints in the middle of the first block approached from the direction of People's Square.

Beyond the junction with Shimen Yi Lu, Wujiang goes upmarket, if only slightly. In place of the small, almost makeshift venues and their doubtful hygiene is a host of more polished, though still cheap and cheerful, Cantonese and other regional restaurants. This stretch of road is off-limits to cars and bicycles. Occasionally you'll catch a street performance or a lowbrow promotion event in the tiny 'square' in its middle. The westernmost stretch of Wujiang Lu is the haunt of street sellers flogging all manner of knock-off items, from DVDs and perfume to designer bags. Weekends and mid evening are the busiest times.

At the point where Wujiang Lu rejoins Nanjing Xi Lu, it is worth a quick detour south down Maoming Bei Lu for some particularly good examples of *shikumen* tenement housing (*see p79* **Changing lanes**). Also down here, in a grid of tiny cramped lanes strung with

washing, where women squat on the doorsteps peeling veg while cigarette-chewing, middle-aged gents putter by on noisy motor scooters, is the little-visited **Chairman Mao's Residence** (*see below*).

### Chairman Mao's Residence

*Lane 120, Maoming Bei Lu, by Weihai Lu (6272 3656). Metro Shimen Yi Lu.* **Open** 8.30-11am, 1-4pm Tue-Sun. **Admission** RMB 5. **No credit cards.** **Map** p243 F5.

This was the most frequently used of three houses that Mao kept during his early years in Shanghai, and is worth a visit. He shared it with his wife, their two children and his mother-in-law. The well-preserved grey- and red-brick *shikumen* dwelling features spartan bedrooms and a large exhibition of photos and letters. The displays are annotated in English. Considering the number of places in China where Mao spent five minutes for a nap that are now historical sites, this Shanghai house stands up as a genuine residence.

## Shanghai Centre & around

In an astonishing contrast that says more about the dynamics of modern Shanghai than any amount of economic analysis, just one turn of the corner is a leap of a century, from the *National Geographic* world of the *shikumen* housing of Maoming Bei Lu to the 21st-century mall culture of central Nanjing Xi Lu. The scenes of hanging washing and women hunched over pots and pans are replaced

**Nanjing Xi Lu.** *See p64.*

# Walk on: Cars, clubs and couture

**Start**: JW Marriott Hotel at Tomorrow Square, 399 Nanjing Xi Lu
**Finish**: Okura Garden Hotel, 58 Maoming Nan Lu
**Length**: One mile (1.5 kilometres)

Some things in Shanghai just don't change – well, not that much anyway. The area around Nanjing Xi Lu, which was developed as a swanky commercial and residential section of the former Western District in the 1920s and early 1930s, is again being redeveloped – and in much the same manner. But a cocktail of historical threads and tracks remains. From its construction in the mid 19th century, the former Bubbling Well Road was the place for an evening drive (horse-driven, of course) and by the 1920s it was home to the classiest car showrooms and garages in town.

Take a look at what's on offer (price on application) in the showroom next to the **JW Marriott**: seductive Ferraris and Maseratis yearning for a diminutive Shanghai femme fatale, wearing sunglasses the size of plasma screens, to take for a ride. On the eastern side of Huangpi Bei Lu, the clocktower of the former Shanghai Race Club, known as '**Big Bertie**' after the club's chairman Bertie Burkill, still keeps as bad time as it did when it was installed in 1934. The Shanghai Automobile Club, of which Bertie was a founding member, used to parade their dressed-up cars on the grounds of the racecourse. That racecourse is now People's Square.

Head westwards on Nanjing Xi Lu where, just across the street, **Ciro's Plaza** (No.388) stands on the site of one of Old Shanghai's classiest nightclubs, Ciro's – owned, naturally, by the legendary Sir Victor Sassoon (*see p12*).

Sassoon was also big at the race club and many of his brethren were buried at the Jewish cemetery where the JW Marriott now stands. Carry on up the road, crossing Chengdu Bei Lu, to reach the **Shanghai TV Station** with its huge LCD display at No.651. It is on the site of the snobby British Country Club, where British Jews like Sassoon were given the brush-off. Almost opposite, however, the building at No.722 briefly housed the Jewish Club in the early 1940s. Opened in 1929, as a sumptuous London-style club, it was originally the home of another horse-racing club before being taken over as club premises for the US Fourth Marines.

Look behind the advertising signs at No.702 to spot the intricate Moorish features of the Star Garage Building next door, built in 1916. The garage, once owned by another Sephardic Jew, Edward Ezra, used to tout Dodge and Hupmobile cars in its showrooms. Cross the road and weave up **Wujiang Lu**, its winding course once that of a creek but now an essential stop for street-side dumplings, and take a left on to **Shimen Yi Lu**. This was Old Shanghai's premier fashion street, formerly known as Yates Road, renowned for its lingerie and lace and for its tailors' deftness in copying the latest Paris fashions. The Brits knew it as 'the land of a thousand nighties'. Its wares speak of polyester today.

Take a right at the **Four Seasons Hotel** on to Weihai Lu. The high-rise tower opposite the hotel houses the headquarters of SAIC, the controlling partner in deals with car giants VW and GM. Just as it was 70 years ago, car parts mechanically materialise from the neighbouring streets and alleys. Take a left at Maoming Bei

by high-heeled, pencil-skirted misses and their dark-suited male counterparts scooting between appointments, streaming rapid-fire speech into palm-sized mobiles. The backdrop is the sheet-glass walls and rounded contours of the Westgate Mall, the CITIC Square, Plaza 66 and the newly arrived Japanese behemoth, Sogo, which overlooks Jingan Temple to the west; for shopping specifics, *see pp132-149*.

After the CITIC Square mall, take Shanxi Bei Lu north to the old **Ohel Rachel Synagogue** (No.500), built in 1920 by Jacob Sassoon and the spiritual home of the city's wealthy Sephardic Jewish community until their departure in 1949. The building was subsequently used as a stable, warehouse and Communist Party

meeting hall until then-US First Lady Hillary Clinton and Secretary of State Madeleine Albright asked to visit the building during a 1998 visit to China. The city had it cleaned up and painted. The synagogue is still not open to the public, but the Shanghai Jewish Centre (6278 0225) can arrange access for groups.

Across the street from the synagogue, at No.525, is a small antiques shop run by a pair of brothers, the **Messrs Li** (6255 7288). The shop is full of original bits and pieces salvaged from pre-Liberation Shanghai, from silverware to pianos and drawing room furniture. If you were wondering how the insides of the old villas you have been walking past once looked, this *Steptoe & Son* den will give you a good idea.

Lu, the 'land of car parts', past a property (No.39) once owned by the Kadoorie family and home to the World Jewish Youth Organisation. Cross over Yanan Zhong Lu on to Maoming Nan Lu, passing an old garage on the eastern corner and the art deco **Lyceum Theatre** (No.57, see p186), the past home of the Amateur Dramatic Club, before ending up at the former French Club – now the **Okura Garden Hotel** (see p38). The over-built block with Italian baroque-style arches at the back of the hotel on Changle Lu, which looks as if it had classy tenants in the past, was nothing more than a showy service garage. Reliving its past, couture is back in the former shops of Sir Victor Sassoon's Cathay Estate – now reborn as the 'Parade on Maoming Lu' opposite the hotel.

● *Peter Hibbard is the author of* Beyond the Bund: Walks in the Old Foreign Areas of Shanghai, *to be published in September 2007 by Odyssey.*

Back on Nanjing Xi Lu, one block west of Plaza 66, is the **Shanghai Centre**, the grandaddy of the city's commercial developments at just 17 years old. More commonly known as the Portman – after its American architect, who is also responsible for the Bund Centre and Tomorrow Square – the complex of apartments and shops was one of the first foreign-backed property ventures in the city after the Communist takeover in 1949. It opened in 1989, shortly after the Tiananmen Square incident. While most other foreigners were cutting ties with China at the unfair matching of tanks versus students, the money behind the Portman honoured its commitment. Because of this, the place has special rights such as its own telephone exchange (operated by US-based BellSouth), the only one in all China. It also boasted the first HSBC branch and automatic teller in Shanghai. In an eerie echo from the old days in Shanghai, we recently heard a young Shanghai resident of the Portman's precincts ask his mother: 'Can we go to China today Mummy?'

The central section of the complex is anchored on the five-star **Portman Ritz-Carlton Hotel** (see p37). Also here is the **Shanghai Centre Theatre** (see p187), which is home to the Shanghai Acrobats, plus a well-stocked, Western-style grocery store on the ground floor; a tailor; the HSBC bank and cashpoint; and – inevitably – a Starbucks.

On the upper level around the forecourt are six airline offices and a Toni & Guy Hair Salon, and the building itself houses several consulates (including that of the United Kingdom) and chambers of commerce.

While the Portman represents Shanghai's embracing of US-style market capitalism, directly across Nanjing Xi Lu is a monument to an earlier ideological union, that between China and the USSR, in the highly Muscovite form of the **Friendship Exhibition Hall** (1000 Yanan Xi Lu, by Tongren Lu, 6247 6980), known as the Shanghai Exhibition Centre and also as the 'wedding cake'. It was the early 1950s and the Chinese Communist Party had just 'saved' the country from the evil Kuomintang (Nationalist Party). China had also recently helped North Korea beat back the 'imperialist' Americans. To show off the first fruits of the new-won socialist paradise, the city government decided on a grand monument to international Communism, which – oh sweet revenge – was built on a site formerly occupied by a villa belonging to one of the Concession era's wealthiest foreigners, Silas Hardoon.

The Exhibition Hall was spruced up in 2001 and now regularly hosts exhibitions of a decidedly unsocialist nature, such as the Shanghai Boat Show, the Dog Show and various other decadent lifestyle exhibitions. When no major event is being held, the side halls are turned into cheap bazaars selling knock-down and knocked-off clothes and knick-knacks. Depending on the event being hosted, entry is free or at a price set by the organisers. Either way it is easy to slip in for a look around. Most of the rooms have long been denuded of their proletariat-lauding mural work, but the Soviet influence remains pervasive in the odd mixture of baroque Bolshevik-cum-beaux arts architecture and crowning red star. All the same, once you have seen one hall, you'll have more or less seen them all.

## Temples

A short walk west of the Portman and the Exhibition Hall, past the busy dim sum restaurant Bi Feng Tang (*see p107*), is the attractive expanse of greenery that is **Jingan Park**, formerly Bubbling Well Cemetery. Now it boasts a scenic lake overlooked by the Bali Laguna restaurant (*see p108*), a copy of an old tram car that is used as a snack bar, and a small but stunning garden (RMB 2) criss-crossed with serpentine pathways. On dry days old men practise big-character calligraphy, with water for ink, on the main path through the park. There's also a re-creation of the well that gave the cemetery and road their names; the original spring was just outside the cemetery gates, at what is now the junction of Nanjing Xi Lu and Wanghang Lu, and was paved over in 1919.

**Jade Buddha Temple.** *See p69.*

**Wujiang Lu**. *See p64.*

The well dated back to at least the third century AD, which was around the time that the first place of worship was erected on the site now occupied by the **Jingan Temple** (Temple of Tranquillity, *see below*). The first temple collapsed in 1216 and was rebuilt in something similar to the form you see today – 'something similar' because not a bit of the old structure remains, having been pulled down in the 1990s and relocated to Tongli in the Jiangsu province, where it survives in the private museum of business tycoon Jeffrey Wong. In Jingan it was rebuilt again from scratch like many historic structures, which have been replaced with concrete-based, gussied-up lookalikes. Jingan's reincarnation came with an inbuilt shopping mall, and the temple itself looks like it is constantly under construction. The main hall is a simple, and extremely ugly, concrete box. The only interesting time to visit is during a festival, when the place fills with worshippers.

West again along Nanjing Xi Lu, just before the junction with Wulumuqi Zhong Lu, the imposing white structure on the south side of the road is the Jingan **Children's Palace**. Each municipal district has one of these institutions, where gifted children receive special tutoring and perform for visiting dignitaries. Talent-show brats aside, what's interesting about the Palace is its former life as the fabled Marble Hall. Built for wealthy Shanghai Jew Sir Elly Kadoorie, the mansion took six years to complete. Its name derives from the massive amounts of Italian stone imported to ornament the fireplaces. It was the first house in the city to have air-conditioning and boasted a 19-metre-high (65-foot) ballroom with 5.4-metre (18-foot) chandeliers. Amazingly, the ballroom and chandeliers have survived and

can be viewed by anyone, so long as they turn up as part of a group and submit to a minder.

A swift 20-minute walk north of Nanjing Xi Lu, along Shanxi Bei Lu, is the **Jade Buddha Temple** (*see below*), or Yufo Si. Built in the 1920s, Jade Buddha Temple is distinctly more temple-like than Jingan Temple, with its quiet courtyards surrounded by effigy-packed halls, and a genuine, 1.9-metre-high (six-foot) Qing Dynasty Buddha statue, which is hidden upstairs and can be viewed for an additional RMB 10 fee. There being no room for a mall here, the shops are actually inside some of the halls, and vendors flog their trinkets while the faithful pray (for money) right beside them.

Worth a sneaky peek, just to see Buddhism's latest incarnation in the Middle Kingdom, is the bank-like office just inside the main gate of the temple on the left. Behind glass windows and computer screens, robed Buddhist monks sit like bank tellers, accepting (according to the titles above the windows) 'donations', 'initiations', 'car cleaning' commissions and 'conversions'. Don't try to change your pounds or dollars at the last one, unless of course you want release from the Wheel of Life in return.

North of the Jade Temple is the arty warehouse district of **Moganshan Lu** (*see p166*).

### Jade Buddha Temple

*170 Anyuan Lu, by Jiangning Lu (6266 3668/www. yufotemple.org). Metro Shanghai Railway Station.* **Open** 8am-4.30pm daily. **Admission** RMB 10 (plus RMB 10 to view Jade Buddha). **Map** p242 D2.

### Jingan Temple

*1686 Nanjing Xi Lu, by Huashan Lu (5213 1586/ www.shjas.com). Metro Jingan Temple.* **Open** 7.30am-5pm daily. **Admission** RMB 10. **Map** p242 C5.

# The Old City

Visit now: the city's historic centre is disappearing quicker than you can say 'modern metropolis'.

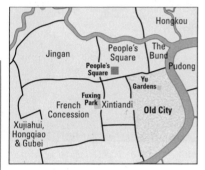

## Maps p248 & 249

The first place that most visitors are shown in Shanghai is the 'Old City'. Look at a map of Shanghai and it's easy to identify where the original settlement once lay: it's the yolk in the egg white of the city. The defining, near circular line of the old walls – demolished but now traced by Renmin Lu/Zhonghua Lu – rebuffs the Cartesian grid of the modern city.

Often called Yuyuan after its famous gardens, the core of the district is actually a modern, open-air shopping complex jam-packed with Chinese tourists and aggressive sellers who tout all manner of Chinese handicrafts to them. Don't be discouraged: there's a lot more of local and historical interest to be discovered within walking distance, and besides, some argue that only the revenue from the tour groups is keeping the place from becoming yet another high-in-the-sky development.

Previously known as Nanshi (Southern City), the site of Old Shanghai has been occupied for around 2,000 years and was well established as a small fishing town long before foreigners arrived to create Concession-era Shanghai. A five-kilometre (three-mile) circuit of walls and a moat were added in the 1550s to keep Japanese pirates at bay. With the arrival of the foreign powers, the Old City remained a wholly Chinese ghetto, squalid and mysterious, a place where few Westerners ever ventured.

Unfortunately, those looking for said wall and other evidence of a long and colourful history will be deeply disappointed. The wall was razed in 1911 at the fall of the last imperial dynasty, the Qing. Further destruction was not far behind: in 1932 and again from 1937-1945 the Japanese invaded and controlled the area, wreaking havoc. Then the Cultural Revolution made mincemeat of many of the district's religious and cultural sites. But by far the most thorough destruction of the Old City is likely to be at the hands of the current authorities in their urgent quest for 'progress'. In anticipation of the 2010 World Expo in Shanghai, most of this part of town is being wiped clean so that Shanghai can (here we quote from the official posters displayed around town) 'Show the world more splendour'.

Venture outside the central shopping area for something more interesting and significantly less noisy, but be mindful that most edifices are far from old and hardly original. Most, if not all, of these Ming- and Qing-styled structures are in fact here courtesy of the authorities, who have spent much of the past decade restoring and in some case totally rebuilding the Old City's cultural and religious buildings.

## Yu Gardens & Bazaar

The most visited part of the Old City is a tightly defined block bounded by Jiujiaochang Lu to the west, Fangbang Zhong Lu to the south, Fuyou Lu to the north and Anren Lu to the east. Taking up a large part of this area is Shanghai's number one tourist attraction, the **Yu Gardens** (218 Anren Lu, 6328 2465, open 8.30am-5pm daily, admission RMB 30) or the Garden of Leisurely Repose – known as Yuyuan to the locals (and, hence, to your taxi driver). The gardens were originally created in the 16th century for the governor of the Sichuan province Pan Yunduan. Neglect followed his demise, but the gardens were rescued and restored in the middle of the 18th century. These days the Yu Gardens are resplendent, with a design that embodies an artistic vision of the world in miniature, ingeniously mingling over 30 pavilions with hillocks and picturesque bridges, stairs, winding paths and carp-laden lotus ponds. Each section of the gardens is separated by curvaceous white walls, crowned with the head and body of a dragon.

One of the key features to look out for is the **Exquisite Jade Rock**, which stands in front of the Hall of Jade Magnificence. The rock was supposedly destined for the imperial park in Beijing, during the reign of Emperor Hui Zong, but by misfortune its cargo boat sank and it ended up languishing at the bottom of the Huangpu River. It was later rescued by the creators of the Yu Gardens.

Of the pavilions, the **Three Ears of Corn Hall** is the largest; symbols of plenty (rice ears, millet, wheat seedlings, melons and fruit) adorn the doors and windows. The nearby **Hall for Viewing the Grand Rockery** is a beautiful two-storey building overlooking a pond. Upstairs is the 'Chamber for Gathering the Rain', which derives its name from a Tang Dynasty poem by Wang Bo. The 'Corridor for Approaching the Best Scenery' (aren't these just the greatest of names?) leads to the heart of the gardens, the **Grand Rockery**, which was built with 2,000 tons of yellow stone quarried from Zhejiang province and the whole thing cemented together with rice glue. At the foot of the rockery is the **Pavilion for Viewing Frolicking Fish** and a neighbouring 200-year-old wisteria, while a gingko tree, reputed to be 400 years old, stands in front of the **Ten Thousand Flower Pavilion**. Also worth a look is the **Hall of Mildness**, which houses a century-old set of furniture skilfully carved from banyan tree roots.

Note that the gardens can get uncomfortably crowded. Our advice is to get there early or visit during the relatively quiet lunchtime period.

## Yu Gardens Bazaar

Just outside the entrance to the Yu Gardens is a large ornamental lake, teeming with carp and crossed by the wonderfully batty **Bridge of Nine Turnings**, which zigzags across the water in lightning-flash fashion. It's built like this to halt evil spirits, which are apparently unable to turn corners. At the centre of the lake sits the **Huxinting Teahouse**, patronised by presidents and queens, and immortalised on dinner plates worldwide as the Willow Pattern Teahouse.

There are a number of speciality eateries in the vicinity, notably **Nan Xiang** (*see p109*), a famous little dumpling shop that sells delicious steamed dumplings near the entrance to the gardens – and it is easy to find simply by following the snaking queues of salivating customers. In a nearby Ming Dynasty-style pavilion, **Lu Bo Lang** (*see p109*) does rather inferior dumplings – the best of them are filled with crabmeat.

Around the lake area is the **Yu Gardens Bazaar** (Yuyuan Shangsha), an area of narrow lanes filled with over 100 small stores. The

# Totally Lupu-y

In April 2006 the Shanghai Yangzi International Travel Agency opened the Lupu Bridge 'Shanghai climb', consisting of a climb up 367 steps to the top of an arch, 100 metres (330 feet) above the Huangpu River. The **Lupu Bridge**, to the south of the iconic Nanpu

Bridge, looks like a more modern version of the Sydney Harbour Bridge. It is officially the world's longest arched bridge and was opened in June 2003 to much fanfare, with Yao Ming, the Chinese NBA basketball star, leading a run across the bridge during the opening ceremony. Now visitors are being encouraged to clamber up its superstructure to enjoy a view previously only experienced by engineers, maintenance workers and seagulls. The hike can only be done in good weather and is unavailable to anybody displaying signs of inebriation or ill health. We're slightly alarmed by the hike's 'emergency route', which (from the look of the site's diagram) involves rappelling down one of the bridge's supports, and by the fact that the agency feels the need to post a number to ring for complaints. For next of kin, perhaps?

*Lupu Bridge, 909 Luban Lu (800 620 0888/ www.shanghaiclimb.com).* **Open** 10am-4pm daily. **Admission** RMB 80. **No credit cards.** **Map** p241 E5.

# NEW TIME OUT
## SHORTLIST GUIDES 2007

**Barcelona**
2007
WHAT'S NEW | WHAT'S ON | WHAT'S NEXT

**London**
2007
WHAT'S NEW | WHAT'S ON | WHAT'S NEXT

**New York**
2007
WHAT'S NEW | WHAT'S ON | WHAT'S NEXT

**Paris**
2007
WHAT'S NEW | WHAT'S ON | WHAT'S NEXT

**Prague**
2007
WHAT'S NEW | WHAT'S ON | WHAT'S NEXT

**Rome**
2007
WHAT'S NEW | WHAT'S ON | WHAT'S NEXT

# The MOST up-to-date guides to the world's greatest cities

**UPDATED ANNUALLY**

**WRITTEN BY LOCAL EXPERTS**

Available at all major bookshops at only
£6.99 and from timeout.com/shop

architecture is traditional in style but modern in execution, and the whole thing comes across as a sort of Disneyfied version of 'ye Olde Shanghai'. Of the few places of genuine interest, look out for **Liyunge Shanzhuang** (35 Yuyuan Lao Lu), a shop specialising in fans that's been around since 1880, and also the city's oldest medicine store **Tong Hang Chun Traditional Chinese Medicine Store** (20 Yuyuan Xin Lu, *see p149*), where you can stock up on bear bile and preserved antlers.

## Temple of the City God

At the heart of the Yu Gardens Bazaar area is what in days gone by was the focal point of the town, the **Temple of the City God** or Chenghuang Miao (249 Fangbang Zhong Lu, 6386 5700, open 24hrs daily, admission RMB 5). Originally built in 1403, the temple was traditionally a venue for fairground activities, where entertainers and vendors would gather at festival times. It was believed that the City God had charge of all the other spirits who had once been embodied in the citizens of Shanghai. Following years of neglect and prior use as a factory and shop, the temple was restored a few years back and people still seek advice from the god on private and business matters.

**Confucius Temple.**
*See p75.*

## Fuyou Lu & Shanghai Old Street

North of the Yu Gardens area is Fuyou Lu, address of an array of warehouse-like jewellery and festival-supply stores; red lanterns are in abundant supply. More culturally noteworthy is the **Chenxiangge Nunnery** (29 Chenxiangge Lu, open 7am-4pm daily, admission RMB 5), which was part of the estate of the gardens' original owner. It was rebuilt as a temple in the early 19th century and, like all religious edifices in the area, ignobly converted into a factory workshop during the Cultural Revolution. Following five years of careful restoration, it reopened as a place of worship in 1994. Visit for the absolute serenity within – seldom is there anyone there – and the massed figurines of the 348 disciples that adorn the surface of a vault enclosing a gilded statue of Buddha. A few minutes' walk west, the **Fuyou Lu Mosque** is one of the oldest surviving buildings in the area. Consisting of three interconnecting halls in traditional Chinese style, it was built in 1870 and reopened in 1979.

South of the Yu Gardens, the street known to locals as Fangbang Zhong Lu is marketed to visitors as **Shanghai Old Street**. It's a picturesque alley of two-storey shop-houses, some of which may be old and most of which were renovated when the street was given a tourist-friendly makeover at the turn of the millennium. Just east of the junction with Jiujiaochang Lu is the **Hua Bao Building**, with an interesting, if expensive, basement antique market.

Travelling west from the junction with Jiujiaochang Lu, Shanghai Old Street is lined with antique, curio and craft stores, one of which is the endlessly fascinating **Seal Military** (361 Fangbang Zhong Lu, by Jiujiaochang Lu, 6311 1297), which stocks Mao memorabilia. Fuyou Lu is home to a lively **antiques market** housed on the north side in the Cang Bao Building, just before the *pailou*, or ceremonial arch, that frames the street. The market comes alive at weekends, and especially on Sundays, with an astounding array of antiques and knick-knacks spread over its four levels. It's best to get there early as many stallholders pack up mid afternoon.

Also on this section of Shanghai Old Street are several teahouses, including the **Old Shanghai Teahouse** (385 Fangbang Zhong Lu, 5382 1202, open 9am-9pm daily), which doubles as a small museum. The 1920s and 1930s artefacts and memorabilia on display include clothing, paintings, photos, posters and some old maps.

# Walk on: The Old City

**Start/finish**: Bridge of Nine Turnings,
Yu Gardens
**Length**: approximately 3.5km (2.2 miles)

On first impressions, the **Yu Gardens**
(Yuyuan) and surrounds seem to have a
lot in common with Disneyland: impressive,
but also gaudy, full of shops selling tat
and bursting at the seams with tourists at all
times. It is overwhelming and underwhelming
at the same time, and before long you'll be
in need of a refreshment break – the perfect
time to explore the surrounding streets
and alleys.

During your visit to Yu Gardens, before
long you'll find yourself at its heart, the
ornamental lake crossed by the **Bridge of
Nine Turnings** (*see p71*). Positioned by the
lake, point yourself due south and head
towards Starbucks (resisting the temptation
to order a double mocha-chocca-lappa-cino)
and veer left. Hang a right at Dairy Queen,
pausing for a peek at the Layang traditional
**picture theatre** (RMB 3). Carry on straight,
then take the next left. In front of you is the

**Temple of the City God** (*see p73*). This is
where the walk proper begins, with a right-
hand turn into the shopping arcade before
the temple, past the cutting-edge shop – it
exclusively sells knives and scissors – also
on your right.

Emerging from the cacophony of
commercialism, turn right and stroll west
down **Fangbang Zhong Lu** (Shanghai Old
Street, *see p73*), a street full of Mao
memorabilia, Chinese paintings, decorated
chopsticks and all-round tourist kitsch. To fuel
your search, pick up a *rou* or *cai baozi* (meat
or vegetable steamed bun) – RMB 0.50-1.20
– or take your pick of the seasonal fruit being
sold by street-side vendors.

After crossing over Jiujiaochang Lu,
stroll north up Houjia Lu, then head right
on Wangyima Nan Nong (take a moment
to admire the *shikumen* dwellings near
the entrance, examples of a pre-renovation
Xintiandi, *see p79* **Changing lanes**) to sample
a slice of what the entire locality used to be
like. At the end of the lane, turn left, and then

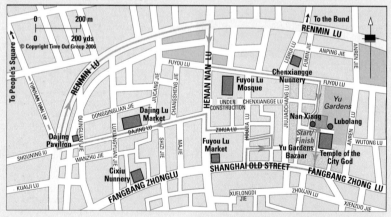

## West of Henan Lu

To escape the tourist version of Old Shanghai,
continue west on Fangbang Zhong Lu across the
major north–south thoroughfare Henan Nan Lu.
This entire area is slated for bulldozing; get in
now to glimpse a slice of undeveloped Shanghai.
About 100 metres along are the ochre-coloured
walls of the new part of the **Cixiu Nunnery**

(admission RMB 10). Continue north around the
nunnery on Zhenling Jie to the older and more
interesting part of the nunnery. There's a richly
decorated small courtyard temple, built in 1870,
with a prayer hall on one side and dormitories
for the nuns opposite. Visitors are welcome. A left
at the top of the lane leads past a row of *shikumen*
housing (*see p79* **Changing lanes**) from the
1920s and to a magnificent old school building.

left again to emerge back out on to Houjia Lu. From here you will keep heading west. First, cross the street to **Zihua Lu** to soak up the busy street life. Then head over Henan Nan Lu, bear right, and then take the first left down Dajing Lu.

At times, it seems as if almost every local resident is out on **Dajing Lu** going about their daily business, and – judging by the abundance of food stalls – their vocation is mostly eating. This is a great place to try *dabing* (a bread similar to a savoury doughnut, sold at RMB 2), grab a snack of fruit, some roast duck, *shandong jiaozi* (RMB 1 for six fried dumplings) or just pick up a couple of *zongzi* (parcels of glutinous rice and meat, wrapped in banana leaf). The local food market (on your right) makes for compelling browsing, though stalls selling snails, eels and chicken's feet may affect your appetite.

The further you walk down Dajing Lu, the more half-demolished houses you pass, until you finally emerge at the **White Cloud Taoist Temple**, adjacent to the **Dajing Pavilion** (for both, *see below*). The latter is the only remnant of the wall that once surrounded the entire Old City. If you're still hungry, take a short detour north up **Yunnan Nan Lu** towards People's Square (Renmin Guangchang) for stalls selling kebabs, *nang* (round bread) and hotpot. Otherwise, follow Renmin Lu as it curves east, past a series of bridal shops on your left (and a gargantuan wedding shopping mall on your right). Take a right on to Henan Nan Lu and a left on Fuyou Lu, where you can stop by the historic **Fuyou Lu Mosque** (*see p73*).

Continue straight to end back at Yu Gardens, where you can pick up that tablecloth/chopstick set/paper-cutting kit you've decided you can't live without.

Take a left on to Dajing Lu and walk west to the impressive **White Cloud Taoist Temple**. It looks like it's seen a bit of history, but was actually only completed in 2004 – and was already being renovated in 2006. Serving as a stage for the daily rituals of Taoist monks, the temple possesses seven unique Ming Dynasty bronze statues. The neighbouring **Dajing Pavilion** adjoins the only surviving section of the Ming Dynasty city wall. It's a two-storey tower that originally served as a battlement from which archers could fire on attacking Japanese pirates in the 16th century. It was subsequently converted into the Guangong Temple and today houses a rather primitive exhibition dedicated to the native city. On the second floor you'll find a small model of the old town and a short series of visuals, annotated in Chinese, that chronicle the area's history.

Across main thoroughfare Renmin Lu, hawker-lined **Yunnan Lu**, with its chain of small food stands, stalls and eateries, makes a beeline north for central People's Square.

## Confucius Temple

South on Zhonghua Lu – the lower half of the Old City 'ring road' – a ceremonial arch marks the entrance to Wenmiao Lu. This is the site of the only **Confucius Temple** (215 Wenmiao Lu, open 9am-5.15pm daily, admission RMB 10) to have survived in the city. The temple's present appearance dates from 1855, days of blood and thunder during which it was occupied by the gangster Small Swords Society for an assault on the city (*see p11*). However, much more damage was done to its majesty and riches during the Cultural Revolution, only some of which was rectified during the extensive restoration work that took place in the mid 1990s.

The centrepiece is the 20-metre-high (66-foot) **Kuixing Pavilion**, which overlooks the 'Sky and Cloud Reflection Pool' and once commanded views over the whole of the Old City (it's now dwarfed by a rash of neighbouring dwellings, all with more than 20 storeys). The temple features a number of exhibition halls with exhibitions of Chinese crafts, including a teapot museum.

As well as being a centre for worship, the compound was a place of learning. It housed the National Library of Shanghai in the 1930s. Students hoping for success in the June national examinations still tie red ribbons around the camphor trees in front of the temple. The main courtyard of the temple also hosts a large and lively parasol-shaded second-hand **book market** each Sunday. While most titles are in Chinese, a good rummage could turn up revolutionary and pre-revolutionary offerings in English. Outside, the street is busy with vendors peddling pirated CDs and DVDs, and also offers some great street eats. There's also a large book market north-east of the complex, just off Xuegong Lu.

A few streets north and east, close to the junction of Fuxing Lu and Henan Lu, is the **Peach Garden Mosque** or Xiaotaoyuan (52 Xiaotaoyuan Lu, open 8am-7pm daily), tucked down an alley of the same name. Completed in 1927, this imposing historic building with Western, Chinese and Islamic architectural adornments is the major centre for the city's growing Muslim population and serves as the headquarters for the Shanghai Islamic Association. Like everything else around here, it has been recently restored to something like its previous state.

## Dongjiadu Lu & Nanpu

South-east of the Old City (as defined by the line of the old walls) is the **Dongjiadu Cathedral**. This is Shanghai's oldest standing, and perhaps most beautiful, place of worship. It was founded in 1849 by a Bishop Besco and a band of Jesuit missionaries. In recent times its magnificent Spanish baroque-style façade and interior have been meticulously restored. The bas-relief on the upper sections of the walls adopts traditional Chinese emblems and the bell tower still holds all four original bells. The surrounding area once housed a huge Catholic community, with its own police force and fire brigade – something like China's very own Vatican – which survived until the early 20th century. Mass is held every morning. At other times just ring the bell; visitors are welcome. A 1914 school building, once attached to the cathedral, stands across the road.

A short walk south of Dongjiadu Lu at 399 Lujiabang Lu is the new site of Shanghai's famous **fabric market** (*see p134*). Until recently located just across the street from the cathedral, this vast but orderly grouping of 200 small shops is Shanghai's best location for fabrics and tailoring.

One of the city's most photographed modern landmarks is the **Nanpu Bridge**. Completed as recently as 1991, this was the first bridge over the Huangpu River. Cars ascend a spiralling access road to reach its distinctive cable-suspended structure; pedestrians and tourists take the lift up to the main span for great views upriver and across the city (open 8.30am-4pm daily). The area to the south of the bridge, down to the new **Lupu Bridge** (*see p71* **Totally Lupu-y**), is being razed to accommodate one of the main sites for the 2010 World Expo.

One hopes that the authorities have sense enough to avoid the destruction of the Sanshan Guild Hall, a precious bit of history that lies in the way of the Expo. Up until the 1920s guilds were very important associations for regulating the economic and social life of migrant workers living in Shanghai. Sanshan, one of the few surviving guild halls, was built in 1909 for its Fujianese community. The magnificent red-brick, stone and wood courtyard building was restored in 2002 and now serves as the **Shanghai Museum of Folk Collectibles** (*see below*). Its central feature is an opera stage with an intricately carved roof.

### Shanghai Museum of Folk Collectibles

*1551 Zhongshan Nan Lu, by Nanchezhan Lu (6314 6453).* **Open** 9am-4pm daily. **Admission** RMB 4. **No credit cards. Map** p248 L11.
The exhibition halls display temporary exhibitions from private collections and offer an intriguing insight into the history of Shanghai through such everyday items as cosmetics, cigarette lighters and cases from the 1920s and '30s, small shoes for bound feet, porcelain and family photos. There are also more general Chinese arts and crafts on display.

**Shanghai Old Street**. See p73.

# Xintiandi

This city-centre commercial development nods to Old Shanghai,
but nearby Dongtai Lu market sells it to you.

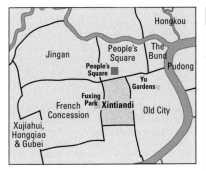

**Map p248**

In the five years since **Xintiandi** (pronounced
'shin-tien-dee') opened to the public, it has
become an unlikely centre of entertainment and
tourism: entertainment, as it houses better-than-
average dining and shopping destinations; and
tourism, because it has become something of a
cultural icon for China, a model for successful
urban development that is being furiously
copied throughout the country. This is quite
a statement for what is essentially an open-air
shopping mall. But think again – China is
devoid of continental-style outside eateries
coupled with boutique shopping for the
leisured classes. And now that China has the
latter, it needs the former. Xintiandi's mix of
retail, entertainment, commercial office space
and residential units is the Shape of Things to
Come for China; many of the tourists at your
side are eager town planners and developers
from Anywhere, China.

Xintiandi's popularity is helped by being
just a ten-minute walk south of central People's
Square, and just off Huaihai Zhong Lu, with its
clustered malls, office towers and department
stores visited by hundreds of thousands of
potential consumers each day.

For commerce of a less brassy nature, a brief
walk east of Xintiandi is the antique and curios
market on **Dongtai Lu** and its side streets,
which offer an authentic slice of Old Shanghai
sans redevelopment. It can only be a matter of
time, though, before the bulldozers get stuck in.

For key sights and streets in Xintiandi
written in **Chinese script**, *see pp252-255*.

## Xintiandi

If the Bund was the showpiece of early 20th-
century Shanghai, then Xintiandi is arguably one
of its 21st-century counterparts. But whereas the
structures on the Bund were all about bombast,
Xintiandi is a celebration of modern Shanghai's
ability to fuse old and new, East and West. Its
28 buildings, grouped into North and South
blocks, are all examples of renovated or wholly
reconstructed *shikumen*. They're a photogenic
fusion of 19th-century English terrace housing
and south-of-the-Yangtze traditional Chinese
residences, originally built in the 1920s and '30s
to house the Chinese middle classes. For more
on *shikumen, see p79* **Changing lanes**.

As part of Xintiandi's redevelopment,
teams of international and local architects
retained – or built anew – the exteriors, while
the interiors were gutted and refitted to modern
requirements. Between the buildings run tiny
*nongtangs* (alleys) that connect with large
open-air plazas suitable for European-style
alfresco dining and drinking. The development
is subject to the most meticulous touches, such
as buttermilk treatment to help grow moss on
bricks and the monthly inspection of manhole
covers to ensure their proper alignment.

However, for all the care and the veneration
of traditional architectural forms, the result in
some areas can resemble a high-end mall (or,
worse, a Disneyfied Shanghai street scene), a
Potemkin village of pretty façades aimed at
seducing affluent visitors and parting them
from their money. Its 100 or so units are filled
with ritzy shops such as Cheese & Fizz, which
sells the likes of Italian wines and French
cheeses, as well as multinational chains of the
ilk of Benetton, French Connection, Starbucks,
Häagen-Dazs and Vidal Sassoon.

There are several worthwhile places to eat
and drink within the complex: we like the
American café **KABB** (*see p109*), superior
lunch venue **Simply Thai** (*see p120*) and, for
top-end dining, **T8** (*see p111*), which are all in
the North Block. The South Block has dim sum
specialist **Crystal Jade** (*see p110*) and the
**UME International Cineplex** (*see p164*).
Cultural representation is otherwise limited
to the **Shikumen Open House Museum**
(*see p78*) and, irony of ironies, the **Museum of**

the First National Congress of the Chinese Communist Party (*see below*) – the humble meeting room in which Chinese Communism was founded now anchors the North Block of this most bourgeois of developments.

East across Huangpi Nan Lu is a fabricated but pretty **lake**. This is also part of the Xintiandi development. When completed in several years' time, it will cover some 20 blocks at the heart of the city. This section is designed for the well-heeled long-term leaseholder and is flanked by modern residential towers (Lakeville at Xintiandi) and grade-A office buildings (on the chillingly named Corporate Avenue). The area east of the lake is pencilled in for more upscale shopping but is for now occupied by real traditional housing, an antiques market (*see below*) and a temple. Visit while you still can.

## Museum of the First National Congress of the Chinese Communist Party

*374 Huangpi Nan Lu, by Xingye Lu (5383 2171).* *Metro Huangpi Nan Lu.* **Open** 9am-4pm daily. **Admission** RMB 3. **No credit cards. Map** p248 H7. Here, on 23 July 1921, the Chinese Communist Party was formed in reaction to foreign domination. A large upstairs exhibition area sets the historical context, displaying hated imperialist, Concession-era icons, such as the seat used by the chairman of the Shanghai Municipal Council. The centrepiece is a lifelike wax diorama immortalising the historic First Congress, with Mao centre-stage. Then it's down to

a small red-brick lane house to see where this gathering actually took place. The gift shop has some excellent memorabilia.

## Shikumen Open House Museum

*No.25, Lane 181, Taicang Lu, North Block, by Xingye Lu (3307 0337/www.xintiandi.com). Metro Huangpi Nan Lu.* **Open** 10.30am-10.30pm Mon-Thur, Sun; 11am-11pm Fri, Sat. **Admission** RMB 20; RMB 10 under-12s, over-60s. **No credit cards. Map** p248 H7.

A small museum devoted to vernacular architecture of the kind seen around Xintiandi, with photographs and models that are labelled in Chinese and English. The foyer doubles as a visitor information centre with assorted bilingual publications on Xintiandi, brochures, free magazines and maps of Shanghai.

# Dongtai Lu Antiques Market

Just a few twists south and east of Xintiandi's lake and park is one of Shanghai's most popular markets. Over 100 booths and shop-houses line Dongtai Lu and Liuhekou Lu, all filled with a mix of antiques (fresh-from-the-factory as well as the genuine article), kitsch and trash. Browse for Mao memorabilia, vintage furniture and locally printed old Tintin books in Mandarin. It's a popular spot with tourists and, although many of the pieces can be found across China, it's a good place to hunt for fragments of Shanghai's past. Most stalls open between 10am and 5pm daily. *See also p134.*

**Dongtai Lu Antiques Market.**

# Changing lanes

Shanghai has long been densely populated. Even during the Concession era, when Shanghai presented a Westernised face to the world, most of the residents were Chinese – and there were a lot of them. Urban planners had to find a way to incorporate their requirements, such as ancestor-worship halls and south-facing gardens, into dense, middle-class neighbourhoods. The result was the *shikumen* or 'stone-gated' house: grey and brown two-storey tenements, which are arranged in terraces.

The appearance is more northern England mill town than archetypal China. The houses typically had five rooms upstairs and five down; family members had the best rooms, while servants and paying lodgers took the undesirable north-facing rooms and roomlets off rear staircases. Gardens were often minuscule and paved. Developers built the *shikumen* in south-facing rows, densely squeezed together, with common bathing facilities at the ends of each lane. The *shikumen* model was standard throughout Shanghai, and by the 1930s almost every part of town was gridded with them.

Sadly, economic pressure to develop Shanghai has had a harsh impact on the *shikumen* lanes. In spite of the fact that most Shanghainese were born and raised in these neighbourhoods, little is being done to protect this key part of the city's shared heritage. Most are overcrowded and poorly maintained by non-owning occupants, which only favours the pro-development lobby. And when it comes to development, the favoured method is to send in the bulldozers. Finding creative ways to preserve the architecture is rarely an option, although there is the odd exception – notably Xintiandi (*pictured above*), where several dilapidated blocks of housing have been overhauled and restyled to create an upmarket mixed-use development. Even here no attempt was made to retain the original community: tens of thousands of long-term residents were evicted to pander to the credit card.

To see a good example of *shikumen* in their original state, visit 200-303 Maoming Bei Lu, which is between Nanjing Xi Lu and Weihai Lu, close to Shimen Yi Lu metro station.

One block east of Dongtai Lu is the **Wanshang Bird and Flower Market** (open 7am-7pm daily), which is where locals come to buy pets – rabbits, hamsters, puppies, kittens and crickets. Bought animals are dropped into plastic bags to be taken home, just like supermarket purchases.

At the southern end of the antiques market, where Ji'an Lu meets Fuxing Zhong Lu, is the **Fangzangjiang Buddhist Temple** (Lanes 2-9, 271 Jian Lu, by Fuxing Zhong Lu, 6311 4971). Built in 1923, it boasts a huge main hall split into two levels. On the lower level worshippers join with monks in prayer, while the upper hall houses giant Buddhist statues and fine bas-

relief murals. Around 1,000 devotees can be accommodated at any one time. Apart from the infectious atmosphere, what sets this temple apart from others is the melange of Western art deco and traditional Chinese styles in the interior and exterior design and decoration. The temple was restored and reopened to the public in 1999 – after years of neglect and, you guessed it, having been used as a factory. The temple adheres to the teachings of the Pure Land Sect, which worships Amitabha Pusa and believes in reincarnation to a Pure Land similar to Heaven. It was cloaked in scaffolding on our lastest visit, but should have unveiled its new façade by the end of 2006.

# French Concession

Eat, drink and shop your way around Shanghai's leafy enclave.

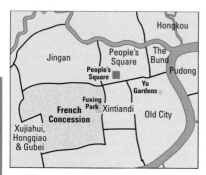

**Map p246 & p247**

It lacks the monuments and majesty of the Bund and the photogenic Chinese scenes of the Old City, and it can't compete with People's Square for cultural institutions, but there's no question that the French Concession is the most enchanting part of Shanghai.

It is predominantly low-rise, thanks to an enlightened bit of colonial-era town planning that ruled buildings must not exceed a height of one-and-a-half times the width of the road, and so far it has escaped the worst excesses of China's 21st-century redevelopment. The streets are narrow, and loop and meander beneath canopies of closely planted trees. Reflecting the cosmopolitan nature of the district's former inhabitants, the architecture mixes elegant French-styled mansion blocks with Spanish villas, Germanic Bauhaus-style apartment buildings with English Tudor country houses, and onion-domed Russian cathedrals with Gothic fantasies. It's all given flavour by a rich scattering of some of the city's best restaurants, and coloured by markets and countless small boutiques. Early mornings are soundtracked by shuffling street hawkers and the setting up of dawn markets; late nights echo with chattering revellers crawling from bar to bar. The French Concession is Shanghai's Marais, its Greenwich Village, its Soho even – but less crowded and prettier.

The French Concession is easily the most pedestrian-friendly part of the city and it is possible to spend days indulging in nothing more structured than aimlessly wandering, nosing down alleys and peering into courtyards, window shopping, and taking lots of time out in cafés and bars. For more on the history of the area, *see p81* **Shaping the Concession**.

Note that to the Chinese, there's no such thing as the 'French Concession' (it is part of the modern administrative districts of Luwan, Xuhui and Da Pu Qiao), but the term still has currency among the many foreign residents, who consider it to mean the area south of Yanan Lu, stretching from the Old City in the east to Xujiahui in the west. This area also includes **Xintiandi**, which, for the purposes of this guide, we have covered in its own chapter; *see pp77-79*.

For key sights and streets in the French Concession written in **Chinese script**, *see pp252-255*.

## Fuxing Park

The French municipality set aside the land for **Fuxing Park** ('foo-shing') in the early 20th century. The park's northern boundary was the Collège Français, one of the city's top public schools, while the central expanse was – and still is – a long rectangle delineated by arcades of tall plane trees. Turn up when the park gates open at 6am to watch the legions of tai chi enthusiasts, or come later to observe games of chess or cards, or the gentle waltzing of the veterans and pensioners who gather here daily. Fellow observers include comrades Engels and Marx, or at least their granite-hewn likenesses. In the north-west corner of the park exit is a well-tended rose garden with a circular fountain, which is overlooked by several posh eateries and nightclubs, including **Park 97** (*see p184* **California Club**).

On the west side of the park is Xiangshan Lu (formerly rue Molière), spiffy address of the **Former Residence of Sun Yatsen**. This is just one of several 'former residences' for the man considered the father of modern China; the house is open to visitors (*see p81*). Running north–south beside the house is **Sinan Lu** (née rue Massenet), one of the city's most attractive thoroughfares, which meanders between arcades of plane trees. Little surprise that several other dignitaries besides Sun Yatsen chose to make their homes here, including Yuan Shikai, the general who assumed the presidency and proclaimed himself emperor in 1912.

At No.73 is the **Former Residence of Zhou Enlai**, Premier and Foreign Minister of China from 1949 to 1976, which is also open to visitors (*see p82*). As with most houses around here, from its external appearance this freestanding, stuccoed home could just as easily originate in northern Europe or America.

Returning north, Sinan Lu is crossed by Gaolan Lu, which is dominated by the golden dome of the former **Russian Orthodox Church of St Nicholas**, built in 1933 and dedicated to the murdered last Tsar and his family. There is a persistent story that during the Cultural Revolution the church was saved

from destruction by a canny priest who added a Mao fresco above the doorway; the portrait is there but the tale is untrue. The church was once used as a washing-machine factory and more recently as a tapas bar and restaurant but, after complaints from the Moscow Patriarchate, the building is to be used for something slightly less sacrilegious.

### Former Residence of Sun Yatsen

*7 Xiangshan Lu, by Sinan Lu (6437 2954/www.sh-sunyat-sen.com). Metro Shanxi Nan Lu.* **Open** 9am-4.30pm daily. **Admission** RMB 8. **No credit cards.** **Map** p247 G8.

# Shaping the Concession

Shanghai's French community presented its claims for territory to the imperial Qing court in 1844, pressing for the same generous rights the British had gained the previous year in the aftermath of the First Opium War. The court allowed the French a muddy plot of less than two kilometres in breadth, south of the International Settlement (now the Bund area) and east between the old walled city of Shanghai and the river. Over the course of the next 70 years 'Frenchtown' expanded westward, eventually taking up about 18 square kilometres (seven square miles).

The Frenchness of the Concession was far from absolute. By the 1930s there were fewer than 10,000 French nationals within its boundaries, compared to 12,000 English subjects and more than half a million Chinese. Main avenue Joffre (now Huaihai Lu) may have been named for Joseph Jacques Césaire Joffre, known as the 'Saviour of France' after his victory in the 1914 Battle of the Marne, but the street was more commonly known as 'Little Moscow' because of the 30,000 Russians who lived there. Even so, there was a distinctly Gallic air about the place. The exclusively French municipal government (Conseil Municipal Français, or CMF) lined each street with French plane trees and enforced zoning regulations designed to make their part of the city more liveable. It's the legacy of these bits of localised legislation that gives today's French Concession a more bucolic and genteel air than much of the rest of the city.

There were, though, less attractive aspects of Frenchtown that contributed heavily to its character. By the beginning of the 20th century Anglo-Saxon sensitivities had largely forced the rampant trades in opium and prostitution out of the International Settlement, so the criminal

element, run by rival Chinese gangs, decamped to the more permissive sphere of French rule. The result was that the French Concession became the crime headquarters of Shanghai, if not all of China.

The gangsters are long gone, ruthlessly suppressed after the Communists took over in 1949. Neither has much of the Russian presence survived, save the two onion-domed Orthodox churches. However, the former Concession area retains an air of genteel sophistication absent from much of the rest of Shanghai. It's the part of town most associated with dining and drinking, and it's still where you'll find croissants (at the French Bakery on the corner of Ruijin Er Lu and Jianguo Xi Lu).

Sun Yatsen (1866-1925), founder of the Kuomintang Party that sought to replace the ailing Qing Dynasty with democratic leadership, lived here with his wife, Soong Qingling, from 1919 to 1925. It's a fairly modest house with simple furnishings, but the place was witness to innumerable historic meetings, including that between Madame Sun's sister, Meiling, and her future husband, Chiang Kaishek. The place is stuffed full of memorabilia, from a fascinating library of over 2,700 volumes to family photos and a Suzhou embroidery of a cat. Recorded English commentaries play in the main rooms.

### Former Residence of Zhou Enlai

*73 Sinan Lu, by Fuxing Zhong Lu (6473 0420).*
*Metro Shanxi Nan Lu.* **Open** 9am-4pm daily.
**Admission** RMB 2. **No credit cards.**
**Map** p247 G9.
Precociously placed in an established Nationalist area, Zhou and his wife, Deng Yingchao, managed and promoted Shanghai's underground Communist movement from here in 1946-7. Meetings were held in the ground-floor reception room, while the upper floors contained Zhou's office (spartan but elegant, with his briefcase and black suit displayed in the corner) and dormitories for Party workers, including the bedroom of Dong Biwu, who went on to become a leading Party figure.

## Taikang Lu

At its very southern end Sinan Lu intersects with Taikang Lu; part way along this busy street, an arch on the north side of the road gives access to a narrow lane known as the **Taikang Lu Art Street**. Since 1998, when a local entrepreneur turned a derelict sweet factory into low-rent studios for artists and designers, developers and aspiring creatives have seized space in neighbouring buildings in an attempt to transform the area into some

# Building a reputation

In 1918 a young Hungarian, Ladislaus Hudec, escaped from a Siberian prison camp and came to Shanghai. Trained in architecture at the Royal Technical University of Budapest, he began his new life in this new city at the practice of American RA Curry. At that time there were fewer than 20 architectural firms in the city and, given the wealth of building work around, it wasn't long before Hudec was able to strike out on his own.

Although his name is little known outside East Asia, Hudec was hands-down Shanghai's most remarkable pre-war architect. His meticulous attention to detail and human comfort – wide stairwells, high ceilings, multi-planar views – bucked the local trend for building functional boxes and slapping a bit of decoration on the outside. He also eschewed the easy route of undertaking repetitive projects for a few choice clients and instead cultivated an extraordinarily diverse portfolio including villas and mansion blocks, churches and hospitals.

The superior nature of Hudec's work has ensured that much of it has survived, notably the **Moore Memorial Church** (*see p63*), the **Joint Savings Society Building** (on the corner of Sichuan Lu and Hongkou Lu) and his masterpiece, the **Park Hotel** (*see p61*; *pictured left*). As well as the **Museum of Arts and Crafts** building (*see p86*), the French Concession is graced by the distinctive **Normandie Apartments** (*see p86*) and modernist **Herbutus Court** apartment block (now a hotel) on Yanan Xi Lu, near the junction with Jiangsu Lu.

Shanghai's present focus on architecture has brought the Hungarian latter-day fame, and he's now one of the few pre-Liberation Westerners officially lauded by the Shanghai Municipal Government. Fame, though, only counts for so much; the house he designed for himself and his family was razed to make way for a flyover in 1998.

**Fuxing Park**. *See p80.*

kind of alternative, low-rent Xintiandi. While the former factory does have some interesting tenants, including **Jooi Design** (*see p141*) and **Marion Carsten** (*see p143*), and there are all kinds of small boutiques, workshops, studios and cafés in the courts off the street, the area has never quite taken off. Unfortunately, it's too far off the beaten track to get much pedestrian traffic, which has meant short lifespans for some of the area's shops.

Also getting in on the arty scene is nearby 'lifestyle centre' **Bridge 8** (8 Jianguo Lu, by Sinan Lu, 6415 0789, www.bridge8.com). After earning their stripes working for the creators of Xintiandi (*see p77*), several employees struck out on their own to trendify an old auto repair centre. The area isn't a consumer paradise like its forebear, but it does have a few quirky design stores, trendy restaurant-nightclub Fabrique (*see p184*) and a pleasant café; across the street, Part 2 promises to bring more boutiques and restaurants.

Five minutes' walk south of Taikang Lu is the morbid yet absorbing **Museum of Public Security** (*see below*), with a gun collection that's reputed to be the largest in the world.

### Museum of Public Security
*518 Ruijin Nan Lu, by Xietu Lu (6472 0256/ www.policemuseum.com.cn). **Open** 9am-4pm Mon-Sat. **Admission** RMB 8. **No credit cards**. **Map** p247 F11.*
Opened in 1999 and housed in a concrete box of a building, the museum chronicles the history of the city's security services, going back to the establishment of its first police department in 1854 – though the emphasis is on post-1949 achievements. Only the introductions to the exhibition areas are in English, but little interpretation is required for the 3,000 items on display, which run from graphic photos of real-life murders to a huge armoury of weapons that includes some fascinating period pieces, such as a cigarette-case weapon made for mobster/police chief Huang Jinrong and an ebony pistol that belonged to Sun Yatsen.

## Huaihai Zhong Lu

Huaihai Zhong Lu, formerly avenue Joffre, is a great bisecting east–west slash across the French Concession. Its four lanes are perpetually gridlocked, and its pavements every bit as crowded with shoppers. The easternmost end, around the Huangpi Nan Lu metro station, is a canyon of shiny glass shopping malls of limited interest. To the west of the elevated Chongqing flyover, Huaihai is lined with pre-Liberation apartment blocks that rise above street-level boutiques catering predominantly to middle-class Chinese. The busiest area is around the junction with **Ruijin Er Lu**, but there's also much of interest at the junctions further west: **Maoming Nan Lu**, **Shanxi Nan Lu** and **Fenyang Lu**. Beyond **Changshu Lu**, the commerce fades and several consulates occupy large villas around here. Finally, at its western extreme, Huaihai is home to local restaurants and small shops as it slides into the neighbouring municipality of Xuhui.

## Ruijin Er Lu

The junction of Huaihai Zhong Lu and Ruijin Er Lu is all blaring 21st-century commerce, but you only have to walk a few minutes south to escape. On the west side of the street are the imposing gates of the **Ruijin Guesthouse**, a walled compound of several colonial-era buildings in a stately garden setting. This was formerly the town estate of HE Morriss Jr, whose father had made his money as founder and owner of the *North China Daily News*, at that time the second-largest English newspaper in Asia. The red-brick main residence became the Italian Embassy in 1938, before being sold to the Japanese. After 1950 it became government property and was used for hosting high-ranking Party leaders. It's now a posh hotel (*see p42*). Another building serves as the Shanghai offices for the *Economist*, while other tenants include the **Art Deco Garden Café** (*see p111*), the fabulous **Face Bar** (*see p129*) and Shanghainese restaurant **Xiao Nan Guo** (*see p116*). You're free to roam the immaculate grounds. Another gateway, on the west side, leads out to Maoming Nan Lu.

South again, Ruijin Er Lu connects with Shaoxing Lu, which is the home of the Shanghai publishing world. Numerous publishers have their offices here, most of them with bookshops attached – and all, of course, selling books in Chinese. For reading matter in English visit the unique and very beautiful **Old China Hand Reading Room** (*see p112*) at No.27, which is a café, bookshop and museum of 1930s Shanghai memorabilia all in one. There are several other attractive cafés along this street too.

## Maoming Nan Lu

Maoming Lu is the most schizophrenic of streets. One end is Shanghai's snobbishly genteel history typified, the other is only too contemporary with its mix of cheap booze, loud music, late licences and lairy behaviour. The junction with Huaihai Zhong Lu is signposted by the art deco spire and vertical lines of the **Cathay Theatre** (*see p163*), very obviously a creation of the 1930s. It remains a cinema, mixing Chinese-language movies with subtitled Hollywood blockbusters. North from here, Maoming Lu appears very much as it must have done in the days when this was rue Cardinal Mercier.

On the west side of the road is the former **Cercle Sportif Français**, one of the most prestigious clubs in Concession-era Shanghai. Ignore the distraction of the looming concrete tower block (added in the 1980s when the building became the Okura Garden Hotel,

*see p38*) and take a walk around the gorgeous gardens, then go inside to view the ballroom and splendid staircase lobbies. Have a drink on the roof of the south-facing porte cochère, and picture the lawn below filled with 20 tennis courts – below those a reinforced concrete nuclear bunker, a hidden reminder that the premises were used as a private guesthouse by Chairman Mao on his visits to Shanghai.

On the opposite side of the road from the Okura is the **Jinjiang Hotel** (*see p35*), which was formerly Sir Victor Sassoon's Cathay Mansions. Built in 1928, this was the first high-rise to be constructed on Shanghai's unstable alluvial mud. It's best known now as the venue in which then-US President Richard Nixon and Chinese Foreign Minister Zhou Enlai signed the Shanghai Communiqué in 1972, the first step toward normalising US-China relations. Flanking the entrance to the hotel grounds is pop-chinoiserie boutique **Shanghai Tang** (*see p141*) and, in the small lane behind the store, highly regarded Shanghainese restaurant **Yin** (*see p117*). Cathay Mansions was such a successful development that Sassoon built an even more luxurious block behind it, Grosvenor House, with a central 21-storey tower flanked by two great batwings. You can access it by going in through the gate beside Shanghai Tang and following the drive round to the right. The lobby is beautifully maintained and absolutely gorgeous.

Facing the Jinjiang across Changle Lu, the **Lyceum Theatre** (*see p186*) was built in the 1930s as the home of the British Amateur Dramatic Society. A young Margaret Hookham danced here, long before she changed her name and found fame as Margot Fonteyn. She was born in England but, at the age of eight, her father's work with the British Tobacco Company took the family to Shanghai. She studied ballet here before returning with her mother to the UK when she was 14. Her father stayed in Shanghai and was interned by the Japanese during World War II.

South of Huaihai, Maoming is lined by small, quality tailoring outfits and numerous cafés and restaurants. South of Fuxing Zhong Lu it is lined by nothing but bars, albeit a rather tawdry array of them; *see p123-131* **Bars & Pubs**.

## Shanxi Nan Lu

Shanxi Nan Lu lacks the charm of neighbouring streets. The junction with Huaihai is dominated by modern shopping plazas, where touts haunt the pavements delivering tugs and rapid-fire pitches of 'BagwatchshoesDVDlookalookalook!' For a bit of escapism, veer north for the fairytale stylings of the **Hengshan Moller Villa** (*see p38*); it's a guesthouse but the management doesn't mind non-guests taking a peek inside. On the corner with Changle Lu is **Garden Books** (*see p138*), selling newspapers, magazines and English-language reading, as well as coffee, teas and ice-cream.

Xinle Lu, running west off Shanxi, is one of the most appealing shopping streets, full of small, own-label fashion boutiques. It runs by Xianyang Park, which is filled all day long with elderly Chinese indulging in 'slow exercises' and playing cards and mahjong. Adjacent is Shanghai's other surviving Russian Orthodox church, the **Cathedral of the Holy Mother of God**. Built in 1931, it is currently empty.

Huaihai is also the site of the infamous Xiangyang Market or the 'fakes market', which – as we went to press – was to close in late 2006 as the government attempts to crack down on the huge trade in copied goods in China.

## Fenyang Lu

An attractive old villa screened by tall trees is home to the **Arts and Crafts Research Institute**, a part of which is the **Museum of Arts & Crafts** (*see p86*). The building itself is in a neo-classical style and was designed by émigré Hungarian architect Ladislaus Hudec (*see p82* **Building a reputation**) as the residence of the manager of the French municipal bus lines. It was later the home of Shanghai's first Communist mayor.

Fenyang Lu connects with **Taiyuan Lu**, which, back in the rum old days when it was known as rue Delastre, boasted not only a French-styled château but also a resident count and countess. The Count de Marsoulies was a lawyer who, along with several community leaders, had a falling out with local mobster Du Yuesheng when they asked him to remove his opium business from the Concession. To show that there were no hard feelings, Big Du invited the Frenchmen to dinner. Within the month several of the dinner guests were dead of a mysterious illness; the rumour was that Big Du had poisoned the mushrooms. The widowed countess remained in the house until 1940. After the war the US army rented the château and it's where General George Marshall stayed while attempting to broker a treaty between the Communists and the Nationalists. Today the château is the **Taiyuan Villa** (*see p42*).

Back where Fenyang meets Yueyang is one of Shanghai's only monuments to a non-Chinese individual, a statue of **Pushkin** (Puxijin), erected in 1937 by the Russian community on the centenary of the poet's death.

**Taikang Lu** 'Art Street'. See p82.

Sightseeing

**Museum of Arts & Crafts**.

## Museum of Arts & Crafts

*79 Fenyang Lu, by Taiyuan Lu (6437 2509). Metro Changshu Lu.* **Open** 9am-5pm daily. **Admission** RMB 8. **No credit cards. Map** p246 D8.

High-quality arts and crafts exhibits form only a small part of this museum. The villa in which the museum sits has been the home of an arts and crafts research institute since 1960, and visitors can observe artisans involved in carving, embroidery and paper-cutting. Much of the work is for sale; there is also an antique store in the basement.

## Changshu Lu & west

As Huaihai dips into the westernmost part of the French Concession the buildings become grander, with plenty of villas and mansions set in their own gardens. This was the 'country manor' part of town. Some of the properties now fly international flags as consulates, but many are bars and restaurants; places such as **Ambrosia** (*see p119*), **Le Garçon Chinois** (*see p117*), **Sasha's** (*see p130*) and **Yongfu Elite** (*see p131*) should be visited for the settings alone. A little out of the way but worth the effort is **Swire House** on Xinggou Lu. George Warren Swire was company chief of Butterfield & Swire, one of the first companies to set up operations in Shanghai. In 1934 he commissioned a new residence from celebrated Welsh architect Clough Williams-Ellis – creator of Port Merion on the Welsh coast, immortalised as the setting for 1960s cult TV series *The Prisoner*. The architect never visited China, instead sending drawings and samples by post. The resulting property was sufficiently magnificent to earn it the nickname

'the Palace'. Post-1949, of course, it became a state guesthouse. Today the house is part of the **Radisson Plaza Xingguo Hotel** (78 Xingguo Lu, by Huashan Lu, 6212 9998, www.radisson.com).

Also in the neighbourhood, just north of the Dingxiang Garden and buried in the basement of one of a group of residential tower blocks, is the **Propaganda Poster Art Centre** (*see p87*) – a must for enthusiasts of political kitsch.

Back on Huaihai Zhong Lu is the **Shanghai Library** (corner of Gaoan Lu), which is Asia's largest book repository. It's not much use if you don't read Chinese, but pass by at around 8am to see the library staff out front doing their tai chi exercises before starting work. Further west is the striking red-brick **Normandie Apartments**, also known as the Intersavings Society Building, which is a dead-ringer for New York's Flatiron Building, only on a smaller scale. On the ground floor (enter from Wukang Lu) is café-bar-restaurant **Arch** (*see p128*).

South across the busy intersection from the Normandie is an evocative slice of social and political history in the shape of the **Former Residence of Soong Qingling**, while a short walk further west it's commerce and industry that's celebrated at the **CY Tung Maritime Museum** (*see p87*), which is housed in a refurbished 19th-century dormitory on the campus of the prestigious Jiatong University, China's second-oldest secular educational institution. Fans of JG Ballard's autobiographical novel *Empire of the Sun* might like to stroll up Xinhua Lu, which angles off Huaihai Xi Lu north of the university; this is the former Amherst Road where both Ballard and his fictional alter ego Jim spent their childhood years.

## CY Tung Maritime Museum

*Jiatong University Campus, 1954 Huashan Lu, by Huahai Xi Lu (6293 2403/www.cytungmm.com). Metro Xujiahui.* **Open** 1.30-5.30pm Tue-Sun. **Admission** free. **Map** p246 A10.

The ground floor plots China's often-understated maritime history from Neolithic times to the present day. Exhibits highlight the maritime route of silk and porcelain during the Middle Ages and China's leading role in naval innovation during the 15th century. The first floor is dedicated to the activities and manifold interests of Shanghai-born shipping tycoon Mr Tung and includes the ship's bell from the ill-fated *Queen Elizabeth*; Tung acquired the old Cunard liner in 1970, only to see her destroyed by fire in Hong Kong two years later.

## Former Residence of Soong Qingling

*1843 Huaihai Zhong Lu, by Yuqing Lu (6474 7183). Metro Hengshan Lu.* **Open** 9am-4.30pm daily. **Admission** RMB 8. **No credit cards**. **Map** p246 B9.

One of China's leading ladies, Soong (1893-1981) was the wife of Sun Yatsen, and a politician of some clout in her own right (for a while she was Vice-President of the People's Republic). This is the house in which she grew up and to which she returned to live fol-lowing her husband's death in 1948. The sitting and dining rooms contain a photographic record of Mao's visit to the house and a large selection of gifts received from foreign dignitaries. Don't miss the garage and its two limousines, a Chinese 'Red Flag' and a Russian 'Jim' presented by Stalin in 1952. Displays include books, family photos and personal correspondence, as well as written exchanges with Mao, Nehru and Stalin. The statue outside was completed in 2003 to commemorate the 110th anniversary of her birth. For more on the Soong family, *see below* **Gone for a Soong**.

## Propaganda Poster Art Centre

*Basement, Building B, 868 Huashan Lu, by Wukang Lu (6211 1845). Metro Changshu Lu.* **Open** 10am-3pm daily. **Admission** RMB 20. **No credit cards**. **Map** p246 B7.

The brainchild of Yang Peiming, the PPAC is two basement rooms in a residential tower block hung floor to ceiling with a stunning collection of original posters from 1949 to 1979. Mr Peimang delights in leading visitors through the collection (there are at least 200 pieces), explaining each bit of artwork. The fact that you may not understand Chinese and he has only four words of English is no impediment: when he comes to the images of ruddy-cheeked Chinese peasants crushing imperialist Uncle Sams underfoot, you worry then that he's going to damage himself from laughing so hard. Some of the posters are also for sale.

**Sightseeing**

# Gone for a Soong

Soong Qingling was the daughter of **Chiaoshun 'Charlie' Soong**, China's most famous dad. Charlie was born in 1866 in Hainan, China. At the age of 14 he stowed away on a sailing ship and began a career as a trader in Boston, Massachusetts. It's here that he developed a strong friendship with an American evangelist who sent him to university and seminary in the American South. Returning to China, Charlie moved to Shanghai. After six years of unrewarding preaching, he embarked on a successful career as a bible publisher, a flourmill comprador and machinery agent. In the 1890s he met another Western-educated Chinese, Sun Yatsen, and joined the young revolutionary in his anti-Qing Dynasty movement. This friendship dramatically changed the fortunes of Charlie and his family.

Charlie's chief legacy is his four children. His three daughters (Soong Ailing, Soong Qingling and Soong Meiling) and his son (TV Soong) were to become some of the most influential people in 20th-century China. Ailing married one of the wealthiest Chinese of the day, HH Kung, who would go on to hold office as China's finance minister – as would TV Soong. The second daughter, Qingling, married her revolutionary idol Sun Yatsen, while the third daughter wed the Nationalist leader Chiang Kaishek. The house on Xiangshan Lu that Qingling and Sun Yatsen shared is now open to visitors (*see p81*).

Charlie's second and third daughters continue to inspire intense love and hate, respectively. Qingling was made honorary president of the People's Republic before her death in 1981. Her name graces children's bookstores and countless children's awards that are bestowed on the gifted throughout China. Her former home (*see above*) is something of a shrine. Meiling, on the other hand, earned China's undying enmity for her loyalty to her husband, the man responsible for the wholesale massacre of Communists in 1937; the unhappy couple fled together to Taiwan in 1949.

# Xujiahui, Hongqiao & Gubei

Suburbia, Shanghai style.

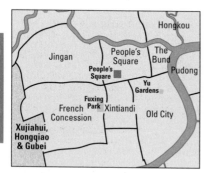

Jingan

People's Square

Hongkou

The Bund

People's Square

Pudong

Yu Gardens

Fuxing Park

French Concession

Xintiandi

Old City

Xujiahui, Hongqiao & Gubei

**Map p240 & p246**
Xujiahui (pronounced 'shoe-jeeah-way'), Gubei ('goo-bay') and Hongqiao ('hong-cheow') make up the great suburban mass that is Shanghai's urban south-west. These areas aren't high on charm, serving more as an introduction to the ills of modern China, with traffic congestion, soulless architecture, gated communities, chain stores and super-sized restaurants. But with careful planning your trip can take in the interesting slices of history that remain, as well as the occasional intriguing landmark.

Bordering the old French Concession, **Xujiahui** offers a veritable merry-go-round of light and sound, with its scores of neon-lit restaurants, office buildings and a cheapy-cheap underground shopping arcade. Many young people think nothing of spending a whole day combing the crowded stalls for a mobile phone tchotchke or glittery fashion accessory. In contrast to high-end Nanjing Lu, Xujiahui is decidedly mass market. Most of the activity is centred on the neighbourhood around Xujiahui metro station.

**Hongqiao** and **Gubei** are where the upwardly mobile move to flaunt their wealth by purchasing gaudy neo-classical flats. Hongqiao begins where old Settlement-era Shanghai ends (roughly where Zhongshan Xi Lu runs today) and extends west to the city's domestic airport. South of Hongqiao and west of Xujiahui lies the relatively new district of Gubei.

Both neighbourhoods are home to large populations of Japanese, Koreans, Indians and corporate Westerners – those who are lured to China with massive housing allowances, personal drivers and maids. As a result, these areas boast some of the city's best Western supermarkets and a good selection of Taiwanese and Korean restaurants, plus Japanese all-you-can-eat *teppanyaki*, which has become something of a Shanghai tradition for rambunctious twentysomethings. Truthfully, there isn't a whole lot happening in these family-oriented neighbourhoods, unless you like golf, and shopping at Carrefour.

## GETTING THERE
The Hongqiao and Gubei folk are too wealthy to need public transport, so the network is often patchy. Bus 911 from Huaihai Lu, corner of Shanxi Lu, runs all the way to the Zoo on Hongqiao Lu, while the No.48 from Jingan Temple runs along Yanan Xi Lu.

The most convenient way to get to Xujiahui is to take Metro Line 1, which stops at Xujiahui. For Longhua Park and temple, get off at Caobao Lu. Metro Line 2 is currently being extended out to Gubei and Hongqiao. By foot, from the French Concession walk south down Hengshan Lu.

For key sights and streets in Xujiahui, Hongqiao and Gubei written in **Chinese script**, *see pp252-255*.

## Xujiahui

Characterised by suburban towers and shopping malls, Xujiahui is the site of Shanghai's oldest Western settlement – a Jesuit centre started by a Chinese Catholic, Paul Xu, in the early 17th century. Xu was a high-ranking Ming official and a committed scholar, who had converted to Catholicism. He donated some of his land in Xujiahui (meaning 'gathering place of the Xu family') to the Church and invited Jesuit missionaries to take up residence.

The nuns and priests held on to various mission buildings throughout the intervening centuries until the Cultural Revolution, at which time they were 'resettled' elsewhere. Some of the structures – all of which were built by orphans under the wing of the Jesuits – are still standing, but many are being pulled down to make way for new towers. The most prominent extant building is the Catholic Cathedral, **St Ignatius** (158 Puxi Lu, by Caoxi Bei Lu, 6438 2595), built in 1910 on the site of earlier churches dating back to 1608. The more permissive political climate today allows the Chinese Catholic diocese to hold masses there for foreign and Chinese Catholics.

Xu was also a keen astronomer/scientist and he operated a meteorological observatory that could transmit its findings to the tower on the Bund (*see p55*). To this day, Shanghai's central weather observatory is in Xujiahui.

## Longhua & south

Just south of central Xujiahui is the bold yellow **Longhua Temple** (*see below*), named after the longhua tree under which Buddha attained enlightenment. Adjacent to the temple is urban Shanghai's only **pagoda**, standing an impressive 44 metres (145 feet) high, with delicate pointed eaves at each of its seven levels on which hang countless small bells.

Night lights in **Xujiahui**.

As tranquil as it appears, the park in which the temple stands has witnessed much bloodshed. In 19th-century Shanghai it was the site of countless public executions. Under the philosophy of 'kill the chicken to scare the monkeys', prisoners were led through the streets to be spat at and pummelled by spectators. Once at Longhua they would receive further gruesome and lengthy torture. During the 'White Terror' of 1927, when Kuomintang forces set about brutally exterminating their Communist rivals in Shanghai (*see p14*), thousands were led to Longhua where, out of sight of the general public, they were executed. These brutal weeks are the background to André Malraux's novel *Man's Fate*.

On the same site during World War II the Japanese ran their largest civilian internment camp in China for British, American and other Allied nationals. The camp – and the pagoda – feature in JG Ballard's book *Empire of the Sun* (and in Spielberg's movie adaptation).

Nearby, **Longhua Martyrs Cemetery** (Lieshi Lingyuan) commemorates the lives of the murdered Chinese Communists. A graceful tree-lined walkway leads up to a pyramidal Memorial Hall, while landscaped gardens are dotted with bizarre statues, such as an enormous torso of a man, half-buried in the earth but with one arm reaching desperately for the sky. The park also has picnic-perfect lawns.

There's more greenery about two kilometres (1.2 miles) further south at the little-visited **Shanghai Botanical Garden** (*see p90*) and also, to the south-west, in the lovely gardens of **Guilin Park** (*see below*).

### Guilin Park
*1 Guilin Lu, near Caobao Lu (6483 0915).* **Open** 5am-6pm daily. **Admission** RMB 2. Map p240 B5. For those who don't make it out to Suzhou (*see p209*), the gardens of Guilin Park offer a little taste of the southern Yangtze style, with stark white walls and grey-tiled roofs. The garden walls create a fitting canvas for slender bamboo stalks and delicate magnolia buds. Don't miss the sweet osmanthus festival (*see p166*) in late September and the darling little teahouse at the rear gate.

### Longhua Temple
*2853 Longhua Lu, Longhua Park (6456 6085). Metro Caobao Lu, then taxi.* **Open** 7am-5pm daily. **Admission** RMB 10. **No credit cards**. Map p240 C5. Shanghai's only fully functioning temple and monastery is scented with incense and contains the usual collection of gold-encrusted Buddhas. The star piece is a gargantuan 6,500kg (14,300lb) bell, which, legend has it, brings good fortune when struck three times (try your luck: RMB 10, RMB 300 on New Year's Eve). Each New Year's Eve the bell is struck 108 times, to address the 108 troubles of Buddhist

**Longhua Temple.** *See p89.*

philosophy. The temple is also the venue for numerous other festivities, including the Birthday of the Queen of Heaven (*see p166*) and the Longhua Temple Fair (*see p163*). **Photo** *above*.

### Shanghai Botanical Garden

*1111 Longwu Lu, Baise Lu (5436 3369). Metro Shanghai South Railway Station.* **Open** 7am-4.30pm daily. **Admission** RMB 15. **No credit cards.** **Map** p240 C6.

Whereas most of Shanghai's green spaces are filled with seasonal flowerbeds and rows of French-inspired plane trees, the Botanical Garden is lush and varied, with ponds, fields, bonsai gardens and greenhouses. Depending on the season, you can see beds brimming with heavy-headed peonies or curly-haired chrysanthemums. It makes for a wonderful picnic ground – arrive early to claim your spot. The only unfortunate aspect is its distance from Shanghai proper; it takes a longish cab ride to get here from a central location, costing around RMB 50.

## Hongqiao Lu & around

Running directly west from central Xujiahui is Hongqiao Lu. In the Concession era this street was lined with the country estates of the stinking rich. One of the most famous of these belonged to the wealthy businessman Sir Victor Sassoon. His Tudorbethan villa is now the **Cypress Hotel** (*see p43*), and sits out near to Hongqiao Airport and **Shanghai Zoo** (*see p159*). Although the government has maintained this house and several dozen others as VIP accommodation, most such opulent reminders of the 1920s and 1930s have either been razed or left to deteriorate slowly. Some former residents have petitioned the government to return the properties to their original owners, but the development frenzy of the past decade has made the land too valuable to relinquish. Only a few villas will survive the next ten years. None are open to the public, except several that are now antique furniture shops (*see p135*).

Just to the south of Hongqiao Lu is the **Soong Qingling Mausoleum** (*see below*). The site was formerly the Wanguo (10,000 Countries) Cemetery, the resting place of many Shanghai notables. The revered Soong Qingling died in 1981; after her body was interred the city changed the name of the cemetery in her honour (her infamous sister Meiling, whose husband Chiang Kaishek was responsible for the wholesale massacre of Communists in 1937, declined to return to China for the funeral; she died in the USA in October 2003, aged 105). Grave-browsing aside, the park surrounding the mausoleum is popular as a social venue. Moongazing parties are held here during the Moon Festival, or Mid Autumn Festival (*see p156*).

Further west is the area commonly known as **Gubei**, a largely residential area occupied in the main by wealthy expatriates.

### Soong Qingling Mausoleum

*Soong Qingling Lingyuan, 21 Songyuan Lu, by Hongqiao Lu (6275 8080 ext 541). Metro Hongqiao Lu.* **Open** 8.30am-4.30pm daily. **Admission** RMB 5. **Map** p240 B4.

Civil and women's rights activist Soong Qingling was made an honorary president shortly before her death and was buried next to her parents in the Soongs' own burial ground – Wanguo Cemetery. The tomb of her beloved maid, Li Yane, lies alongside. Also lying at Wanguo is Talitha Gerlach, an American Christian minister, whose bravery and devotion to Communist causes (and her anti-foot-binding campaign) earned her the respect of the Chinese government and one of the first green cards issued to a foreigner in Shanghai. Not far from Gerlach's grave are the prominent stones of Jewish families, the Kadoories and Sassoons; the original Jewish cemeteries in other parts of town were destroyed during the Cultural Revolution. A well-presented exhibition room portrays Soong Quingling's life and dedication using old school exercise books, clothing and an epitaph for her friend, the author Edgar Snow. A foreign and a Chinese cemetery are also housed within the park. For more on the Soong family, *see p87* **Gone for a Soong**.

# Pudong

Super-high-rise Pudong is Shanghai's modern showpiece.

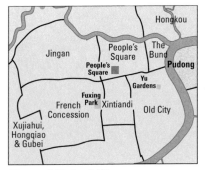

**Maps p241 & p245**

Modern Pudong is at the very heart of Shanghai's bid to become the most important international economic and trading centre in 21st-century East Asia. Visually, it's a staggering sci-fi landscape of spaceship towers, 88-storey pagodas, vast globes the size of rogue meteorites and golden skyscrapers where the whole side of the building acts as a giant video screen. As construction continues to stretch further and further east, some of the streets, apartment blocks and parks are still waiting to be inhabited, meaning that, in contrast to the hustle and bustle of Puxi (the areas west of the river), there is an eerily quiet, clean and institutional feel to Pudong. That said, Pudong's cultural life has developed substantially over the past few years, sprouting several key new cultural centres, such as the beautiful **Shanghai Oriental Art Centre** and the cutting-edge **Zendai Museum of Art**.

Just 20 years ago Pudong was nothing more than empty marshland with some shabby warehousing at the water's edge – and the distinct entity that was Shanghai stopped abruptly on the west bank of the Huangpu River. The development of these 530 square kilometres (205 square miles), stretching out to the East China Sea, has been so intense that the city is rumoured to be sinking under the weight of Pudong's towering new office blocks, hotels, apartment buildings and roads.

Pudong's riverfront skyline, incorporating some of the world's highest and newest towers, is iconic. The completion of the **World Financial Centre** in October 2007 will serve only to reinforce the area's high-flying status,

as it will surpass Taiwan's Taipei 101 building as the tallest building in the world. The 101-storey building, designed by Kohn Pederson Fox Associates, will even have a rectangular opening at its top levels.

For more about Pudong and the intensely accelerated development of Shanghai, *see pp25-28* **Megalopolis Now**.

### GETTING THERE

The **Bund Tourist Tunnel** is certainly one of the more entertaining ways of crossing the Huangpu River (5888 6000, open 8am-10.30pm daily in summer, 8am-10pm daily in winter, tickets RMB 30). Clear-glass shuttles take you underground through a 647-metre (2,123-foot) tunnel, in which you're flanked by bright technicolour lights and lots of strobes. For an additional RMB 25, the tunnel includes an exhibition of rare deep-sea creatures, a sound extravaganza and the infamous China Sex Culture Exhibition (*see p92*).

Further down the Bund are the **ferries**, which cost as little as RMB 2 (from a terminal just south of the Meteorological Tower). Boats leave every 15 minutes and berth at the southern end of the Binjiang Dadao in Pudong.

By **taxi**, the ride from People's Square or thereabouts takes 15 to 20 minutes and costs RMB 20-25. Buses No.3 and No.518 (RMB 2) depart from opposite the Shanghai Museum and drop off in front of the Jinmao Tower.

## The riverfront

Stretching for 2.5 kilometres (1.5 miles) along Pudong's waterfront is **Binjiang Dadao**, a riverbank walkway lined with cafés such as Starbucks and Häagen-Dazs, plus the German bar-restaurant **Paulaner Brauhaus** and the recently opened teppanyaki restaurant **Fuga**, directly in front of the **Shanghai International Convention Centre**. Fuga's outdoor decking and glass-enclosed interior offer sweeping views of the Bund and Suzhou Creek. The Bund Tourist Tunnel surfaces nearby, which is where you'll find the **China Sex Culture Exhibition** (*see p92*), with 500 'sex antiques' showcasing some 5,000 years of Chinese sexual life. Nearby – and impossible to miss – is the wonderfully kitsch **Oriental Pearl Tower** (*see p94* **Pearl of the East**), with its great pink spheres and gaudy 1980s

Pudong's sensational skyline.

music blaring out in every direction. At the base of the tower is the **Shanghai History Museum** (*see p93*).

West along Fenghe Lu is the **Natural Wild Insect Kingdom** (*see p158*), with over 200 different kinds of creepy-crawly. East along Yincheng Xi Lu is the simple yet well-designed **Shanghai Ocean Aquarium** (*see p158*), home to penguins, sharks and an underwater glass tunnel.

Lujiazui metro station is on the intersection of Pudong's great Shiji Dadao (Century Boulevard) and Lujiazui Lu and beside it the ten-storey **Super Brand Mall**, jam-packed with big-brand shops and eateries. Next to it is the newly revamped **Pudong Shangri-La** (*see p44*). Enjoy a pre-dinner drink or dinner at the hotel's swanky new **Jade on 36** bar-restaurant (*see p122*) for spectacular night views of the city. For greater elevation, walk one block east on Century Boulevard to Shanghai's pride and joy, the sky-scraping **Jinmao Tower**. The building incorporates oriental pagoda-like geometric detailing in its protruding eaves, stepped structure and delicate roof; the observation deck is on the 88th floor (5047 5101, open 8.30am-10pm daily, admission RMB 50). For an equally awesome view, but without the throngs of tourists, try the restaurants and bars of the luxurious **Grand Hyatt** (*see p44*), which starts on the 53rd floor of the tower and finishes on the 87th, making it the highest hotel in the world. The interior of the Hyatt is an extraordinary sight in itself, one best viewed

from the Patio Lounge on the 56th floor, at the base of the 33-storey atrium. It breathtakingly resembles a Senate scene from the *Star Wars* prequels. Up on the 87th floor is the aptly named **Cloud 9** cocktail bar (*see p131*), a surreal and expensive option for a drink with a view. The **Jinmao Concert Hall** (booking hotline 5047 2612, www.jinmaoconcerthall.com, tickets RMB 80-500) is located on the first floor of a square building, the **JLife** annexe, built adjacent to the tower. JLife also houses yet another shopping plaza, albeit an extremely upmarket one, with fabulous see-through escalators.

Not far away is the **Lujiazui Development Museum** (15 Lujiazui Lu, by Shiji Dadao), just a few minutes' walk east of the Jinmao Tower. The museum is currently closed to the public, but the house (which is easily viewed from the outside) was once one of the largest residences in Shanghai. A red cobblestone path at the back of the house leads right into the heart of **Lujiazui Central Green** (also known as Lujiazui Park), an expanse of green grass containing a variety of trees and plants, plus fountains and a man-made lake.

### China Sex Culture Exhibition

*Located next to the Bund Tourist Tunnel exit, 2789 Binjiang Dadao (5888 6000). Metro Lujiazui.* **Open** *Summer* 8am-10.30pm daily. *Winter* 8am-10pm daily. **Admission** RMB 20. **Map** p245 N4.
Controversy has surrounded the exhibits in this collection of sexual antiquities since it first went on show in 1999. The museum showcases hundreds of pieces, including erotic statues and ancient sex

symbols, and covers the areas of sexual identity, ancient sex worship, marriage, the sexual oppression of women and sexual health. More than 500 people visit the museum each day.

### Oriental Pearl Tower

*1 Shiji Dadao (5879 1888). Metro Lujiazui.* **Open** 8am-9.30pm daily. **Admission** *1st Sphere only* RMB 70. *All spheres & museum* RMB 100 Mon-Fri; RMB 135 Sat, Sun. **No credit cards. Map** p245 O4.
This 468m (1,535ft) tower is undeniably the principal icon of Shanghai and, with its gaudy pink spheres, a much-loved fixture on the city's skyline. Completed in 1994, tourists come to the tower both to admire its unusual structure and to look out over Puxi and Pudong from inside its pink spheres. The spheres contain exhibitions, shops, restaurants and conference halls. There is even a rotating Chinese/Western buffet inside the middle bubble. *See also p94* **Pearl of the East.**

### Shanghai History Museum

*Gate 4, Oriental Pearl Tower, 1 Shiji Dadao (5879 1888). Metro Lujiazui.* **Open** 8am-9.30pm daily. **Admission** RMB 35. **No credit cards. Map** p245 O4.
Situated at the base of the Oriental Pearl Tower (*see above*), this museum makes use of some extraordinary memorabilia to illustrate the city's rich history. Stacked with historical artefacts, life-size dioramas, models, photos and paintings, the History Museum puts the spotlight on all aspects of life in post-1840s Shanghai, from the city's famous cinema industry to its opium houses and curious forms of criminal justice. Even one of the precious bronze lions that once guarded the Hongkong & Shanghai Bank on the Bund (*see p51*) is here on display. The collection is, however, incomplete: there are plans afoot to build a new history museum that is big enough for all of the 30,000 artefacts (many of which are in storage) to be displayed on a single site. The completion of the new museum is, of course, expected to coincide with the World Expo in 2010.

## Lujiazui & Century Park

**Shiji Dadao** (Century Boulevard) is Pudong's vast eight-lane avenue, supposedly modelled on the Champs-Elysées in Paris. Starting at the Oriental Pearl Tower, it runs for four kilometres (2.5 miles) in a dead-straight line culminating at **Century Park** (*see p95*). This grassy parkland has trees (albeit spindly ones), lakes, an open-air theatre, a children's amusement park and a fishing area.

Before hitting the park, Century Boulevard is intercepted by the impressive feat of modern architecture that is Shanghai's **Science & Technology Museum** (*see p95*). On weekends small children gather in the big open areas in front of the museum and outside metro exits 1, 2, 7 and 8 to rollerskate and fly kites.

**Lujiazul**, making midgets of the trees.

**Sightseeing**

# Pearl of the East

Catching, if not blinding, the eyes of the millions of onlookers who stroll the Bund each year is the rather bizarre spectacle that is the **Oriental Pearl Tower** (see p93). Reaching 468 metres (1,535 feet) into the Pudong sky like a rocket waiting to launch, the tower's pink and purple lights and lasers light up the night sky, representing perfectly Shanghai's mania for everything kitsch. It was created back in 1994 by Shanghai civic leaders eager to give the city a landmark that could be recognised the world over, and would lead the new building explosion in Shanghai. As one of the first buildings to have been erected in the now-burgeoning Pudong, and the subject of countless tourist snaps every month, it's fair to say that it's done the trick.

The Oriental Pearl's design is said to be based on a Tang Dynasty poem about the haunting sounds made by the ancient Chinese lute; the eleven huge 'pearls' that are distributed along its height are said to represent Shanghai's booming pearl trade. Opinions about the architect's real inspiration, however, are divided: some suggest that he watched too many episodes of The Jetsons, others that he was making up for his own physical inadequacies, still others that he was seeking to create Thunderbird 7. Whatever the truth may be, the tower now proudly adorns every postcard, magazine article and T-shirt associated with Shanghai.

With costs, for what is essentially a TV transmitter tower, spiralling towards $100 million, additions were made to the building in an attempt to recoup revenue. These include observation decks in the three accessible spheres, a revolving restaurant, a 20-room 'Space Hotel' and a shopping mall. And recoup revenue they certainly do, bringing in over three million visitors every year, which easily surpasses the Eiffel Tower in Paris in terms both of money and volume of visitors.

Most tourists head to the observation deck in the central pink sphere/pearl, 263 metres (863 feet) off the ground and 45 metres (148 feet) in diameter. But to avoid getting a poke in the eye from the Chinese tour group leaders' flags and being deafened by their megaphones, head to the smaller Space Module situated at 350 metres (1,150 feet) for a higher and more relaxed view across the sprawling city.

Opposite the Science & Technology Museum on Dingxiang Lu is the butterfly-inspired **Shanghai Oriental Art Centre** (see p95), one of the newest and most beautiful concert halls to grace the city. Shanghai's municipal government invested huge amounts of money in building the centre, which boasts a café, a French restaurant, state-of-the-art concert halls and the delightful **Shanghai Gallery of Antique Music Boxes** (see p95).

A 30-minute walk (or a five-minute taxi journey) north-east of here is the Zendai Thumb Plaza. This outdoor mall contains a Carrefour, as well as upmarket home decor shops, bakeries, and Chinese, Japanese and Indian restaurants. More unusually, it also contains the Immaculate Conception Church and the excellent new **Zendai Museum of Modern Art** (see p95).

Further down Metro Line 2 is Longyang Lu station. This is the terminus for Shanghai's super-slick train, the **Maglev**, which runs the 30 kilometres (19 miles) out to Pudong Airport in seven minutes. Although inconveniently located and linked to only one metro line, the RMB 50 return trip (RMB 40 for same-day air ticket holders) is worth it just to travel on the fastest train in the world, reaching speeds of up to 430km/h (that's nearly 270mph). Trains depart every 15 minutes from 7am to 9pm.

## Century Park

*Gate 1, 1001 Jinxiu Lu (3876 0588 ext 8210). Metro Century Park.* **Open** *Summer* 7am-6pm daily. *Winter* 7am-5pm daily. **No credit cards. Admission** RMB 10. **Map** p241 H4.

Hawkers sell kites outside the entrance to the park, but, ironically, kite flying (along with football) is strictly prohibited. Nor are animals permitted in the park. Still, the paths that zigzag across the park make it ideal for rollerskating or cycling on the tandems that are available for hire. The roughly 5.5km perimeter (3.5 miles) of the park is best jogged on the quieter footpaths. Small pedalos and slow motorised boats are also available for hire.

## Science & Technology Museum

*2000 Shiji Dadao (6854 2000). Metro Shanghai Science & Technology Museum.* **Open** 9am-5.15pm Tue-Sun (last admission 4.30pm). **Admission** RMB 60. **Credit** MC, V. **Map** p241 G4.

This other-worldly glass-and-steel facility cost RMB 1.75 billion to build. It contains hundreds of high-tech, interactive attractions, focused on natural history, health, science and technology, and the earth's place within the galaxy. The complex also boasts a space theatre (tickets RMB 40), two IMAX 3D cinemas and an Iwerks '4D' theatre – incorporating regular 3D technology with the addition of environmental effects such as moving seats, water-spray rain simulations, air blowing through the cinema like wind and even leg-ticklers built into the seats. Sadly, there are still no films screened with subtitles in English.

## Shanghai Gallery of Antique Music Boxes

*3rd floor, Shanghai Oriental Art Centre, 425 Dingxiang Lu, by Shiji Dadao (6854 7647/ www.shoac.com.cn). Metro Shanghai Science & Technology Museum.* **Open** 11am-6.30pm daily. **Admission** RMB 50. **No credit cards**. **Map** p241 G4.

On the third floor of the impressive Shanghai Oriental Art Centre is this charming collection of European music boxes, with examples from the 19th and 20th centuries. English titles and explanations are provided.

## Shanghai Oriental Art Centre

*425 Dingxiang Lu, by Shiji Dadao, Pudong (6854 1234/www.shoac.com.cn). Metro Shanghai Science & Technology Museum.* **Map** p241 G4.

This spectacular 'blossoming flower' concert hall was designed by French architect Paul Andreu. Opened in July 2005, it houses a state-of-the-art performance hall, concert hall and opera theatre, as well as the music-box collection on the third floor (*see above*). You can wander into the lobby at will, but the place really comes into its own for concerts,

during which more than 880 inlaid lights decorating the roof change colour in response to the music being played. The dress code strictly stipulates 'no slippers'. *See also p188.*

## Zendai Museum of Modern Art (Zendai MoMA)

*Zendai Thumb Plaza, No.28, Lane 199, Fangdian Lu (5033 9801/www.zendaiart.com). Metro Century Park.* **Open** 10am-8pm Tue-Sun. **Admission** RMB 20; free Sun. **No credit cards. Map** p241 H3.

This small but very contemporary art museum is worth seeking out. It is under the directorship of Shen Qibin, also director of Shanghai's better-known Doland: Shanghai Duolun MoMA (aka Duolun, *see p97*), which is a promising sign. The Zendai hosts a range of international modern art exhibitions that aim to encourage young people to enjoy and consume art by being as interactive as possible. There is no permanent exhibition, but the visiting works are of a superior calibre; the inaugural exhibition, Electroscape, featured a fantastic variety of new media works, including Text Rain, an interactive piece with falling letters and a motion-sensor fishpond. The museum also hosts concerts, as well as lectures by foreign artists and curators. Check the website for the exhibition schedule.

Shanghai Oriental Art Centre.

*Sightseeing*

# Hongkou

Where the Jewish diaspora, a Chinese literary legend and a developing waterfront meet.

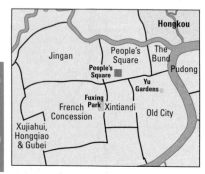

Hongkou

Jingan

People's Square

People's Square

The Bund

Pudong

Yu Gardens

Fuxing Park

French Concession

Xintiandi

Old City

Xujiahui, Hongqiao & Gubei

**Maps p241, p244 & p245**

While most visitors spend time exploring the Bund, Hongkou – just across Suzhou Creek to the north – remains a relatively unknown part of old Shanghai. The grey view across to Hongkou may not inspire much enthusiasm but don't let that put you off, as the area has an intriguing history, with interwar remnants of Chinese, Japanese and Jewish urban settlements.

Hongkou's known history is quite brief. In 1853 the Americans founded the American Concession on the then-swampy Hongkou waterfront and, a decade later, this merged with the British Concession to form the International Settlement. By the beginning of the 20th century the district had gained 30,000 Japanese residents, earning it the nickname 'Little Tokyo'. After the Japanese invaded Manchuria, Chinese unrest in Hongkou led Japanese troops to occupy this part of the city. A few years later, upheavals in fascist Europe saw Ashkenazi Jews flee to this remote safe haven, with several thousand remaining here for the duration of the war.

### GETTING THERE

Most of what's interesting lies in the vicinity of Duolun Lu (which is just off Sichuan Bei Lu) and Lu Xun Park; to get here take Metro Line 3 from Shanghai Railway Station to Dong Baoxing Lu. Alternatively, bus No.21 runs by Duolun Lu from Sichuan Zhong Lu, one block in from the Bund. A taxi to Duolun Lu picked up around People's Square will cost around RMB 15.

## Suzhou Creek

North from People's Square, Suzhou Creek runs roughly parallel to Nanjing Dong Lu, emptying alongside the Bund next to the old British Consulate. Early European traders called it Suzhou Creek because that's where they thought it might take them. They were wrong, but locals still favour the Concession-era term to the official name 'Wusong Creek'.

Before urban development restarted in the early 1990s, the creek was lined with neo-Gothic and art deco *godowns* (warehouses). The few that remain among the new high-rise tower blocks now house posh loft flats and design studios. Also remaining from the 19th century are the low gunwale barges that transport goods to and from Shanghai along the peaceful waterway. Families still live in them and grow herbs and flowers on the top decks.

Over the past decade the municipal authorities have poured a considerable amount of time and money into a rejuvenation project. The first phase improved water quality; subsequent phases included height restrictions on all new construction, as well as generous provision of green space on both sides. The ultimate goal is to remake Suzhou Creek (including the currently People's Navy-occupied Hongkou waterfront) as one of the most picturesque waterfronts in the world. No faulting the ambition.

## Duolun Lu & Lu Xun Park

L-shaped Duolun Lu has been spruced up since it provided a home for various famous writers, most notably Lu Xun, the 'father of modern Chinese literature'. It now bears the rather nebulous designation 'Cultural Celebrities Street'. Passing between rows of charming *shikumen* lane housing, the street forms a pedestrianised thoroughfare laid with cobblestones set in geometric patterns. The street furniture includes gleaming bronze statues of said cultural celebrities.

At the eastern end of Duolun is a welcome addition to the city's arts scene in the form of the **Doland: Shanghai Duolun Museum of Modern Art** (*see p97*), known to locals and expats simply as 'Duolun'. Although the institutional grey cubist architecture doesn't do much for the scenery, the exhibits tend to be refreshingly provocative. At the point where the street curves north are two fine old mansions, both of which are now cafés. The **Old Film Café** (*see p122*), at No.123, is the most famous java house in the area, but the nearby **Reading Room Café** at No.195 is also worth a visit.

The ground floors of many of Duolun's houses have been turned into art and antique stores, heaped high with collections of old magazines, crockery, watches, posters and assorted aged miscellanea. At **Nos.179-181 Duolun Lu** is one of the city's finest collections of memorabilia from early 20th-century Shanghai and the Cultural Revolution years. Duolun Lu also has several **mini museums** devoted variously to chopsticks (No.191), porcelain (No.185) and, at No.183, Wang Zaoshi's collection of 10,000 Mao badges – which some zealous revolutionaries wore pierced into their skin as proof of their loyalty.

A little to the north-east of Duolun is the **Former Residence of Lu Xun** (*see below*), the creator of modern Chinese vernacular literature – as opposed to age-old classical Chinese literature, which has always been unintelligible to most ordinary people. A supporter of the Chinese cause against foreign exploitation, Lu Xun (1881-1936) was also one of the masterminds behind the 4 May Movement (*see p13*). It's in this elegant 1924 mansion that the Chinese League of Leftwing Writers was founded in March 1930. Walk out into the courtyard garden to see a quintet of statues of young writers, looking very earnest and revolutionary among the bushes. The five were secretly murdered by Nationalists in 1931.

A short walk from Duolun is **Lu Xun Park**, also known as Hongkou Park, which is one of the city's most pleasant green spaces. In addition to a couple of lovely lakes it contains the tomb of Lu Xun, fronted by a giant seated bronze of the writer and with memorial calligraphy inscribed by Chairman Mao himself. There's also a museum, the **Lu Xun Memorial Hall** (*see below*) and, flanking the north-west corner of the park, the contemporary art museum **Zhu Qizhan** (*see below*).

### Doland: Shanghai Duolun Museum of Modern Art

*27 Duolun Lu, by Sichuan Bei Lu (6587 6902/ www.duolunart.com). Metro East Baoxing Lu.* **Open** 9am-5.30pm daily. **Admission** RMB 10; RMB 5 concessions. **No credit cards**. **Map** p241 E2.
The first state-owned museum in China devoted entirely to modern art is an impressive seven-storey affair. Run by the culture bureau of the Hongkou district, it opened in 2003 but has already become one of the city's most active cultural institutions. It has brought in several big-name shows, including such artists as Jean-Michel Basquiat, and frequently collaborates with other Asian museums. It boasts an active artist-in-residence programme; visitors are encouraged to pop into the artists' studios on the fifth floor. There are regularly changing temporary shows, workshops, screenings and music events.

### Former Residence of Lu Xun

*No.9, Lane 132, Shanying Lu, by Duolun Lu (5666 2608). Metro East Baoxing Lu.* **Open** 9am-4pm daily. **Admission** RMB 8. **No credit cards**. **Map** p241 E1.
Replete with original furniture and a collection of Lu Xun's belongings. Conspicuous by their absence are his books – the writer's secret library was housed elsewhere and found its final home in Beijing.

### Lu Xun Memorial Hall

*200 Tianai Lu, by Sichuan Bei Lu (6540 0009). Metro East Baoxing Lu.* **Open** 9am-4pm daily. **Admission** RMB 8. **No credit cards**. **Map** p241 E2.
This spacious new museum opened in 1999. The second level displays a voluminous collection of Lu Xun's books, letters, hand-scripted essays and personal artefacts, including his hawk's-bill-rimmed glasses and a plaster-cast death mask still embedded with a few strands of his facial hair. Signs are in English and Chinese. The museum shop sells Lu Xun's books in English-language editions.

### Zhu Qizhan Art Museum

*580 Ouyang Lu, by Dalian Xi Lu (5671 0741/www. zmuseum.org). Metro Hongkou Stadium or Dalian Xi Lu.* **Open** 10am-5pm Tue-Sun. **Admission** RMB 10. **No credit cards**. **Map** p241 E1.

Cultural icons on **Duolun Lu**.

Originally named after a renowned ink-brush painter, Zhu Qizhan has since remodelled itself as a contemporary art museum. Directed by former Duolun staffers, it offers similar material, with less of a focus on installations and new media art. It tends instead to favour traditional media, but has been known to host the occasional experimental show, such as Chinese rocker Douwei's experimental jazz outfit.

## Huoshan Lu

The heart of Jewish Shanghai is Huoshan Lu – not to be confused with Huashan Lu, which is in the French Concession. Get here by crossing Garden Bridge then walking east along Dongdaming Lu or take a taxi from the Bund.

At 65 Huoshan Lu is what was once the **Broadway Theatre**, which had a Jewish-owned roof garden called the Vienna Café. Now the big neon sign in Chinese reads 'Broadway Disco'. East along the street are some charming brick almshouse-like townhouses with small gardens in front; this was formerly Jewish housing during the war. **Huoshan Park** (open 6am-6pm daily), a nondescript leafy area, has the distinction of bearing the city's one public monument to the area's historic role as a Jewish haven; the inconspicuous stone engraved in English, Chinese and Hebrew alludes to the Hongkou neighbourhood as a 'designated area for stateless refugees'.

Zhoushan Lu is one of Huoshan's crossroads; its brick townhouses with arches over the windows are lovely, if run-down. Michael Blumenthal, the US Secretary of the Treasury from 1977 to 1979 and now director of the Jewish Museum Berlin, once lived at No.59.

Follow Zhoushan Lu north to Changyang Lu and track back west for the **Ohel Moshe Synagogue**. Built in 1927, Ohel Moshe was run by Meir Ashkenazi, the spiritual leader of the Russian Jewish community and chief rabbi of Shanghai from 1926 to 1949. The hollow ground floor has a small display of grainy photos of Jewish buildings from China's past. Out back is a small exhibit donated by Canadian artists of Jewish or Chinese descent to honour the friendship between the Jews and the Chinese. The third floor is now the tiny **Jewish Refugee Museum** (62 Changyang Lu, by Zhoushan Lu, 6541 5008), the only Jewish museum in China, holding period photos, a historical video and books on Jewish Shanghai. The elderly Mr Wang oversees the exhibits and speaks fluent English. On the east side of the street a high wall hides a jail built in 1901 by the British and later used by Japanese for military intelligence. It's an active jail once more, allegedly holding 20,000 inmates.

# Jewish Shanghai

Not much has been done to mark Shanghai's historic Jewish ghetto, where some 8,000 Jews fleeing the Holocaust once found unlikely refuge under the strict but comparatively benevolent eye of the occupying Japanese. The six-block area in Hongkou now looks like any other crowded Chinese neighbourhood, but the Jewish history is there if you know where to look. Despite development in anticipation of the 2010 Expo – generally meaning anything of historic interest gets ploughed back into the earth – efforts to enhance the historic character of the space have thankfully been undertaken both by the municipal planning authorities and by several preservation groups.

Jews first arrived in Shanghai in the late 19th century on the coat tails of the British. This first community numbered only around 800 – although the impact they made on the city was far out of proportion to their small number (see p12 **The Jewish dynasties**). In the early 20th century came another wave: Russian Jews fleeing the pogroms and service in the Tsar's army and, shortly after that, when the Tsar had been defeated, the vindictiveness of the Red Army. They were doctors, musicians, writers and intellectuals who had left almost everything behind and they found a cheap residential area in Hongkou's townhouses. The third and last influx was that of the Holocaust refugees. They fled central and eastern Europe to Moscow and from there took the Trans-Siberian railway to Vladivostok and thence passage on a ship to Shanghai.

In July 1942 the Nazis sent Josef Meisinger to present to their Japanese allies a 'Final Solution' plan for Shanghai that involved mass drowning of the city's Jewish citizens. The Japanese refused to implement the plan. However, they did herd the city's refugee Jews (as well as 10,000 other stateless individuals) into one designated area in Hongkou from 1943 to 1945.

**Dvir Bar-Gal** (1300 214 6702 mobile, www.shanghai-jews.com), an Israeli based in Shanghai, gives an insightful tour of Jewish Shanghai, including the Hongkou district; call for further details.

# Eat, Drink, Shop

**Suzhou Cobblers**. *See p144*.

# Restaurants & Cafés

Is this the world's liveliest food city?

Like the city itself, Shanghai's dining scene is nothing if not dynamic. It feels like there's a hottest, hippest, most it-est restaurant opening every night, all aimed at feeding the city's rapidly expanding band of nouveaux riches and the constant stream of international businessmen and moneyed visitors.

The superchefs are here, headed by Jean-Georges Vongerichten (**Jean-Georges**, see p102) and the Pourcel Brothers (**Sens & Bund**, see p102), who have all set up shop on the Bund. There they find themselves in the company of only slightly less high-flying kitchen captains such as David Laris (**Laris**, see p103) and Jereme Leung (**Whampoa Club**, see p102). This little gathering at Three on the Bund represents one apex of the city's dining scene – quite literally if you dine in the domed corner tower, a stunning dining space so exclusive (and small) that it can only accommodate two diners and the butler (Tom Cruise and Katie Holmes dined here when filming in town in 2005).

However, just as exciting, and certainly more affordable, are the restaurants influenced by immigrants from more than 30 Chinese provinces, plus Hong Kong and Taiwan, and other East Asian territories including Singapore. Restaurants like **South Beauty** (majoring in spicy Sichuan cuisine, see p116), **Crystal Jade** (Cantonese, see p110) and **Shanghai Uncle** (Shanghainese, see p121) combine terrific regional cuisine with jaw-droppingly stylish decor. Interestingly, all three of these restaurants are chains. And just as there is no stigma attached to eating in a chain restaurant, neither is there any shame in dining at a hotel: sample the excellent eateries at the Grand Hyatt (**Cucina**, see p122), Portman Ritz-Carlton (**Palladio**, see p107) and Pudong Shangri-La (**Jade on 36**, see p122) if you don't believe us.

Where Shanghai perhaps disappoints is with its lack of good street food. City government clean-ups have chased off most itinerant vendors and forced stall traders into roofed premises. There are just a handful of food streets left. **Yunnan Nan Lu**, which links the

**Tan Wai Lou**. See p102.

Old City and People's Square, has lots of kebab sellers, small seafood diners and hotpot sellers; **Huanghe Lu**, which runs north beside the Park Hotel, is also good for meat on a stick and fresh *la mian* (pulled noodles); and **Wujiang Lu**, which loops off main Nanjing Xi Lu, is lined with plastic-covered tables where locals consume *zongzi* (glutinous rice dumplings) and beer. Still, no one who has spent time in Hong Kong, Singapore or KL is likely to be impressed.

But this isn't to say that you can't get good cheap food. Places like **Bao Luo** (see p112), **Bi Feng Tang** (see p107), **Di Shui Dong** (see p113) and **Nan Xiang** (see p109) all serve great food for about the price of a McDonald's Happy Meal back home.

## DINING ETIQUETTE

The dos and don'ts of Chinese dining in Shanghai are not as elaborate as you might imagine, but there are a few points to note. Your coat won't be taken, so just hang it on the back of your seat – a plastic covering will be slid over to protect it. Most meals will be served communal-style, with platters in the centre of the table, so usually only one menu is given, and that to the host, presuming he or she will

❶ Purple numbers given in this chapter correspond to the location of each restaurant or café as marked on the street maps. See pp240-249.

order for everyone. Your plate is for food that you serve yourself with chopsticks from the main dishes, and also for scraps. The bowl and spoon is for soup and for dishes that are difficult to eat with chopsticks, such as slippery tofu. For anyone who finds chopsticks awkward, there is no shame in asking for a fork (*chazi*) or spoon (*shaozi*).

Cold dishes come first. Next come meat and vegetable dishes, followed by fish. Soup comes last. Shanghainese are big fans of soup, and if you don't order it the waitstaff may prompt you to do so. Rice is average everyday food, and most locals won't order it in restaurants. Tea is refilled as many times as you drain your cup. Dessert is usually a plate of watermelon slices to cleanse the palate. Toothpicks will be provided to clean your teeth (while covering your mouth with your hand).

Except at extremely formal official dinners, dining Chinese-style is casual. People will smoke or talk on mobile phones while eating, often shovelling and slurping food, and even tossing bones right on to the table. The only real no-nos are superstitious in nature and usually only apply to dining with older Chinese. For example, don't stab your chopsticks into a pile of food or bowl of rice and leave them – this evokes funeral incense sticks. Don't turn a whole fish over – this is like a boat capsizing. Don't reach across the table for food and never take the last piece from a dish – bad manners in any part of the world, really.

If you are being treated to dinner by locals, remember that hosts always pay for their guests, and try everything you are offered, as leaving a dish untouched implies your host did a poor job of ordering. You won't offend if you leave something on your plate that you didn't like.

If you are offered *baijiu*, the very strong rice spirit used for toasting, you may have to toss it down when your host shouts 'Gangbei!' ('empty glasses'). You can plead illness (*wo bu shufu*) if you really don't want to drink any more, or say that you want to drink at your own pace (*suiyi*). For more on general issues of attitude and etiquette, *see p224* **Attitude problems.**

### PRACTICALITIES

While most of the restaurants listed in this guide have English menus, some local places will not. Our advice in this case is simply to point to the things you see on other tables. It's what the locals do.

The Chinese tend to eat early by Western standards. Most local restaurants serve lunch between 11am and 2pm, dinner between 5pm and 8pm. Some kitchens close even earlier than that. It is advisable to book in advance for the popular restaurants, particularly at weekends.

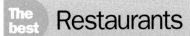

# The best Restaurants

### Crystal Jade
A Singaporean chain serving superb dim sum, crisp pork belly and succulent roasted meats. Stylish surroundings, efficient service and a decent wine list. See p110.

### Jade on 36
Cerebral, boundary-crossing cuisine – and the best view in town. The Shangri-La's fine-dining flagship is unique. See p122.

### Jean-Georges
This restaurant disproves the common claim that fine dining can't be franchised. The complexity of Jean-Georges's nuanced dishes are painstakingly recreated in this breathtaking space by executive chef Eric Johnson. See p102.

### Jishi
Simple, satisfying Shanghainese home cooking is what you'll get at Jishi. Try the red-cooked pork with cuttlefish – it's the best in town. See p115.

### Shintori
Shintori is a modernist theatre of (Japanese) food, where busy chefs roll sushi and shake salad in a futuristic warehouse space. A combination of style and substance that is pure Shanghai. Unmissable. See p120.

### Whampoa Club
Jereme Leung could well be Asia's hottest chef: his 'new Shanghai' style has put Shanghainese food in the fine-dining spotlight. Expect gorgeous tasting menus that present classic dishes in refined fashion. See p102.

### Xinjiang Fengwei Restaurant
Worth seeking out to sample the flavours of Xinjiang on China's western frontier. The lamb-centric menu is probably unlike anything you've ever tried, and the spirited service unlike anything you've ever experienced. See p121.

### Yin
Classic, Concession-era decor, well-mixed cocktails and Shanghainese food freed of MSG and excess grease. Every detail has been attended to – from the unique tableware to the 1930s jazz soundtrack and the superior ingredients. See p117.

**Eat, Drink, Shop**

Credit cards are accepted in most international restaurants, but otherwise Shanghai is largely still a cash economy – always carry enough money on you to cover the meal. Tipping is not necessary in local places (if you do want to tip, tell the staff it's a *xiaofei* if they are confused), although the custom of leaving 10 or 15 per cent is creeping in at top-end venues. Most hotel restaurants will add a 15 per cent service charge to the bill.

# The Bund

The grid of streets back from the waterfront is full of small eateries, but the Bund itself is all about high-end dining. For less formality try the burgers, steaks and other pub food at jazz bar **Five** (*see p124*), situated in the basement level of **M on the Bund**. **Zhapu Lu**, just north of the Bund across Suzhou Creek, is an excellent food street with dozens of small restaurants. There's also a branch of **Shanghai Uncle** (*see p121*) near the Natural History Museum.

## Chinese

### Tan Wai Lou

*5th floor, Bund 18, 18 Zhongshan Dong Yi Lu, by Nanjing Dong Lu (6339 1188/www.bund18.com). Metro Henan Zhong Lu.* **Open** 11am-2pm, 5-10pm daily. **Main courses** RMB 48-3,580. **Credit** AmEx, DC, MC, V. **English menu. Map** p245 M5 ❶
Cantonese
Enjoy Bund views with a side of shark's fin and a helping of tender, braised abalone. Tan Wai Lou, one of the city's most elegant Chinese restaurants, was designed by Italian architect Filippo Gabbiano to capture the spirit of the city's meteoric rise. The menu, which incorporates Taiwanese and Cantonese classics, and demonstrates a flair for fusion (think foie gras and sashimi), reflects the tastes of the big spenders in its midst, who finish off a business banquet with a cognac and a Cohiba. **Photo** p100.

### Whampoa Club

*5th floor, Three on the Bund, 3 Zhongshan Dong Yi Lu, by Guangdong Lu (6321 3737/www.threeonthe bund.com). Metro Henan Zhong Lu.* **Open** 11.30am-2.30pm, 5.30-10pm daily. **Main courses** RMB 168-200. **Credit** AmEx, DC, MC, V. **English menu. Map** p245 M5 ❷ Shanghainese
One of Asia's pre-eminent chefs, Jereme Leung, breathes new life into traditional Shanghainese cuisine in a dazzling modern deco setting created by celebrated Hong Kong designer Alan Chan. The extensive menu features everything from soups and seafood to shark's fin and Leung's signature slow-cooked Australian abalone. His adaptations of classic dishes include drunken chicken with Shaoxing wine, shaved ice and house-smoked tea eggs, plus a dollop of caviar. Leung also breaks new ground with dishes such as almond and cocoa fried spare ribs and

seared goose liver on glutinous red dates. If you can stretch to it, the five-course tasting menu (RMB 550) is superb. Diners can also choose from over 50 special teas for a traditional ceremony served at the table or in one of the opulent private tearooms. Reservations are required for dinner. **Photos** p103.

## European

### Sens & Bund

*6th floor, Bund 18, 18 Zhongshan Dongyi Lu, by Nanjing Dong Lu (6323 9898/www.bund18.com). Metro Henan Zhong Lu.* **Open** 11.30am-2.30pm, 6.30-10.30pm daily. **Main courses** (dinner) RMB 238-598. **Set menu** (lunch) RMB 188, RMB 228. **Credit** AmEx, DC, MC, V. **English menu. Map** p245 M5 ❸ French
The Pourcel Brothers – those silent, determined twins of Jardin de Sens fame – churn out fine dining restaurants like plates of seared foie gras. And this sleek white space, the flagship restaurant at the restored neo-classical Bund 18 building, is their new restaurant du jour. Expect a refined Michelin-style French menu (many recipes originate from their two-Michelin-starred restaurant in Montpellier), from which Shanghai's Frenchmen and local fashionistas select beautifully presented dishes with a refined Mediterranean flair, while sipping wines from Shanghai's strongest list of Gallic grapes. Try the fillet of turbot with vanilla-scented potato cream and grilled baby artichokes, and finish with roasted spiced pineapple and rose butter sorbet. A feast for the senses indeed.

## Fusion

### Jean-Georges

*4th floor, Three on the Bund, 3 Zhongshan Dong Yi Lu, by Guangdong Lu (6321 7733/www.threeonthe bund.com). Metro Henan Zhong Lu.* **Open** 11.30am-2.30pm, 6-11pm daily. **Main courses** RMB 238-330. **Credit** AmEx, DC, MC, V. **English menu. Map** p245 M5 ❹
Jean-Georges being Jean-Georges Vongerichten, the Alsace-born chef lauded for his New York restaurants Vong and 66. Long a fan of Shanghai cuisine, in April 2004 he put the money where his mouth had been and introduced the city to his fragrant, Asian-infused take on traditional French cuisine. The location is Michael Graves-designed Three on the Bund (*see p50*). Decorated with eel-skin sofas and pony leather armchairs, the restaurant is part Gothic Shanghai gentlemen's club, part Manhattan Martini bar. Diners can order à la carte or select one of two seven-course tasting menus. Start with crisp foie gras brûlée, juicy scallops with a caramel caper-raisin sauce, or divine red snapper sashimi with fresh wasabi and rose gêlée. Exquisite mains include lobster infused in lemongrass and fenugreek broth. Alternatively, the RMB 188 lunch menu is a less painful way to introduce yourself to the experience. Reservations are required for both lunch and dinner.

Trad Shanghainese cuisine and updated deco meet at **Whampoa Club.** *See p102.*

### Laris

*6th floor, Three on the Bund, 3 Zhongshan Dong Yi Lu, by Guangdong Lu (6321 9922/www.threeonthe bund.com). Metro Henan Zhong Lu.* **Open** 11.30am-2.30pm, 5.30-10.30pm daily. **Main courses** RMB 190-388. **Credit** AmEx, MC, V. **English menu.** **Map** p245 M5 **5**

The prevailing trend in restaurant decor is retro-chic Old Shanghai, but not at Laris – this place is all about 'new Shanghai' and the money that goes with it. It's the first signature restaurant of aspiring celebrity chef David Laris, formerly executive chef of Terence Conran's London restaurant Mezzo, and it taps into the nouveau Shanghainese love of luxe: cue bright marble interiors and fat velvet couches, cocktails in the sexy Vault Bar, followed by fresh oysters, lobster and Russian caviar at the marble Claws, Wings & Fins bar. The menu dresses up Asian flavours in nouvelle fine-dining fashion: crab with avocado salsa and lemongrass gazpacho or Sichuan peppercorn and coriander-seed crusted tuna. Laris seems to spend his time honing the media persona and plugging Martini nights, but Austrian exec chef Gerhard Passrugger ably steers the marble-clad ship.

### M on the Bund

*7th floor, 20 Guangdong Lu, by Zhongshan Dong Yi Lu (6350 9988/www.m-onthebund.com). Metro Henan Zhong Lu.* **Open** 11.30am-2.30pm, 6.15-10.30pm daily. **Main courses** RMB 182-288. **Credit** AmEx, DC, MC, V. **English menu.** **Map** p245 M5 **6**

Before Jean-Georges (*see p102*), there was M on the Bund. Named after the city's networking tour de force Michelle Garnaut, M has been a bellwether for Shanghai's giddy economic growth since opening in 1999. The art deco revival venue is stunning, with sweeping views of the historic Bund and across the Huangpu River to the mighty skyscrapers of Pudong. The North African-meets-Mediterranean menu is hearty at dinner, but lighter at lunch; for the former you might try couscous royale or suckling pig, finished off with Egyptian orange cake with English lemon curd, for the latter perhaps carrot and ginger soup or vinegared chicken salad with artichokes, green beans and herbs. M serves a simple, no-frills menu, so if you're a gastronome pining for a degustation menu you might be happier across the street at Three. That said, it does have the best service in town and a fantastic wine list. Toast the Shanghai skyline with a glass of champagne or raise a pinky at Sunday high tea. Late cocktails and desserts are accommodated downstairs at the Glamour Bar (*see p125*). Reservations required for lunch and dinner.

### New Heights

*7th floor, Three on the Bund, 3 Zhongshan Dong Yi Lu, by Guangdong Lu (6321 0909/www.three onthebund.com). Metro Henan Zhong Lu.* **Open** 11am-2.30pm, 6-10.30pm daily. **Main courses** RMB 110-240. **Credit** AmEx, DC, MC, V. **English menu.** **Map** p245 M5 **7**

**Eat, Drink, Shop**

# great food!
# great places!
# great people!

appetizers - salads - sandwiches - asian sets - pasta - dinner - smoothies - fresh juice

**nan jing xi lu (shanghai centre/portman)**
112 retail, shanghai centre, 1376 nan jing xi lu
南京西路店(上海商城/波特曼) 上海 南京西路1376号
上海商城#112室 200040 tel 6279 8682

**huai hai zhong lu (KWah centre)**
4th & 5th floor, KWah house, 1028 huai hai zhong lu
淮海中路店(嘉华中心) 上海 淮海中路1028号
嘉华坊4楼至5楼 200031 tel 5403 8865

**lu jia zui (super brand mall)**
ground floor, northwest corner, super brand mall
lu jia zui xi lu & fu cheng lu
陆家嘴店(正大广场) 上海 陆家嘴西路富城路口
正大广场底层西北角 200122 tel 5047 2060

www.elementfresh.com

element fresh®
新 元 素

In what seems an almost socialist gesture for such an unreservedly fat-cat capitalistic city, New Heights – the cheapest of the quartet of eateries situated in Three on the Bund – occupies the top floor of the development, bagging the best views and a wonderful roof terrace complete with 180° panorama of the river and Pudong. The menu amuses with its division into 'Wet things', 'Things that swim', 'Things that walk' and 'Farinaceous things', which (dictionary to hand) we can tell you means 'things made of starch' – pasta, in other words. The other categories embrace everything from such Western favourites as steak, ale and mushroom pie or fish and chips, to Asian standards like the scrumptious Malaysian Hainan chicken, which comes with garlic fragrant rice, or a rich Indonesian laksa. If you visit at lunchtime you can tuck into quality burgers and croque monsieur. Food and service are both terrific, and afterwards you can retire to the bar (see p125), Martini in hand, for possibly the best bar experience you can have in Shanghai.

## International

### CJW

*50th floor, Bund Centre, 222 Yanan Dong Lu (6339 1777/www.cjwchina.com). Metro Henan Zhong Lu.* **Open** 11.30am-3pm, 6-10.30pm daily. **Main courses** RMB 152-248. **Credit** AmEx, MC, V. **English menu. Map** p244 L5 **8**

In a city in which stunning views are no longer enticing bonuses but prerequisites for any new dining or drinking venture, CJW out panoramas the lot. It's a whole 43 floors higher than any other building on the Bund. Luck out with a window seat (or book in advance) and check out the Bund, a tiny, wrong-end-of-a-telescope jagged roofscape that's dwarfed by the massive sweep of the Huangpu River. The food isn't quite as impressive, but the set lunch is a good deal (two courses, RMB 78; three courses, RMB 88). The half a dozen mains don't include anything too exciting, but your Caesar salad, vegetarian pasta, ribeye steak or grilled sea bass does come with that free side order of vertigo. Brunch, served on Saturdays and Sundays from 11.30am to 3pm for RMB 128 per person, is very popular.
**Other locations**: Unit 4, No.2, Lane 123, Xingye Lu, by Madang Lu, Xintiandi (6385 6677).

## People's Square

As a main bus and metro terminus, People's Square has a clutch of cheap noodle joints, Western fast-food outlets and Japanese or Chinese chain restaurants plus, in season, some prime crab outlets. **Huanghe Lu**, beside the Park Hotel, has plenty of Shanghainese eateries big and small, as does **Yunnan Nan Lu**. For more upmarket fare, there's a branch of **Xiao Nan Guo** (*see p116*) just to the north of the square.

## European

### Kathleen's 5

*5th floor, Shanghai Art Museum, 325 Nanjing Xi Lu, by Huangpi Bei Lu (6327 2221/www.kathleens5. com.cn). Metro People's Park or Square.* **Open** 11.30am-midnight daily. **Main courses** RMB 120-260. **Credit** AmEx, DC, MC, V. **English menu. Map** p244 H5 **9**

American-born Chinese Kathleen Lau is an old hand in Shanghai – she was involved in setting up monthly magazine *that's Shanghai*, as well as a number of previous dining and drinking ventures. In fact, this is her fifth, hence the name. It's a stunning venue – a glass box on top of the Shanghai Art Museum building, which was, back in the day, the clubhouse of Shanghai's colonial-era racecourse (*see p57*). Since opening in 2004 the food hasn't quite managed to live up to the exhilarating surroundings. A new menu introduced at the start of 2006 may turn things around, with starters of chilled crab tower and pan-fried fois gras with onion jam, and mains of braised lamb shank provençal on a bed of baby carrot, turnip and potato or porcini mushroom. Two- and three-course set lunches are offered at RMB 100 and RMB 130, respectively. If the restaurant doesn't lure you, at least visit the bar for a drink (*see p125*).

## Jingan

In addition to the places listed below, Jingan has a branch of the ever-popular Shanghainese **Xiao Nan Guo** (*see p116*) and the city's most vibrant locale for street food, **Wujiang Lu**. As expat central, Jingan also has plenty of Western-friendly restaurants, particularly around the neighbourhood of the Shanghai Centre/Ritz-Carlton. At the Centre itself is rib and burger joint **Tony Roma's** (6279 7129), along with Californian-style pizza kitchen and burgers galore at **Malone's** (*see p127*) around the corner. The **Brazil Steakhouse** (1649 Nanjing Xi Lu, by Huashan Lu, 6255 9898) is just up the street, opposite the Jingan Temple.

## Cafés & snacks

### Element Fresh

*Shanghai Centre, 1376 Nanjing Xi Lu, by Xikang Lu (6279 8682/www.elementfresh.com). Metro Jingan Temple.* **Open** 7am-11pm Mon-Thur, Sun; 7am-midnight Fri, Sat. **Main courses** RMB 88-138. **Credit** AmEx, DC, MC, V. **English menu. Map** p243 E5 **10** Bistro

A smart, bright and informal Californian-style deli attached to the Shanghai Centre, this is possibly the best spot in town for breakfast: go 'cowboy' (omelette, cornbeef hash, potatoes and endless coffee) or healthy (egg-white omelette and broccoli), or plump for one of many in-between options. There's an excellent juice bar, which also does superb

Eat, Drink, Shop

# Shanghai dumplings

The *xiaolongbao*, literally the 'little basket bun', is a key feature of Shanghainese street food. This tiny bun, whose delicate skin cradles a juicy filling of pork and a fragrant, rich soup, is found everywhere – from delicious but dingy roadside stalls to fancy dim sum eateries. It takes practice to fold these tiny packets, which are about an inch in diameter and filled with pork or a mixture of pork and crab. The soup in the buns is actually gelatin, which is in the meat filling and melts during the steaming process. The result is a broth of incredible richness, which should be eaten with caution (fresh off the steamer, *xiaolongbao* are scaldingly hot).

Bun etiquette is an exercise in taste-bud preservation: first, carefully peel the bun off the steamer and place it in a spoon. Then gently dip the dumpling in a bit of vinegar, and bite a hole in the wrapper to allow steam and a bit of soup to escape. Drink the soup, then gobble down the tender pork filling and wrapper.

While the *xiaolongbao* is the best known of the Shanghai dumplings, the *shengjianbao* is equally revered in the city; it's the sturdy and filling cousin of the steamed bun. *Shengjianbao* fall somewhere between a fried pot sticker and a steamed bun; cooked over high heat in huge, flat pans, they're topped with a large wood lid that allows the bun to steam during the frying process. Golden brown and crisp on the bottom, with fluffy dough and a topping of sesame seeds

and chives on top, the buns are also filled with a rich, meaty soup and an unctuous mix of pork, garlic and ginger.

For good, safe *xiaolongbao*, try **Ding Tai Fung** (*see p110*) – or, if you're more adventurous, look for the nearest street stall. The best *shengjianbao* in town can be found at **Yang's Fry Dumpling** (*see p107*).

smoothies and 'nutrition boosters'. At lunch or dinner choose between gourmet sandwiches (cold or hot, including a terrific duck breast and apple), bagels, salads, pasta dishes or Asian set specials, supplemented by a handful of more substantial options after 6pm. Alcohol is served, and the outdoor terrace overlooking Nanjing Xi Lu is popular for early-evening cocktails (especially the fantastic Bloody Mary). The sole drawback is the often lengthy wait for a table at weekends. No smoking during the day. **Other locations** 279 Wuxing Lu, Xujiahui (5116 9887); 5th floor, 1028 Huaihai Zhong Lu, by Donghu Lu, French Concession (5403 8865); Shop 17, 2nd floor, Building 2, Co-operate Avenue, 202 Hubin Lu, Xintiandi (6340 6966); Unit 2, 2nd floor, Headquarters Building, 168 Xizang Zhong Lu, People's Square (6361 6966).

### New York Style Pizza

*Shop J16, 1699 Nanjing Xi Lu, by Huashan Lu (3214 0024). Metro Jingan Temple.* **Open**
10am-11pm daily. **Average** RMB 88/pizza, RMB 10/slice. **No credit cards. English menu. Map** p242 D6 ⑪ Pizza

Hungry for a wide slice of thin-crust, New York-style pizza, dripping with greasy cheese and pepperoni? The kind of straight-out-of-Brooklyn slice you fold in half to fit in your mouth, the kind that's divine after a night out and perfect for lunch on the run? Then check out this pizza joint just next to the subway entrance at Jingan Temple, which has become a favourite for homesick Americans. With its slipshod decor, NYSP isn't the place for a perfect pie it can't be beat. Another bonus is the free toppings (jalapeño peppers, artichokes, anchovies).

### Wagas

*Room LG12A, Underground Floor 1, CITIC Square, 1168 Nanjing Xi Lu, by Shanxi Bei Lu (5292 5228). Metro Shimen Yi Lu.* **Open** 7.30am-11pm daily. **Average** RMB 38-58. **Credit** AmEx, DC, MC, V. **English menu. Map** p243 E5 ⑫ Sandwich bar

A prime venue for snack lunches, Wagas is a big hit with time-strapped office workers. The fare is all healthy – fresh salads, great pastas, soups and sand-wiches, plus daily blackboard specials, as well as fresh juices, non-dairy frappés and smoothies. The coffee's excellent, and there's always a good selection of cakes. The interior is smart and clean, its utilitarian nature softened by the couches and magazines for browsing. Breakfast is served daily.

## Chinese

### Bi Feng Tang

*1333 Nanjing Xi Lu, by Tongren Lu (6279 0738).* *Metro Jingan Temple.* **Open** 10am-5am daily. **Dim sum** RMB 8-18. **Credit** AmEx, DC, MC, V. **English menu. Map** p243 D5 ⑬ Cantonese

The local answer to McDonald's, BFT is a city-wide chain that draws round-the-clock crowds with cheap Cantonese dim sum and similar savoury snacks. This branch is hugely convenient for guests at the Ritz-Carlton, which is just over the road. It's kitted out like a traditional fishing village, with an outdoor seating area of small wooden huts draped with nets and festive lights. Expect the usual dough-wrapped suspects from steamed shrimp and pork dumplings to barbecue pork buns, as well as various congees and, for dessert, baked egg-custard tart. Late-night clubbers are a significant portion of the custom at the 24-hour French Concession branch (175 Changle Lu, by Ruijin Yi Lu, 6467 0628).
**Other locations**: throughout the city.

### Meilongzhen

*No.22, 1081 Nanjing Xi Lu, by Jiangning Lu (6253 5353). Metro Shimen Yi Lu.* **Open** 11am-1.30pm, 5-9pm daily. **Main courses** RMB 22-880. **Credit** AmEx, DC, MC, V. **English menu. Map** p243 F5 ⑭ Shanghainese

The kitchens at Shanghai's most famous local restaurant have been churning out dishes since 1938. The building was once home to the Chinese Communist Party and the restaurant remains state-run. The classic decor consists of mahogany and marble furniture, carved wood panels and paper lanterns. Sichuan dishes are prepared in Shanghai style (that is, sweeter and oilier). Highlights include Meilongzhen special chicken and deep-fried sweet and sour fish. First-timers might enjoy the Sichuan convention of serving tea at a distance of several paces by means of a long-spouted teapot. Service can deteriorate as the night wears on, so an early book-ing is advised.
**Other locations**: Westgate Mall, 77 Jiangning Lu, by Nanjing Xi Lu, Jingan (6255 6688); 2nd floor, 2550 Zhongshan Bei Lu, by Wuning Lu, Putuo (6245 7777).

### 1221

*1221 Yanan Xi Lu, by Panyu Lu (6213 6585). Metro Jiangsu Lu.* **Open** 11.30am-2pm, 5-11pm daily. **Main courses** RMB 18-168. **Credit** AmEx, DC, MC, V. **English menu. Map** p240 C3 ⑮ Shanghainese

Owner Michelle Liu was raised by Shanghainese parents in Hong Kong and her mixed background is expressed in diverse local and Cantonese dishes, with a few other regional specialities thrown in. The menu is very Western-friendly and the cooking isn't as heavy on the oil as elsewhere, so the bulk of the clientele are expats. The food is also consistently excellent. It's hard to go wrong, but we particularly like shredded chicken with peanut sauce and sautéed beef with fried dough sticks. Dessert of hot rice frit-ter with chopped banana comes on the house. It's a classy looking place with white starched tablecloths, chalkboard-black floor and big daubings of modern art for colour. It's also a little difficult to find, being located some way from central Jingan; look for the Howard Johnson Apartment Hotel on the north side of Yanan Xi Lu, and the restaurant is just a tiny bit further, slotted down at the end of a small alleyway.

### Yang's Fry Dumpling

*54 & 60 Wujiang Lu, by Shimen Xi Lu, Jingan (6267 6025). Metro Shimen Yi Lu.* **Open** 10.30am-11.30pm daily. **Average** RMB 3 for 4 dumplings. **No credit cards. Map** p243 F5 ⑯ Dumplings

It's easy to spot this Shanghai institution, despite the street being crowded with food stalls – look for the lines that snake across Wujiang Lu. At Yang's they only make one thing: *shengjianbao*, a delicious shallow-fried dumpling topped with sesame and chives that is crisp on the bottom and fluffy on top. Inside lies ginger-tinged ground pork and flavour-ful soup. Be careful not to spill any of the scalding liquid on your shirt, and pack some napkins.

## European

### Bella Napoli

*140 Xikang Lu, by Beijing Xi Lu (6253 8358). Metro Jingan Temple.* **Open** 11am-3pm, 6-11pm daily. **Main courses** RMB 75-170. **No credit cards. English menu. Map** p243 D4 ⑰ Italian

The era of small, family-run restaurants has nearly come to a close in this corner of China, but two Italian chefs are bucking the trend. Bella Napoli is a cosy, no-frills, family-style trattoria, and all the ingredients – from the cheeses and meats on its ample antipasto platter to the olives in the pungent puttanesca – are imported from Italy. But don't expect import prices: this is one of the most afford-able places in town, with a brief but inexpensive wine list, huge portions of pasta, like the creamy rocket pesto on fusilli, and meat-heavy mains such as osso bucco milanese that are designed for shar-ing. All this in a smart, stripped-down dining room popular with just about everyone.

### Palladio

*1st floor, Portman Ritz-Carlton, 1376 Nanjing Xi Lu, by Tongren Lu (6279 7188). Metro Jingan Temple.* **Open** 11.30am-2.30pm, 5.30-10.30pm Mon-Sat; 5.30-10.30pm Sun. **Main courses** RMB 220-450. **Credit** AmEx, DC, MC, V. **English menu. Map** p243 E5 ⑲ Italian

Eat, Drink, Shop

Did Italy import the notion of spaghetti noodles from China or was the exchange in the reverse direction? Either way, the bond between the two countries that was secured by those thin strips of dough remains strong, and Shanghai has more than its fair share of Italian eateries, in all price categories. For the top-drawer experience, check the balance on the credit card and, if favourable, head to Palladio. Its location at the Portman Ritz-Carlton makes it a favourite for high-powered business lunches, while dinner sees hotel guests mix with local glamour as moneyed city residents dress up for chef Giovanni Terracciano's seriously delicious dishes, such as nutty risotto and squid ink pasta. Alternatively, test the limits of your plastic on veal with goose liver and black truffles. Further trappings of *la dolce vita* include grappa and cigars, as well as Shanghai's best selection of Grand Crus and premium Italian bottles.

## Fusion

### 239

*239 Shimen Yi Lu, by Weihai Lu (6253 2837). Metro Shimen Yi Lu.* **Open** 11am-3pm, 6pm-midnight Mon-Fri; 10am-4pm, 6pm-midnight Sat, Sun. **Main courses** RMB 80-270. **Credit** AmEx, MC, V. **English menu. Map** p243 F6 **⑲**
Brad Turley, the founding chef at New Heights (*see p103*), has taken his style of big flavours and fresh ingredients to this striking dining room just off Nanjing Lu. 239's all about strong cocktails, big portions and good times. Expect a crowded dining room

of young professionals sharing family-style dishes, downing drinks and making a night of it. The menu warns diners that dishes are meant to be shared, and in rich dishes like beef carpaccio with quail egg, parmesan toast and potato confit, or gnocchi with blue cheese cream, this advice rings true. With a deft combination of casual chic and deliciously creative fusion fare, 239 is a number you'll want to remember when the weekend rolls around.

## South-east Asian

### Bali Laguna

*189 Huashan Lu, in Jingan Park (6248 6970). Metro Jingan Temple.* **Open** 11am-2.30pm, 6-10.30pm daily. **Main courses** RMB 40-138. **Credit** AmEx, DC, MC, V. **English menu. Map** p242 C6 **⑳** Indonesian
Scented blooms, exotic statuary and carved teak furniture in a pretty residence beside a lily-carpeted lake in the middle of Jingan Park – this place makes a fair stab at the notion of a Balinese island paradise. No wonder, then, that it's full of couples and is a perennial second-date spot. On warm summer nights the beautiful lakeside tables are normally all reserved, but if it's cold or raining the second-floor lofted dining room, with views of treetops, is hardly less attractive. Dishes include plenty of seafood and pork with coconut and lemongrass. Waitstaff – pretty in brightly coloured sarongs – are slow and the food isn't terribly authentic but the sublime atmosphere means that nobody minds. Reservations are required for dinner.

11pm daily. **Main courses** RMB 50-200. **Credit** AmEx, DC, MC, V. **English menu**. Map p249 M7 ㉒

Shanghainese

Housed in a classical Ming Dynasty-style pavilion overlooking the Yu Gardens and the teahouse pond (*see p70*), this place gets the tourists flocking in to soak up the history and gawk at the admittedly impressive decor. They are in good company: previous rubberneckers have included Bill Clinton, Queen Elizabeth and Fidel Castro, their visits commemorated in photos gracing the walls of the second- and third-floor corridors. However, as with most state-run enterprises in China, the service and food are entirely underwhelming. House speciality is dim sum; order individually from a vast menu or opt for a set meal (RMB 50-100).

### Nan Xiang

*85 Yuyuan Lu, Yu Gardens (6355 4206). Metro Henan Lu.* **Open** *1st floor* 10am-9pm daily. *2nd floor* 6.30am-8pm daily. *3rd floor* 10.45am-6.30pm daily. **Average** RMB 8-30 per dumpling. **Credit** AmEx, DC, MC, V. **English menu**. Map p249 M7 ㉓

Dumplings

At the heart of the Yu Gardens, this three-storey shrine to *xiaolongbao* (dumplings) is one of the city's most famous eateries. It features on every tourist itinerary, as evidenced by the permanent, lengthy queues. The basic dumpling varieties are steamed pork and crabmeat, but the higher the floor, the more elaborate the offerings; the third floor is where to go for the crab roe filling. We prefer the second floor, which boasts the best views of the nearby lake and its zigzag bridge. The minimum spend (to eat in) is RMB 60 per person.

## Xintiandi

In addition to the places below, Xintiandi has branches of the excellent **Simply Thai** (*see p120*) and of Shanghainese favourite **Jishi** (*see p115*).

## Cafés & snacks

### KABB

*House 5, North Block, Lane 181, Huangpi Nan Lu, by Taicang Lu (3307 0798/www.bluefrog.com.cn). Metro Huangpi Nan Lu.* **Open** 7am-1am Mon-Fri; 7am-2am Sat, Sun. **Main courses** RMB 35-120. **Credit** AmEx, DC, MC, V. **English menu**. Map p248 H7 ㉔

American

A multi-functional American-style casual diner, KABB starts the day with large platters of carb-intensive breakfasts. Lunches include sizeable snacks like burgers (RMB 65-75), pastas and stir-fries (RMB 65-80), and other good stuff like a Reuben on rye or a Philly cheese steak sandwich. Come evening KABB is more of a bar-diner, doing a good trade in dinners but with heavier accent placed on booze and even the occasional appearance of a DJ. Bring your laptop – the premises are Wi-Fi-enabled.

**Crystal Jade**. *See p110.*

## Thai Gallery

*127 Datian Lu, by Beijing Xi Lu (6217 9797). Metro Shimen Yi Lu.* **Open** 11am-2.30pm, 5.30pm-midnight daily. **Main courses** RMB 50-128. **Credit** AmEx, DC, MC, V. **English menu**. Map p243 G4 ㉑ Thai

In a town full of Thai restaurants, Thai Gallery sets itself apart from the pack with its decor. Within, the sleek, minimal lines and steel-grey concrete are brightened by colourful canvases imported from Bali by owner Edwin Ng, also proprietor of Bali Laguna (*see p108*). Lie down on the floor-cushions with your date and nibble on wonderful salads flecked with verdant herbs and laced with tangy fish sauce and chillies, or a rich red duck curry with chunks of roasted pineapple – the flavours are as vibrant as the surrounding artwork. Thai Gallery has become a haunt of Shanghai's stylish set – and for very good reason.

## Old City

Dining in the Old City is synonymous with touristy dumpling restaurants, many of which have seen better days. Eschew the Western fast-food franchises for a visit to **Yunnan Nan Lu**, on the western fringe – great for cheap eats.

## Chinese

### Lu Bo Lang

*115-131 Yuyuan Lu, south shore of the teahouse pond (6328 0602). Metro Henan Lu.* **Open** 7am-

Eat, Drink, Shop

## Visage

*Unit 3, House 1, North Block, Lane 181, Taicang Lu, by Huangpi Nan Lu (6385 4878). Metro Huangpi Nan Lu.* **Open** 10.30am-midnight daily. **Average** RMB 45. **Credit** AmEx, DC, MC, V. **English menu. Map** p248 H7 ㉕ French pastries

Shanghai's sweetest little shop, Visage is the creation of pastry-chef extraordinaire Eric Perez, who has done more for pâtisserie in Asia than just about anyone. Visage is one of precious few places in town where customers can enjoy perfect croissants and coffee, perhaps a late-night snack of ethereal tiramisu or a lemon meringue tart. But that's just for starters: this South-east Asian-styled sweet shop has beds for you to sit on, simple Thai-inspired dishes (Perez has several stores in Thailand) and the best own-made chocolates in town.

**Other locations**: Room 101, 808 Hongqiao Lu, by Huaihai Xi Lu, Changning (6448 1233).

## Chinese

### Crystal Jade

*Unit 12A & 12B, 2nd floor, House 6-7, Lane 123, Xingye Lu, South Block, by Zizhong Lu, Xintiandi Plaza (6385 8752). Metro Huangpi Nan Lu.* **Open** 11.30am-3pm, 5-11pm Mon-Sat; 10.30am-3pm, 5.30-11pm Sun. **Main courses** RMB 46-580. **Credit** AmEx, DC, MC, V. **English menu. Map** p248 H8 ㉖ Cantonese

Part of a Singaporean chain with restaurants in Hong Kong, Jakarta and Saigon, Crystal Jade is wildly popular for its inexpensive but incredibly good Cantonese and Shanghainese dim sum. Top picks are the baked barbecue pork bun, the steamed pork dumplings, spicy Sichuan noodles and the spicy wontons. The regular menu features superb Hong Kong barbecue fare, especially the suckling pig and roast duck combination. Break off from eating to watch the mesmerising performance of kitchen staff making noodles by hand (it's all in the wrist), which can be seen through a long slot of a window at the entrance to the massive dining room. The design of the restaurant is also something to behold: screens of red slats divide various dining spaces and lustrous woods and natural stone have been employed in the furnishings. Booking is essential for lunch and dinner, although at busy times you may have to wait even if you have a booking. **Photo** *p108 and p109*.

**Other locations**: B110, Hong Kong New World Plaza, 300 Huaihai Zhong Lu, by Madang Lu, Xintiandi (6335 4188); 7th floor, Westgate Mall, 1038 Nanjing Xi Lu, by Jiangning Lu, Jingan (5228 1133).

### Ding Tai Fung

*11A (inner Alexander Health Club), 2nd floor, No.6, South Block, 123 Xingye Lu (6385 8378). Metro Huangpi Nan Lu.* **Main courses** RMB 28-138. **Credit** AmEx, DC, MC, V. **English menu. Map** p248 H8 ㉗ Taiwanese

This Taiwanese restaurant, whose Taipei branch was once voted one of the 'World's Ten Best

Restaurants' by the *New York Times*, serves chic street food in pristine bamboo steamers. In this branch, decorated with cartoon caricatures of Chinese celebrities, well-off locals munch on an upscale take on Shanghai's venerable *xiaolongbao*. These unctuous pork and crab dumplings, filled with a mouth-watering broth of pork juice and tender meat, accented with garlic and ginger and encased in an impossibly thin wrapper, are dipped in strong black vinegar. The place also offers a great double boiled chicken soup, with the rich intensity of a consommé, and refreshing cold salads. It all makes a perfect lunchtime repast after browsing Xintiandi's boutiques, and is a safe foray into Shanghainese street food that will have you wishing they'd open a branch in a city near you.

**Other locations**: 1st floor, 12 Shuicheng Lu, by Hongqiao Lu, Gubei (6208 4188).

### Yè Shanghai

*Unit 1, House 6, North Block, Lane 181, Taicang Lu, by Huangpi Nan Lu (6311 2323). Metro Huangpi Nan Lu.* **Open** 11.30am-2.30pm, 5.30-11pm Mon-Thur, Sun; 11.30am-2.30pm, 5.30pm-midnight Fri, Sat. **Main courses** RMB 48-580. **Credit** AmEx, DC, MC, V. **English menu. Map** p248 H7 ㉘ Shanghainese

Named after a hit song of the 1940s, recorded by popular local songstress Zhou Xuan, Yè Shanghai ('Shanghai Night') is a nostalgic trip of red lanterns, antique furniture and sepia-toned images of old Bubbling Well Road and the pre-war racecourse. The menu features such typical Shanghainese dishes as drunken chicken and steamed pork dumplings, as well as chef's specials such as sautéed river shrimp and king prawns with chilli sauce. This is a good spot for an introduction to Shanghai's food, before heading out to more foreign territory.

## French

### Shikumen Bistro

*Unit 2, House 2,3,5, Lane 181, Taicang Lu, by Huangpi Nan Lu (6386 7100/www.shikumen bistro.com). Metro Huangpi Nan Lu.* **Open** 11.30am-2.30pm, 6.30-10.30pm Mon-Fri; 11.30am-3.30pm, 6.30-11.30pm Sat, Sun. **Main courses** RMB 160-212. **Credit** AmEx, DC, MC, V. **English menu. Map** p248 J8 ㉙ Bistro

San Francisco restaurateur George Chen was drawn to Shanghai after having opened two successful Asian restaurants in California. For his new enterprise, he enlisted the help of award-winning chef Jean Alberti, a classically trained French chef who was roundly praised for his new take on Greek cuisine at SF's lauded Kokkari. The two have joined forces here to create a casual space for straightforward, Mediterranean French fare that is satisfying rather than spectacular. There are hints of Alberti's Greek pedigree in dishes like zucchini fritters over a cucumber and yogurt salad with tomato confit, and a grilled whole sea bass with fresh thyme and lime vinaigrette. Shikumen shines at brunch, when

Eat, Drink, Shop

diners can sit on the outdoor terrace overlooking Xintiandi and sample traditional bistro fare like steak tartare, bubbly in hand.

## Fusion

### T8

*House 8, North Block, Lane 181, Taicang Lu, by Huangpi Nan Lu (6355 8999/www.ghmhotels.com). Metro Huangpi Nan Lu.* **Open** 11.30am-2.30pm, 6.30pm-midnight Mon, Wed-Fri; 6.30pm-midnight Tue; 11.30am-4pm, 6.30pm-midnight Sat, Sun. **Main courses** RMB 208-428. **Credit** AmEx, DC, MC, V. **English menu. Map** p248 H7 ③ Mediterranean
T8 looks South-east Asian, has an Australian chef and tastes Mediterranean. Hefty slate slabs laid over fish-filled pools make for a striking entrance, while the main dining area is sleek lacquered furniture with a warm, Thai touch. Central to the action is the large open kitchen, where half a dozen young chefs sear, sauté and flash-fry in front of diners seated at counter tables. On the beautifully presented degustation menus, the punchy food is worthy of all the superlatives it gets, as seen in dishes such as green pea cappuccino with goat's cheese foam and truffles or tuna tataki. Accompany with something from a fine Australian-accented wine list and be sure to reserve for dinner.

## French Concession

### Cafés, snacks & teahouses

**Arch** (*see p128*) isn't just a bar. It's also a performance space, a place to browse design mags and a film club, all in one of the city's most striking historic buildings (the Normandie Apartments, *see p86*). It serves very good food too, including what is for our money (RMB 58, and worth every yuan) the best burger in China.

### Art Deco Garden Café

*Building 3, Ruijin Hotel, 118 Ruijin Er Lu, by Maoming Nan Lu (6472 5222 ext 3006). Metro Shanxi Nan Lu.* **Open** 8.30am-1am daily. **Average** RMB 25-45. **Credit** AmEx, DC, MC, V. **English menu. Map** p247 F8 ③ Café
There is absolutely nothing art deco about the Art Deco Garden Café, but there is a baize-like green lawn stretching out front. It's all part of the grounds of the Ruijin Hotel (*see p41*), where the café is lodged in an elegant glass-fronted pavilion with terrace, just inside the Maoming Lu entrance. It consists of two or three high-ceilinged rooms, which in themselves are nothing special at all, but there are the great big windows and the outdoor seating, and on a warm afternoon it's all just blissful in its peacefulness. Just you, a book and a severely priced cappuccino or cocktail.

### Citizen Bar & Café

*222 Jinxian Lu, by Shanxi Nan Lu (6258 1620). Metro Shanxi Nan Lu.* **Open** 11am-1am Mon-Fri;

10am-1am Sat, Sun. **Main courses** RMB 80-180. **No credit cards. English menu. Map** p247 F7 ㉜ Italian
Come to this artsy little spot for a bit of San Francisco style at reassuringly affordable Shanghai prices. Downstairs is a swanky bar with claret velvet sofas, walnut tables and bracing Martinis; the upstairs dining room serves classic bar snacks, simple brunches and tasty sandwiches. Citizen, with its gentrified neighbourhood vibe, is where the city's hipsters nibble on seared ahi tuna sandwiches with pickled ginger and wasabi mayonnaise, a simple salade niçoise or salt and pepper calamares with chilli lime dipping sauce. Perfect for a pre-dinner drink and superb bar snacks or a laid-back dinner for two followed by a few cocktails on the sofas.

### La Casbah

*1554 Huaihai Zhong Lu, by Gaoan Lu (6471 2821). Metro Hengshan Lu.* **Open** 8am-10pm Mon-Thur; 8am-11pm Fri-Sun. **Main courses** RMB 28-38. **No credit cards. English menu. Map** p246 C8 ㉝ Café

**Citizen Bar & Café.**

# Chinese cuisines

Chinese people have a well-deserved reputation for eating practically anything. But each region is different. The Cantonese certainly aren't picky (civet cat, anyone?), while northerners do, in fact, eat dog, believing that it keeps them warm in winter. Shanghainese diners, meanwhile, are notoriously fussy, and do not like to be thought of as indiscriminate eaters. Still, it's all relative: delicacies such as crab sperm, snake's blood and turtle shells are considered Shanghainese specialities and served at many restaurants.

Just as in the West nobody would say 'Let's go eat European', but instead specify French, Italian or whatever, the Shanghainese don't go out for a Chinese – they eat Cantonese, Shanghainese or Sichuan. Cuisines from most provinces of China are available in Shanghai, although some are more popular than others.

## SHANGHAINESE

As you'd expect, this is the most popular cuisine in town, rich both in flavour and texture. Heavy, unctuous brown sauces are used for braising meat such as pork shanks or knuckle, or to simmer fatty pork balls with vegetables. Dumplings are popular, and very different from the lighter Cantonese variety. The most famous Shanghainese dumplings are *xiaolongbao* (*see p106* **Shanghai dumplings**), which are dipped in a sauce made with Shanghainese brown vinegar and shreds of ginger. This unusual vinegar is an essential flavouring in many other dishes as well – it's an ingredient in some braising sauces and stir-fries, and is drizzled over seafood, including delicate freshwater shrimp.

While the main starch of Chinese from the south is rice, the Shanghainese prefer bread. The poetically named 'silver threads' bread (so-called because the interior dough is formed into long, thin strands and then wrapped in a flat sheet of dough) is subtly sweet and comes either steamed or fried; the former is better for sopping up juices.

Shanghainese also specialise in so-called 'cold dishes', which are actually served tepid or at room temperature. They're most often eaten as an appetiser but are so delicious and varied it's easy to make an entire meal of them. They include jellyfish flavoured with sesame oil, mashed soybeans with preserved vegetables, sweet and crispy fried eel, and 'drunken' chicken or pigeon, which has been marinated in rice wine until the flavour permeates the meat.

Shanghai means 'by the sea' and the region's own peculiar sea cucumber is served braised with shrimp roe. Similarly, shark's fin soup is usually served with braised chicken and ham giving it a curious taste (one not enjoyed by all).

A tiny café just a dictionary's heave from the Shanghai Library, La Casbah is ideal for a pitstop on a walk around the French Concession, especially if you're not keen on paying the expat prices of the eateries on Hengshan Lu. Casbah does good basic lunch fare such as generously sized, thin-crust pizzas with meat and vegetarian toppings, plus salads and grilled sandwiches on toasted breads. Fresh juices, good coffee and ice teas are also available. Service is friendly and staff speak some English.

### Old China Hand Reading Room

*27 Shaoxing Lu, by Shanxi Nan Lu (6473 2526/ www.han-yuan.com). Metro Shanxi Nan Lu.* **Open** 10am-midnight daily. **Credit** MC, V. **English menu. Map** p247 F9 ㉞ Café
A beautiful space owned by the Old China Hand Press, a joint venture between photographer/collector Deke Erh and writer/historian Tess Johnston. They specialise in the architectural heritage of the Concession-era, documented in a series of self-published coffee-table volumes (sold here). The café

is decorated in Ming Dynasty fashion with salvaged bits of wood latticing, period furniture, antiques and glass-fronted cabinets of books. Far from musty, the place is light and airy courtesy of big picture windows overlooking the street, although the atmosphere is hushed with tables typically taken by studious types, heads buried in books. The menu is limited to beverages of flower teas, coffees and soft drinks, with nothing available to eat.

## Chinese

### Bao Luo

*271 Fumin Lu, by Changle Lu (5403 7239). Metro Changshu Lu.* **Open** 11am-6am daily. **Main courses** RMB 16-158. **No credit cards.** **English menu. Map** p246 D7 ㉟ Shanghainese
Packed day and night, Bao Luo is brash, loud, smoky Shanghai dining at its best. A tiny frontage of a single room and reception desk leads to a cavernous dining hall and a grand staircase leading to a warren of tiny rooms above. Waitstaff dash and rush

## CANTONESE

Cantonese is the cuisine of the south, exported worldwide via Hong Kong. In this type of cooking, the freshness of ingredients is paramount and cooking techniques (especially steaming) highlight this freshness. Because subtlety of flavours is so important, Cantonese cooks use a light, delicate hand with seasonings. To those who prefer more robust flavours, Cantonese food might seem bland.

Traditional Cantonese cooking techniques include steaming and stir-frying – which seals in the flavour of food by cooking it quickly over high heat for no more than a minute – producing dishes such as delicate rice noodles, dumplings and a variety of deep-fried savoury pastries.

## DONGBEI

Dongbei is the name of the cuisine from Beijing and the north-east region of China. It is rich and oily, with plenty of meat, vegetable and aubergine dishes, all flavoured with lashings of spring onions and garlic. Lamb and mutton are popular, and stir-fried slivers of meat and vegetables are frequently served stuffed into pockets of sesame-coated baked breads. The cuisine's most famous dish is Peking duck. It is always served with great ceremony by a white-gloved waiter carving off the deep, mahogany-coloured skin, wrapping the pieces in a thin pancake with a dab of plum sauce and a sliver of spring onion. When it's good, the skin is the best part of the duck – it should be crisp, flavourful and with just a hint of fat.

## HUNANESE AND SICHUAN

China's western spice-belt provinces of Hunan and Sichuan have similar base ingredients, but the source of the spice is different. Hunanese dishes use chilli, but Sichuan mixes dried chillies with gum-numbing, metallic-tasting pink peppercorns harvested from prickly ash trees. Sichuan food is hearty and rich, with sauces that ideally blend sweet, sour and spicy flavours. Hot and sour soup is probably the Sichuanese dish best known in the West – it combines vinegar, pepper and chillies to make a powerful, sinus-clearing broth. Dumplings and breads are also popular. Steamed buns are usually served with tea-smoked duck; meat dumplings look similar to Cantonese won ton, but instead of being served in a subtle broth, they're smothered in a sauce of soy, garlic and chillies.

## XINJIANG

The autonomous region of Xinjiang is situated south-east of Kazakstan and Afghanistan, thus the influences in the Xinjiang cuisine are more Central Asian than Chinese. Lamb stews and skewers are combined with naan bread, spicy salads, dark beer and live entertainment.

**Eat, Drink, Shop**

bearing massive metallic trays of steaming food. This landmark restaurant can be intimidating if you've never been and don't speak Chinese; the manual-thick menu's English-language descriptions are no help and range from the perplexing ('Stewed pork intestine with eating able grass') to the nonsensical ('Acctle show immerged in bitern'). We can recommend the braised pork hoof Shanghai style (RMB 30), which is just the most succulent and tender meat, and the stir-fried vegetables and mushrooms 'for monks' (RMB 25), which – once you've dealt with the hairnet-like membrane stretched over the top – is delicious. Otherwise, take a few chances: prices are cheap. And pity the waitresses, who have to wear red dresses with a funny pleat that makes it look like they've got the backs caught in their knickers.

### Di Shui Dong

*2nd floor, 56 Maoming Nan Lu, by Changle Lu (6253 2689). Metro Shanxi Nan Lu.* **Open** 11am-1am daily. **Main courses** RMB 18-88. **No credit cards. English menu. Map** p247 F7 ❸ Hunanese

A Shanghai veteran, Di Shui Dong is a throwback to dining in the days before 'design'. Expect oily floors, menu items written in big characters on streamers pasted to the wall and large tables with checkered cloths. Dishes are listed on a bilingual menu, although for some reason those in English are often unavailable. Try spicy staples such as fried chicken with chillies, sour beans with minced pork or sweet and spicy twice-cooked pork in red sauce – Mao's favourite. The lack of humidity in the Hunan region is not only good for drying chillies, but also favours citrus fruits, so pitchers of freshly squeezed orange juice are served in season. Reserve for dinner. **Other locations**: Unit B, 5 Dongping Lu, by Yueyang Lu, French Concession (6415 9448); 626 Xianxia Lu, by Shuicheng Lu, Changning (3207 0213).

### Dongbei Ren

*1 Shanxi Nan Lu, by Yanan Zhong Lu (5228 9898/ www.dongbeiren.com.cn). Metro Shanxi Nan Lu.* **Open** 11am-10pm daily. **Main courses** RMB 10-98. **No credit cards. English menu. Map** p243 F6 ❸ Dongbei

# 乐·名牌世界

2006.05 总第 90 期 6.50RMB

# Top 50 Unique
# Designer Stores
## 50家上海设计师店

## 本城最食尚的
## 露天餐厅

ISSN 1006-7027

9 771006 702038

# Time Out
## Shanghai

附送奥地利旅游指南

"Your monthly guide to the city - in Mandarin"

In Chinese there is a word, *renao*, that means warm, noisy and hearty, all at the same time. *Renao* is the concept on which the owners of Dongbei Ren ('the people from Dongbei') appear to have based their business. On a recent visit we were greeted by the waitress with a cry of '*Waiguo pengyou lai le!*' ('Foreign friends coming in!'). As we ordered she proceeded to share the information with the surrounding tables. Not a place for shy, retiring types then. Nor for those with less than hearty appetites: typical Dongbei dishes include *jiaozi* (heavy dumplings) and *guobaorou* (fatty, crispy pork in a tasty sweet and sour sauce). Wash it all down with the excellent northern dark beer Snow.

**Other locations:** 555 Shuicheng Lu, by Tianshan Lu, Gubei (6233 0990); 46 Panyu Lu, by Yanan Xi Lu, Changning (5230 2230); 20 Zhendan Dong Lu, by Guoji Lu, Yangpu (6530 8011).

### Guyi

*87 Fumin Lu, by Julu Lu (6247 0758). Metro Jingan Temple.* **Open** 10.30am-2pm, 5.30-10.30pm daily. **Main courses** RMB 20-148. **Credit** AmEx, DC, MC, V. **English menu. Map** p242 D6 ⑥ Hunanese

Guyi is one of a few restaurants equally popular with (affluent) locals and with expats. It's always packed, so if you turn up without a reservation be prepared to wait anything up to an hour (pass the time with a drink at nearby Manifesto, *see p129*). The decor juxtaposes traditional China with modern Shanghai and creates a classy setting for classic spicy Hunanese fare. Standouts include the spicy beans with ground pork and the king-sized grilled shrimp. Portions are sized to share, so bring friends. Fresh lemon sodas nicely take the edge off the chilli.

**Other locations:** 2nd floor, No.66, Lane 999, Changshou Lu, Putuo (6232 8677).

### Jishi

*41 Tianping Lu, by Huaihai Xi Lu (6282 9260). Metro Hengshan Lu.* **Open** 11am-midnight daily. **Main courses** RMB 22-368. **Credit** AmEx, DC, MC, V. **English menu. Map** p246 B9 ⑥ Shanghainese

Dishing up superb home-style Shanghainese cuisine, this no-frills, two-storey shack now has a side annexe to accommodate the throngs of lively locals. Chatty diners sit elbow to elbow, while the efficient waitstaff shout orders as they stomp up and down the narrow rickety staircase. No oil, sugar or MSG is spared and must-eats include air-dried eel with horsebean paste, deep-fried bamboo shoots, wild herbs with beancurd, jellyfish with vinegar and house speciality pork knuckle, which is braised for five hours in soy sauce, sugar and salt. Reservations are required for dinner.

**Other locations:** throughout the city.

### Pin Chuan

*47 Taojiang Lu, by Wulumuqi Nan Lu (6437 9361). Metro Changshu Lu.* **Open** 11am-2pm, 5-11pm daily. **Main courses** RMB 32-159. **Credit** AmEx, DC, MC, V. **English menu. Map** p246 C8 ⑥ Sichuan

Recipient of numerous 'best restaurant' awards from the local press, Pin Chuan is perhaps the finest Sichuan restaurant in town. It sits beside a small green park opposite the US Consulate in an old Shanghai house made bright with paint and manned by friendly waiters, some of whom speak enough English to offer novices guidance in this spiciest of Chinese cuisines. All the classics are here, including fish with sliced beef in chillies and peppercorn oil, cold peppery noodles and claypot spicy bean with beef and pork. For the real Sichuan burn, though, go for the *lazi ji*, small knuckles of golden deep-fried chicken on the bone buried in a bowl of crimson dried chillies; beautiful to behold, explosive to taste.

### Shu Di Lazi Yu Guan

*187 Anfu Lu, by Wulumuqi Zhong Lu (5403 7684). Metro Changshu Lu.* **Open** 11am-2.30pm, 5-11.30pm daily. **Main courses** RMB 12-68. **No credit cards.** **English menu. Map** p246 C7 ⑥ Sichuan

A Shanghai restaurant that is innovative yet serves spicy, home-style Sichuan food is more than rare; it's nearly unheard of. Some claim this isn't an authentic Sichuan restaurant, which is probably true – it's much more than that. The chain is owned by famous Sichuan actor Ren Quan, a foodie who has picked his favourite dishes from his home province, as well as a collection of classics from the north-east and other regions. Expect downhome Chinese cooking as inexpensive as it is delicious. The speciality dish, spicy fish (*lazi yu*), comes in large crocks that are set to simmer on the table, teasing your tastebuds as they emit wafts of ginger, peppercorns and chillies (ask the waitress to scoop out the chillies if you struggle with fiery food). Try the *zhuxiangji*, meaty spring chickens that are diced, marinated and deep-fried, then combined with crunchy leeks, young green onions, fennel seeds and chillies in a bamboo basket, and fried once more. It's just one of a slew of fabulous dishes at this run-down place, its greasy-looking floors overshadowed by great food.

**Other locations:** throughout the city.

### Sophia's Tea Restaurant

*480 Huashan Lu, by Wulumuqi Zhong Lu (6249 9917). Metro Jingan Temple.* **Open** 11.30am-2.30pm, 5.30-10.30pm daily. **Main courses** RMB 25-298. **Credit** AmEx, DC, MC, V. **English menu. Map** p246 C7 ⑥ Shanghainese

Tucked into a modest terrace house, just around the corner from the Hilton, Sophia's bucks the Shanghai trend for cavernous food palaces with large tables and boisterous patrons. Its intimate atmosphere makes it a favourite for low-key business lunches or quiet family dinners. Diverse Chinese dishes have their stronger flavours toned down for the Shanghainese palate, and the chefs go easy on the oil. Standouts include hearty northern-style pancakes with aubergine or chicken, and subtly spiced Sichuan-style lemon fish. The prawns are also good: try them crisp and deep-fried with longjin tea leaves, or fat, steamed and juicy with rose petals. Portions lean towards tiny, so order more than you would at your neighbourhood Chinese restaurant. There are excellent teas too. Reservations are necessary.

Eat, Drink, Shop

## South Beauty

*28 Taojiang Lu, by Baoqing Lu (6445 2581/ www.qiaojiangnan.com). Metro Changshu Lu.* **Open** 11am-10pm daily. **Main courses** RMB 22-788. **Credit** AmEx, DC, MC, V. **English menu. Map** p246 D8 🉐 Sichuan

Shanghai restaurateurs really go a bundle for design gimmicks. At this branch of the respected spice vendor South Beauty, diners have to parade down a long, water-fringed catwalk towards a large mirror that eventually slides back to reveal itself as a door. The restaurant is a little more straightforward than the approach route, with an airy main dining area downstairs and light-filled private rooms upstairs, both of which overlook a street-side bamboo garden. Despite Shanghai's reputation for being spice-shy, there is no holding back on the heat here: dishes such as chicken with spring onions and vinegar, and tripe and peanuts in pepper oil have a high singe factor. When it's time for dessert, the 'Chinese calligraphy set' is so visually magnificent you'll hesitate to eat it. The Yanan Zhong Lu branch of South Beauty (*see p131*), which opened in summer 2005, is – if anything – even more impressive, occupying a sprawling villa and its grounds, all deftly refitted by Japanese design wizards Super Potato, complete with a rooftop deck overlooking the skyline, private dining rooms and a sweeping lawn for outdoor events. If spice isn't your thing, then at least visit the lounge bar for a drink.

**Other locations:** 881 Yanan Zhong Lu, by Shanxi Nan Lu, Jingan (6247 5878); 5th floor, Times Square, 93 Huaihai Zhong Lu, by Liulin Lu, Xintiandi (6391 0890); 10th floor, Super Grand Mall, 168 Lujiazui Lu, Pudong (5047 1817); B7B8, 100 Zunyi Lu, by Hongqiao Lu, Hongqiao (6237 2887).

## Uighur Restaurant

*1 Shanxi Nan Lu, by Yanan Zhong Lu (6255 0843). Metro Shanxi Nan Lu.* **Open** 10am-2am daily. **Main courses** RMB 30-118. **No credit cards. English menu. Map** p243 F6 🉐 Xinjiang

When the house band at the Uighur starts to play, nobody is allowed to remain sitting. Uniformed waiters drag diners away from their mounds of *yangrou paofan* (saffron rice with chunks of lamb) to link yellow-stained fingers (Xinjiang is a hands-on cuisine) and join in the ring dancing – shy visitors should sit as far away from the restaurant's stage as possible. Other than dancing, expect huge mounds of fatty lamb, eaten with bread, tomatoes and grapes. It's very basic and wouldn't be your first-choice restaurant if you're only in town for a couple of days, but as something far, far removed from Shanghainese food yet still Chinese, it's certainly worth investigating. Reservations are required for dinner.

## Xia Wei Guan

*Oriental Gardens, 9 Zhenging Lu, by Huashan Lu (6212 6797). Metro Changshu Lu or Jiangsu Lu.* **Open** 11.30am-10.30pm daily. **Main courses** RMB 28-888. **Credit** AmEx, DC, MC, V. **English menu. Map** p246 B7 🉐 Shanghainese

A haunt of Hong Kong celebs and sundry moneyed Shanghainese, this place certainly looks the part, with a glass staircase entrance suspended over a pond. Small portions of (pricey) refined local cuisine are served in delicate china in the polished setting of elegant teahouse tables and chairs. Choice dishes include an exceptional crabmeat tofu and what is arguably the city's best 'lion's head' meatball with crabmeat (*xiefen shizitou*). Other top dishes are fried beancurd skin with enoki mushrooms and sautéed spring bamboo shoot with chopped greens.

## Xiao Nan Guo

*2nd floor, Ruijin Hotel, 118 Ruijin Er Lu, by Yongjia Lu (6466 2277). Metro Shanxi Nan Lu.* **Open** 10.45am-2pm, 4.45-10pm daily. **Average** RMB 125-150. **No credit cards. English menu. Map** p247 F8 🉐 Shanghainese

This is the flagship branch of a city-wide chain known for terrific food and efficient service. In a gorgeous garden setting, it's an airy hangar of a dining hall – a refreshing change from the typical cramped and smoky Shanghainese joint. Tables are correspondingly huge and designed for sharing (couples will feel very lonely here). Standout cold dishes include drunken chicken and the chopped wild herbs with diced tofu, while of the hot fare we recommend spring onion pancakes, roasted pigeon, claypot of crabmeat and roe, and sautéed pea shoots. Intrepid diners can test their mettle against dishes

**Nepali Kitchen.** *See p119.*

such as turtle with sticky rice, roasted snake or marinated snake skin. You'll need to make a reservation if you're coming for dinner.
**Other locations**: throughout the city.

### Yin
*1st floor, Jinjiang Gourmet Street, 59 Maoming Nan Lu, by Changle Lu (5466 5070). Metro Shanxi Nan Lu.* **Open** noon-3pm, 6-10pm daily. **Main courses** RMB 30-150. **Credit** AmEx, DC, MC, V. **English menu. Map** p247 F7 ⑰ Shanghainese
Part of the 1929 Jinjiang Hotel complex (*see p41*), Yin riffs on an 'Old Shanghai' theme, with decor of cherrywood floors and antique screens, a stage and piano at one end of the room (never used in the dozen or more visits we've made) and a long bar at the other, which is staffed by *qipao*-clad girls who know their way round a cocktail list. But Japanese-born restaurateur Takashi is also canny enough to bring the place into the 21st century with warm lighting and splashes of colour, courtesy of Pop artist Zeng Fanzhi. The food is superb with a menu that roams through the best of China's regional cuisine, from the far west's Xinjiang-style lamb with cumin to eastern seafood dishes such as fat Shanghainese-style shrimp. Food is served on the restaurant's own flatware, which colourfully updates traditional Asian square-cut plates and tea beakers. We recommend this place highly. The Japanese restaurant Zen (*see p120*) is just upstairs.

### Yuan Yuan
*201 Xingguo Lu, by Taian Lu (6433 9123). Metro Hengshan Lu.* **Open** 11am-11pm daily. **Main courses** RMB 22-680. **Credit** AmEx, DC, MC, V. **English menu. Map** p246 B8 ㊽ Shanghainese
Yuan Yuan is a two-storey casual eaterie that is especially popular among well-to-do locals. It serves all the Shanghai classics, from jellyfish with sesame oil to spongy bean thread. Signature dishes here include red-cooked pork and glutinous rice-stuffed red dates. There's also a branch at the terminus of the Maglev in Pudong.
**Other locations**: 7th floor, Westgate Mall, 1038 Nanjing Xi Lu, by Jiangning Lu, Jingan (6272 6972); 550 Wanping Nan Lu, by Lingling Lu, Xujiahui (6438 1015); 108 Xiangyang Bei Lu, by Huaihai Zhong Lu, French Concession (5108 3377).

## European

### Le Garçon Chinois
*No.3, Lane 9, Hengshan Lu, by Dongping Lu (6445 7970). Metro Changshu Lu or Hengshan Lu.* **Open** 6.30-11.30pm daily. **Main courses** RMB 58-138. **Credit** AmEx, DC, MC, V. **English menu. Map** p246 C9 ㊾ Spanish
Still the most romantic little eaterie in town, Le Garçon is in an old French villa secreted down a winding, leafy alleyway. Sparsely decorated with commissioned murals painted by local artists, it boasts a delightful, pocket-sized bar, invariably packed with devotees of owner Takashi's throwback style where old jazz, great service and traditional takes on Vietnamese and Spanish cuisine are the order of the day. On the first floor a young Basque chef cooks wonderful tapas, accented simply with sea salt, garlic and olive oil, and squid served in squid ink sauce with crusty slices of bread. Upstairs expect Northern Vietnamese dishes like *cha ca*, turmeric-fried fish with dill and herbs, and light, but interesting salads. Le Garçon Chinois is everything a villa restaurant should be, but the secret's out now – so make sure you reserve for dinner.

## Fusion

### A Future Perfect
*No.16, Lane 351, Huashan Lu, by Changshu Lu, inside the Old House Inn (6248 8020). Metro Changshu Lu.* **Open** 7am-2am daily. **Main courses** RMB 53-155. **Credit** (over RMB 500) AmEx, DC, MC, V. **English menu. Map** p246 C7 ㊿
Bury your nose in the latest edition of *Wallpaper** at this ever-crowded restaurant and bar, tucked inside a boutique hotel (*see p41*), and popular with a crowd of architects, artists and scenesters. The slick urbanity of AFP is exemplified by its decor of cardboard chairs designed by Frank Gehry and green pixellated graffiti, by a logo that shows a sperm swimming upstream and a menu that reads like a clever exercise in creative writing. The food is simple and

**Eat, Drink, Shop**

filling, a quirky amalgamation of Western faves from stuffed grape leaves and smoked salmon to thin shavings of roast beef plus Caesar salad and pasta. The on-site bakery churns out crusty breads and desserts, and there's a sunny patio for outdoor dining. It isn't yet perfect, but if AFP's popularity is any indication then its future is bright.

### Mesa

*748 Julu Lu, by Fumin Lu (6289 9108). Metro Jingan Temple.* **Open** 6-11pm Mon; 11.30am-2pm, 6-11pm Tue-Sun. **Main courses** RMB 128-238. **Credit** AmEx, DC, MC, V. **English menu.** **Map** p243 D6 ⑤

Mesa is a former factory warehouse that has been beautifully reappointed as a chic, airy and light-filled dining room, although the original function of the building is still apparent in the high ceilings, deco picture windows and unusual explosion-proof hanging lights, once common in the city's factories. It's a striking space, and one that provides the setting for some of the best Western cuisine in town. Visit for classy, well-executed Mediterranean-style dishes enhanced with delicate Asian flavours, such as soy-, star anise- and ginger-baked salmon, and save room for desserts like spiced black rice and coconut risotto with banana jam. Reservations are required for dinner at weekends. Mesa's all-day weekend brunch is excellent and ace bar Manifesto (*see p129*), a sibling venture, is next door.

### Viva/Azul

*18 Dongping Lu, by Baoqing Lu (6433 1172). Metro Changshu Lu.* **Open** 11am-11pm daily. **Main courses** RMB 48-178. **Credit** AmEx, DC, MC, V. **English menu.** **Map** p246 C9 ⑤

Peruvian chef Eduardo Vargas garnered almost cult following at Xintiandi tapas and cigar bar Che. Now he has his own bar-restaurant, just off Hengshan Lu. Azul is the drinking part of the operation, where lime Margaritas and Sangria are served up alongside Vargas's signature tapas (mussels in decadent cream-chilli sauce is fantastic). Upstairs is the restaurant, Viva, a languid affair of couches and throw cushions, much softer than the assembly of granite slab tables downstairs. You can order tapas up here too, but there's also a solid menu of New World cuisine. Dishes play on sweet and sour flavours – spicy duck breast with chilli-honey glaze, for example, or blue cheese bavarois with char-grilled asparagus and nut oil dressing. Chocolate soup makes for a sinful finale. Reservations required for dinner.

## Indian & Nepali

### Indian Kitchen

*572 Yongjia Lu, by Wulumuqi Nan Lu (6473 1517). Metro Hengshan Lu.* **Open** 11.30am-2.30pm, 5-11pm daily. **Main courses** RMB 110-115. **Credit** AmEx, DC, MC, V. **English menu.** **Map** p246 C9 ⑤ Indian

**Coconut Paradise** – for fiery Thai cuisine in stylish surroundings. *See p120.*

Of the ever-increasing number of Indians in town – well into double figures now – this remains our favourite. Part of a China-wide chain established by a Goan-born entrepreneur, it adheres to a simple but winning concept of attractive surroundings, impeccable service and reasonably authentic Indian food, prepared by authentic Indian chefs on view in the open kitchen. The menu is all Indian classics, although flavours are tailored to a broad Chinese palate, so curries are not especially spicy. We particularly like the tandoori chicken, and the rich and creamy kormas. The streetside patio is a bonus. **Other locations**: 600 Lantian Lu, by Yunshan Lu, Pudong (5030 2005); House 8, 3911 Hongmei Lu, by Yanan Xi Lu, Hongqiao (6261 0377); 480 Minsheng Lu, Zhangyang Lu, Lujiazui (5821 9875).

### Nepali Kitchen

*No.4, Lane 819, Julu Lu, by Fumin Lu (5404 6281). Metro Jingan Temple.* **Open** 11am-2pm, 6-11pm daily. **Main courses** RMB 44-50. **Credit** AmEx, DC, MC, V. **English menu.** **Map** p246 D7 ㊴ Nepali
A few years ago diners mourned the passing of the Nepali Kitchen, which had closed its doors on Xinle Lu. But just a month later it was back, and had dropped the shabby Himalayan guesthouse get-up for a four-storey colonial villa with hardwood floors, creaky staircases and comfy floor seating. In three tasteful dining rooms, adorned with Nepali folk art and panoramas of the Anapurna Range, friendly waitstaff serve curries that are flavourful but lighter than the Indian variety – try the wonderful mushroom pea curry and the famous cheese balls, rich potato and cheese croquettes served with a cumin and chilli dipping sauce. The restaurant has a good, reasonably priced New World wine list, and is vegetarian-friendly, with a meat-free tasting menu. Be sure to reserve a table, then curl up on the comfy cushions and prepare yourself to enjoy Nepali's subtle charms. **Photos** *p116 and p117.*

### Vedas

*550 Jianguo Xi Lu, by Wulumuqi Nan Lu (6445 8100/www.vedascuisine.com). Metro Hengshan Lu.* **Open** 11am-3pm, 6-11.30pm daily. **Main courses** RMB 45-145. **Credit** AmEx, DC, MC, V. **English menu.** **Map** p246 D10 ㊵ Indian
Not long ago, furniture importer and first-time restaurateur Anoop boasted he would open the best Indian restaurant in town. A year later, his promise rings true. Vedas is a big success, catering to a loyal clientele of Indian families and fashionable French Concession expats, in a simple space where the open kitchen is the main attraction. As the heady scent of copper pot curries surrounds you, watch the team of five-star chefs from Delhi pluck spears of the succulent Kesari chicken out of the tandoor – these otherworldly boneless chunks of yogurt-marinated chicken are not to be missed. Richly spicy lamb rogan josh, creamy dal makhni (black lentils slow-cooked in clarified butter and spices) and a cooling dessert of frozen yogurt kulfi round out some of the best Indian cuisine you'll find.

# Hairy crabs

As the autumn winds begin to blow, crab connoisseurs from across Asia make their annual pilgrimage to Shanghai to feast on the region's most famous delicacy. The season runs from the ninth through the tenth lunar month (roughly early October through November), during which the roe-filled females mature in the first half, and the fleshy, spermatic males in the second.

For the uninitiated, eating the crabs is a challenge. The first step is to remove the top shell by sliding either a fingernail or fork under the belly flap and prying it open. Females will reveal a reddish or orangey mass of roe, while males will contain a sticky, grey substance – the most prized part for gourmets. Next, the legs are pulled off and snapped in two, allowing a chopstick to be pushed inside to dislodge the meat. Finally, the body can be broken in half and all the flesh inside eaten, minus the air sacs and other internal organs.

Hairy crab is traditionally accompanied by black vinegar and fresh ginger, and Shaoxing and yellow wine is often drunk with the meal, with sweet ginger water served at the end.

Hairy crabs can be sampled in season at most of the city's high-end hotels, and most People's share at **Wangbaohe Restaurant** (603 Fuzhou Lu, by Zhejiang Lu, People's Square, 6322 3673) or **Xin Guang** (512 Tianjin Lu, by Guangxi Bei Lu, People's Square, 6322 3978). Reservations are recommended.

## Japanese

### Ambrosia

*150 Fenyang Lu, by Yueyang Lu (6431 3935). Metro Changshu Lu.* **Open** 11.30am-2pm, 5.30-11pm daily. **Main courses** RMB 38-1,200. **Credit** AmEx, DC, MC, V. **English menu.** **Map** p246 D9 ㊳
Set in sumptuous, baize-lawned grounds, the grand triple-decker villa that is home to Ambrosia was built by a wealthy French merchant in 1930. It's now a very impressive Japanese restaurant, where top-quality sashimi, sushi, tempura and yakiniku compete for superlatives with marble architecture and a gallery's worth of fine paintings and antiquities. Show curiosity about the surroundings and staff will present a descriptive brochure, along with a handout celebrating the restaurant's appearance on the *Condé Nast Traveller* world hot list of 2003.

**Eat, Drink, Shop**

### Shintori

*803 Julu Lu, by Fumin Lu (5404 5252). Metro Changshu Lu or Shanxi Nan Lu.* **Open** 5.30-10.30pm Mon-Fri; 11.30am-2pm, 5.30-10.30pm Sat, Sun. **Main courses** RMB 50-300. **Credit** AmEx, DC, MC, V. **English menu. Map** p246 D6 **57**

As good as the food is, it's not what you remember from a visit to Shintori. Instead, what you take away is a mental slide show of impressions of what is the city's most laughably wonderful interior. The restaurant is approached along a ghostly lit pathway that snakes through a thicket of slender bamboo. Entrance is through two silently sliding clouded-glass doors. The restaurant itself is like one of Ken Adams's designs for a James Bond submarine hangar – a sunken pool-like main space with steps up to side galleries and a vast open stainless-steel kitchen, with a surrounding upper gallery connected by a bannisterless stair and serviced by platform elevators. Everything is in grey, wet-look concrete. It really is quite startling. That the food holds its own is a great tribute to the white-hatted chefs, armies of whom busy themselves chopping, rolling and flash-frying. The cuisine is Japanese and it's fabulous, particularly the presentation: sashimi is served on granite platters, cold noodles come in sculpted ice bowls. We'd put dinner at Shintori high on our list of Shanghai must-dos.

### Zen

*2nd floor, Jinjiang Gourmet Street, 59 Maoming Nan Lu, by Changle Lu (5466 5070). Metro Shanxi Nan Lu.* **Open** noon-3pm, 6-11pm daily. **Average** RMB 200. **Main courses** RMB 28-88. **Credit** AmEx, DC, MC, V. **English menu. Map** p247 F7 **58** Japanese

Situated upstairs from the Shanghainese eaterie Yin (*see p117*) is Japanese restaurant Zen. The design isn't Zen at all: it's much warmer – a mix of art deco, Shanghai style and sympathetic modern additions, including lovely pendant light fittings. Dishes are classic Japanese – sushi, sashimi, tempura, yakitori and noodles – consumed in the company of discerning locals, Westerners and Japanese. Service is impeccable and prices are very reasonable. Reservations required.

## South-east Asian

### Coconut Paradise

*38 Fumin Lu, by Julu Lu (6248 1998). Metro Jingan Temple.* **Open** noon-2pm, 5pm-midnight daily. **Main courses** RMB 38-170. **Credit** AmEx, DC, MC, V. **English menu. Map** p246 D7 **59** Thai

Tucked away in a tastefully restored villa, this is an effortlessly elegant Thai restaurant where every detail is attended to, from the first-rate wine list to the lemongrass scent that washes over you as you step through the teak doors. With an old Chiangmai lady pounding curry pastes in the kitchen, expect fiery, authentic and affordable Northern Thai fare, including a perfectly complex green curry and an infernal beef larb salad with Thai basil and coriander. The place also boasts a tranquil garden that feels more Sukhothai than Shanghai. One drawback is sluggish, unreceptive service, but for a combination of great looks and balanced Thai flavours, Coconut Paradise lives up to its lofty moniker. **Photos** *p118*.

### Lan Na Thai

*Building 4, Ruijin Hotel, 118 Ruijin Er Lu, by Fuxing Zhong Lu (6466 4328). Metro Shanxi Nan Lu.* **Open** noon-2.30pm, 5.30-10.30pm Mon-Thur, Sun; noon-2.30pm, 5.30-11pm Fri, Sat. **Main courses** RMB 65-198. **Credit** AmEx, DC, MC, V. **English menu. Map** p247 F8 **60** Thai

Opened in 1999, Lan Na Thai is decked out with elegant Ming Dynasty furniture and serene Buddhist sculptures, and boasts gorgeous views of the guesthouse gardens. No wonder Shanghai first-timers find the languid, colonial air of the place irresistible. Long-termers get sniffy, take umbrage at the high prices and stay downstairs in the splendid Face Bar (*see p129*), but everyone has to do Lan Na at least once. The food is Thai Thai, as opposed to the Chinese Thai that is the norm around here. Even so, if you like your chicken larb spicy or your green curry hot, then you still need to ask for it to be prepared that way. Reservations required for dinner.

### Simply Thai

*5 Dongping Lu, by Hengshan Lu (6445 9551/ www.simplythai-sh.com). Metro Changshu Lu or Hengshan Lu.* **Open** 11am-11pm daily. **Main courses** RMB 45-108. **Credit** AmEx, DC, MC, V. **English menu. Map** p246 D9 **61** Thai

The ever-expanding 'Simply' group includes flower and lifestyle stores, but what it did first – and still does best – is Thai food. The menu at its restaurants covers all the staples: curries in red, green and yellow flavours, laksas, tom yam dishes and plenty of seafood. Spicing is light but flavours are abundant. The surroundings at Dongping Lu are lovely – a cosy two-storey house decorated in a minimalist fashion with some courtyard seating looks out on a picturesque tree-lined street. It's perfect for quiet, candlelit dinners; the Xintiandi branch is more business-like and better suited to lunch. Consistent cooking, reasonable prices (most non-seafood mains cost around RMB 45) and a decent wine list make this a regular favourite with the city's expats – as a collection of awards from listings magazines testifies. **Other locations:** 27 Madang Lu, by Xingye Lu, Xintiandi (6326 2088); No.28, Lane 3338, Hongmei Lu, Changning (6465 8955).

## Xujiahui

Although it's not a dining destination as such, Xujiahui's myriad shopping malls do host a good range of eateries. Among them you'll find a handful of good-quality regional specialists: try **Fwu Luh Pavilion** for some classy Yangzhou seafood, perhaps, or **Yunnan**

Jade on 36. *See p122.*

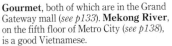

**Gourmet**, both of which are in the Grand Gateway mall (*see p133*). **Mekong River**, on the fifth floor of Metro City (*see p138*), is a good Vietnamese.

## Chinese

### Shanghai Lao Zhan (Old Station)

*201 Caoxi Bei Lu, by Nandan Dong Lu (6427 2233). Metro Xujiahui.* **Open** 11.15am-2pm, 5-9.30pm daily. **Main courses** RMB 28-280. **Credit** AmEx, DC, MC, V. **English menu. Map** p246 A11 ® Shanghainese
Housed in an ex-convent that dates back to the 1920s, the dining rooms here are graced by classic decor of dark wood, whitewashed walls, tiled floors and ornate light fixtures. Waiters in traditional jackets deliver typical Shanghainese fare, the best of which includes smoked dried fish, asparagus soup and 'eight treasure' duck. Request a table by the window for a view of the garden with its two antique train carriages. One was once used by the Empress Dowager, the other by Soong Qingling.

### Shanghai Uncle

*211 Tianyaoqiao Lu, by Nandan Lu (6464 6430). Metro Xujiahui.* **Open** 11.15am-2pm, 5.15-10pm daily. **Main courses** RMB 22-280. **Credit** AmEx, DC, MC, V. **English menu. Map** p246 B12 ® Shanghainese

Owned by Shanghai-American Li Zhongheng (who is the son of a *New York Times* food critic), the Uncle is a favourite with locals before 8.30pm and with the Hong Kong and Taiwanese set after that. Its classic Shanghai dishes – illustrated on a colourful picture menu that also bears delightful Chinglish descriptions – are heavily influenced by other regional and foreign cuisines. Book ahead if you want to sample house specialities such as 'Uncle's crispy pork of flame' and the 'six-pounder onion duck'. The traditional Shanghainese cold dish of smoked fish is also terrific. Diners can choose from the second-floor sprawl of loud red floral chairs or one of the third-floor private eating dens, complete with TV. Making a reservation is advisable.
**Other locations**: 8th floor, Time Square, 500 Zhangyang Lu, by Pudong Nan Lu, Pudong (5836 7977); 222 Yanan Dong Lu, by Henan Zhong Lu, the Bund (6339 1977).

### Xinjiang Fengwei Restaurant

*280 Yishan Lu, by Nandan Lu (6468 9198). Metro Yishan Lu.* **Open** 10am-2am daily. **Main courses** RMB 10-60. **No credit cards. English menu. Map** p240 C4 ® Xinjiang
Xinjiang cuisine is one of China's best-kept secrets, a Middle Kingdom meets the Middle East blend of flavours and techniques. The Uighur minority, who live in the western deserts bordering Pakistan and Afghanistan, cook complex stews like *da pan ji*

(chicken in a heady tomato braise accented with star anise, *tsaoko* cardamom, tomatoes, onions and peppers) and huge hunks of roasted mutton, which pair perfectly with the region's dense, unleavened breads. This is the best place in town to eat these hearty dishes, washed down with a malty black beer, in delightfully tacky surroundings. You'll need to bring your dancing shoes as well: dinner is a riotous affair with waiters breaking into song, and frequently dragging diners on to the dancefloor. Reservations are required for dinner.

## Pudong

In addition to the places listed below, Pudong has branches of Shanghainese restaurants **Xiao Nan Guo** (*see p116*) and **Shanghai Uncle** (*see p121*).

### Chinese

#### Minghao Seafood Restaurant

*POS Plaza, 480 Pudian Lu, by Shiji Dadao (5820 3333). Metro Dongfang Lu.* **Open** 11am-2.30pm, 5-10.30pm daily. **Main courses** RMB 28-over 6,000. **Credit** AmEx, DC, MC, V. **English menu. Map** p241 G4 **⑮** Seafood

An extravagant seafood palace among the skyscrapers of Pudong. The decor is ridiculously OTT, with ceilings and mouldings pressed with gold leaf and great aquatic tanks filled with marine life – nice to look at, but gradually emptied during the course of an evening for the assorted sea life to be fried, baked and steamed. This is no place to play safe with a bit of salmon or tuna fillet; try rarer treats such as octopus, eels and even snake (fried with spicy salt). Other delicacies are Indonesian bird nests, shark's fin and abalone. None of which comes cheap (abalone costs RMB 198-698).

### European

#### Cucina

*56th floor, Grand Hyatt, 88 Shiji Dadao (5049 1234 ext 8908). Metro Lujiazui.* **Open** 11.30am-2.30pm, 5.30-10.30pm Mon-Thur, Sun; 11.30am-2.30pm, 5.30-11pm Fri, Sat. **Main courses** RMB 230-270. **Credit** AmEx, DC, MC, V. **English menu. Map** p245 O5 **⑯** Italian

Two floors above the world's highest hotel lobby (at the Grand Hyatt, *see p44*) is On56, a trio of restaurants where only sheets of glass separate diners from the wreaths of high-altitude fog that usually envelope Pudong skyscrapers. Make reservations well in advance to get a good table by the floor-to-ceiling windows. **Kobachi** is Japanese with sashimi, tempura and noodles, the **Grill** has arguably the best steak in Shanghai and **Cucina** majors in well-executed, inventive mod Italian cuisine. Its offerings include delicate pastas and risottos, piquant salads and velvety desserts to finish. The wine list is about

as good as it gets in Shanghai; alternatively, have a few drinks in the amazing **On56** bar, where you can sink back into the sofas and gaze all the way up to the 88th floor. Prices are not as stratospheric as the high altitude would suggest, but do reserve.

### Fusion

#### Jade on 36

*36th floor, Tower Two, Pudong Shangri-La, 33 Fucheng Lu (6882 8888/www.shangri-la.com). Metro Lujiazui.* **Open** 6-10.30pm. **Set menu** RMB 480-888. **Credit** AmEx, DC, MC, V. **Map** p245 O5 **⑰**

When the Shangri-La unveiled its new Tower Two, which overlooks the Bund, it did it in style, uncorking bottles of bubbly with Adam Tihany, the world's foremost restaurant designer, in this magnificent space on the 36th floor. The restaurant and lounge are nearly as breathtaking as the view: a private elevator whistles you to the top of the tower and you disembark in a hallway with ornate Venetian marble floors and eccentric design elements (an upturned rice bowl, say). Chef Paul Pairet's unique food is the ideal complement to such rarified surroundings; expect nouveau fine dining with a deft, playful touch. The foie gras lollipop, a creamy foie gras terrine coated in crunchy caramel and served on the end of a stick, melts in your mouth with a shot of hot spiced tea that is then cooled by a final layer of fluffy champagne foam. The lemon tart, a whole candied lemon stuffed with creamy lemon sorbet, makes a beautiful finale to one of the four degustation menus. There's no à la carte here, only the set menus, but who wants to settle for three courses when the food on offer is this much fun? **Photos** *p121*.

## Hongkou

### Cafés & teahouses

#### Old Film Café

*123 Duolun Lu, by Sichuan Bei Lu (5696 4763). Metro East Baoxing Lu.* **Open** 10am-2am daily. **No credit cards. English menu. Average** RMB 30. **Map** p241 E2 **⑱**

Perhaps not worth a special trip, but if you happen to be up around beautifully restored Duolun Lu in Hongkou, then the Old Film Café (which actually bears the name 'Old Film Coffee', but we think they mean café) is the place to break for refreshments. The name is justified by framed black and whites of Golden Age movie stars on the walls, continuous screenings of vintage Chinese movies and by – with no explanation proffered – a near life-size bronze statue of Charlie Chaplin out front. Apart from that, it's a beautiful, small, grey-brick house with seating on three dimly lit floors all with the look of an old English tearoom. In addition to teas, coffee and fresh juices, booze is served.

# Bars & Pubs

Espresso Martinis at a style bar or cheap and cheerful disco night – you decide.

Shanghai's bar scene is one big game of musical chairs, only it's not the punters that are doing the circling, it's the bars themselves. The pace of transition in the city, allied with a municipality decidedly prone to rezoning and redeveloping according to whim, means that not just individual businesses but whole streets of boozy premises can disappear or appear almost overnight.

The city's long-standing bar strip is **Maoming Lu** in the French Concession, a 200-metre stretch of beer-fuelled raucousness. Old favourites like the **Blue Frog** party on, but perennial threats of a crackdown have spread the revelry elsewhere, notably to **Tongren Lu**, where a string of bars has recently settled round the corner from the Portman Ritz-Carlton. This son-of-Maoming strip boasts the same good-time vibe, with cheap beer, loud sounds and lots of local ladies happy to lighten things up, ideally by removing some of the weight from your wallet.

There's a stretch of **Hengshan Lu** that's similar, lined with all-you-can-drink joints where RMB 100 buys oblivion. However, if you prefer to enjoy what you drink and retain control of your basic motor functions while in polite company, this area also has some of the town's most convivial bars in the shape of **Sasha's, O'Malley's**, the **Blarney Stone, Cotton's** and **Senses**. The formerly moribund Bund is now the address for destination bars. The **Glamour Bar** has been congratulating itself for being so damn fabulous for several years now, but it has been joined by **New Heights** and **Bar Rouge**, where the air is so rarefied and the ambience so intoxicating that you're punch-drunk before that immaculate Cosmopolitan has even moistened your lips.

It's still very much the expat community who made sure that bartending is not an unrewarded profession in Shanghai, but increasingly the local Chinese have both the money and the inclination for cocktail carousing and beer-fuelled benders.

As well as the venues listed below, many of the venues described in the **Music** and **Nightlife** chapters double as drinking dens.

> ❶ Pink numbers given in this chapter correspond to the location of each bar and pub as marked on the street maps. See pp240-249.

**Top five** Bars

### Arch
Come for breakfast. Stay for lunch. Go online. Have a sundowner. Stick around for the film or reading. Take a nightcap. Shame it doesn't do accommodation. See p128.

### Cotton's
Friendly atmosphere, open fires in winter, a great garden in summer and heart-starting espresso Martinis all year round. See p128.

### Face Bar
If ever a Bacardi ad were to be filmed in Shanghai, it would have to be here. Beautiful venue, beautiful people and a thumping good-time ambience come the weekend. See p129.

### New Heights
For a table with the most amazing view of Pudong by night, we'd drink tap water out of a dog's bowl if that was all that was on offer. Happily, it does alcohol. See p125.

### YY's
One of the few genuinely laid-back bars in town and an institution in Shanghai's fickle nightlife scene. Come here for easy conversation and the possibility that things might turn out wild in the end. See p131.

## The Bund

Back in the old days Fuzhou Lu was the city's bar and brothel street. For better or worse, not a trace remains. Nostalgists can wallow at the **Peace Hotel Bar** (see p32), to the tune of octagenarian jazz, but these days the smart money is at new developments such as Three on the Bund and its house bar **New Heights** or near-neighbour **Bar Rouge** at 18 The Bund.

### Bar Rouge
7th floor, 18 Zhongshan Dongyi Lu, by Nanjing Dong Lu (6339 1199). Metro Henan Lu. **Open** 6.30pm-1.30am Mon-Thur, Sun; 6.30pm-4am Fri, Sat. **Credit** AmEx, DC, MC, V. **Map** p245 M4 ❶

Eat, Drink, Shop

Bar Rouge. *See p123.*

The cocktails, much like the clientele at this über-chic bar atop the Bund, are fabulous. Bar Rouge is the second half of the globe-hopping Pourcel Brothers' Shanghai project (the first being Sens & Bund, *see p102*) – and the culinary genius of the Michelin-starred twins lends itself well to a stylish nightspot. In one of the many chandeliered booths you can nibble on high-class canapés while watching the impressive skills of the show bartenders, who mix up strong cocktails with fresh elixirs of ginger, wasabi, mango and other tongue-tickling ingredients. These days it's tough to get a drink, though, and the Euro-trash factor will prove too much for some. But Bar Rouge makes up for it with an incredible outdoor terrace that boasts one of the city's best views of Pudong.

### Captain Bar

*6th floor, 37 Fuzhou Lu, by Sichuan Zhong Lu (6323 7869/www.shcaptain.com). Metro Henan Lu.* **Open** 11am-2am daily. **Credit** AmEx, DC, MC, V. **Map** p245 M5 ❷

Not so long ago the house bar of the Captain Hostel (*see p35*) used to be called Noah's and you could get a Tsingtao for RMB 15, but after an unnecessary makeover introduced hardwood floors, wicker chairs and sampan theming, prices have escalated. It's now a sort of three-star hotel bar, attached to a backpackers', with the curious result that boarders can enjoy a cocktail at their lodgings that costs almost as much as their bed for the night. Non-residents should visit for the scenery: although set back off

the Bund, the bar terrace boasts an uninterrupted view of the Huangpu and river traffic. It's not as good as the view at Bar Rouge or New Heights, but the crowd is far more relaxed and less likely to curl a lip at your saggy jeans and yellowing T-shirt.

### Fest Brewhouse

*11 Hankou Lu, by Sichuan Zhong Lu (6323 0965). Metro Henan Lu.* **Open** 11am-2am daily. **Credit** MC, V. **Map** p245 M5 ❸

Fest brings a Chinese twist to the microbrewery concept – a strong focus on food. When you take a seat waitstaff hand you a dining menu rather than a drinks list, and every table is set with placemats and condiments. However, there are two massive copper vats dominating the centre of the otherwise saloon-like room and these are used to produce the two house beers: the Fest Light and Fest Dark, both sold at RMB 38 for half a litre and brewed 'in accordance with the German Purity Law of 1516 and Bavarian recipes'. We're not sure what that means other than the Light is a little tasteless and the Dark is rich and hoppy. Nice venue, though, immaculately clean and very spruce. Maybe that's the German Purity Law.

### Five

*Basement, M on the Bund, 20 Guangdong Lu, by Zhongshan Dong Yi Lu (6329 4558/www.number five.cn). Metro Henan Lu.* **Open** 10am-2am daily. **Credit** AmEx, DC, MC, V. **Map** p245 M5 ❹

The remarkably casual Five brings to the Bund a welcome loosening of the collar. While the folks upstairs (Five is in the basement of the ultra-chic M on the

Bund building) are raising their little pinkies to French bubbly, there's a clued-up crowd down below having a blast on cheap Shanghai beer and live jazz five nights a week (the band strikes up at 9.30pm, no cover). The leather club chairs are the most comfortable bar seating in all Shanghai, and the atmosphere swings between dimly lit and sultry and, well, dimly lit and swinging. Things are helped along by early-evening happy hours and cheap lunch deals (RMB 50-75). With a couple of pool tables and an easygoing atmosphere, this is an ideal spot to take five.

### Glamour Bar

*6th floor, M on the Bund, 20 Guangdong Lu, by Zhongshan Dong Yi Lu (the Bund) (6350 9988/ www.m-onthebund.com). Metro Henan Lu.* **Open** 5pm-midnight daily. **Credit** AmEx, DC, MC, V. **Map** p245 M4 ❺

There are only a handful of places in Shanghai for which a gal can frock up, and a night of cocktails at the aptly named Glamour Bar is one. Originally a small adjunct of class-act restaurant M on the Bund (*see p103*), Glamour outgrew its space and moved in 2006 into a thoroughly expansive new home on the sixth floor. No shorts, only smart-casual couture, please – all the better to blend in with your fellow corporate players lounging around a bar that was designed to look like something out of a Golden Age Hollywood gangster flick. It may be pretentious and it's certainly pricey but the drinks go down easily, mixed as they are by premier-league barstaff. Glamour also regularly hosts jazz acts and readings by prize-winning authors.

### New Heights

*7th floor, Three on the Bund, 3 Zhongshan Dong Yi Lu (the Bund), by Guangdong Lu (6321 0909/ www.threeonthebund.com). Metro Henan Lu.* **Open** 10am-2am daily. **Credit** AmEx, DC, MC, V. **Map** p245 M5 ❻

Both bar and restaurant (*see p103*), New Heights offers the quintessential Shanghai experience – G&Ts at sunset overlooking the Huangpu River, a tradition that started, two doors up at the long-departed Shanghai Club, back in the formative years of the 20th century. There is a glass-enclosed bar area, with well-stocked bar shelves and DJ decks, but – in all but the bitterest of January freezes – the place to be is the rooftop deck. The views are pinch-me-I'm-dreaming magical. Pudong glitters and twinkles opposite: 16 floors of the Aurora building transformed into the world's biggest TV screen and an endless stream of alternately Christmas-tree bright and stealthy, sinisterly black shapes passing on the river below. Management could charge two front teeth as admission and we'd join the queue at the dentists, but it doesn't – drinks are no more expensive than almost anywhere else in town and neither are the excellent bar snacks. One of the world's best spots for a drink. Seriously. **Photo** *p127.*

## People's Square

The arrival of Moroccan-themed **Barbarossa** in 2004 doubled the number of decent drinking options around the square at a stroke; the splendid **Sky Bar Dome** has increased the choice by another 50 per cent; and **Kathleen's 5** is as good as ever. Although the options are scant hereabouts, there is some compensation in quality, with all three bars ranking as essential stops on any exploration of Shanghai's drinking scene.

Panoramic views of the city lit up in neon can be had at the JW's Lounge bar high up in the **JW Marriott** (*see p35*).

### Barbarossa

*231 Nanjing Xi Lu (6318 0220). Metro People's Square.* **Open** 11am-2am Mon-Thur, Sun; 11am-3am Fri, Sat. **Credit** AmEx, DC, MC, V. **Map** p244 H5 ❼

In a city that freely mixes hard-nosed commerce with pure fantasy, Barbarossa is still a pretty wild concept – a Moroccan-style, mountain kasbah built from scratch in a park in central Shanghai. But it's a fantasy that has clearly been seized on by the city's high-times crowd, as this is one of the loudest and liveliest venues in town. Laid-back on the ground floor, where a dining area opens to the park and an ornamental lake, there's no holding back upstairs, where a boudoir accommodates horizontal water-pipe smokers and a terrace bar encourages vertical drinking. Prices are steep (bottled Tsingtao RMB 45; cocktails RMB 60) and staff overly pushy, but the music is spot-on and, for the moment at least, there's the buzz that comes with the certainty that you're partying at the place that out-parties the others. To find Barbarossa, take the path just to the south of the main entrance to the Shanghai Art Museum (*see p60*) and follow your ears.

### Kathleen's 5

*5th floor, Shanghai Art Museum, 325 Nanjing Xi Lu, by Huangpi Bei Lu (6327 2221/www. kathleens5.com.cn). Metro People's Square.* **Open** 11.30am-midnight daily. **Credit** AmEx, DC, MC, V. **Map** p244 H5 ❽

When you're done with views of the Huangpu River and Pudong, visit Kathleen's for equally fabulous panoramas of downtown Shanghai. Ms (Kathleen) Lau's establishment is perched, pigeon-like, five floors up on the roof of the Shanghai Art Museum (*see p60*). If the restaurant side of the operation has yet to find its feet (*see p105*), the bar's a well-established venue for escaping the cacophony of People's Square. Settle on a stool at the long, smoked-glass bar counter and peer over the barman's shoulder and across People's Park to the fringe of surrounding skyscrapers – gorgeous by night. By day, for most of the year, the favoured seating is out on the front terrace, which is the perfect place for languid afternoons with a Pimm's, a fancy sandwich and a healthy resolve to write off the rest of the day.

**Eat, Drink, Shop**

# OUR CLIMATE NEEDS
# A HELPING HAND TODAY

Be a smart traveller. Help to offset your carbon emissions
from your trip by pledging Carbon Trees with Trees for Cities.

All the Carbon Trees that you donate through Trees for Cities
are genuinely planted as additional trees in our projects.

Trees for Cities is an independent charity working with local
communities on tree planting projects.

**www.treesforcities.org   Tel 020 7587 1320**

**Trees for Cities**
Charity registration number 1032154

New Heights. *See p125.*

(including the disco-tastic **Studio 78**, *see p185*). Near its junction with **Nanjing Xi Lu**, this street attracts a younger and more mixed crowd than its forebear.

The **Long Bar** (1376 Nanjing Xi Lu, by Shanxi Nan Lu, 6279 8268) at the Shanghai Centre is a popular post-work spot for unwinding foreign businessmen, drawn in by several 'model' nights a week, when leggy women in bikinis parade along the bar counter.

### Malone's

*255 Tongren Lu, by Nanjing Xi Lu (6247 2400/ www.malones.com.cn). Metro Jingan Temple.* **Open** 11am-2am daily. **Credit** AmEx, DC, MC, V. **Map** p242 D5 ⑩

When Malone's opened in 1994 it was command central for the city's few expats, who'd gather here to wolf burgers and wallow in homesickness. These days, with the city awash with international bars, the big M has to try a little harder. Cue pushy staff coaxing punters into ordering food, spirits and expensive foreign beers (RMB 40 a bottle) and the Filipino covers bands with manic female vocalists prone to dragging middle-aged Western men up to dance with demands of 'C'mon guys, let's party'. Despite all this/because of all this, the place retains a devoted swarm of barflies, gathered for the free pool, big-screen TV sports and 18 kinds of burger (RMB 48 with fries and salad).

## Xintiandi

The polished version of Old Shanghai, Xintiandi's narrow *nongtangs* (lanes) provide prime retail space for boutiques, as well as some rather plastic restaurants and bars. But among the ersatz, there are a handful of venues worth your beer money; as well as the places reviewed below, take a look at diner **KABB** (*see p109*).

### DR Bar

*No.15, North Lane, Lane 181, Taicang Lu, by Huangpi Nan Lu (6311 0358). Metro Huangpi Nan Lu.* **Open** 4pm-1am Mon-Thur, Sun; 4pm-2am Fri, Sat. **Credit** AmEx, DC, MC, V. **Map** p248 H7 ⑪

Not 'Doctor Bar' (so, alas, no chesty barmaids in white-rubber nurse outfits) but DR Bar, which stands, we are informed, for 'Design Resources'. Appropriately enough, tables are furnished with copies of *Wallpaper** (not to be taken away) and other similar cred-enhancing reads. It looks like somebody spent a good deal of time immersed in these magazines before decorating, because the bar is a stylish little assemblage of dark wood, black lounge sofas and subdued lighting. It's a smart-date sort of venue, intended as a setting for good-looking people comfortable with cocktails (from RMB 55) and shooters, which arrive packed in ice.

### Tou Ming Si Kao (TMSK)

*House 11, North Block, Lane 181, Taicang Lu, by Huangpi Nan Lu (6326 2227). Metro Huangpi*

### Sky Dome Bar

*Radisson Hotel, 88 Nanjing Xi Lu, by Xizang Zhong Lu (6359 9999). Metro People's Square.* **Open** 5pm-1am daily. **Credit** AmEx, DC, MC, V. **Map** p244 J4 ⑨

The latest place to get high in Shanghai is right up on top of the new Radisson hotel, which means on top of the building whose 45 storeys are capped by a ridiculous grounded UFO. In fact that ridiculous grounded UFO is the Sky Dome Bar. It takes not one but two lifts to get all the way up there, and when you arrive it feels as though you've been planted in the heavens. The bar sits under a glass dome, with 360° views over Shanghai. It will reduce vertigo sufferers to quivering blobs but for everybody else the place is a complete knock-out. The decor is a little cheesy, but just settle into one of the very comfortable, oversized lounge chairs and soak up the view. House cocktails are cosmically themed and go for close to RMB 70 (plus 15% service), which isn't cheap, but then what do you expect at this altitude? Live jazz nightly too.

## Jingan

With the concrete towers of the American Centre setting the corporate tone of the neighbourhood, Jingan's bars have traditionally been geared towards those foreign businessmen who need to blow off steam after a day being wrongfooted by local business etiquette. But since a crackdown in 2004 shook up Maoming Lu, many bars have relocated to **Tongren Lu**

**Eat, Drink, Shop**

*Nan Lu.* **Open** 2pm-midnight Mon-Wed, Sun; 2pm-1am Thur-Sat. **Credit** AmEx, DC, MC, V. **Map** p248 H7 ⓬

Dreamt up by Taiwanese actress Yang Hui Shan and her husband, TMSK is two parts tack to one part delirium. The happy couple are both 'glass artists', which means their bar has oversized glass sculptures and a luridly multicoloured bar that's like stained glass on acid. Far-out, but also quite beautiful – and definitely worth a look, whether you decide to stay for a drink or not. Martinis are served in glasses inspired by ancient Chinese symbols. Come after 8.30pm any night for the house band, who play techno-inspired Chinese folk music while wearing cast-off outfits from *Star Trek*. We're not making this up. Honest.

## French Concession

Despite repeated threats to its existence, **Maoming Lu** hangs on as the Concession's nightlife central but, to be frank, it's all a bit tawdry and desperate. Most of the better bars (including **Cotton's**, **Sasha's**, **O'Malley's** and the **Blarney Stone**) are up around the northern end of Hengshan Lu.

Tang Hui (*see p180*), newly relocated from Hongqiao, is a friendly spot to kick back with a few (cheap) beers and some live music.

### Arch
*439 Wukang Lu, by Huaihai Zhong Lu (6466 0807). Metro Hengshan Lu or Xujiahui.* **Open** 10.30am-2am Mon-Fri; 8.30am-2am Sat, Sun. **No credit cards.** **Map** p246 B9 ⓭

Shanghai's bar for web-savvy, Le Corbusier-loving, cargo-panted, *Wired*-reading, would-be intellectuals, Arch is a diner-styled affair with a long bar counter facing banquette seating and big windows. It's long, narrow and feels like a train carriage – but an

# Baijiu

The Shanghainese aren't fussy drinkers. They are wholly unimpressed by a noble Bordeaux and beer is nothing more than a lightweight beverage for washing down a good bowl of *shuijiao* (dumplings). In fact, there's only one drink that commands China's respect: the toe-numbing national booze, *baijiu*. This evil grain spirit tastes like a mixture of saké and Domestos and can clock in at up to 65 per cent ABV. If that's not sufficiently kamikaze for you, some drinkers mix it with fresh snake's gall bladder, which is apparently like tossing back a natural Viagra. It sure beats a splash of soda and a slice.

extremely stylish train carriage at that. By day it's a fine café-restaurant (*see p111*); by night it's a sophisticated drinking den offering European beers by the bottle (Chimay, Duvel, Erdinger, Hoegaarden, all RMB 25 a pop), wines by the glass and a short-list of cocktail classics and improbables (a 'Sheep Go to Heaven' of gin, Malibu, Martini, Cointreau and sparkling wine, anyone?) at RMB 45-50. There are occasional free movie screenings or literary salons down in the basement.

### Blarney Stone
*5A Dongping Lu, by Yueyang Lu (6415 7496). Metro Hengshan Lu.* **Open** 4pm-1.30am Mon-Wed; 11am-1.30am Thur-Sun. **Credit** AmEx, DC, MC, V. **Map** p246 D9 ⓮

Funnily enough, of the city's quartet of Irish pubs, this is the one with the least blarney about it. Yes, there's a live Irish band every night bar Tuesday. There are multiple Saw Doctors CDs on the jukebox, as well as the Chieftains, Pogues and Van Morrison. Guinness (albeit a locally brewed variety) and Kilkenny are prominent on the bar counter. And posters advertise screenings of rugby clashes involving Connacht, Leinster, Munster and Ulster. All that aside, it's simply a pleasing and comfortable drinking hall – a long, stone-flagged room with a polished-wood bar at one end and a small raised stage at the other, with a chain of tables stretching between. What's not to like?

### Blue Frog
*207-206 Maoming Nan Lu, by Fuxing Lu (6445 6634/www.kabbsh.com). Metro Shanxi Nan Lu.* **Open** 11am-late daily. **Credit** AmEx, DC, MC, V. **Map** p247 F9 ⓯

There's now a quadruplet of little Blue Frogs in Shanghai, but the Maoming Lu site is the original (opened in 2002). It remains a (relatively) civilised place from which to launch an evening of high jinks around the French Concession. Screen doors open directly on to the street, making this a perfect spot to observe the action. For those seeking respite from the fun and games outside, cosy nooks and couches upstairs provide a quiet alternative. The Frog occasionally arranges popular booze cruises along the Huangpu River: check the website for details. **Other locations:** 86 Tongren Lu, by Nanjing Xi Lu, Jingan (6247 0320); No.3, Lane 3338, Hongmei Lu, by Hongxu Lu, Changning (5422 5119); Green Sports & Leisure Centre, R3-633 Bi Yun Lu, by Lantian Lu, Pudong (5030 6426).

### Cotton's
*132 Anting Lu, by Jianguo Xi Lu (6433 7995). Metro Hengshan Lu.* **Open** 11.30am-2am. **No credit cards.** **Map** p246 C10 ⓰

A great place to beat the blistering summer heat or the damp winter, this laid-back bar features four fireplaces in an old villa and quite possibly the best garden for outdoor drinks in town. Cotton's is located on a quiet street, and the beautifully restored villa is home to deliciously stiff concoctions served by the friendly proprietor Cotton and her brother Mondy.

**Barbarossa.** *See p125.*

Try the espresso Martini, a rich blend of vodka, espresso and Kahlua, or the spicy Chairman Mao shot, which has become the bar's trademark. Utterly lacking in pretension and with character to spare, this is a bar you'll want to make your own.

### Face Bar

*Building 4, Ruijin Guesthouse, 118 Ruijin Er Lu, by Fuxing Zhong Lu (6466 4328). Metro Shanxi Nan Lu.* **Open** noon-1.30am Mon-Thur, Sun; noon-2am Fri, Sat. **Credit** AmEx, DC, MC, V. **Map** p247 F8 ⓱
What is arguably Shanghai's most famous bar owes a lot to a sublime villa setting in the gardens of the 1920s Ruijin guesthouse (*see p41*). On a warm summer evening there's no finer place to be than at a table on the forecourt, beside a lawn so immaculately manicured it would put a Cruft's winner to shame. It's even better if you're there between 5pm and 8pm for the half-price drink deals. Inside, the red-leather couches, opium beds and lounge chairs, French windows with drapes wafting in the breeze, and walls the colour of over-ripe fruit allow patrons to indulge in colonial fantasies. Come weekends, though, and old-fashioned courtesy is thrown to the wind in the scrabble for bar space as Face becomes party central. Upstairs is restaurant Lan Na Thai (*see p120*).

### Manifesto

*748 Julu Lu, by Fumin Lu (6289 9108). Metro Changshu Lu.* **Open** 6pm-midnight Mon-Thur, Sun; 6pm-2am Fri, Sat. **Credit** AmEx, DC, MC, V. **Map** p243 D6 ⓲
While Julu Lu by Changshu Lu is known for its parade of girlie bars, the same street just one block east is altogether classier. Grouped here are the designer diner Shintori (*see p120*) and concrete cool

People 7 (*see p130*), as well as the pairing of Mediterranean-flavoured eaterie Mesa (*see p118*) and this, its sibling bar. The place consists of a single grand room, dominated by a large oval bar strung with softly glowing orange lamps. Dim recesses harbour cushion-filled daybeds, perfectly decadent surroundings for sipping white chocolate Martinis. Take a seat at the bar counter and request your chosen poison from smart, friendly barstaff unlikely to be stumped by any sensible request. It's a far sexier proposition than anything on offer down the other end of the street.

### O'Malley's

*42 Taojiang Lu, by Wulumuqi Lu (6474 4533/ www.omalleys-shanghai.com). Metro Changshu Lu.* **Open** 11am-2am daily. **Credit** AmEx, DC, MC, V. **Map** p246 C8 ⓳
O'Malley's big draw is its massive walled garden with lawn and a large patio filled with bench seating. There's also a children's playroom, a performance space for live bands and a pull-down screen for international sports. On summer afternoons the scene's like a village green, as expats arrive with their offspring and lolloping dogs for long-drawn-out boozy lunches and good-natured trading of insults over Premiership football. Inside is quite lovely too: the 19th-century building that houses the pub was, apparently, an infant school from 1949 to the mid 1990s and, although not entirely free of the occasional bit of juvenile behaviour, is an enchanting collection of tiny rooms, corners and coves squirrelled over two floors. Real fires burn in winter, folkies busk in side rooms and, although the place is a rarity in not having any kind of happy hour,

Tuesday is curry night – all you can eat and a pint of Carlsberg for RMB 100.

## People 6

*150 Yueyang Lu, by Yongjia Lu (6466 0505).* Metro Hengshan Lu. **Open** 11.30am-1am daily. **Credit** AmEx, DC, MC, V. **Map** p246 D9 ⑳

The first thing you need to know about People 6 is how to get in. No amount of shoving or sliding will budge the big silvery metal door. Instead, turn to the adjacent steely block and slide your hand, palm down, into the crack. *Voilà*, and open sesame. Inside is more shiny metal and lots of glass, including big people-watching windows and washrooms almost totally covered in mirrored surfaces. It's hip and smart, but also quite comfortable, with lots of big white sofas and armchairs. The drinks list is enticing and includes an array of reasonably priced saké cocktails (RMB 35-50).

## People 7

*805 Julu Lu, by Fumin Lu (5404 0707). Metro Changshu Lu.* **Open** 11.30am-1am daily. **Credit** AmEx, DC, MC, V. **Map** p246 D6/7 ㉑

If People 6 is hip, People 7 is hipper. If the secret door-release gimmick at People 6 is baffling but fun, then it is doubly so at People 7, where there are two sliding doors (slip your hand into the centre of the nine round holes, twice). The interior has plenty of wow: a shell of a two-storey building, with the raw concrete beams and walls exposed in their seemingly unfinished state and a corrugated steel ceiling. The bar counter is one immensely long and eerily glowing lightbox. The drink to go for is the 'tube wine' (RMB 160), a fruit bowl heaped with ice embedded with two dozen test-tube shots of booze. But don't be foolish – it's meant to be shared. The toilets are also deliberately designed to perplex alcohol-addled

minds: the doors are hinged in the opposite fashion to how they appear and there's no light switch… just close the door behind you and ta-da! What a lark.

## Sasha's

*House 11, 9 Dongping Lu, by Hengshan Lu (6474 6167/www.sashas-shanghai.com). Metro Changshu Lu.* **Open** 10am-1am Mon-Thur, Sun; 10am-2am Fri, Sat. **Credit** AmEx, DC, MC, V. **Map** p246 C9 ㉒

Sasha's combines the laid-back nonchalance of a Maoming Nan Lu bar with all the classy stylings appropriate to its setting – the old Concession-era villa that houses the bar is said to have belonged to TV Soong, at one time the richest man in the world. Thankfully, the lurid red paint job is confined to the exterior and the interior is feet-up comfortable with hardwood floors, wicker chairs, and a nice long bar counter with stools for singletons, sofas for groups and a pool table for anyone feeling competitive. The beer on offer includes bottled Tsingtao at RMB 40 (ouch) and John Smith's and Guinness on draught (RMB 60). Given the prices, it's a good idea to turn up in time for the 5-7pm Monday-Friday happy hour. There's a bar menu of decent pizzas (RMB 45-60) and other assorted standards, plus a more formal restaurant upstairs. The large garden patio is a big plus on summer nights.

## Senses

*515 Jianguo Xi Lu, by Wulumuqi Nan Lu (5492 1655/www.senseswinelounge.com). Metro Hengshan Lu.* **Open** 11am-late daily. **Credit** AmEx, DC, MC, V. **Map** p246 D10 ㉓

China has a flourishing wine industry – and industry is the operative word, with leading producer Great Wall turning out in the region of 35 million bottles annually. However, there are an increasing number of boutique operations that, with a little help from abroad, are producing some very drinkable

**Cloud 9**. *See p131.*

wines. Wine fans should look out in particular for bottles carrying the labels of Grace and Taillan. Both of those should be available here, at Shanghai's only dedicated wine bar. It has a good selection of mostly imports by the glass and bottle (a Frontera Cabernet Sauvignon is RMB 200, while a Wolf Blass Gold Label is RMB 510), supplemented by regular specials and wine-tasting events. Monday nights feature wine at RMB 25 a glass, while Tuesday sees a 30% reduction on bottles.

### South Beauty

*881 Yanan Zhong Lu, by Shanxi Nan Lu (6247 5878). Metro Shanxi Nan Lu or Shimen Yi Lu.* **Open** 11am-2am daily. **Credit** AmEx, DC, MC, V. **Map** p243 E6 ㉓

South Beauty is a restaurant chain that mixes high-concept design with fiery Sichuan cuisine (*see p113*). The latest addition to the Shanghai stable is the most stunning of the lot, a many-roomed villa set in beautiful lawns with gurgling fountains. It has an equally gorgeous stand-alone bar. One blogger has described it as like being a guest at a ritzy country house where the owners have said, 'We'll be back in a few hours. Just relax and the staff will look after you.' You could be gauche and ask said staff to fetch you a bottled beer, but that's not really playing the game – especially when they go to the trouble of loading the Martinis with not one, or even two, but three olives. There is even a blackjack table at which patrons can play for drinks.

### Time Passage

*No.183, Lane 1038, Huashan Lu, by Fuxing Xi Lu (6240 2588). Metro Jiangsu Lu.* **Open** 5pm-2am Mon-Fri; 2pm-2am Sat, Sun. **No credit cards**. **Map** p246 A7 ㉕

A small bar hidden down a nondescript alley next to a tennis court, Time Passage is divinely unpretentious. It's a real neighbourhood bar – a category that's highly uncommon in Shanghai – dark, poky and popular with students. Staff are friendly, the beers are cheap and the choice of music is unobjectionable going on great. Aspiring local musicians, usually a guitar duo, belt out unplugged rock covers from 10pm on Fridays and Saturdays.

### Yongfu Elite

*200 Yongfu Lu, by Hunan Lu (5466 2727). Metro Changshu Lu.* **Open** 11.30am-midnight daily. **Credit** AmEx, DC, MC, V. **Map** p246 B8 ㉖

Yongfu Elite has the honour of being housed in a building once occupied by the British Consulate. But that's probably the least remarkable thing about the place. Since the civil servants left in 1998, the villa, twin pavilions and gardens have been renovated and decorated in the most extraordinary fashion. Interiors feature European vintage along the lines of green Gucci leather sofas, Chinese vintage like Ming Dynasty furnishings, deco chandeliers and drapes decorated with peacock feathers. The garden sports a massive Buddha, a carved wooden temple gateway and an original Beijing Opera outdoor

theatre. It took two-and-a-half years to bring all this together, creating what may well be the most fabulous hangout in all Asia. Cocktails start at RMB 50 (plus obligatory service), and they aren't particularly good, but you do get to swan around feeling like Dietrich (and that's just the boys).

### YY's (Yin Yang)

*125 Nanchang Lu, by Maoming Nan Lu (6466 4098). Metro Shanxi Nan Lu.* **Open** 2pm-4am daily. **Credit** AmEx, DC, MC, V. **Map** p247 F8 ㉗

Around the end of the 1990s, YY's was the place. Under the stewardship of owner Kenny, it was the haunt of subculturals, artists and radicals – characters like Mian Mian (author of banned sex 'n' drugs novel *Candy*) and Wei Hui (author of *Shanghai Baby*, who was once gloriously condemned by Chinese state media as 'decadent, debauched and a slave of foreign culture'). It's no longer quite so essential, but the sparse and well-worn ground-floor bar still serves as a sort of common room for the city's young and not-so-young chain-smoking, alternative set. In fact, for refugees from hip hop and Cantopop, from all-you-can-drink-till-you-die girlie bars and interminable Filipino covers band, this still is the place.

## Gubei

### The Door

*4th floor, 1468 Hongqiao Lu, by Yanan Xi Lu (6295 3737).* **Open** 6pm-2am daily. **Credit** AmEx, DC, MC, V. **Map** p240 A3 ㉘

A veritable exhibition of Chinese antiques, Buddhist sculpture and quirky Victorian touches, this huge Gubei loft is at once an eclectic fusion restaurant and a jaw-dropping lounge. The huge restored Tudor mansion draws a moneyed crowd of Hongqiao expats and local tycoon types, who nibble on the not-so-spectacular food and lounge in the crowded but gorgeous interior. A bit off the beaten track, but worth it for the unique aesthetic.

## Pudong

The bar at swanky restaurant **Jade on 36** (*see p122*), in the revamped Shangri-La Hotel, features stunning design and superb views.

### Cloud 9

*87th floor, Grand Hyatt, Jinmao Tower, 88 Shiji Dadao (5049 1234). Metro Lujiazui.* **Open** 6pm-1am Mon-Thur, Sun; 6pm-2am Fri, Sat. **Credit** AmEx, DC, MC, V. **Map** p245 O5 ㉙

At 420m (1,386ft) above sea level, Cloud 9 is reputedly the highest bar on earth. Be warned, though, the heavenly views that this height suggests can often be obscured by clouds. It's pretty spectacular all the same – and the cool, dark and steely interior is a sight in itself. Prices match the altitude, with an imposed minimum spend of RMB 120 per person after 8pm. **Photo** *p130*.

**Eat, Drink, Shop**

# Shops & Services

Skip the local obsession with big Western labels and dig into the city's idiosyncratic bargains.

Eat, Drink, Shop

Shopping in Shanghai can be an enlightening experience. Even out of the teeming markets (*see p134*) and smart downtown shopping drags the streets are packed with tiny, eclectic shops. Modest boutiques turn out to be dens of designer factory overruns; budget houseware stores become treasure troves for quirky fashion accessories (who could resist high-heeled, pointed Wellington boots for just RMB 10?). Even the least passionate shoppers will find themselves tempted by rows of miniature tea sets, piles of sequinned slippers, stacks of bamboo steamers, yards of pashminas and the odd repro Buddha head. In short, Shanghai will pack your present drawer for years.

It seems every small-scale entrepreneur has their finger in Shanghai's ballooning retail pie. But, despite the burgeoning economy, they live in difficult times: ruthless price wars, rising rents and the rise of the mega-mall make it tough for small – and even medium-sized – shops to stay in business. The upside for the consumer is that many goods can be bought incredibly cheaply. The Chinese even bargain in high-street shops, so always try for something off the asking price, even if haggling breaks your heart. Haggling techniques vary but it's generally accepted that good humour is essential; pooh-poohing the vendor's wares will get you nowhere. Decide on how much you want to pay before you begin haggling, and if you aren't getting your desired price, remember to walk away – you may find the price instantly drops.

Outside of high-end stores, prices are cheap and often negotiable. Cash is king (although credit cards are accepted in all the swankiest places), but be sure to try before you buy as there are no refunds and rarely will goods be exchanged, with or without a receipt.

If it's clothes you're after, bear in mind that Chinese sizes are minuscule. XL is equivalent to a UK size 12 or US size 10. And the shop assistant will look at you as though you truly are extra large.

## THE RISE OF LUXURY GOODS

China has a fast-growing market for luxury goods, with Shanghai firmly at the helm. *Vogue* China launched in March 2005 and, like the luxury brands it showcases, the style bible picked Shanghai for its country

Grand Gateway mall.

headquarters. China's most international city is quickly becoming the big-brand testing ground for the rest of the country. As a result scruffy Beijing misses out on a good proportion of the top international brand launch parties and must wait longer for the stores to open.

The luxury emporiums on the Bund (Bund 18, Three on the Bund and the soon-to-open Bund 6) are crammed with old and new luxury labels from Armani and Cartier to Seven for Mankind and Ann Demeulemeester. In addition, shopping malls along the western tip of Nanjing Xi Lu are brimming with smart boutiques and even smarter shoppers lining up outside Lanvin, Todd's, Piombo, Moschino, Louis Vuitton, Gucci, and edgier brands like Costume National, Paper Denim & Cloth, DSquared2 and Cacharel.

At present Chinese brands aren't really competing in the luxury market – but that is bound to change. Taiwanese high-end brand Shaitzy Chen occupies a fantastic building on the Bund and Bund 18 has done its bit with collections from Lu Kun, Jenny Ji and Zhang Da at **Younik** (*see p142* **Created in Shanghai**).

Note that as a general rule import taxes on luxury goods make prices as much as 20 per cent greater than elsewhere.

### SHOPPING AREAS

For the highest concentration of cool per metre cubed, head straight to the boutique-lined streets of the **French Concession**, especially – in order of abundance – **Nanchang Lu, Shanxi Nan Lu, Xinle Lu, Changle Lu, Maoming Lu** (for Chinese silk and embroidered items) and **Julu Lu**. Here you can get your hands on the latest trends, some local brands and international designer labels at low prices. For well-known international streetwear brands, focus on the area's main shopping artery **Huaihai Lu** (between Shanxi Lu and Ruijin Lu).

Dinky Lane 210 off **Taikang Lu** (the 'art street') is much smaller scale and a more hassle-free way to browse for something different. Several local designers have located here and the rest of the boutiques do their best to fit in with the creative vibe. The lane itself is quiet – a relief for weary tourists but a little worrying for shop owners.

For something more bustling, visit the 'lifestyle' development of **Xintiandi**. Here you can do lunch, catch a movie, purchase high-end souvenirs, pick up a dress from Vivienne Tam or Zuczug (*see p142* **Created in Shanghai**) and slip into it ready for alfresco sundowners.

Another lifestyle hub that's more luxe in taste than Xintiandi is the flourishing **Bund**, the waterfront strip. Splash out on luxury international and local designer brands (*see p142* **Created in Shanghai**), high-end restaurants and contemporary Chinese art. Luxury goods can also be had at the western end of **Nanjing Lu** in Jingan. There's Hermès, Louis Vuitton, Versace, Gucci, Marc Jacobs, Jean Paul Gaultier, Kenzo, Burberry, and so the list goes on. Head to the Shanghai Center complex and the two pristine malls either side: Plaza 66 (east) and City Plaza (to the west.)

The concentration of shopping malls at **Xujiahui** was designed with monsoons in mind. Metro Line One delivers its passengers directly into the major shopping destinations of the Pacific Department Store and Grand Gateway. Here you'll find a mix of foreign and Asian high-street brands.

## One-stop shopping

### Shanghai Friendship Store

*68 Jinling Dong Lu, by Jiangxi Nan Lu, the Bund (6337 3555).* **Open** *9.30am-9.30pm daily.* **Credit** AmEx, DC, MC, V. **Map** p245 M6.

Established in 1958 in the darkest red-dyed days of international isolation, the Friendship Store was historically the only store authorised to receive foreign guests, the only place that the rare visitor could spend his or her specially issued Foreign Exchange Certificates. Local Chinese were rebuffed at the door. These days it's the official China gift shop, peddling everything from miniature terracotta warriors to impressively sized dildos. Jewellery, cosmetics, books, luggage and 'sex health' implements fill the ground floor, with silk and cashmere on the second. On the third are carpets, jade and colourful kites. Prices are a little more than you'll pay elsewhere, but quality is guaranteed. Best buys are silk robes and pyjamas (RMB 380-480), and 100% cashmere sweaters (RMB 800-2,000).

## Malls

These big, shiny, air-conditioned boxes are taking over Shanghai's retail landscape. For the locals the mall is *the* place to hang out at the weekend and, during the rainy season (mid June to mid July), you'll probably be joining them. Food courts are usually found on the top or bottom floors and they can be good places to sample a range of local dishes. **Metro City** in Xujiahui (1111 Zhaojiabang Lu, by Caoxi Bei Lu) has a particularly wide range of food stalls.

Nanjing Xi Lu in Jingan is home to the big three (**CITIC Square, Plaza 66** and **Westgate**) with more along Huaihai Zhong Lu in the French Concession and in the western district of Xujiahui, where four malls square up to each other at the junction of Hengshan Lu and Zhaojiabang Lu. The **Super Brand Mall** (168 Lujiazui Xi Lu, by Yincheng Xi Lu) in Pudong is super-sized.

### Grand Gateway

*1 Hongqiao Lu, by Huashan Lu, Xujiahui (6407 0794/www.grandgateway.com). Metro Xujiahui.* **Open** 10am-10pm daily. **Map** p246 A11.

Shanghai's most popular shopping destination, where the atmosphere is enthralling even if the shops aren't. Most high-street brands are here: Oasis, Mango, Lacoste, Hong Kong's izzue.com and, on the ground floor, multibrand store Double Park. For local design check out Zuczug and Decoster (both on the second floor) and Croquis (fourth floor). The cinema at the top screens English-language films.

### Plaza 66

*1266 Nanjing Xi Lu, by Shanxi Bei Lu, Jingan (6279 0910/www.plaza66.com). Metro Shimen Yi Lu.* **Open** 10am-10pm daily. **Map** p243 E5.

**Eat, Drink, Shop**

There are few faster ways to blow your holiday budget than taking your plastic for a spin here. Stores include Fendi, Louis Vuitton, Moschino and Prada; Diesel and multibrand store IT are on the third floor. High-quality dining options include dim sum at Zen (no relation to the Zen in the French Concession, *see p120*), and there are conveyor-belt soup noodles at Red Door, aka Xiamien Guan. The Atrium café is good for people-watching, but not so good for food.

### Raffles City

*268 Xizang Zhong Lu, by Fuzhou Lu, People's Square (6340 3600). Metro People's Square.*
**Open** 10am-10pm daily. **Map** p244 J5.
Raffles City is Shanghai's funkiest mall so far. Its most successful outlet is the multibrand store Novo Concept, which carries Miss Sixty, Quiksilver and a handful of Hong Kong brands.

---

# Markets

Stockpiling everything from fashion and fabrics to antiques and live animals, the city's markets are a haggler's paradise. Food and flowers excluded, the starting price is generally four times the local, and ultimately acceptable, price.

Even if you're not self-catering, it's worth checking out one of the city's **wet markets**. They're usually teeming with fresh vegetables, live animals and even livelier vendors. It's best to eat before you venture in, though, as a wink from a freshly chopped fish head or a pile of skinned frogs may turn the stomach. There are good wet markets on Yanqing Lu by Xinle Lu and Jianguo Xi Lu by Taiyuan Lu.

As we went to press, the future of one of Shanghai's most popular markets (with visitors, at least), **Xiangyang Market** (the infamous 'Fakes Market'), was uncertain. In an effort to clean up Shanghai's shopping and reduce the market in fake products, officials closed the market in 2006. Meanwhile, the much-loved Dongjiadu Lu **Fabric Market** (*see below*) was moved, also in 2006, to a more modern site.

### D Mall

*Renmin Dadao, by Xizang Zhong Lu, People's Square. Metro People's Square.* **Open** 10am-9pm daily. **Map** p244 J5.
Beneath the grass and concrete parades of People's Square lies a warren of passageways packed with low-cost fashion and accessory stores. There's also an infinity of little shops selling cosmetics, bags and shoes. Best buys are the colourful wigs (roughly RMB 50), hair extensions and glittery hairclips, which can be found just off the row of cheap manicure stalls. Locals call this market 'Dimei'.

### Dongtai Lu Antiques Market

*Dongtai Lu & Liuhekou Lu, by Xizang Nan Lu, Xintiandi. Metro Huangpi Nan Lu.* **Open** 9am-6pm daily. **Map** p248 J7.

Only a fraction of what you see here could qua as antique, but this is still a great place to pick Mao memorabilia, fake propaganda posters, im tion porcelain, little Buddhas, snuff bottles and o interesting curios. Reputable dealer Chine Antiq has an outlet at 38 Liuhekou Lu. *See also p78.*

### Fabric Market

*399 Lujiabang Lu, by Liushi Lu, Old City.*
**Open** 8am-5pm daily. **Map** p249 M10.
If you really want to get carried away with tai made clothes, this fabric market should be your f port of call. It houses over 100 stalls carrying a w range of fabric, domestic and imported, natural a synthetic fibres. Nearly all stalls have tailors hand but the quality, though generally of a h standard, varies considerably (for tips, *see p* **Made to measure**). The market moved to this n air-conditioned venue in summer 2006 but, as went to press, it was slated to move again. If the c government sticks to its word it should end up no of Suzhou Creek (35 Guoqing Lu, by Xizang Lu); updates on the new location call 6380 6624.

### Jingan Xiaoting

*68 Yuyuan Lu, by Changde Lu, Jingan. Metro Jing Temple.* **Open** 10am-5.30pm daily. **Map** p242 C5.
This market is tucked away behind the giant C Plaza mall on Nanjing Xi Lu. It never gets unbe ably crowded and is a relaxing option for bud independent boutiques, good fake denim and colc ful hair extensions. If you're there at lunch, ge the queue for *mala tang*, the best rendition of t spicy soup in town.

### Qipu Lu Market

*168 & 183 Qipu Lu, by Henan Bei Lu, Hongkou.*
**Open** 9am-5pm daily. **Map** p244 L2.
Getting round Qipu Lu requires stamina, but dizzying choice and silly prices make it all wor while. There are two five-storey buildings, cramm with clothing, shoes and accessories, mostly pric between RMB 30 and RMB 50. When you've push elbowed and bargained enough through the sta destress on the streets around the market, which a full of life and sizzling food stalls.

### Yuyuan Bazaar (Yuyuan Shangsha

*Corner of Fuyou Lu & Jiujiachang Lu, Old City.*
**Open** 8.30am-8.30pm daily. **Map** p249 M7.
If you can bear the crowds, the inflated prices a the cloying stench of tofu, then this is a great pla to stock up on Chinese souvenirs. Stalls are cramm with embroidered silk jackets (RMB 100) and dress gowns (RMB 60), Lake Tai pearls (RMB 60), ceram tea sets (RMB 40), imitation Cultural Revoluti posters (RMB 40), rattan, wooden fans (RMB 40) a painted scrolls (RMB 50). Shops along Fangbang offer more of the same. Persistent souls have be known to unearth the odd treasure at the Fuy Antiques Bazaar (No.459), which is also the locati of multi-storey jewellery enterprises Lao Miao a First Asia.

# Antiques

In terms of antiques, Shanghai is best known for the restoration of old furniture, although it also has a good reputation for high-quality reproductions. Along **Hongqiao Lu** and **Wuzhong Lu** in the far-western Hongqiao/Gubei district are a number of reputable dealers with immense warehouses of furniture both old and new. For antiques of a smaller and more portable nature, it's worth scouring the junkier stalls and shops of **Dongtai Lu Antiques Market** (*see p134*). Note that foreigners are not allowed to take anything out of the country that's more than 200 years old; it is thus essential you make sure that your piece carries the official seal that marks it as OK for export.

### Annly's Antique Warehouse

*No.68, Lane 7611, Zhongchun Lu, by Hu Song Lu, Hongqiao (6406 0242). Metro Xujiahui.* **Open** 9am-6pm daily. **Credit** AmEx, DC, MC, V.

If you are good at bargaining, there are plenty of deals here. There's a wide choice of pieces from the close of the 19th century, and fewer reproductions than in the other warehouses along this stretch.

### Henry Antiques

*359 Hongzhong Lu, by Wuzhong Lu, Hongqiao (6401 0831). Metro Xujiahui.* **Open** 9am-6pm daily. **Credit** AmEx, DC, MC, V.

If it's choice you want, make a beeline for this furniture emporium. We're talking 4,000sq m (43,000sq ft) of warehouse, displaying over 2,000 pieces. A local favourite, due to the respected after-sale service.

### Hu & Hu Antiques

*No.8, Lane 1885, Caobao Lu, Hongqiao (3431 1212/ www.hu-hu.com). Metro Xujiahui.* **Open** 9am-6pm daily. **Credit** AmEx, DC, MC, V.

Since 1998 sisters-in-law Lin and Marybelle Hu have been combing the countryside for stylish bits of antiquity to fill their large showroom and warehouse. There's a wide selection of furniture, from Anhui wedding beds to Shandong wine cabinets. Pieces are tastefully restored to customer specifications.

They aren't authentic but they sure are cheap: street-side shopping in Shanghai.

# Arts & handicrafts

China is famed for its production of fine silk, embroidery and ceramics, but while you're here it's also worth taking a look at the folk paintings, batik, carpets and rattan. There are heaps to choose from at the **Yuyuan Bazaar** (*see p134*), but the goods are mainly mass-produced on the cheap so be sure to bargain hard and keep the prices low.

See also *p146* **Gifts & interiors**.

## Brocade Country

*616 Julu Lu, by Xiangyang Lu, French Concession (6279 2677). Metro Shanxi Nan Lu.* **Open** 10am-7pm daily. **No credit cards. Map** p243 E6.
Liu Xiaolan has filled this store with handicrafts from her minority group the Miao, who inhabit the southern province of Guizhou. Pick up intricate tapestries or second-hand embroidered jackets, even some antique items for RMB 100-1,000.

## Calico Cat

*835 Jiangsu Lu, by Huashan Lu, French Concession (1300 313 5546 mobile/calicocat@sina.com). Metro Jiangsu Lu.* **Open** 10.30am-8.30pm daily. **Credit** AmEx, DC, MC, V. **Map** p246 A7.
Just as you might expect from the name of the shop, this is a fun place. Using the blue and white fabric that is characteristic of Jiangsu province, designer Xing Xiuping has created a whole range of playful designs. Tailor-made outfits can be prepared within a week for around RMB 600 a set, or choose from the good selection of bags.

## Chinese Handprinted Blue Nankeen Exhibition Hall

*No.24, Lane 637, Changle Lu, by Changshu Lu, French Concession (5403 7947). Metro Changshu Lu.* **Open** 9am-5pm daily. **Credit** AmEx, DC, MC, V. **Map** p246 D7.
Established by Japanese artist Kubo Mase, this museum-cum-shop has been selling fine blue and white cotton products for over 20 years. Originating in the Jiangsu, Zhejiang and Guizhou provinces, the handmade blue calico, akin to batik, carries traditional Chinese patterns. The delicate designs adorn everything from clothing to curtains and mobile phone cases. Expect to pay in the region of RMB 18 to RMB 70 per metre.

## Eddy Tam's Gallery

*20 Maoming Nan Lu, by Jinxian Lu, French Concession (6253 6715). Metro Shanxi Nan Lu.* **Open** 9am-9pm daily. **Credit** AmEx, DC, MC, V. **Map** p247 F7.
Specialising in the acquisition and custom framing of Chinese art, Eddy Tam's is the pick of the numerous galleries along this stretch of Maoming Nan Lu. It carries lots of hand-painted Jinshan stencils (brightly coloured folk images) and is also the exclusive agent for local artist Xie Weimin, whose oeuvre includes watercolours of Shanghai buildings.

## Shanghai Art Museum Store

*Shanghai Art Museum, 325 Nanjing Xi Lu, People's Square (6327 2829 ext 422). Metro People's Square.* **Open** 9am-4pm daily. **Credit** AmEx, DC, MC, V. **Map** p244 J6.
A large space containing everything from painted scrolls and calligraphy sets to embroidered slippers and assorted silk apparel. The lower level has an impressive assortment of ceramics from Jingdezhen, including reproductions of items in the museum's Zande Lou Ceramics Gallery. There are also attractive jade pendants, agate teapots and blue calico.

## Spin

*Building 3, Lane 758, Julu Lu, by Fumin Lu, French Concession (6279 2545). Metro Changshu Lu.* **Open** 11.30am-10.30pm daily. **Credit** AmEx, DC, MC, V. **Map** p246 D6.
Spin capitalises on the rich ceramic heritage of China's clay capital Zhingdezhen in Jiangxi province. The cool open interior stocks pieces designed by: Gary Wang (USA), Langshen Li and May Zhao (both Shanghainese). Their works incorporate Chinese themes but in a sophisticated and subtle way. Wang's very contemporary angular tea-set (RMB 880), for example, uses the traditional Chinese rice grain motif. Prices are, for the most part, reasonable: salt and pepper shaker, say, for RMB 50 each or a presentation dish for around RMB 240. Check out the bamboo charcoal water and air purifier (from RMB 40) – give it a spin in your drink to remove the impurities.

# Books, movies & music

Most high-end hotels carry a basic selection of international press; the best is offered at the newsstand at the **Portman Ritz-Carlton** (*see p37*), but for a massive range of both magazines and books **Chaterhouse** (*see below*) is your best bet. People may want to direct you to the traditional booksellers' street, **Fuzhou Lu**, which runs between People's Square and the Bund, but there's not a whole lot of joy there for English-language readers.

For movies and music (DVD, CD) you're spoilt for choice. Of course it's all fake and quality varies, so never pay more than RMB 7.

## Chaterhouse

*Shop B1-E, Shanghai Times Square, 93 Huaihai Zhong Lu, by Liulin Lu, Xintiandi (6391 8237/ www.chaterhouse.com.cn). Metro Huangpi Nan Lu.* **Open** 10am-10pm daily. **Credit** AmEx, DC, MC, V. **Map** p248 J7.
Although small, this bookshop offers Shanghai's best range of newly published fiction and non-fiction titles. There's even a stock of Biggles books from around 1940, and a vast selection of magazines on more contemporary topics (starting at RMB 80).

**Other locations:** Unit 68, 6th floor, Super Brand Mall, 168 Lujiazui Xi Lu, by Yincheng Xi Lu, Pudong (5049 0668).

### China National Publications Import-Export Corporation (CNPIEC)

*5th floor, CITIC Square, 1168 Nanjing Xi Lu, by Jiangning Lu, Jingan (5292 5214). Metro Shimen Yi Lu.* **Open** 10am-10pm daily. **Credit** AmEx, DC, MC, V. **Map** p243 E5.

This minuscule foreign-language bookstore, which is located on the fifth floor of the CITIC Square mall, majors in mostly non-fiction English titles. It also stocks a selection of international publications, including *The Economist, Newsweek,* the *Wall Street Journal* and *Wallpaper\**.

### Foreign Languages Bookstore

*390 Fuzhou Lu, by Fujian Zhong Lu, People's Square (6322 3200). Metro Henan Lu.* **Open** 9.30am-6pm daily. **Credit** V. **Map** p244 L5.

Come here for maps and books about Shanghai. There are also Chinese-language learning materials on the ground floor and English-language fiction, with a focus on the classics up on the fourth.

### Garden Books

*325 Changle Lu, by Shanxi Bei Lu, French Concession (5404 8729). Metro Changshu Lu.* **Open** 10am-10pm daily. **Credit** AmEx, DC, MC, V. **Map** p247 E7.

A friendly place to sit and browse while sipping a coffee or tucking into a bowl of Italian ice-cream. General-interest books on Shanghai are well represented, and there's a decent fiction section upstairs, as well as more art and architecture titles on the ground floor.

### Kade Club

*483 Zhenning Lu, by Yuyuan Lu, French Concession (5239 8920). Metro Jingan Temple.* **Open** 11am-11pm daily. **No credit cards. Map** p243 F6.

This well-established, smoothly shop is a must on every tourist's list. Prices are a little higher than other outlets, at RMB 10 per DVD, but these guys have the widest selection of current movies and television series. Be sure to ask if the copy is good or not before you buy.

### Shanghai's City of Books

*465 Fuzhou Lu, by Fujian Zhong Lu, People's Square (6391 4848). Metro People's Square.* **Open** 9.30am-8pm daily. **Credit** AmEx, DC, MC, V. **Map** p244 K5.

Given that it covers seven storeys, it's no surprise that this place scores points for its fantastic range of subjects. Take time out in the café after browsing more than 200,000 books, video and audio products.

## Electronics

While still not as cheap as Hong Kong, prices for electronics have fallen dramatically here in recent years thanks to a proliferation of quality local brands. You can score good deals on home-grown DVD and MP3 players, portable CD players and digital cameras. Even international brands can be got for around ten per cent less than in the UK. In addition to the places below, try the **electronics market** at Fuxing Zhong Lu and Xiangyang Nan Lu. Always ask to see the original boxes.

### Baoshan market

*Qiujiang Lu, between Baoshan Lu & Sichuan Bei Lu, North Hongkou. Metro Baoshan Lu.* **Open** 9am-5.30pm daily.

Tiny stalls sprawl over several streets and cluster in packed indoor nooks – even if you aren't a techie, this market is fun to wander round. There's a ton of second-hand (and possibly stolen) appliances to sift through, and plenty of local and fake brands, but your best bet are the little gadgets, such as MP3 players, which go for a fraction of the price elsewhere (prices seem to drop every week, but when we last checked it was RMB 200 for 256KB).

### Cybermart

*282 Huaihai Zhong Lu, by Huangpi Nan Lu, Xintiandi (6390 8008/www.cybermart.com.cn). Metro Huangpi Nan Lu.* **Open** 10am-8pm daily. **Credit** V. **Map** p248 H7.

Impossible to miss with its deafening music booming from the massive speakers outside, Cybermart is the best place for high-quality electronic and digital devices. Computers, printers, memory sticks and digital music players occupy the first floor, while mobile phones, blank CDs, webcams and computer components for techie DIYers are on the second and third. The place is ISO 9001-certified, signifying high quality overall.

### Metro City

*1111 Zhaojiabang Lu, by Caoxi Bei Lu, Xujiahui (6426 8380/www.shmetrocity.com). Metro Xujiahui.* **Open** 10am-10pm daily. **Credit** AmEx, DC, MC, V. **Map** p246 A11.

Hidden in the basement of this futuristic mall (look for the giant glass sphere) is a buzzing, bleeping electronic market. Make sure you do the rounds before purchasing, and remember to bargain.

## Photography

Film processing is cheap in China, costing around RMB 20 for a 24-exposure film. A good bet is **Guanlong** (*see below*), but Kodak has outposts at Xintiandi and on Huaihai Zhong Lu near the Shanghai Library.

### Guanlong Photographic Equipment Company

*180 Nanjing Dong Lu, by Jiangxi Zhong Lu, the Bund (6323 8681). Metro Henan Lu.* **Open** 9am-9pm daily. **Credit** AmEx, DC, MC, V. **Map** p244 L4.

A shutterbug paradise, this massive electronics store has everything from high-end digital and point-and-shoot cameras to MP3 players and

# Made to measure

Half the fun of being in Shanghai is ordering a brand new wardrobe of tailor-made clothes. The city is justly famed for its skilled tailors, and you'll spot them tucked away down the side streets, beavering away at their antique sewing machines.

The best place to kick-start the creative process is the city's fabric market (see p134), one of the most colourful places in Shanghai. You can find anything here, from formal suit cloth to disco-sequinned chiffon. But, before you get lost in the kaleidoscope, there are a few things to remember that will ensure you end up with the real deal.

● Don't be fooled by vendors lighting the fibres to prove they are selling real **wool** (RMB 80 per metre). That old trick only signals the presence of natural hair (remember the last

time you singed your fringe?), it doesn't actually show the percentage of wool in the fabric. A better test is to roll the material between your fingers, if little bobbles start to form then you can be pretty sure it's not pure.

● **Silk** (approximately RMB 60 per metre) should be ultra-thin and fine, but still weighty. When you scrunch the silk up in your hand, if it doesn't wrinkle, it's a polyester blend.

● When you go shopping for **cashmere** (approximately RMB 150 per metre), beware of hairy/furry weaves. If you can't stroke the furry fibres in the opposite direction, then you know it's not real.

● Stall holders will try to sell you excessive amounts of cloth. Remember that a pair of trousers requires roughly 2.5 metres (8 feet), a jacket 2 metres (6.5 feet) and a shirt 1.5 metres (5 feet).

While every stall markets a nifty tailor, not all of them are gifted. **Xiao Li** (1304 167 3841 mobile) works in the market and can come to your home or hotel for fittings (add RMB 30). Expect to pay around RMB 40 for a pair of trousers and RMB 80 for a shirt, but keep it simple with copies. Otherwise, stick to the local English-speaking heroes **Danielle**, **XiaoYu** and **Silk King**. For conservative tastes, **Danielle** (99 Fahuazhen Lu, by Panyu Lu, French Concession, 6282 0925) can make a two-piece suit in two days for RMB 2,000. Her tiny store is towards the west of town and has a selection of formal-wear fabrics; her prices include the material. **Silk King** (819 Nanjing Xi Lu, by Shimen Yi Lu, Jingan, 6215 3114, www.silkking.com) is the best place for *qipaos* and other traditional Chinese designs; expect to pay around RMB 1,000 for a *qipao*, including the fabric. For the city's fashionistas, **XiaoYu** (Room 101, 88 Fengxian Lu, by Maoming Lu, Jingan, 1300 219 5532 mobile, by appointment only) can recreate a designer item in a week; a two-piece suit with fabric costs around RMB 1,000 – less for consecutive sets.

## USEFUL PHRASES
**copy exactly** *qing anzhao yuanyang fuzhi*
**too big/too small** *tai da le/tai xiao le*
**Can I have the leftover fabric?** *Wo keyi ba sheng xia de buliao na zou ma?*
**Please deliver to my hotel** *Qing songdao wo de jiudian*
**Please come to my hotel** *Qing dao wo de jiudian lai*

**Eat, Drink, Shop**

Jooi Design.

camcorders. Prices aren't low, but you're paying for reputable brands such as Sony and Nikon. On-site photo processing is available, as are other professional photographic services.

## Fashion

Shanghai stores do carry an increasing array of international designer labels, but high taxes on imported goods mean that you'll end up paying more than you would back home. If you simply must purchase luxury goods in China, head to **Plaza 66** (*see p134*) and, just up the road, **City Plaza** (1618 Nanjing Xi Lu, by Huashan Lu, Jingan). The best deals, however, are to be found among the designer surplus items and seconds of the boutiques in the French Concession (*see p146* **Always read the label**), especially along Changle Lu, between Chengdu Nan Lu and Maoming Nan Lu. The city is also home to a handful of local fashion designers, not yet quite the next Issey Miyake but promising much (*see p142* **Created in Shanghai**).

### IT

*Suite 1 (1st floor) & Suite 2 (2nd floor), Shanghai Xintiandi, Lane 123, Xingye Lu, by Madang Lu, Xintiandi (6336 5131). Metro Huangpi Nan Lu.* **Open** 11.30am-11pm daily. **Credit** AmEx, DC, MC, V. **Map** p248 H8.

This successful Hong Kong retail group gave the Shanghainese their first taste of designer gear when its multibrand store opened back in 2002. Although the city is now home to many designer-brand flagships, IT still offers the more fashion-forward collections that are new to China, such as Costume National, Paper Denim & Cloth, DSquared2, Cacharel, Tsumori Chisato, Martin Margiela and APC.

**Other locations**: 3rd floor, Plaza 66, 1266 Nanjing Xi Lu, by Shanxi Bei Lu, Jingan (6288 4270).

### Jooi Design

*Studio 201-203, Lane 210, Taikang Lu, by Sinan Lu, French Concession (6473 6193). Metro Shanxi Nan Lu.* **Open** 9am-6pm daily. **Credit** AmEx, DC, MC, V. **Map** p247 G10.

Danish design company Jooi adapts traditional Chinese techniques and detailing to modern sensibilities. Bestsellers include silk evening bags and scarves with delicate hand-embroidered butterflies,

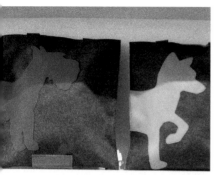

The famous Hong Kong brand (with outlets in New York, London, Paris, Bangkok…) excels in traditional China with a kitsch twist. The shop itself is a sultry space of dark wood, bright chinoiserie and delicate wafts of ginger flower essence. Wares range from leather coats to silk-covered diaries, but the most popular buys are the signature reversible 'double fish' motif velvet Tang jackets and custom-made *qipaos* from the Imperial Tailor department. The labels may read 'Made by Chinese' but, be warned, prices are wholly Fifth Avenue.
**Other locations**: No.15, North Block, 181 Taicang Lu, by Xingye Lu, Xintiandi (6384 1601).

### Three Retail

*Three on the Bund, 3 Zhongshan Dong Yi Lu, by Guangdong Lu, the Bund (6323 3355 ext 2/ www.threeonthebund.com). Metro Henan Zhong Lu.* **Open** 11.30am-10.30pm daily. **Credit** AmEx, DC, MC, V. **Map** p245 M5.

Three Retail's loft-style space on the first floor is home to cherry-picked collections of such exclusive labels as Alain Mikli, Yohji Yamamoto, Han Feng and Ann Demeulemeester. The open-plan space is arranged with free-standing racks and open shelves, and instead of bland changing rooms there are floor-to-ceiling rattan dressing niches with sliding panels. If you feel the urge to do even more serious financial damage, head downstairs to the ground floor where you can pay through the nose at Giorgio Armani's flagship China store. Jean-Georges, Whampoa Club (for both, *see p102*) and New Heights (*see p103*) offer high-end drinking and dining on the premises.

## Fashion accessories & services

The city's markets are a good place to stock up on low-cost pashminas, fun jewellery, stylish belts, all types of bags and snazzy tights. Visit the places recommended below if you want to be sure of the quality.

### Dry cleaning

One of the city's boom industries is dry cleaning, so if you keep an eye out, you'll probably find one within walking distance of where you are staying. Prices are low, around RMB 30 per item, and the time taken can vary from one day to five. Well-known chains to look for are **Meifeng** (often located in the corner of the local Lianhua or Hualian supermarket chains) and **Elephant King** (*see below*).

### Elephant King

*107 Nandan Dong Lu, by Tianyaoqiao Lu, Xujiahui (6469 9773). Metro Xujiahui.* **Open** 8.30am-9pm daily. **No credit cards**. **Map** p246 B12.

This Taiwanese chain is well established and trustworthy. Expect to pay around RMB 35 for your items, with service requiring five days.

---

blossoms and filigree coins. Lifestyle and home-decor products are also popular, among them place settings, cushion covers, silk robes and hand-crocheted silk blankets. Bags range in price from RMB 200 up to RMB 1,000.

### Shiatzy Chen

*Nine on the Bund, 9 Zhongshan Dong Yi Lu, by Guangdong Lu, the Bund (6321 9155/www. shiatzychen.com). Metro Henan Zhong Lu.* **Open** 10am-10pm daily. **Credit** AmEx, DC, MC, V. **Map** p247 F7.

This Taiwanese brand – a newcomer to Shanghai – takes the Qing Dynasty collars and intricately embroidered silk one step further with very traditional, formal-looking garments straight out of the Forbidden City. Perfect for that high-class costume party, men's jackets go for around RMB 5,000.
**Other locations**: Unit D, 59 Maoming Nan Lu, by Changle Lu, French Concession (5466 1266).

### Shanghai Tang

*59 Maoming Nan Lu, by Changle Lu, French Concession (5466 3006/www.shanghaitang.com). Metro Shanxi Nan Lu.* **Open** 10am-10pm daily. **Credit** AmEx, DC, MC, V. **Map** p247 F7.

# Created in Shanghai

Once you've stuffed your suitcase full of fake North Face jackets and Fendi bags, it may be time for you to think about investing in gear that has actually been designed in China. There are passionate Shanghai-based fashion designers who are way ahead of their international-brand-obsessed city – and could seriously do with your support. Unlike the fashion-forward shoppers of cities such as Tokyo, Hong Kong and Seoul, the Shanghainese turn their noses up at local design. The local government is no better: it hosts **Shanghai Fashion Week** (6208 2155, www.shfashionweek.com.cn) twice a year, but the budget is all spent on wowing the crowds with big (and not-so-big) Western brand names instead of promoting home-grown talent. Which is a terrible shame, since there is some genuinely interesting design to be found. For visitors, there's the additional cachet of being able to sport gear fresh out of Shanghai when you get home.

Wang YiYang is the daddy of the city's emerging design generation, with two brands: **Zuczug** (on the second floor of Grand Gateway, see p133) and the more alternative **Cha Gang**; think simple shapes and unrefined fabrics, sometimes with a cartoon-like twist. **He Yan** (www.heyan.org, appointments 1367 196 7749 mobile) is a new face on the local scene – and is causing quite a stir with her simple, kooky designs and strong Communist influences: think military with red lipstick. **Lu Kun** is adored

by the city's fashion gang for sexy garments that give a nod to 1930s Shanghai, while Zhang Da makes you step into a geometry class when you try his collection: think prism skirts in buff fabrics, with a raw industrial finish. The best places in the city to find them are **Younik** and **AIAIA**.

Jenny Ji pushes the boundaries of fashion with interesting cutting and complicated, colourful embroidery. Her collection at Younik is more conservative than own-brand **La Vie**. **Yi Hui** is less edgy, with a reputation for classy suits and evening wear that rejoice in ancient Chinese aesthetics at a fraction of the prices of **Shanghai Tang** (see p141).

**insh** (*pictured right*) is inspired by the funny side of the city – jackets reference the city's taxi drivers and there are posh dresses that are made out of bed sheets. **Shirt Flag**, though more involved with graphic design than fashion design, can provide you with various quirky, Communist pop art-inspired T-shirts and bags.

## AIAIA

*161-5 Taiyuan Lu, by Yongjia Lu, French Concession (6467 9102). Metro Hengshan Lu.* **Open** 10am-8pm daily. **Credit** AmEx, DC, MC, V. **Map** p246 D10.

## Cha Gang

*No.1, Lane 299, Fuxing Lu, by Huashan Lu, French Concession (6466 1089).* **Open** 10am-9pm daily. **Credit** AmEx, DC, MC, V. **Map** p246 B7.

**Other locations**: No.15, 228 Anfu Lu, by Wulumuqi Lu, French Concession (5403 6322); 336 Jianguo Dong Lu, by Madang Lu, Luwan (6384 8292); 515 Fahuazhen Lu, by Dingxi Lu, Hongquiao (6281 1333); 1219-1221 Xianxia Lu, by Hami Lu (6290 2782).

## Shanghai Jazz Cleaner

*Unit 203A, Shanghai Centre, 1376 Nanjing Xi Lu, by Xikang Lu, Jingan (1333 193 5332 mobile). Metro Jingan Temple.* **Open** 7.30am-9.30pm daily. **No credit cards**. **Map** p243 E5.
Shanghai Jazz Cleaner is an established favourite of the expat community, who are more than happy to hand over their cherished evening gowns and dinner jackets. Service takes three days, the average price is RMB 35 per item.
**Other locations**: Carrefour, 269 Shuicheng Nan Lu, by Yanan Xi Lu, Gubei (1391 658 6519 mobile); 1500 Huaihai Zhong Lu, by Huashan Lu, French Concession (6437 4862).

## Jewellery

The Old City and the pedestrianised section of Nanjing Dong Lu that runs inland of the Bund are home to several multi-storey, state-run jewellery operations. Unfortunately the counters in these places are typically tended by staff who are surly and generally off-putting. If you want to brave it, try **Lao Miao** (462 Nanjing Dong Lu, by Shanxi Nan Lu) and **Chow Tai Fook** (300 Huaihai Zhong Lu, by Madang Lu), both of which can offer you the choice from heaps of precious metals, diamonds, jade and pearls.

For smoother service and appropriately higher prices, visit **Tiffany & Co** (D116, City Plaza, 1618 Nanjing Xi Lu, by Jiaozhou Lu, Jingan, 6288 2748), the **Cartier** flagship that is to be found on the ground floor of

580 南京路

### insh
*200 Taikang Lu Art Street, French Concession (6466 5249). Metro Shanxi Nan Lu.* **Open** 10.30am-9pm daily. **Credit** AmEx, DC, MC, V. **Map** p247 G10.

### La Vie
*No.7, Lane 210, Taikang Lu Art Street, French Concession (6445 3585). Metro Shanxi Nan Lu.* **Open** 10.30am-8.30pm daily. **Credit** AmEx, DC, MC, V. **Map** p247 G10.

### Lu Kun Fashion of Mirror Studio
*2nd floor, 60 Anlan Lu, by Xizang Nan Lu, Old City (6378 2120).* **Open** 9am-6pm daily. **No credit cards**. **Map** p248 K9.

### Shirt Flag
*330 Nanchang Lu, by Maoming Nan Lu, French Concession (5465 3011). Metro Changshu Lu.* **Open** 10.30am-10pm daily. **Credit** AmEx, DC, MC, V. **Map** p247 F8. **Other locations**: Unit 8, 7 The Yard, Lane 210, Taikang Lu, Da Puo Qiao (6466 7009).

### Yi Hui
*No.15, Lane 210, Taikang Lu Art Street, French Concession (6466 5249). Metro Shanxi Nan Lu.* **Open** 11am-9pm daily. **Credit** AmEx, DC, MC, V. **Map** p247 G10.

### Younik
*2nd floor, Bund 18, 18 Zhongshan Dong Yi Lu, by Nanjing Dong Lu, the Bund (6323 8688). Metro Henan Lu.* **Open** 10am-10pm daily. **Credit** AmEx, DC, MC, V. **Map** p245 M4.

Bund 18 (18 Zhongshan Dong Yi Lu, by Nanjing Dong Lu, 6323 5577) or the multitude of pearl stalls that throng **Pearl City** (Century Square, 558 Nanjing Dong Lu, Pudong).

### AmyLin's Pearls & Jewellery
*3rd floor, 580 Nanjing Xi Lu, by Chengdu Lu, Jingan (1391 631 3466 mobile). Metro Shimen Yi Lu.* **Open** 9am-8.30pm daily. **Credit** AmEx, DC, MC, V. **Map** p243 G5.

Graced by pictures of the foreign dignitaries, celebrities and VIPs who have all shopped here, this is Shanghai's foremost pearl dealer. Here you'll find natural pink, white and lilac varieties or, for those with more adventurous tastes, dyed green, yellow and black Zhejiang freshwater strands. If that isn't enough, South Sea salties and semi-precious stones are also available. Amy's prices (around RMB 80 to RMB 250) include custom stringing and the staff speak good English.

### Marion Carsten Silver Jewellery
*Suite 106, Building 3, 210 Taikang Lu, by Ruijin Er Lu, French Concession (6415 3098). Metro Shanxi Nan Lu.* **Open** 10am-6pm daily. **Credit** AmEx, DC, MC, V. **Map** p247 F10.

German expat Marion Carsten spent four years studying the art of the goldsmith in Dusseldorf. Her chokers and matching bracelets are hand-assembled and finished, using inventive combinations of silver, suede, leather and pearl.

### Q&W Design
*Unit 3, No.25, North Block, 181 Taicang Lu, by Huangpi Nan Lu, Xintiandi (6326 2140). Metro Huangpi Nan Lu.* **Open** 10.30am-10.30pm daily. **Credit** AmEx, DC, MC, V. **Map** p248 H7.

Shanghainese designer Qionger Jiang says that her aim is to 'bridge the abyss separating the commonplace and the extraordinary'. Quite right too. What that means in practice is bold, striking necklaces and earrings fashioned out of such mundane elements as stainless steel, screw nuts and even washers. You will be able to find a different collection from the same designer at the Younik boutique in the Bund 18 building (18 Zhongshan Dong Yi Lu, by Nanjing Dong Lu, the Bund).

## Shoes

Shanghai's affordable and delightfully designed footwear is enough to bring out the Imelda Marcos in all of us – although sizes can be a problem. Chinese have dinky feet, so even if a size 39 is in stock it's going to feel like a 38. Quality is also variable. Don't be fooled by upmarket-looking boutiques: they'll take your RMB 300 and your shoes will still fall apart in a few months. The best tip is to bargain hard and remember the same shoes can be got for RMB 60 a pair in the markets. For cheap shoes (RMB 70) and sizes up to 41 (UK: 7; US: 9½), head to the market-style shoe stall at Shanxi Nan Lu metro station (exit 2) by the entrance to the Parkson department store's supermarket.

### Change & Insect 100

*318 Nanchang Lu, by Maoming Nan Lu, French Concession (6467 3677). Metro Shanxi Nan Lu.* **Open** 10.30am-10.30pm daily. **No credit cards.** **Map** p247 F8.
For something really fresh, head to this Hong Kong chain. Don't worry too much about the name: the designs are fashion-streets ahead of the rest of the city's offerings. For both men's and ladies' collections you can expect to pay around RMB 300 for shoes, double that for boots.

### Hot Wave

*108 Shanxi Nan Lu, by Changle Lu, French Concession (5403 6909). Metro Shanxi Nan Lu.* **Open** 10am-10pm daily. **No credit cards.** **Map** p247 E7.
Hot Wave stocks a broad assortment of discounted men's and ladies' footwear from such international favourites as Nine West, Timberland, Merrell, Prada and Fendi. The crowded store also stocks casual-wear from Miss Sixty, Tommy Hilfiger and Morgan at cut prices and boasts a decent selection of outdoor and camping gear.
**Other locations:** 390 Shanxi Nan Lu, by Nanchang Lu, French Concession (6472 0376).

### Suzhou Cobblers

*Room 101, 17 Fuzhou Lu, by Zhongshan Dong Yi Lu, the Bund (6321 7087/www.suzhou-cobblers.com). Metro Henan Lu.* **Open** 10am-6pm daily. **Credit** AmEx, DC, MC, V. **Map** p245 M5.
Suzhou Cobblers is an emporium of exquisite hand-made silk slippers, which can be worn both at home and around town. Mary Janes and mules feature Suzhou embroidery, including 'double fish', floral and vegetal designs with charming bags to match. Purchases can also be made at the online store.

### Trend

*218 Shanxi Nan Lu, by Huaihai Zhong Lu, French Concession (5403 1374).* **Open** 9am-10pm daily. **Credit** AmEx, DC, MC, V. **Map** p247 E7.
This reliable chain has supermarket aisles of choice, and its flagship on Huaihai Lu is a great place to come when you've had enough of bargaining. Prices are marked and very reasonable (RMB 80-250). The quality isn't fantastic, but the shoes will more than last you the season.
**Other locations:** 1336 Sichuan Bei Lu, by Wujing Lu, Hongkou (6324 4252); 1981 Huashan Lu, behind the Pacific Department Store, by Zhaojiabang Lu, Xujiahui (6447 4791).

## Food & drink

**Shanghai No.1 Foodstore** (*see p146*) and **Shanghai Changchun Foodstore** (*see below*) and **Shanghai No.2 Foodstuff Shop** (955-965 Huaihai Zhong Lu, by Shanxi Nan Lu, French Concession) are as much sightseeing experiences as shops – the same goes for the city's many wet markets (*see p134*). For Western-style foodstuffs, try **City Supermarket**, which has outlets at the Shanghai Centre (map p243 E5) and in Printemps department store (939-947 Huaihai Zhong Lu, by Shanxi Nan Lu, French Concession), or French *hypermarché* **Carrefour**, whose flagship is in Gubei (269 Shuicheng Nan Lu, by Yanan Xi Lu).

### Cheese & Fizz Gourmet Shop

*Unit 105, North Block, 119 Madang Lu, by Taicang Lu, Xintiandi (6336 5823). Metro Huangpi Nan Lu.* **Open** 10am-12.30am daily. **Credit** AmEx, DC, MC, V. **Map** p248 H7.
Imported and pricey delicacies (RMB 60-80 for 100g of cheese) ranging from over three dozen French cow, goat and ewe-milk cheeses to Italian marinated artichoke hearts, olives and biscuits. French/Chinese duo Clarence and Glendy also sell freshly baked quiches, rustic pâté and crusty baguettes to eat in or take away.

### Huangshan Tea Company

*605 Huaihai Zhong Lu, by Gusi Nan Lu, Xintiandi (5306 2974). Metro Huangpi Nan Lu.* **Open** 9am-10pm daily. **Credit** AmEx, DC, MC, V. **Map** p248 H7.
Specialist in high-grade Chinese teas, sold by weight. The store also carries an assortment of classic teapots, made in the town of Yixing 193km (120 miles) north-west of Shanghai. After a few years' use you can brew tea supposedly just by pouring water into the pot, such is their ability to absorb flavour.

### Shanghai Changchun Foodstore

*619-625 Huaihai Zhong Lu, by Sinan Lu, French Concession (5386 4940). Metro Shanxi Nan Lu.* **Open** 9am-10pm daily. **No credit cards.** **Map** p247 G7.
This local classic is a good place to check out favourites like dried meats (often spicy) or super-sweet sesame or mixed nut cakes. It usually offers

Eat, Drink, Shop

**Q&W Design**. *See p143.*

# Always read the label

It may come as some surprise, but not everything in Shanghai is fake. And with just a small dose of manufacturing savvy, you can uncover real gems. Factory seconds that haven't made it through quality control and factory overruns (not always accidental) are often released into the local market at just above cost price. These usually have the brand name snipped out of the label or blacked out with a marker pen – always a good sign for the bargain hounds. Otherwise, all manner of dodgy dealings take place between those who have *guanxi* (connections) with factory or export personnel. In which case a garment might slip out of the back door in perfect condition.

The most reliable way to tell whether an item is the genuine article is to go straight to the label. If it says 'Made in China' or 'Made in Hong Kong' (a way of getting around the quota system), you can be sure it's real. Chinese customers shun 'Made in China' garments, so copies always have 'Made in Italy' or 'Made in USA' labels. It's that simple.

For the biggest cluster of outlets, head to the unassuming stores along Nanchang Lu between Shanxi Nan Lu and Ruijin Er Lu (map p247 D7 & E6). Most mix the factory extras with their own-name brand collection.

## Africa Copa
*316 Nanchang Lu.*
This trendy ladieswear store stocks Nine West, Banana Republic, Mango, Rebecca Taylor and Guess, plus its own brand – the rather funky IP PURPURIN. Dresses cost RMB 360, jackets RMB 180.

## Around Tips
*280 Nanchang Lu.*
Miss 60, Diesel, DSquared2, Energy, Abercrombie & Fitch and Replay men's and women's jeans and tops for around RMB 250.

## Star Place
*340 Nanchang Lu.*
Very frilly and girlie pieces from Cacharel, Kookai and own-brand Star Place. Beware the Moschino: it says 'Made in Italy'. Sizes are on the petite side.

## U Fit
*348 Nanchang Lu.*
Some Mango, DKNY, Lee and sexy Diesel minis (RMB 150) mixed with U Fit's own hippie-chick gear.

## Coat Mountain
*117 Nanchang Lu.*
Compact selection for men and women: Zegna suit jackets for RMB 450, DSquared2 jeans RMB 260 and G-Star Raw hoodies RMB 200.

## Dense City
*328 Nanchang Lu.*
A good selection of menswear in large sizes. DSquared2 and Replay jeans are here for around RMB 200, and Paul Smith and Tommy Hilfiger shirts at RMB 80.

## Hot Wave
*360 Shanxi Nan Lu, by Fuxing Lu.*
Good selection of menswear, plus some womenswear and shoes. Levi and Energie jeans go for RMB 200; Armani Jeans, Versace and Calvin Klein tops around RMB 300.

---

tastings, but beware, what looks like chocolate may turn out to be red bean or, worst of all, sweetened meat. Crikey.

## Shanghai No.1 Foodstore
*720 Nanjing Dong Lu, by Guizhou Lu, People's Square (6322 2777). Metro Renmin Park or People's Square.* **Open** 9.30am-10pm daily. **Credit** AmEx, DC, MC, V. **Map** p244 K4.
Operating since 1954, this massive food store on the pedestrian stretch of Nanjing Dong Lu west of the square sells domestic and imported products. The ground-floor sprawl stocks everything from fresh-baked goods and dried fungus to salted fish and Dove chocolate bars. Pay-by-weight nuts and pre-served fruits are particularly popular. Tobacco and spirits are available, in addition to supplies of Eastern and Western health remedies.

## Gifts & interiors

**Mitsukoshi** at the Okura Garden Hotel (*see p.38*) stocks a good selection of popular local products, including designs by Annabel Lee, Shanghai Trio and Simply Life. Otherwise, the place to browse is the **French Concession**, particularly along Fuxing Xi Lu, Dongping Lu and around the area of Taikang Lu.

## Annabel Lee
*Unit 3, North Block, Lane 181, Taicang Lu, Xintiandi (6320 0045/www.annabel-lee.com).* **Open** 10am-10.30pm daily. **Map** p248 H7.
Local designer and owner Feng Bo has spent a lot of time in Japan, and it shows in her minimalist approach. Her simple but elegant designs include

fine linen place settings, raw silk travel pockets and business card holders, plus graceful candles, and sleek silk pyjamas with jade buttons.

### Blue Shanghai White

*Unit 103, 17 Fuzhou Lu, by Zhongshan Dong Yi Lu, the Bund (6323 0856). Metro Henan Zhong Lu.* **Open** 10.30am-6.30pm daily. **No credit cards.** **Map** p245 M5.

This is the sales space for Shanghai native Wang Hai Chen's distinctive furnishings, which combine blue and white porcelain with hand-polished antique pear wood. Fine celadon tea cups with handwoven tassles are popular, as is the crockery with painted images of *shikumen*, the celebrated but vanishing architecture of Old Shanghai.

### Jin

*614 Julu Lu, by Xiangyang Lu, French Concession (6247 2964). Metro Shanxi Nan Lu.* **Open** noon-9pm daily. **No credit cards.** **Map** p243 E6.

A colourful mix of larger furniture pieces and cute Chinese trinkets. Between the travelling chests (RMB 600) and refined wood and rattan emperor's chairs (RMB 2,000), you'll find silk bags and delicate blue and white ceramics (RMB 100-300), plus cushions and little notebooks (RMB 40-60).

### Lapis Lazuli

*9 Dongping Lu, by Hengshan Lu, French Concession (6474 3219). Metro Hengshan Lu.* **Open** 11am-11pm daily. **Credit** AmEx, DC, MC, V. **Map** p246 D9.

Attached to this stylish fusion eaterie is an equally eclectic gift/lifestyle boutique. Stock is always on discount (a cunning marketing ploy) so you can get good deals on its range of bamboo treasure chests (RMB 1,500), mini tea sets (RMB 200), rattan trays (RMB 168) and minimalist vases.

### Lilli's Shanghai

*174 Xiangyang Lu, by Nanchang Lu, French Concession (6474 5336). Metro Shanxi Nan Lu.* **Open** 10am-9pm daily. **Credit** AmEx, DC, MC, V. **Map** p247 E8.

Not the cheapest spot, but a treasure trove of Chinese silk, pearls (RMB 380) and handmade jewellery. Current favourites are a seriously stylish black silk clutch (RMB 280) and Lilli's blue and white ceramic bracelet designs (RMB 1,500).

**Other locations**: Maosheng Mansion, Suite 1D, 1051 Xinzha Lu, by Canghua Lu, Jingan (6215 5031).

### Madame Mao's Dowry

*70 Fuxing Xi Lu, by Yongfu Lu, French Concession (6437 1255). Metro Changshu Lu.* **Open** 10am-7pm daily. **Credit** AmEx, DC, MC, V. **Map** p246 C8.

Its English and Chinese owners conceived this as the kind of store in which Madame Mao – head of art and culture during the Cultural Revolution – might have shopped with her daughters. Two floors are filled with vintage posters, paintings and industrial propaganda, as well as antique furniture and lifestyle products.

### Shanghai Trio

*House 6, 37 Fuxing Xi Lu, by Wulumuqi Nan Lu, French Concession (6433 8901/www.shanghaitrio. com.cn). Metro Changshu Lu.* **Open** 9am-6pm Mon-Fri. **Credit** AmEx, DC, MC, V. **Map** p246 C8.

Located in a charming old residence, this showroom is a sublime setting for the innovative creations of French owner/designer Virginie Fournier. Customer favourites include Fournier's vibrantly coloured silk pouches and her small silk cases in the shape of rice baskets. These – as well as other products such as the tablecloths (RMB 1,300), cushion covers (RMB 300) and baby clothes (RMB 200-500) – are fashioned from all-natural Chinese fabrics such as cashmere, linen, silk and cotton.

**Other locations**: Unit 5, Building 1, Lane 181, Taicang Road, by Huangpi Nan Lu, Xintiandi (6355 2974).

### Simply Life

*Unit 101, 159 Madang Lu, by Taicang Lu, Xintiandi (6387 5100/www.simplylife-sh.com). Metro Huangpi Nan Lu.* **Open** 10.30am-11.30pm daily. **Credit** AmEx, DC, MC, V. **Map** p248 H7.

A city-wide chain that provides one-stop shops for high-quality and pricey Chinese-style home decor products and gifts. Choice items include house-brand silk boxes, place settings, appliqué greeting cards, embroidered pillows and glazed ceramic crockery sets and vases. The flagship store is in Xintiandi; on top of the usual range it also stocks local fashion brand insh (*see p142* **Created in Shanghai**), as well as such high-end imports as Alessi and Bodum.

**Other locations**: 9 Dongping Lu, by Hengshan Lu, French Concession (3406 0509).

## Health & beauty

**City Supermarket** and **Carrefour** (for both, *see p144*) both stock decent selections of branded Western beauty and personal-care products. Otherwise, try one of Shanghai's several outlets of the **Sephora** chain (*see below*) or the department stores in the various **malls** (*see p133*).

## Cosmetics

### Carpenter Tan

*75 Xiangyang Nan Lu, by Huaihai Zhong Lu, French Concession (1331 188 6907 mobile/www.crpttan. com). Metro Shanxi Nan Lu.* **Open** 10am-8pm daily. **No credit cards.** **Map** p247 E8.

Aka Combs 'r' Us. From humble origins, this head-grooming franchise now boasts over 300 stores throughout China. By stimulating blood flow to the scalp, combing (so it's claimed) promotes quicker hair growth and prevention of dandruff. The kaleidoscope of choice here includes combs made from peach wood (*tao mu*) and poplar (*huangyang mu*), plus intensely fragrant sandalwood (*tanxiang mu*).

Eat, Drink, Shop

## Sephora

*629 Huaihai Zhong Lu, by Ruijin Lu, French Concession (5306 6198). Metro Shanxi Nan Lu.* **Open** 10am-10pm Mon-Thur; 10am-11pm Fri, Sat. **Credit** AmEx, DC, MC, V. **Map** p247 F7.

This flagship store of the respected French multi-brand store arrived in Shanghai in 2005 to the joy of its cosmetics-starved citizens. The range here is far greater than in any of the department stores.

**Other locations:** 1st floor, 268 Shuicheng Nan Lu, by Yanan Xi Lu, Gubei (6270 5698); 1st floor, Super Brand Mall, 138 Lujiazui Xi Lu, by Yincheng Xi Lu, Pudong (5047 2318).

# Hairdressing

## Eric Paris Hairdressing & Beauty

*4 Hengshan Lu, by Wulumuqi Lu, French Concession (6473 0900). Metro Hengshan Lu.* **Open** 10am-8pm daily. **Credit** AmEx, DC, MC, V. **Map** p246 C9.

A refuge for expat ladies who've experienced far too many bad China-hair days to take any more risks. Relax in the safe hands of Eric and his well-trained, English-speaking staff. A cut and blow-dry goes for around RMB 400.

**Other locations:** 3N 4-5, J-Life Mall, Jinmao Tower, 88 Shiji Dadao, by Yincheng Lu, Pudong (1376 139 0706 mobile).

## Esprit Salon

*301B CITIC Square, 1168 Nanjing Xi Lu, by Jiangning Lu, Jingan (5292 8800). Metro Shimen Yi Lu.* **Open** 10am-10pm daily. **Credit** AmEx, DC, MC, V. **Map** p243 E5.

Favoured by in-the-know expats for its affordable yet cutting-edge hairstyles. All the stylists have trained at Esprit in Hong Kong and most can speak English. Even better, discontented customers can return to the salon within seven days for the same service free of charge. Women's haircuts start from RMB 400; if that is too steep, the salon often runs promotional deals for up to 50% off.

**Other locations:** Super Brand Mall, 168 Lujiazui Xi Lu, by Yincheng Xi Lu, Pudong (5049 3988).

## Nanjing Cosmetology & Haircut Co Ltd

*784 Nanjing Xi Lu, by Shimen Yi Lu, Jingan (6253 2958). Metro Shimen Yi Lu.* **Open** 9am-9pm daily. **No credit cards. Map** p243 F5.

In business for more than 70 years, Nanjing is considered by locals the best in men's and women's hairdressing. The place has more than a whiff of history about it, with traditional barber stations on the ground floor, and ladies' cuts and colouring on the second, up a sweeping, balustraded staircase. Apart from the RMB 50 cut/wash/shave for men,

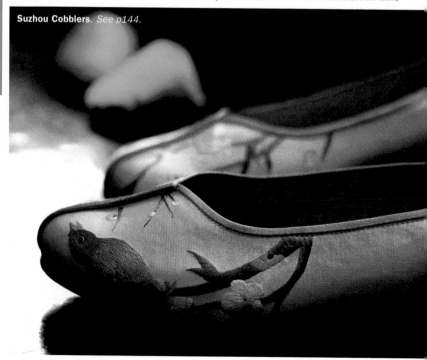

**Suzhou Cobblers.** *See p144.*

prices are steep – a hairwash/massage (*toubu anmo*) will set you back RMB 75, but the package includes a 15-minute special head and upper body massage. The list of services is available in English.

## Health stores & pharmacies

Shanghai is packed with pharmacies, most of which sell both Western and Chinese medicine. They are also often open 24 hours, but there's an especially safe all-night bet in the middle of the French Concession (973 Huaihai Zhong Lu, by Shanxi Nan Lu, 6473 6810, map p247 E7).

For **opticians**, see *p221*.

### Fulintang Xinyidai

*Unit 3, Suite 1A, South Block, 123 Xingye Lu, by Madang Lu, Xintiandi (6384 5987/www.fulintang. com). Metro Huangpi Nan Lu.* **Open** 10am-midnight daily. **Credit** AmEx, DC, MC, V. **Map** p248 H8.
Although it has been around since the days of the Qing Dynasty, this venerable institution has these days adopted a modern approach to Chinese herbal medicine. Healthy ingredients are administered in the form of convenient snacks and floral teas. You could go for liver-relieving osmanthus tea, perhaps, or buy some soup packs and Chinese mushrooms coated with sweet sesame.

### Tong Hang Chun Traditional Chinese Medicine Store

*20 Yuyuan Xin Lu, by Jiuxiao Lu, Old City (6355 0308).* **Open** 8.30am-9pm daily. **Credit** AmEx, DC, MC, V. **Map** p249 M7.
Established in 1783, Tong Hang Chun is the city's oldest medicine store. Large glass jars containing sea horses, antlers and placentas share space with modern-day over-the-counter medication. With everything labelled in Chinese and no English-speaking staff, you're best bringing someone who can translate or just browse through the bear bile powder and gnarly ginseng.

### Watson's

*787-789 Huaihai Zhong Lu, by Ruijin Yi Lu, French Concession (6431 8650). Metro Shanxi Nan Lu.* **Open** 9.30am-10.30pm daily. **Credit** AmEx, DC, MC, V. **Map** p247 F7.
Born in Hong Kong, this Western-style chain drugstore is a one-stop shop for toiletry and personal-care needs. In addition to deodorants, razors and the like, it also carries affordable make-up brands such as Maybelline, L'Oréal and Revlon, Chinese and Western health remedies, and teas, basic first aid supplies and the entire Scholl footcare line.
**Other locations**: 218B Westgate Mall, 1038 Nanjing Xi Lu, by Jiangning Lu, Jingan (6218 0465).

## Sports & outdoor gear

Many malls reserve an entire floor for sporting gear, notably **Grand Gateway** (*see p133*) and **Raffles City** (*see p134*), and **Hot Wave** (*see p144*) is good for outdoor and camping gear. Otherwise, you can find knock-offs of all major sporting brands in the city's markets.

### Decathlon

*393 Yinxiao Lu, by Longyang Lu, Pudong (5045 3888). Metro Longyang Lu.* **Open** 9am-9pm daily. **Credit** AmEx, DC, MC, V.
It's a bit of a trek to Decathlon, but well worth it for the best choice of sportswear and sports equipment in the city, at reasonable prices.
**Other locations**: 88 Xianxia Xi Lu, by Jianhe Lu, Hongqiao (6238 5511); 600 Lantian Lu, by Yunshan Lu, Pudong (5030 7558); 2 Shenbei Lu, by Humin Lu, Hongqiao (5442 5585).

### Ye Huo

*296 Changle Lu, by Ruijin Yi Lu, French Concession (5386 0591/www.yehuo.com). Metro Shanxi Nan Lu.* **Open** 10.30am-10pm daily. **Credit** AmEx, DC, MC, V. **Map** p247 F7.
A camping store that stocks all the goods necessary for a weekend with Mother Nature. Quality local brands – of which the best are Backpackers, Zealwood and Zebra – are cheap, and flawed or last-season foreign brands are also reasonably priced, but apart from that there are few bargains. English-speaking staff can suggest the best places in China to pitch your tent.

**Eat, Drink, Shop**

# Time Out
# Travel Guides

## Far East

**Available at all good bookshops
and at timeout.com/shop**

**Time Out**
Guides

# Arts & Entertainment

**Science & Technology Museum**.
*See p95.*

# Festivals & Events

Ignore the organisational hiccups and raise a glass of Shaoxing wine.

Yippee! It's the **Anting Kite Festival**. *See p154*.

Once, there were 24 holidays in the Chinese calendar, each marking a significant agricultural event. Mangzhong, for example, brought peasants out into the paddies to plant rice seedlings in early June. Failing to properly attend to these dates was thought to bring agricultural ruin and, although imminent starvation is no longer a threat for most Chinese, the influence of the old calendar persists. **Qingming Jie** ('grave-sweeping festival', *see p154*) and not **Chinese New Year** (Chunjie or Spring Festival, *see p156*) marks the beginning of spring, while Xiaoshu still acknowledges the start of the 'mouldy days' (muggy weather) at the beginning of July. Religious holidays such as the birthdays of **Sakyamuni Buddha** (*see p154*) and the **Queen of Heaven** (*see p155*) are virtually unheard of outside the temple walls.

As traditional holidays wane, Shanghai's cultural festivals have yet to take hold. They are disorganised at best; at worst they can be cheesy, commercial and so poorly promoted that they often pass unnoticed. Most suffer chronic mismanagement at the hands of corrupt

government officials, and prices are steep to compensate for the thousands of tickets given away to clients, officials and the police in exchange for their co-operation. The flipside of this is that there are usually many tickets available from the *huangniu* ('yellow cows' or touts), often at reduced prices. As long as you're not expecting world-class entertainment, you might even be pleasantly surprised by such events as the **Shanghai International Literary Festival** (*see p153*) or the high-profile **Formula 1** race (*see p156*). The **World Expo**, due to be hosted in Shanghai in 2010, is already generating all sorts of crazy plans. The website www.expo2010china.com should have details of any confirmed events.

For the Chinese, most holidays are family affairs. Typically, people gather around the mah-jong table and while away the afternoon chewing through a packet of melon seeds. Around 5pm, the table is laid with a plastic tablecloth and piled high with a dozen different dishes. Families mow through the food, and toast each other with Shaoxing rice wine. Sufficiently inebriated, they lay into the firecrackers, setting the lanes ablaze with paper and smoke. Various public events are, however, staged for the traditional Chinese holidays. They are often extremely crowded, but the **Longhua Temple Fair** and **Lantern Festival** (for both, *see below*) are impressive.

## PRACTICALITIES

Traditional Chinese holidays follow a lunar calendar, meaning the dates change year by year, and although **Labour Week May Holiday** (*see p155*) and **National Week** (*see p156*) are predictable, business hours during the celebrations vary, with many places closing for the whole week. Make travel plans well in advance: tickets sell out, prices can increase by as much as 50 per cent and many travel agents are closed. It's best to avoid tourist destinations altogether unless you enjoy the company of megaphone-wielding tour groups. For a list of national public holidays, *see p230*.

Up-to-date and accurate information on forthcoming events is hard to find, but the *Shanghai Daily* and *Shanghai Star* newspapers are good sources, as are monthly English-language magazines such as *that's Shanghai* (www.thatssh.com), *City Weekend* (www.cityweekend.com.cn) and *Shanghai Talk*. Concierge staff at high-end hotels usually speak English and keep a what's on list.

Purchasing tickets in advance may require sleuthing around. Try the theatre box offices, especially the **Shanghai Grand Theatre** (*see p187*), which is one of the largest and has some English-speaking staff.

## Spring

### Lantern Festival

*Yu Gardens, 115 Yuyuan Lu, Old City (6328 0602).* **Date** 4 Mar 2007; 21 Feb 2008. **Admission** RMB 10. **Map** p249 M7.

In Chinese it's called Yuanxiao Jie, and marks the end of winter. It is customary to display a red lantern outside the home so that the Taoist Lord of Heaven will visit to bestow luck and happiness. The tradition of people making paper lanterns and wandering the streets has largely died out, but Yu Gardens (Yuyuan) has a wonderful selection of exquisitely crafted creations, including the *tangyuan* – sweet dumplings filled with bean paste, meat or, our favourite, *zhima* (black sesame paste). The Gardens fill up quickly and the doors are shut to prevent overcrowding, so it's best to arrive by late afternoon. **Photo** *p155*.

### Shanghai International Fashion Week/Culture Festival

*Various venues (6279 2828 ext 234 or 236/ www.fashionshanghai.com).* **Date** mid Mar.

Glamourati and fashionistas strut around town in full regalia, on their way to fashion shows and model competitions all over town. But, unless you're an industry insider, you won't get anywhere near the action. Various Fashion Week trade fairs offer a good array of local design and modest catwalk shows.

## Shanghai International Literary Festival

*Glamour Bar, 6th floor, 20 Guangdong Lu, by Zhongshan Dong Yi Lu, the Bund (6350 9988). Metro Henan Lu.* **Date** 2 or 3 weekends in Apr. **Admission** RMB 50 (incl 1 drink). **Map** p245 M5.

Riding piggyback on the Man Hong Kong International Literary Festival, this is one of Shanghai's best-loved festivals. The 2006 version featured Booker Prize-winner John Banville, Pico Iyer and Robert Elegant, along with a slew of local and locally based authors such as Tess Johnston, Paul French and Ma Jian.

## Longhua Temple Fair

*Longhua Temple, 2853 Longhua Lu, by Longhua Park, Xuhui (6456 6085).* **Date** Apr. **Admission** RMB 15. **Map** p240 C5.

The Temple Fair dates back to the Ming Dynasty and is the largest of its kind in Shanghai. Rites are performed for Maitreya (the Buddhist messiah) and a grand Buddhist ceremony is held. The fair includes street theatre, paper-cutting, calligraphy, Chinese opera, vegetarian food stalls and a parade of Chinese mythological figures.

# Mooning around

Glazed golden cakes stamped with lovely Chinese designs, mooncakes certainly look delightful, but beware the taste. Fillings range from palatable lotus, chocolate, red bean and sesame paste to revolting egg yolk and salty pork. At worst they can be like wet canned cat food with the consistency of an ice-hockey puck.

It's no surprise, then, that few people seem to enjoy eating them, in spite of their abundance. Every **Mid Autumn Festival** (*see p156*) fancy boxes are lined with satin and packed with gold-wrapped mooncakes. From companies to employees and clients, among family and friends, round they go. Where do they stop? Some in the stomachs of committed mooncake-lovers; others in the cupboard where they petrify until Spring Festival. In fact, the endurance of the mooncake seems puzzling: certainly tradition plays a part, but importantly the giving of mooncakes is about *guanxi*, as they say in Chinese – about strengthening connections. Sending mooncakes generates *guanxi* points, which may be redeemed at some appropriate moment in the future.

**Arts & Entertainment**

### Qingming Jie
*Various temples & graveyards (6972 0010).*
**Date** 4 or 5 Apr.
Qingming ('grave-sweeping day') is an ancient and very important festival. Relatives visit the tombs of ancestors, lay flowers and do some spring-cleaning. Joss paper is folded into shapes that are burned for the dead as 'Hell Bank Notes', in various ludicrous denominations; these provide a yearly 'living'

# CNY

For many foreigners the thought of **Chinese New Year** conjures up festive images of red and gold dragons gaily wagging their heads to the sound of clanging cymbals. A quaint picture, certainly, but hardly representative of Chinese New Year (CNY) in modern China. Traditions have been increasingly abandoned, with home-cooked dinners replaced by huge banquets in gilded, rococo-crazy seafood restaurants – and the soundtrack is provided less by cymbals than by the cacophonous Chujie Lianhua Wanhui, or Spring Festival variety show. It features garishly dressed Cantopop crooners, obnoxious child performers and full-on song and dance numbers extolling the virtues of the Chinese military.

China's new-found prosperity has – for better or worse – played a part in altering the traditions of CNY. In the past, when people said *nian nian you yu* ('may there be fish to eat every year') they really meant it. *Yu* ('fish') is a homophone for abundance, and during Mao's Great Leap Forward, CNY was the only time many families ate meat of any kind. In those days families began to prepare months in advance, travelling miles back to their *jiaxiang* ('home town'), painting New Year poems to hang either side of the front door, buying food, and wrapping dumplings and rolling *tangyuan* (doughy dumplings served in soup). People took the time to make everything, including their own Yuanxiao lanterns, from scratch. There was even a small New Year's Eve held three days before New Year's Eve proper, and an even smaller New Year's Eve held six days in advance. In fact, the festival was such a momentous event that its end brought a profound come-down. On that last day people would sweeten the pain of returning to work with delectable *shouxin huntun* – 'take back the heart' wontons.

allowance for the deceased. Although not an official holiday, hospitals and stock exchanges are noticeably quieter because, with so many spirits wandering the earth, the day is considered inauspicious for medical procedures or business dealings. Traffic jams can cause acute gridlock on the city's outer roads, so many families celebrate before or after the actual date.

### Birthday of Sakyamuni Buddha
*Jingan Temple, 1686 Nanjing Lu, by Wanghangdu Lu, Jingan (6256 6366). Metro Jingan Temple.*
**Date** 24 May 2007; 12 May 2008. **Admission** free. **Map** p242 C5.
Public displays of faith are rare in Shanghai, but the birthday of Sakyamuni Buddha ('Shijiamuni' in Mandarin) is an exception. Monks chant prayers and perform a ritual cleaning of their Buddhas.

### Anting Kite Festival
*Auto Park of Shanghai International Automobile City, 228 An Li Lu, Anting, Jiading (6289 5855). Buses run from People's Square.* **Date** mid Apr.
About half an hour west of the city, Anting is host to a thrilling kite-flying competition at which the contestants strive to go faster, higher and further. When the neck strain gets too much, try kite culture exhibitions and DIY kite-making at ground level. **Photo** *p152.*

### Nanhui Peach Blossom Festival
*286 Beimen Lu, Huinan Town, Nanhui (5801 8877 ext 2008/6801 9541). No.2 bus from Shanghai Stadium.* **Date** 10 days in mid Apr. **Admission** RMB 48. **Map** p241 H6.
The Nanhui district contains hundreds of hectares of peach trees, which come into full bloom in April. People flock here to enjoy the pink blossom and take in folksy festivities including singing, dancing and a 'Farmer's Wedding Performance'. The posh city folk also like to marvel at quaint peasants tending the trees and engaging in manual labour, many of them rolling up their sleeves and heading to the Nongjia Le ('Peasant Happiness Home'), a kind of model farm where city slickers can pick fruit and sample home-cooked pumpkin cakes and green onion pastries. Nearby Shanghai Flower Port boasts a version of Dutch tulip garden Keukenhof Park.

### International Tea Culture Festival
*Various venues, Zhabei (3303 0071). Metro Shanghai Railway Station.* **Date** mid-late Apr.
Tea fanatics from around the world pour into Shanghai to attend tea ceremonies, seminars, tastings and exhibits. There are tours of nearby tea fields for those who want to escape the city, and folk performances are held around Zhabei train station.

### International Flower Festival
*Changfeng Park, 451 Daduhe Lu, Changfeng (6286 0458).* **Date** Apr 2008 (biennial). **Map** p240 A3.
See Changfeng Park carpeted with exotic spring flowers, such as peonies and tulips, and rare herbs. There's folk dancing and singing at the aquarium too.

*Arts & Entertainment*

The **Lantern Festival**. *See p153*.

## Labour Week May Holiday

*Daning Lingshi Park, 228 Guanzhong Xi Lu,*
*by Gonghe Xin Lu (6437 2020). Metro Shanghai*
*Circus World.* **Date** 1-5 May. **Map** p240 C1.

In years past the heroic achievements of workers
and farmers were celebrated on May Day with
parades and government rallies. Today this 'golden
week' has been lengthened to generate some tourist
dollars and is thus one of the worst times to travel.
Expect a crush at all airports and train and bus stations, although the city itself tends to clear out.
Those looking for something with more spark would
do well to check out the International Musical
Fireworks Games at Daning Lingshi Park.

## Birthday of the Queen of Heaven

*Longhua Temple, 2853 Longhua Lu, by Longhua*
*Park, Xuhui (6456 6085).* **Date** 9 May 2007; 28 Apr
2008. **Admission** free. **Map** p240 C5.

The birthday of Mazu, the Queen of Heaven, is fêted
with the arrival of merchants from the Fujian
province. They bring traditional gifts of joss-paper
money and incense to be burnt in her honour, and
pray for safety and wealth. Devotees stage special
theatre performances.

## Shanghai Spring International Music Festival/Jazzy Shanghai

*Various venues (6386 8686/www.culture.sh.cn).*
**Date** early May.

Hitherto famous for their failings, these two festivals decided to join forces in an attempt to regroup.
The music is a mixed bag of Chinese classical and
B-grade Western jazz. The event usually passes
pretty much unnoticed, but there may be bigger acts
to look forward to in the future.

## BMW Asia Open

*Thomson Shanghai Golf Club, 1 Longdong*
*Dadao, by Luoshan Lu, Pudong (5833 8888).*

Golf is increasingly popular in China, and this tournament hopes to establish itself as the region's major
event. $1.5 million in prizes certainly attracts the big
hitters. Tiger Woods, David Howell and home-grown
talent Zhang Lianwei have all competed.

# Summer

## Dragon Boat Festival

*Suzhou Creek (6355 3788).* **Date** 19 June 2007;
8 June 2008.

The festival celebrates poet Qu Yuan, who drowned
himself in 278 BC to protest government corruption.
Legend has it that a fisherman threw small packets
of rice wrapped in bamboo leaves into the water to
prevent the fish eating his body. These rice snacks,
*zongzi*, are still served as a reminder of Qu Yuan's
noble sacrifice; bean paste, egg or pork varieties can
be found steaming in little crock-pots at convenience
stores. Exhilarating dragon boat races are held on the
Huangpu River and Suzhou Creek. To join in, call 138
0166 2148 (mobile) or visit www.shanghaiexpat.com.

## Shanghai International Film Festival (SIFF)

*Various venues (6253 7115/www.siff.com).*
**Date** mid June.

SIFF features Chinese movies, plus a few Hollywood
offerings. Foreign films may be dubbed into Chinese
and Chinese films may not have English subtitles,
and buying tickets can be a challenge (especially for
premières, which sell out quickly). *See also p163*.

### Founding of the Chinese Communist Party

*Museum of the First National Congress of the Chinese Communist Party, 374 Huangpi Nan Lu, by Xingye Lu, Xintiandi (5383 2171). Metro Huangpi Lu.* **Date** 1 July. **Map** p248 H7.

Government newspapers run front-page editorials extolling the supreme glory of the People's Party and old stagers organise ceremonies around the city, focused at the museum.

## Autumn

### Shanghai Biennale

*Shanghai Art Museum, 325 Nanjing Xi Lu, People's Square (6327 2829/www.shanghai biennial.cn). Metro People's Square.* **Date** Sept-Nov 2008 (even yrs). **Admission** RMB 20. **Map** p244 H5.

The Shanghai Biennale was launched in 1996, as a showcase for Chinese art, but it is now an international affair. *See also p168.*

### Kunshan Beer Festival

*Kunshan Stadium, Kunshan (6875 8536 ext 1647/ www.china.ahk.de/beerfestival). Buses run from Jinjiang Hotel.* **Date** mid-late Sept. **Admission** free. **Map** p240 A1.

A sterile man-made canal town, Kunshan rarely sees as much fun as during the Beer Fest. Expats from Shanghai flood the town for a weekend drowning themselves in suds. The festival features several *biergarten*, complete with Chinese waitresses in *lederhosen*. Which is as authentic as it gets: the food is passable, the beer selection limited and the antics fairly tame – Shanghai is a long way from Germany.

### Mid Autumn Festival

*Various venues.* **Date** 25 Sept 2007; 14 Sept 2008.

The Moon Festival (in Chinese, Zhongqiu Jie) is a time for family gatherings, moon-gazing and eating mooncakes (*see p153* **Mooning around**). Children are told the originary myth: a fairy, who lives alone on the moon with her jade rabbit, is visited by a celestial general for whom she dances. Shadows visible on the moon during the festival are thought to be their silhouettes.

### Formula 1

*Shanghai International Circuit, Anting, Jiading (9682 6999/www.icsh.sh.cn/www.f1china.com.cn).* **Date** 3 days in late Sept. **Admission** RMB 180-3,980.

The latest and most high-profile addition to the city's sporting calendar brings many glamorous events and Chinese celebs to town. Those without VIP invitations can catch a blurred glimpse of Schumacher and Alonso at the circuit, a 40-minute drive north-west of the city centre.

### Shanghai Sweet-Scented Osmanthus Festival

*Guilin Park, Caobao Lu, by Guilin Lu, Caohejing (6483 0910).* **Date** late Sept-early Oct. **Admission** RMB 120. **Map** p240 B5.

Around the time of the Mid Autumn Festival (*see above*), thousands of trees bloom in Guilin Park in the south-west of the city, releasing a heady, blissful fragrance. The former pleasure garden of gangster Du Yuesheng hosts film screenings, martial arts demonstrations, acrobatics and fashion shows.

### National Week

*The Bund, by Nanjing Dong Lu. Metro Henan Lu.* **Date** 1-5 Oct. **Map** p245 M4.

National Week brings with it a similar exodus as Labour Week (*see p155*). Those who stay behind roam Nanjing Lu or Huaihai Lu assaulting each other with giant inflatable plastic hammers.

### Shanghai International Arts Festival

*Various venues (6272 0702/0455/www.artsbird.com).* **Date** mid Oct-mid Nov.

When compared to Hong Kong's world-class arts festival, Shanghai's seems a bit shabby. Classical music is the main draw (with some big names, such as Yo-Yo Ma and Sir Simon Rattle), but there's also dance and theatre from little-known international groups.

### Tennis Masters Cup

*Qi Zhong Centre Court Stadium, 5500 Yuanjiang Lu, by Kunyang Lu, Minhang (962 288/962 388/ www.masters-cup.com).* **Date** 12-19 Nov. **Admission** RMB 36-176.

Held in a gorgeous stadium (*see p191*), the Masters should attract top global talent – but it's at the end of the season, so most players are too knackered to make it. In 2005 Roddick, Hewitt and Agassi all pulled out, which – along with expensive tickets – left stands half full. Never mind: the Masters looks like it's going to stick around until at least 2009.

### Toray Cup

*The Bund (6629 8808/www.shmarathon.com). Metro Henan Lu.* **Date** last Wed of Nov. **Map** p245 M4.

In conjunction with the Health Promotion Festival, die-hard runners risk their lungs in the city's biggest street marathon. The event includes a less intense 21km (13-mile) half-marathon – plus a 4km (2.5-mile) fun run – for those not up to the long haul. Expect congested traffic as many roads, including the Bund, are closed to accommodate the 10,000 racers.

## Winter

### Chinese New Year

*Various locations.* **Date** 18 Feb 2007; 7 Feb 2008.

It's Yuandan or Chunjie (Spring Festival) in Chinese; either way, it's the biggest fixture on the Chinese calendar. CNY officially lasts three days. On the first day, families gather to eat special meals symbolising good fortune, prosperity and health. Typical dishes include dumplings (for luck), blood clams (wealth) and fish balls (family harmony). Fireworks are set off to scare away evil spirits; to experience the pyrotechnic blowout, get a window seat in a tall building or hotel. *See p154* **CNY**.

# Children

Tots might be bewildered but at least they won't be bored.

**Science & Technology Museum**. *See p158.*

Shanghai may be the Pearl of the Orient, but for travellers with children it can seem rather lacklustre. For a megacity with millions of little emperors and empresses, Shanghai has surprisingly few dedicated kids' attractions. Nor were there any major new ones in the pipeline as we went to press, despite the grand ambitions of city planners, who have thus far not delivered on their promise of theme parks. Even rumours about Disney coming to town have gone quiet.

The oppressive humidity in summer and the chilling dampness in winter tend to drive tourists with children back into their climate-controlled hotel rooms. Fight the urge to cocoon. Instead, make the most of Shanghai's excellent shopping scene (with kids' bargains galore), vibrant markets, few but well-executed museums, river cruises and its genuinely awe-inspiring acrobat troupes (*see p188* **Turning tricks**). With some effort, Shanghai can take on a shine for visitors of all ages.

**PRACTICALITIES**

It is a good idea to give your children a copy of the hotel address written in Chinese characters and the hotel phone number, just in case you get separated while out; English isn't widely spoken. The standards of public toilets range from revolting to reasonable, so carry pocket tissues (many toilets lack toilet paper) and hand sanitiser, and aim for bathroom breaks in major hotels or chain restaurants.

Prepare your children for the likelihood of being stared at by locals. Foreign children, especially those with blond hair and blue eyes, are still curiosities for many Chinese, particularly the older generations. It's a harmless fascination, but still a bit alarming when a stranger closes in to get a better look.

## Where to stay

Shanghai's hotels are geared primarily towards business travellers, and their facilities are tailored accordingly. With advance notice, most high-end hotels can provide cribs, cots, highchairs and babysitting (RMB 40-60 per hour). But few hotels have play areas, and some may refuse to admit children to their swimming pools if there is no shallow end. Others, like the **Hilton** (250 Huashan Lu, French Concession, 6248 0000) and the **JW Marriott** (*see p35*) admit children with parental supervision into the pool area.

The **Portman Ritz-Carlton** (*see p37*) and the **Westin** (*see p31*) are both extremely accommodating towards young travellers. Both have kids' menus, offer activity kits upon check-in, encourage children to participate in treasure hunts on site and allow children in the pool area (with adult supervision). In addition, the Westin has the best kids' brunch in town and provides a Kid's Heavenly Crib, a junior version of the chain's mega-comfortable, trademarked Heavenly Bed. The Portman has a playroom on the eighth floor, and its Tea Garden restaurant has healthy mains for children.

The **Novotel Atlantis** (728 Pudong Dadao, by Fushan Lu, Pudong, 5036 6666, www.novotel.com) is the best kid-friendly choice in Pudong. Its pool is open to children, and its brunch offers half-price grub for six- to 12-year-olds (free for under-sixes), along with a play area with games, puppet and magic shows.

For families staying five days or more, a better bet may be a serviced apartment. Try the **Shanghai Centre Serviced Apartments** (Shanghai Centre, 1376 Nanjing Xi Lu, Jingan,

6279 8502), which are in the heart of downtown surrounded by shops and restaurants. Two blocks from Xintiandi, the **Somerset Grand Shanghai** (8 Jinan Lu, by Taicang Lu, Xintiandi, 6385 6888, www.somersetgrandshanghai.com, rates from RMB 1,450) offers cosy one- to three-bedroom apartments with kitchens, plus a pool and children's play area for guest use.

## Sightseeing

For kid-friendly activities in Shanghai, go with the flow: the Huangpu River and the Bund and Pudong riverfronts hold the greatest concentration of attractions with child appeal. There are **riverboat tours** (*see p48*) and the surreal sound and light show of the **Bund Tourist Tunnel** (*see p91*) under the river. Once on the other side of the water in Pudong, there's the **Oriental Pearl Tower** (*see p94* **Pearl of the East**), with its fantastic views and sci-fi looks, as well as the **Natural Wild Insect Kingdom** and **Shanghai Ocean Aquarium** (for both, *see below*). Underneath the Pearl Tower is the **Shanghai History Museum** (*see p93*), which contains numerous interesting reconstructions of Old Shanghai streets, including Chinese medicine stores, tailor shops and old trams and cars. Another museum that justifies a trip to Pudong is the interactive **Science & Technology Museum** (*see p95*; **photo** *p157*) three stops past the Oriental Pearl Tower on Metro Line 2. It boasts two IMAX theatres, sound and light displays, an indoor rainforest, a robot theatre and a hands-on children's 'technoland'.

On People's Square, the **Urban Planning Centre** (*see p61*) has a huge scale model of what city planners envisage for their buzzing metropolis by 2020.

### Changfeng Ocean World

*Gate 4, 21 Changfeng Park, 451 Daduhe Lu, by Jingshajiang Lu, Putuo (5281 8888/6286 6399 for English/www.oceanworld.com.cn). No.6 Tour Bus Line from Shanghai Stadium/Metro Zhongshan Park.* **Open** 8.30am-5pm daily. **Admission** RMB 110; RMB 80 children; free children under 1m. **Credit** AmEx, DC, MC, V. **Map** p240 A3.

Still waters run deep at Changfeng Park, located a half-hour drive north-west of the city centre. Beneath its boating lake lies Ocean World (formerly Aquaria 21), an impressive Australian-owned aquarium with more than 10,000sq m (107,500sq ft) of tanks filled with fish, penguins and sharks, plus an adjoining 2,000-seat stadium with daily beluga whale shows. The foyer is designed like an aircraft cabin, and the aquarium's galleries then take visitors on a flight of fancy to South America, through Inca temples, past waterfalls and across the Amazon basin before reaching fresh- and saltwater tanks. The park offers

fine entertainment for all ages and is more interactive than its competitor, Shanghai Ocean Aquarium (*see below*). Visitors can take a glass-bottom boat tour or a simulator ride on an underwater roller-coaster, and older guests (over-tens) can arrange to swim with the whales or dive with the sharks. There is limited English signage, but exhibits speak for themselves. Highly recommended.

### Natural Wild Insect Kingdom

*1 Fenghe Lu, Lujiazui, Pudong (5840 5921). Metro Lujiazui.* **Open** 9am-5pm Mon-Fri; 9am-5.30pm Sat, Sun. **Admission** RMB 35; RMB 20 children; free children under 0.8m. **No credit cards**. **Map** p245 O4.

Slithering snakes, leaping lizards and snapping turtles fill the cages at the Insect Kingdom, which boasts 200-plus species of insects from as far afield as Africa and South America. Creepy crawlies are joined by monkeys, ferrets and rabbits; bunnies are also sold in the gift shop.

### Shanghai Ocean Aquarium

*158 Yincheng Bei Lu, by Dongyuan Lu, Lujiazui, Pudong (5877 9988/www.aquarium.sh.cn). Metro Lujiazui.* **Open** 9am-6pm daily. **Admission** RMB 110; RMB 70 children 0.8m-1.4m; free children under 0.8m. **Credit** MC, V. **Map** p245 P4.

Shanghai Ocean Aquarium has what you might call tunnel vision. The highlight of this state-of-the-art Chinese-Singaporean venture, one of the largest attractions of its kind in Asia, is a 155m (509ft) underwater clear viewing tunnel, which offers 270-degree views of sharks, turtles and exotic fish. The surrounding nine galleries plumb the depths of four oceans and five continents, and feature 15,000 fish representing 360 species, with a special section devoted to species from China's own Yangtze River.

**Century Park.**
See p159.

### Shanghai Zoo

*2381 Hongqiao Lu, by Hami Lu, Hongqiao (6268 7775/www.shanghaizoo.cn). Bus 925 from People's Square/No.4 Tour Bus Line from Shanghai Stadium.* **Open** 6.30am-5.30pm. **Admission** RMB 30; RMB 24 children; free children under 1.2m. **No credit cards.** **Map** p240 A4.

Compared to snazzy Western counterparts, the atmosphere of Shanghai's zoo is drab and institutional. Even star attractions among its 600-plus species, like the giraffes and giant pandas, occupy enclosures that resemble World War II bunkers. Fortunately, the extensive green grounds help to compensate. Once a British golf club, the former fairways now make pleasant picnic spots, and the water hazards provide a quaint home for geese, swans and other birds. While the children's zoo is lacklustre, the elephant and sea lion shows are entertaining, and a Ferris wheel provides a bird's-eye view of the park.

### Gardens, parks & playgrounds

Because Shanghai is an unremittingly urban city, public parks and squares are popular gathering spaces and great for people-watching. Head with the kids to the Bund (*see pp49-56*) to watch the sword- and fan-wielding tai chi groups in the morning and to People's Square (*see pp58-60*) for kite flyers in the afternoon. These activities are not staged for tourists' benefit; they are poignant glimpses of life in the 'real China' that the children will not soon forget.

### Century Park

*1001 Jinxiu Lu, by Shiji Dadao, Pudong (5833 5621/ www.centurypark.com.cn). Metro Century Park.* **Open** 16 Mar-15 Nov 7am-6pm daily. 16 Nov-15 Mar 7am-5pm daily. **Admission** RMB 10; free children under 1.2m. **No credit cards.** **Map** p241 H4.

A veritable triathlon of fun awaits kids at Shanghai's largest park. They can pedal their way through the park's 1.4sq km (0.5sq mile) on rented bicycles, covered pedal cars and tandems (RMB 20-80/hr), navigate the park's canals by electric boat (RMB 30-50) and soar through the skies on the kiddie rollercoaster in the new amusement park. You can also engage in more traditional pursuits in a variety of designated areas, including fishing and picnic grounds. *Photo p158*.

### Fuxing Park

*2 Gaolan Lu, by Sinan Lu, French Concession (5386 0540 ext 0). Metro Huangpi Nan Lu.* **Open** 6am-6pm daily. **Admission** free.

This park's broad promenades remain unchanged since families from the surrounding French Concession pushed their prams under the same towering plane trees a century ago. More modern additions include a rose garden, amusement rides and remote-controlled model boats. In all, a nice old-fashioned retreat that's conveniently central.

### Zhongshan Park

*780 Changning Lu, by Yuyuan Lu, Hongqiao (6210 5806). Metro Zhongshan Park.* **Open** Oct-Mar 6am-6pm daily. Apr-June 5am-6pm daily. July-Sept 5am-7pm daily. **Admission** free. **Map** p240 B4.

This park offers good year-round entertainment for kids. Its spectacular indoor playground, Fun Dazzle (open 9am-5pm) – with tunnels, mazes and slides galore – is a great fallback when it's too cold to wander the park's meandering paths or ride the outdoor carousel, dodgem cars and other amusements.

## Eating & drinking

Shanghai has plenty to appease small, grumbling stomachs – and knives and forks are available more often than not. When it comes to fast-food fixes, Chinese children are just as crazy for McDonald's, KFC and Pizza Hut as their Western peers. If you're visiting the child-friendly sights of Pudong, check out the neighbouring **Super Brand Mall** (168 Lujiazui Xi Lu, by Yincheng Xi Lu, 5049 0668), which houses fast-food standbys, a wide range of Asian fare and a branch of the reliable expat favourite **Blue Frog** (*see p128*). For a snack with a view, you can stroll along the riverside promenade for ice-cream at **Häagen-Dazs** (Binjiang Garden, Lujiazui Xi Lu, by Lujiazui Huan Lu, 5888 0621) or hot pretzels and other German food at the **Paulaner Brauhaus** (2967 Lujiazui Xi Lu, next to the Pudong Shangri-La, 6888 3935).

Back over the river in downtown Shanghai, expat magnet the **Shanghai Centre** (*see p65*) houses familiar chains such as **Tony Roma's** (6279 7129), a barbecue restaurant with a children's menu; **California Pizza Kitchen** (6279 8032), whose children's menu doubles as an activity book; and another branch of **Element Fresh** (*see p105*), purveyor of healthy pan-Asian and European food.

Put your chopstick skills to the test at family-friendly Chinese chains like **Bi Feng Tang** (*see p107*); its English and photo menu makes it easy to assemble a dim sum meal, and the few boat-shaped tables are a hit with kids. Perennial expat favourite **1221** (*see p107*) is used to accommodating families. It has highchairs on hand and a vast English-language menu of basic Chinese dishes.

Many upscale hotels and restaurants cater their mammoth Sunday brunches towards families by offering supervised kids' play clubs and junior menus. The **Westin**'s (*see p31*) brunch is the current favourite among expat families. Its free, nanny-supervised kids' corner has its own menu, cartoons and activities, plus half-price grub for six- to 12-year-olds (free for under-sixes). The **Yi Café** at the **Pudong Shangri-La** (*see p44*) is a huge hit with kids for its extensive dessert bar, with candy floss, ice-cream and takeaway boxes of sweets. The **Novotel Atlantis** (728 Pudong Nan Lu, 5036 6666) and the **Portman Ritz-Carlton** (*see p37*) are worth checking out, as are the panoramic **M on the Bund** (*see p103*), which offers an abbreviated kids' brunch menu, and **Mesa** (*see p118*), which has a nanny-supervised play area.

Elsewhere, the Irish pub **O'Malley's** (*see p129*) has a huge sunny garden with a play area, and baby-changing facilities in the (clean) toilets. **Park 97** (5383 2328), inside Fuxing Park (*see p159*), serves Italian and Japanese fare, as well as a Western-style brunch at the weekend with a kids' table and activity packs. A few tables outside overlook the park, where kids can let off steam while parents linger over coffee. The open-air mall that is **Xintiandi** is usually a big hit with youngsters for its myriad fast-food outlets, cafés and ice-cream.

To put together a picnic, the Gourmet Corner at the **Hilton** (250 Huashan Lu, by Changshu Lu, French Concession, 6248 0000) has ready-made sandwiches, quiches and other bakery items, as does the Treats bakery at the **Westin** (*see p31*). In the basement of **Parkson Department Store**, on the corner of Huaihai Zhong Lu and Shanxi Nan Lu, you'll find a good, cheap supermarket, which also carries a decent variety of baby food and supplies. For a splurge, stop at **City Shopping**, which has a convenient branch in the Shanghai Centre, as well as other locations. The store's wide range of imported food items may light up your taste buds, but it will lighten up your wallet too.

# Shops

Good things really do come in small packages in Shanghai; greatly discounted children's gear goes for a song. Most of the world's biggest children's brands for clothes and shoes, plus some toys, are made in factories outside Shanghai. As a result, you will find samples, overruns, fakes and plenty of the real thing in the wealth of small shops around the French Concession (try Changle Lu for a concentration of kids' clothes stores) and in the markets. English-language children's books can be picked up at the **Foreign Languages Bookstore** (*see p138*) on Fuzhou Lu.

The huge **Decathlon** store (*see p149*) in Pudong is a good place to stock up on cheap trainers and sportswear for children.

### Bao Da Xiang
*685 Nanjing Dong Lu, by Zhejiang Zhong Lu, People's Square (6322 5122). Metro Henan Lu.* **Open** 9.30am-10pm daily. **Credit** MC, V. **Map** p244 K4.

Tucked between department stores on the tourist-packed Nanjing Pedestrian Road, this kids' emporium has an arcade in the basement and five more storeys filled with goods for infants to teens. It sells a mix of imported toys and clothes, great-value Chinese brands and popular Asian names such as Playwell and T.O.T.S.

### Ni Hong Children's Plaza
*10 Puan Lu, by Yanan Dong Lu, Xintiandi (5383 6218/www.shnhgc.com). Metro Huangpi Nan Lu.* **Open** 9.30am-8pm daily. **No credit cards. Map** p244 J6.

There is much buried treasure to be found in this underground children's market. Nearly 200 shops sell cheap, brand-name shoes and clothes for newborns up to eight-year-olds, as well as toys, costumes and accessories. Prices are negotiable, especially when buying multiple items from one store. Enter by the stairway near the corner of Jinling Lu and Puan Lu, by the bus station.

### Orient Shopping Centre
*8 Caoxi Bei Lu, by Zhaojiabang Lu, Xujiahui (6487 0000). Metro Xujiahui.* **Open** 10am-9.30pm Mon-Thur; 10am-10pm Fri-Sun. **Credit** MC, V. **Map** p246 A11.

Dwarfed now by the newer, bigger neighbouring malls of Xujiahui, the Orient remains a top destination for foreign-brand toys and baby supplies. Finds range from Gameboys to strollers to art supplies.

# Services

## Childminding

Temporary childcare can be difficult to arrange at short notice; check with your hotel before you book an evening out. The more upscale hotels will generally offer babysitting services in-house for RMB 40-60 per hour, plus a taxi surcharge if the session lasts past 11pm.

## Health

Shanghai has two special children's hospitals, both good. Generally, some English-speaking staff will be on hand. For more general information on healthcare, *see p220*.

### Children's Hospital of Fudan University
*Opposite Zhongshan Hospital, 183 Fenglin Lu, by Qingzhen Lu, French Concession (5452 4666/www.ch.shmu.edu.cn).* **Credit** AmEx, MC, V. **Map** p246 D11.

### Shanghai Children's Medical Center
*3rd floor, 1678 Dongfang Lu, by Pujian Lu, Pudong (5839 5238/5873 2020 ext 6172/www.scmc.com.cn). Metro Dongfang Lu.* **Credit** MC, V. **Map** p241 G4.

# Film

A promising future and idyllic past are both central to Shanghai's film present.

In April 2006 the outspoken London mayor Ken Livingstone visited China. With him went representatives from FilmLondon, the body responsible for encouraging filmmaking in the UK capital, who were looking to forge links with Chinese filmmakers. With its prestigious Film Academy, whose alumni include virtually every successful native actor, director and cinematographer since 1980, Beijing was the obvious place for FilmLondon to focus its energies. Instead, the UK delegation fobbed off the Chinese capital with a few DVD screenings and opted for a base in Shanghai.

Chances are FilmLondon's decision was influenced by the films themselves. Once upon

Cruise control in **Mission: Impossible III**.

a time Shanghai wasn't just the Paris of the East, it was also its Hollywood. China's first full-length feature was produced in Shanghai in 1923 and by the 1930s the city had a studio system cranking out scores of silent melodramas, acted out by its own pantheon of tragic starlets – none more tragic than **Ruan Lingyu** (*see p164* **The goddess of Shanghai**). The glamour travelled and the city's filmic fame was perpetuated worldwide by such vehicles as 1932's *Shanghai Express* and 1947's *The Lady from Shanghai*, never mind that the two corresponding stars, Marlene Dietrich and Rita Hayworth, barely ventured beyond California. In fact, a quick search on the Internet Movie Database (www.imdb.com) reveals that there are over 130 films with Shanghai in the title, few of which will have been set in the city but all of them wanting a piece of the image.

## ON LOCATION

Everything went dark under the hard-line Communists, but it wasn't that long after they'd gone that Steven Spielberg came to town for what is arguably his best film, *Empire of the Sun* (1987), sections of which were shot on the Bund. Spielberg inspired a trickle of intrepid producers to give Shanghai a go. In 2002 director John Dahl (*The Last Seduction, Red Rock West*) plumped for the Shanghai Film Studio backlot to shoot a large chunk of his World War II epic *The Great Raid*. With its Hollywood-sized budget and enormous crew, the film injected much-needed morale (and money) into the local industry. Perhaps most importantly, the Miramax-backed flick was not set in China at all: Shanghai was a stand-in for 1940s Manila, in the Philippines. 'We made the right choice,' said producer Marty Katz at the time, 'Shanghai just had the right look.' It also had the right look for 2005's *The White Countess*, but then that's hardly surprising given that the Merchant Ivory film is a 1930s period piece, set in Shanghai.

It's not just a colourful past that sells. The giddy vision of the 21st century that is Pudong gave Shanghai the role of anonymous futurescape in Michael Winterbottom's dystopian sci-fi chiller *Code 46* (2003), while the same glittering architecture provided a suitably wow-factor backdrop for Tom Cruise's skyscraper-diving antics in *Mission: Impossible III* (2006).

Local filmmakers are also starting to take to their city. In 1995 director Zhang Yimou (*Hero*) put the city back on the map with his 1930s gangster flick *Shanghai Triad*, starring Gong Li. For a few years after that, you couldn't turn a corner without bumping into film sets peopled by men in trilbies and women in *qipaos* and feather boas. In 2002 Lou Ye's *Suzhou River* brought present-day Shanghai back into fashion. An edgy tale of love gone wrong set on the banks of the city's main waterway, the movie gave Shanghai a new filmic voice. Underground filmmakers – who work under the keen radar of the official censors – are starting to reclaim Shanghai as their own; stories about sex, drugs and disillusionment are back with a vengeance.

And it can all only get better. In 2004 the city's movie credentials received a boost with the opening of the **Shanghai Film Academy**, the city's first dedicated film school since the days of the Cultural Revolution. The aforementioned *The White Countess* was also a notable landmark, being the first English-language European-Chinese co-production (made in partnership with the Shanghai Film Studios) to be shot in Shanghai for decades. The film might have earned Merchant-Ivory some of its worst reviews ever in the US and UK, but its legacy might one day be seen as the start of an exciting East-meets-West filmic friendship.

### GOING TO THE FLICKS

With fewer than 3,000 screens nationwide, China suffers from a serious lack of cinemas. Shanghai is doing its best to compensate, with a multitude of new multiplexes – most of them located in shopping malls – desperately trying to wean the masses off pirate DVDs. With film exhibition now open to foreign investment, Warner Bros, UME, Kodak and Golden Harvest all operate swanky city-centre cinemas.

Film buffs are likely to be disappointed with the limited fare, however. China's movie laws restrict foreign film imports to 20 a year, and most of those are Hollywood blockbusters. Beijing's Film Bureau has a strict 'No Sex Please, We're Chinese' policy, so films are likely to suffer the attentions of the censor's scissors. (In March 2006 the planned world première of *Mission: Impossible III* in Shanghai had to be cancelled because US distributors neglected to get the film to the Chinese censors in time to be reviewed.) Anything remotely controversial is likely to be banned altogether, as was the case with *Memoirs of a Geisha*, which upset state controllers with the casting of two of China's most famous actresses as Japanese prostitutes. Despite the quota, foreign productions dominate at the box office, taking 60 per cent or more of total revenue each year.

Dubbing is the norm for foreign films, though the cinemas listed below regularly play original language versions. It pays to call ahead and check which print will be playing at what time. Most Chinese films are not subtitled in English.

Multiplexes have brought with them international multiplex prices: expect to pay RMB 50 and upwards for a ticket, more during opening week and at the weekend. Online and phone bookings are usually possible – though service in most places is in Chinese only. Credit cards aren't accepted.

Shanghai Film
Art Centre

merchant, it bears a characteristic art deco vertical brick façade and once attracted film-goers from as far away as Japan. It showed mostly American films until the Revolution, at which point both the sign and the films on offer switched to Chinese. During the Cultural Revolution, it became the People's Theatre, and accordingly showed a mix of Soviet, Chinese and North Korean films. Today it screens all manner of movies and in 2006 it hosted the wildly successful Philippines Film Festival.

### Kodak CinemaWorld
*5th floor, Metro City, 1111 Zhaojiabang Lu, by Caoxi Bei Lu, Xujiahui (6426 8181 ext 168/http://cinemaworld.kodak.com/english.htm). Metro Xujiahui.* **Tickets** RMB 50-60. **No credit cards. Map** p246 A11.
One of Shanghai's better-established multiplexes, Kodak does its best to show a decent mix of local and international fare, as well as hosting special film events including Maria's Choice nights (*see above*). English-language films are played almost exclusively in their original version. The cinema's website is in English, providing profiles of forthcoming international releases and listing show times.

### Paradise Theatre (Yongle Gong)
*308 Anfu Lu, by Wukang Lu, French Concession (6742 2606). Metro Changshu Lu.* **Tickets** RMB 40. **No credit cards. Map** p246 B7.
The Paradise is a taste of what cinemas used to be like in Shanghai. A decade ago it was the only venue in town playing undubbed foreign films. Those days are long gone, and the drab-looking entrance, dingy railway waiting-room lobby and cramped screening halls don't bear comparison to the city's newer, shinier multiplexes. But nestled on beautiful tree-lined Anfu Lu, the cinema still has its plus sides: it gets most of the big-hitting foreign movies on or fairly close to their Chinese release date, it's hardly ever sold out and it features some wonderful retro tiling.

### Paradise Warner Cinema City
*6th floor, Grand Gateway, 1 Hongqiao Lu, by Huashan Lu, Xujiahui (6407 6622/www.paradise warner.com/index-en.htm). Metro Xujiahui.* **Tickets** RMB 50-60. **No credit cards. Map** p246 A11.
Warner Bros' first foray into China looks and feels like a top-notch multiplex. Nestled on the sixth floor of a mall, it's rapidly gaining popularity, with even late-night screenings often close to full. All the trimmings are here: thick carpets, lots of screens, popcorn by the bucketful and foreign films screened alternately in English and dubbed Mandarin. Paradise was also the first cinema in China to install a digital projector. Check the website for details.

### Shanghai Film Art Centre
*160 Xinhua Lu, by Huaihai Xi Lu, Changning (6281 7017). Metro Xujiahui.* **Tickets** RMB 50-60. **No credit cards. Map** p246 A9.
About as close to an arts cinema as you'll get in this city, the Film Art Centre is home to most of the major screenings during the Shanghai International Film

## FILM FESTIVAL
In business since 1993, the **Shanghai International Film Festival** (SIFF; information: 11th floor, STV Mansions, 298 Weihai Lu, Jingan, 6253 7115, www.siff.com, mid-late June) is China's only recognised film festival, and it usually attracts a few stars. The offerings have become increasingly local and of unpredictable quality in recent years, but it's worth noting that films shown during SIFF are outside the official import quota and thus largely uncut by the censors.

## Cinemas

For the more adventurous programming, you'll have to look beyond the licensed cinema chains. The **Canadian Consulate** (6279 8400) and **German Consulate** (6391 2068 ext 602) both organise regular screenings of films from, unsurprisingly, Canada and Germany; **Ciné-Club de l'Alliance** (6357 5388) does the same for Francophiles. For underground local (often subtitled) and international cinema, check out **DDM warehouse** (*see p168*) and **Arch** (*see p128*). **Maria's Choice** is a film club that meets monthly to watch screenings of Chinese movies subtitled in English; email mariaschoice-subscribe@topica.com to get on the mailing list.

### Cathay Theatre
*870 Huaihai Zhong Lu, by Maoming Nan Lu, French Concession (5404 0415/www.guotaifilm.com). Metro Shanxi Nan Lu.* **Tickets** RMB 15-70. **No credit cards. Map** p247 F7.
Known in Chinese as the Guotai, the Cathay has a long and rich history. Built in 1930 by a Cantonese

Arts & Entertainment

# The goddess of Shanghai

The late 1920s and early 1930s were the Golden Age of Chinese cinema. Films mirrored the social mores of the time – heroes were poor but honourable, villains were rich and ruthless. The leading studio at the time was Ming Xing, and it was to its call for auditions, advertised in a newspaper in 1926, that a maid's daughter named Ruan Lingyu responded. By the time of her suicide less than ten years later, she had starred in 29 silent films and become the greatest Chinese film star of her day.

In truth, Ruan did not hit her straps until 1931, by which time she was under contract to Lianhua. That year she starred in four films, with *Lian'ai Yu Yiwu* (*Love and Duty*) standing out for her portrayal of a woman at different stages of her life, from a young girl through to an old lady. Her next milestone was *Sange Modeng Nuxing* (*Three Modern Women*), a film within a film, which, with its left-wing tendencies, is seen as the forerunner to a wave of Chinese films glorifying the workers' struggle. In 1934 she starred in perhaps her most famous film, *Shennü* (*The Goddess*), where she gave a sympathetic performance as a prostitute single-handedly raising her young son. By this time Ruan's private life, as well as her work

on screen, was receiving vitriolic attention from the so-called 'mosquito press', many of whom regarded actresses as little better than prostitutes.

Ruan had been dogged by the story of her tumultuous relationship with Zhang Damin, an inveterate gambler whom she met before becoming a star. Their ongoing lawsuit became a source of malicious press coverage that revealed intimate details of Ruan's private life. Faced with this and other problems, on the night of 7 March 1935 Ruan penned a note addressed 'To Society' in which she wrote that 'Gossip is a fearful thing'. She then poured the contents of three bottles of sleeping pills into a bowl of rice porridge, which she ate. Ruan Lingyu was dead at the age of 24. Her death, announced the next day, made the front page of every Shanghai newspaper. After lying in state for five days her funeral procession, which stretched over ten miles, brought parts of Shanghai to a standstill. Mourners lining the street numbered more than at Rudolph Valentino's funeral in Hollywood: *Variety* put the number at 300,000. They watched in silence as the goddess of Shanghai slipped from their view forever.

---

Festival (*see p163*) in June, when it gets its fair share of VIPs. Film buffs should enjoy its retro-styled lobby, featuring a shop that stocks Chinese-language film books as well as, bizarrely, irons. All the latest films, local and foreign, are screened here. **Photo** *p162*.

## UME International Cineplex

*5th floor, No.6, Lane 123, Xingye Lu, by Madang Lu, Xintiandi (6384 1122 ext 807). Metro Huangpi Nan Lu.* **Tickets** RMB 50-60. **No credit cards.** **Map** p248 H8.

One of Shanghai's newest multiplexes, UME is also located in one of its trendiest areas, Xintiandi, fitting in perfectly among the hip boutiques, bars and nightclubs. With mainly moneyed local and international customers, the cinema plays foreign films in their original versions, as well as screening most current Chinese films.

# Galleries

Highly commercial but occasionally cutting-edge,
the Shanghai art scene is booming.

Artist Ji Wenyu's take on city life, displayed at **ShanghART**. *See p167.*

Though certainly well-meaning, the fanfare in the Western press about Shanghai's art scene has been mostly to its detriment. Mediocre artists have been raised on to pedestals and greedily snapped up by collectors. These first movers, supported by prominent galleries such as **ShanghART** and **Shanghai Gallery of Art**, have tended to obscure some of the more interesting art the city has to offer.

The commercial art market has also created a distorted output, where works reflect the desires of Western collectors rather than Chinese artists. Political Pop – painting which uses Cultural Revolution iconography – is a case in point. The ironic use of Communist icons expresses a certain rebel spirit, a retro-commie chic, that is irresistible to Western collectors, who make up close to 90 per cent of buyers.

Shanghai is a brand-conscious city and the signature on the canvas is often more important than the painting itself. It's common to see the same names – Xue Song, Ding Yi, Zhou Chunya – on the walls of a number of galleries. Very few exhibitions are organised around coherent creative themes.

But the fact that Shanghai's art scene is so market-oriented is no great surprise. With little government support, the scene was built brick by brick by small galleries such as **Eastlink** and **ShanghART**. They are now enjoying the fruits of their labour, with artists selling canvases for tens of thousands of dollars.

These founding galleries have inspired hordes of imitators, and even the government has begun to take notice. It not only halted its plans to demolish **Moganshan Lu**, an alternative art area (*see p166*), but also

# Moganshan Lu

New York has its Meatpacking District and London has Hoxton: Shanghai has Moganshan Lu. In a grim industrial park beside the fetid Suzhou Creek, Moganshan's chill warehouses offer a solution to the high rents and cramped spaces faced by artists elsewhere in the city. So it's here that Shanghai's underground art scene began – and is now blossoming.

The artists moved in towards the end of the 1990s and about 35 now have studios in the area. They've gradually been joined by a handful of major galleries (some of which are listed below). These spaces used to host some of the most edgy art in the city but are increasingly being filled with galleries of a more commercial bent.

Places like **DDM warehouse** (see p168) and the **Museum of Contemporary Art Shanghai** (see p60) are starting to eclipse Moganshan Lu as sources of innovation. Nonetheless, Moganshan still offers one-stop shopping for art initiates, and its recently opened local design boutiques, art deco furniture store and cafés bring added value. Stroll through its newly renovated gates and pop into **Bandu Music** (see p179), a shop that sells Chinese music and hosts free concerts every Saturday at 8pm.

The easiest way to get to Moganshan Lu, which is just north of the Jade Buddha gave it a facelift; other creative centres and museums have been established too.

Since 2002, Shanghai has gained four new art museums – **Doland: Shanghai Duolun Museum of Modern Art** (see p97), **Zendai Museum of Modern Art** (see p95), **Museum of Contemporary Art Shanghai** (MOCA; see p60) and **Zhu Qizhan Art Museum** (see p179) – and some 30 new commercial galleries. They may not all be world-class institutions, but they have nonetheless expanded Shanghai's artistic horizons dramatically.

International exhibitions are also on the rise. In 2005/6 Shanghai hosted Picasso, Basquiat and Warhol exhibitions, with Keith Haring on the horizon for late 2006. The quality of locally curated exhibitions has also improved. Recent highlights include the 'New Rise of Painting', an excellent show of young Chinese painters at the Zendai Museum, and 'Shanghai Apartments', Hu Yang's photographic take on the city's increasing social stratification.

Shanghai's photography scene is showing promise, with three solid galleries (**Art Sea**, **epSITE** and **Aura**) and an array of budding photographers to fill them. Video art ('DV art'), though often shoddy, is also finding space in the Duolun, BizArt and MoCA. A glance around the city may indicate the contrary, but Shanghai is developing a growing respect for design. Duolun kicked off 2006 with 'Shanghai Cool', a pan-Asian design show, followed by 'Get It Louder', curated by Jiji, Shanghai's design darling. Then there was MVRDV (Shanghai Gallery of Art), a conceptual architecture exhibition; Swiss Design Now (MoCA); and Droog Design from the Netherlands at **Bund 18 Creative Centre** (4F Zhongshan Dong Yi Lu, by Nanjing Dong Lu, the Bund, 6323 7066 ext 3202, www.bund 18.com), which holds intermittent shows in its stylish space.

Temple, is by taxi. It's best to visit in the afternoon and, given the erratic hours of many of these places, it's also worth calling ahead.

## Art Sea Studio & Gallery

*2nd floor, Building 9, 50 Moganshan Lu, by Aomen Lu, Jingan (6227 8380). Metro Xinzha Lu, then taxi.* **Open** 10am-6pm daily. **Map** p242 D1.
Dvir Bar-Gal, an Israeli photojournalist and documentary maker, created this gallery as a platform for cutting-edge photography and his shows rarely disappoint.

## BizArt

*4th floor, Building 7, 50 Moganshan Lu, by Aomen Lu, Jingan (6277 5358/www. biz-art.com). Metro Xinzha Lu, then taxi.* **Open** 11am-6pm Mon-Fri. **Map** p242 D1.
Despite the corporate moniker, BizArt has built a strong reputation for conceptual art since opening in 1998. In 2005 it staged a 'courier' exhibition, in which interested parties could 'dial an artwork' and have it delivered to their home complete with artistic explanation from the courier. It has a strong residency programme and often stages workshops and installation.

## Eastlink

*5th floor, Building 6, 50 Moganshan Lu, by Aomen Lu, Jingan (6276 9932/www.eastlink gallery.com). Metro Xinzha Lu, then taxi.* **Open** 10am-6pm daily. **Map** p242 D1.

Founded by a local returnee, who lived 12 years in Sydney, Eastlink used to be the most avant-garde of the city's galleries (with animal carcasses and self-mutilation themes in the early days) but it has gone rather quiet of late. The exhibitions, though a little haphazard, usually provide something of interest.

## H Space

*Building 18, 50 Moganshan Lu, by Aomen Lu, Jingan (6359 3923). Metro Xinzha Lu, then taxi.* **Open** 1-6pm daily. **Map** p242 D1.
ShanghART's revolving exhibition space features reliable shows from some key artists on the Shanghai scene.

## ShanghART

*Building 16, 50 Moganshan Lu, by Aomen Lu, Jingan (6359 3923/http://china.shangh artgallery.com). Metro Xinzha Lu, then taxi.* **Open** 10am-6pm daily. **Map** p242 D1.
Lorenz Helbling, Shanghai's Swiss godfather of contemporary art, founded ShanghART in 1995. His warehouse is the closest thing Shanghai has to a permanent collection of contemporary Chinese art. It has an excellent website, including some 3,000 images of its stable of artists. Ask the staff to show you some of Ji Wenyu's work (*pictured p165*); his gaudy painting, composed of adverts and logos, leaves no question about his take on Shanghai's consumer culture.

Though still dominated by commercially successful painters, Shanghai's art scene is finally beginning to mature. Artists such as Tang Maohong and Yang Yong are exploring new styles and concepts and, most importantly, they are beginning to challenge society.

For more traditional collections of art visit the **Shanghai Art Museum** (*see p60*) at People's Square and the **Doulun** (*see p97*) in Hongkou. For details of what's on where, check the listings in *that's Shanghai* (www.thatssh.com), *City Weekend* and *SH* magazine.

# Galleries

## Art Scene China

*No.8, Lane 37, Fuxing Xi Lu, by Wulumuqi Zhong Lu, French Concession (6437 0631/www.art scenechina.com). Metro Changshu Lu.* **Open** 10am-6.30pm Tue-Sun. **Map** p246 C8.

Housed in a beautiful 1930s villa, this gallery hosts regular exhibitions by the 25 or more Chinese artists it represents. Their work is almost uniformly figurative and safe – ensuring that openings are hugely popular with the expat crowd.
**Other locations**: Art Scene Warehouse, 2F Building 4, 50 Moganshan Lu, by Aomen Lu, Jingan (6277 4940/www.artscenewarehouse.com).

## Aura Gallery

*5th floor, 713 Dongdaming Lu, by Gaoyang Lu, Hongkou (6595 0901/www.aura-art.com).* **Open** 10am-6pm Tue-Sun.
Founded in 2000 by art buff William Zhang, Aura majors in young artists born in the 1960s and '70s (the YCAs, as it were). The emphasis is on photography, from Han Lei's Chinese ink brush-style creations to Hong Lei's meditations on the degradation of traditional Chinese culture. The gallery itself is housed in 700sq m (7,500sq ft) of warehouse space on the banks of the Huangpu River; it's a five-minute taxi ride from the Peace Hotel.

### DDM warehouse

*3rd floor, 713 Dongdaming Lu, by Gaoyang Lu,*
*Hongkou (3501 3212/www.ddmwarehouse.cn).*
**Open** 11am-7pm Tue-Sat.

Two floors below Aura (*see p167*) is the lovably
grungy DDM, which hosts exhibitions of contemporary paintings, photography, video art and sculpture; past shows have included German mixed
media artist Horn$leth and LED screen artist Teddy
Lo. The art displays are supplemented with an innovative programme of cultural events, including poet-
ry readings, electronic music and performance art
festivals. The gallery site lacks polish and some
exhibitions are lacklustre, but for certain art lovers
this only adds to the 'underground' appeal.

### epSITE

*B/1, Benetton Building, 651 Huaihai Zhong Lu,*
*by Sinan Lu, French Concession (5306 7711/*
*www.epsom.com). Metro Shanxi Nan Lu.* **Open**
10am-9pm daily. **Map** p247 G7.

EpSITE hosts many shows by local photojournal-
ists and documentary photographers, providing a
panorama of life in China.

### Room With a View

*12th floor, 479 Nanjing Dong Lu, by Fujian Lu, the*
*Bund (6352 0256/www.topart.cn). Metro Henan Lu.*
**Open** 3-10.30pm daily. **Map** p244 K4.

RWV is a bar (a weird combination of frosted glass,
black leather and corrugated iron) with a small
exhibition space attached. Exhibitions are plentiful but unpredictable, as the space is often given to
young and/or emerging artists. Nonetheless, director Holly Zhao has created a wonderfully inclusive
atmosphere, which attracts both Chinese and
foreign visitors.

### Shanghai Gallery of Art

*3rd floor, Three on the Bund, 3 Zhongshan Dong*
*Yi Lu, by Guangdong Lu, the Bund (6321 5757/*
*www.threeonthebund.com). Metro Henan Lu.*
**Open** 11am-11pm daily. **Map** p245 M5.

The city's ritziest gallery, SGA is part of the Three
on the Bund complex and so shares lodgings with
the likes of Armani and celeb chef eaterie Jean-
Georges (*see p102*). It boasts 1,000sq m (10,750sq ft)
of floor space and a staggering ziggurat-like atrium
designed by Brit architect Michael Graves. The
policy seems to be to roll out the 'greatest hits' of
contemporary Chinese art – those who are well
established, but not necessarily cutting-edge.

### Shanghai Sculpture Space

*570 Huaihai Xi Lu, by Hongqiao Lu,*
*Xujiahui (6280 5629). Metro Hongqiao Lu.*
**Open** 10am-4pm Tue-Sun.

This huge site – a beautifully converted steel factory – opened in late 2005 with a much-visited
inaugural show ('Sculpture a Century') featuring
the cream of Chinese sculpture in the 20th century. Though much of the space is taken up by
bronze statues of political luminaries, at least
half is given over to young, adventurous sculptors

such as Yu Xiaoping, who built a three-dimen-
sional mountain landscape into a massive take-out
food container.

### Unique Hill Studio

*Room 301, Tian Long Apartments, 907 Tianyaoqiao*
*Lu, by Zhongshan Nan Er Lu, Xujiahui (5410 4815).*
*Metro Shanghai Indoor Stadium.* **Open** 10am-5pm
Tue-Sun.

Unique Hill is a must-see for those with an interest
in Shanghai's colonial era. It specialises in sleek and
sexy advertisements from the 1920s and '30s. These
designs, known as cigarette card posters, feature
Chinese women clad in *qipaos* with spit curls, wan
eyes and smoky smiles. Along with the posters, it
also hosts historical photography exhibitions.

## Festivals & events

### Shanghai Art Fair

*Shanghai Mart, 99 Xingyi Lu, by Loushanguan Lu,*
*Hongqiao (6225 4977/www.cnarts.net/sartfair).*
**Date** Nov. **Admission** RMB 30.

This is the biggest art fair in Asia, typically featuring some 600 exhibiting galleries from China and the
rest of the world, from traditional to contemporary.
It's no Art Basel, but it's a good place to pick up a
Salvador Dali lithograph or a Picasso print. Part of
the Shanghai International Arts Festival.

### Shanghai Biennale

*Shanghai Art Museum, 325 Nanjing Xi Lu,*
*People's Square (6327 2829/www.shanghai*
*biennial.cn). Metro People's Square.* **Date** Sept,
Nov (even yrs). **Admission** RMB 20. **Map** p244 H5.

The Shanghai Biennale launched in 1996 but it
wasn't until 2000 that international artists were invited. The 2004 edition featured Yoko Ono, Bill Viola
and Cindy Sherman, alongside local artists such as
Xu Zhen, Jin Shan and Yang Fudong. The 2006
Biennale, with three simultaneous exhibitions in
Singapore, Gwangju and Shanghai, will include fewer
heavyweights to make a last time but Matthew Barney is
scheduled to make a long-awaited appearance. Also
on the bill are Paul de Marinis and Rebecca
Cummings with their Light Rain (a kind of musical
sprinkler that emits a rainbow of fine vapour), and
Dutch artist Theo Jansen, who will contribute his
massive wooden animals powered by wind.

### Shanghai Spring Art Salon

*Shanghai Mart, 99 Xingyi Lu, by Loushanguan Lu,*
*Hongqiao (6217 2011/www.cnarts.net/artsalon).*
**Date** 5 days May. **Admission** RMB 25.

Launched in 2003, the Spring Art Salon is a five-day
event that in its first year brought together works
by nearly 200 Chinese and German artists under the
banner 'Kann man Seele sehen' ('Is the soul visible').
Despite that bit of portentousness, the event is
unashamedly populist with crowd-pulling names
and even a kids' salon. In 2006 it featured a series of
sculptures by Dali, which was seen by some as an
attempt to retrieve credibility.

# Gay & Lesbian

From a Communist closet big enough for 15 million to
My Big Gay Asian Wedding?

**Shanghai Studio**. *See p172.*

While life for China's gay and lesbian
community still isn't easy (nor particularly
visible), social norms are evolving quickly.
The state media are becoming increasingly
daring, approaching the sensitive topic of
homosexuality in a less derogatory – and more
challenging – way. Newspapers, magazines
and TV documentaries are saying that it's
OK to be gay, and the long-held stance of
complete censorship of homosexual love
is beginning to be disputed on the front
pages. Fudan University even offers an
oversubscribed course in gay studies. All
this a mere five years since homosexuality
was removed from the national list of mental
disorders in China, and only nine years since
sodomy was decriminalised.

The sudden pinkish hue descending on
Red China may have set gay tongues wagging,
but equality is still a very long way off. The
press – though testing the boundaries –
remains heavily restricted in its portrayal of
homosexual lifestyles. There are no gay and
lesbian support groups, and Pride marches

are banned. (Then again, marches of all kinds
are banned here.) There are no laws to protect
China's homosexuals from discrimination and,
as a result, secrecy is the rule rather than the
exception. Particularly in the countryside, most
gays will end up married for fear of family
rejection and discrimination in the workplace.
In Shanghai you can see the poorer gay guys
around People's Square, and at the seedier
joints, desperately flogging their sex appeal.

Although caution is still recommended,
Shanghai is one of the best places to be gay in
China, as tolerance is relatively high. Shanghai
has long been an international city, and is more
open-minded as a result. The current economic
and cultural renaissance in Shanghai has made
it a sponge for those attracted to a Western
lifestyle – and the freedoms that come with
it. There is a multitude of bars, clubs and
saunas to suit every gay taste, and gay
establishments are now seldom 'closed for
renovations' by the local officials. While the
bars may seem primitive – and a little tame –
to Westerners, Shanghai has some of the

# The queer dynasties

It's easy to forget that homosexuals weren't persecuted in China before the advent of Communism – in fact, there is a very long and open history of Chinese yang-yang relationships. On formation of the People's Republic in 1949, however, homosexuality was condemned as contributing to the 'mouldering [sic] lifestyle of capitalism' and during the Cultural Revolution gays and lesbians were actively persecuted. They were not only publicly criticised, but also received jail sentences for fictional crimes.

In China's long and colourful history, more than a few major episodes are shaded pink. Homosexual love has been portrayed extensively in Chinese art – many explicit paintings and prints survived the Cultural Revolution – and literature. Indeed, 19th-century Chinese attitudes to sexual behaviour shocked the early European settlers. While Christianity denounced homosexuality as a sin, this was never the case with Taoism and Confucianism, China's major religions.

In ancient times the 'Yellow Emperor' Huang Di (2697-2597 BC), the disputed founder of Chinese culture, was thought to have kept male lovers. More widely acknowledged, and testified to in official literature from the period, is the series of openly bisexual emperors who ruled over two centuries of the Han Dynasty. Emperor Ai (*pictured left*), for instance, was evidently enamoured of his male concubine, Dong Xian. One night, while he slumbered in the arms of his lover, Dong Xian lay on the emperor's sleeve. Emperor Ai needed to get up – things to do, people to see – but, not wanting to wake his lover, cut his sleeve to free himself from the embrace. Terribly sweet… if a little costly in tailoring bills. This story created the phrase *duanxiu* ('the cut sleeve'), which is a term meaning gay love, now commonly known as 'the passion of the cut sleeve'.

Still more famous is the earlier story of Duke Ling of Wei and his handsome male favourite Mi Zixia. One fine day, when they were in an orchard, Mi Zixia was so struck by the sweetness of a peach that he insisted on giving the other half to the duke. The phrase 'to be fond of the leftover peach' became a euphemism for same-sex love.

Nowadays, the preferred slang term for homosexuals is *tongzhi*, while *tongxinglian* is the formal term meaning same-sex relations.

friendliest and most excitable gays in the world, celebrating their new-found freedoms each and every night.

Although rejected by Congress twice, scholars claim that gay marriage is a real possibility in China, on account of the lack of religious opposition. Who knows if, in years to come, Shanghai could become the Asian mecca for big pink weddings? In the meantime, China's gays are fighting a quiet revolution, mainly involving tight tops and disco-pop.

## OUT AND ABOUT

Aside from bars and clubs, there are plenty of other venues that draw a significant gay crowd. The city's bathhouses, for example, are actually used for bathing, but are also typically segregated. Such an all-male, nearly nude and literally steamy scenario makes for a charged atmosphere. Fumblings and sexual play are no-nos, but there's no ban on looking. In a similar vein, there are certain gyms that are notoriously cruisey, including **Ambassy Club** (1500 Huaihai Zhong Lu, 4437 9800), **MegaFit** (398 Huaihai Zhong Lu, 5383 2252) and **Total Fitness** (*see p196*).

Given that Lady Shanghai is more a culinary queen than a boozer, much gay socialising goes on over food. There are a handful of dining spots that fall under the heading gay-friendly, including **Kevin's Bar & Restaurant** (No.4, Lane 946, Changle Lu, French Concession, 6248

Arts & Entertainment

8985) and **Canteen** (407 Dagu Lu, French Concession, 6327 1227), which is opposite the current hottest gay club **Home&Bar** (*see p172*). Other gay-friendly eateries are **Arch** (*see p128*), **KABB** (*see p109*), **M on the Bund** (*see p103*) and **Simply Thai** (*see p120*). Some of these places are gay-owned, some just have cute staff – either way, you'll find a significant gay clientele there.

### INFORMATION

All press is heavily censored and controlled, pushing gay groups and information exchange on to the internet. Nonetheless, several **magazines** on the market, while not explicitly marketed as gay, feature a remarkable number of photos of men with their clothes off. Most notable of these are *Mensbox* and *Men's Style*.

Adult-rated **www.gaychina.com** is a bulletin-board site with several forums for personals, photos and general postings; it has an English portal. The Chinese portal is more heavily visited. Expect plenty of ads from college students offering 'companionship' in exchange for financial aid. South-east Asia's largest portal for its gay community, **www.fridae.com**, has member profiles in English for those looking to connect before or during a visit to Shanghai. Highly recommended is **www.utopia-asia. com**, which is one of the most current and useful gay Asia resources; from the navigator bar choose China, then Shanghai for the latest online news and gossip. It is also a good place to find out where you can meet up with lesbian social and clubbing groups.

The international gay forum site **www.gay.com** includes a Shanghai chat room frequented by Chinese and the city's gay expats. Gay dating site **www.gaydar.co.uk** allows members to seek fellow members listed as local to China or those travelling in the area.

### Bars & clubs

The Shanghai scene may seem to have few nightspots in comparison to other world cities, but 2006 saw a huge expansion, with several renovations and openings, and it's easy to forget that ten years ago there was nothing. Most bars are a pleasing mix of Chinese, Western and Asian expats, plus, of course, the ever-present rent boys. It's a tight-knit crowd and newcomers will receive plenty of curious attention. There are a few mixed bars in town, but discretion is advised – if you fancy a gay night out, it's best to stick to the gay places. Lesbian haunts are few and far between, with some bars having disappeared. The scene is very eclectic, though, with girls more than welcome at predominantly male gay bars.

In recent years, Shanghai has enjoyed the arrival of several big gay party nights, which sweep into town roughly once a month: **Club Deep** (*see below*) has become a permanent fixture and another night is still going strong. If you're lucky enough to be here at the right time, then make these nights a priority– you'll get to enjoy go-go dancing hotties, drag acts and big-name DJs. To check out the dates, go to www.godshanghai.com.

### Bo Bo

*307 Midst, Bugaoyuan Club, Shanxi Nan Lu, by Jianguo Lu, French Concession (6471 2887). Metro Shanxi Nan Lu.* **Open** 7pm-2am daily. **Admission** free. **No credit cards. Map** p247 F10.
If you think the Shanghai gay scene is too small for cliques, think again: Bo Bo is a bear bar – or should that be a panda bar? Relocated in 2005 from Suzhou Creek, this funky little bar, with giant bear paws on the walls, has a mix of high stools and comfy sofas, and boasts an impressive dancefloor complete with bear cage. Bo Bo-goers are mainly bears and bear hunters, but everyone is warmly welcomed. Music is eclectic, jumping from 1960s-style retro Chinese pop to the latest Western dance tunes. The bar is located in a residential complex; walk past the security guard at 307 Shanxi Lu, cross the lake bridge, enter the glass building, descend the stairs and head behind the black curtain. Then belly up to the bar and discover your inner panda.

### Club Deep

*1649 Nanjing Xi Lu, by Huashan Lu, inside Jingan Park, Jingan (6248 7034/www.clubdeep.cn). Metro Jingan.* **Open** 8pm-late Tue-Sun. **Admission** free. **No credit cards. Map** p242 C6.
The R & G circuit parties were some of the biggest events of the gay nightlife calendar, and the organisers quickly realised they were on to a good thing. In June 2006 R & G became a permanent part of Shanghai's growing gay club scene, with Club Deep opening in Jin An Park. Subtle doesn't come easily to Club Deep, with its male model fashion shows and 'manhunt'-themed nights – and the Shanghai scene is all the better for it. The lush decor comprises red lanterns, long white sofas and dark honeycomb screens; it is new, sleek and gives Home&Bar (*see p172*) a run for its money. The competition for gay clientele just stepped up a gear.

### Eddy's

*1877 Huaihai Zhong Lu, by Tianping Lu, French Concession (6282 0521/www.eddys-bar.com). Metro Hengshan Lu.* **Open** 8pm-3am daily. **Admission** free. **No credit cards. Map** p246 A9.
Eddy's has been the gay venue of choice in Shanghai for more than ten years. From its humble beginnings as the first gay bar in town, it has changed location no fewer than six times on the way to becoming the stylish and bold gay mecca you see today. The red under-lit bar, high stools and Chinese-style interiors are impressive, but it is the atmosphere that is the

real draw here. The lively vibe is in no small part due to the ever-present Eddy, who goes a long way to making sure everyone is happy, and barman Wayne's legendary cocktails (RMB 50). You can't fail to make friends here, and lesbians are just as welcome as the boys.

### Frangipani Bar & Café
*399 Dagu Lu, by Shimen Yi Lu, Jingan (5375 0084). Metro Shimen Yi Lu.* **Open** 6pm-late daily. **Admission** free. **No credit cards. Map** p243 G6.
Frangipani, new in 2006, is a mixture of bar and café that's situated right in the city centre. The bar is fresh and relaxed, offering light snacks and booze to gay expats and visitors alike. There's plenty of room and the industrial feel, exposed concrete and long bar create something of a space-age vibe. Mix this with smiling service from the waiters and dice-playing upstairs, and the Frangipani experience sits somewhere between a futuristic funky hangout and a friendly local.

### Home&Bar
*18 Gaolan Lu, by Ruijin Er Lu, French Concession (7002 102 1038/www.barhome.com). Metro Shanxi Nan Lu.* **Open** 9pm-2am Wed-Thur, Sun; 9pm-4am Fri, Sat. **Admission** RMB 25 Fri; RMB 30 Sat. **Credit** MC, V. **Map** p247 F8.
In an unlikely location next to a Russian Orthodox church, Home&Bar is Shanghai's most popular gay club, and for good reason. The boys (and some girls) get to throw themselves into great dance music, with their chests proudly displayed. The alcohol is cheap both in price and quality: RMB 40 will get you a spirit and mixer, and a monster hangover to boot. At the time of writing, the club was undergoing renovation and was due to reopen in July 2006 with a much-needed bigger dancefloor and a separate lounge bar. Hopefully, the expansion won't mean losing the small garden, one of the only places in Shanghai where you can sit on the grass.

### Hunter Bar
*86-90 Nanyang Lu, by Xikang Lu, Jingan (6258 1438). Metro Jingan Temple or Shimen Yi Lu.* **Open** 8pm-2am daily. **Admission** free. **No credit cards. Map** p243 E4/5.
What used to pitch itself as the gay, blue-collar veterans' club, with wooden furniture and neon signs, finally relented to the gay Shanghai hipsters a year ago. Still in the same location, hidden behind Nanjing Lu's Plaza 66 (*see p133*) in a quiet lane off Xikang Lu, the bar is now a shiny, blue-lit, trendy hangout, popular with a younger but still mainly Chinese crowd. The latest films can often be seen showing at the end of the bar, while the local boys drink themselves into a frenzy.

### Shanghai Studio
*No.4, 1950 Huaihai Zhong Lu, by Xingguo Lu, French Concession (6283 1043/www.shanghai-studio.com). Metro Hengshan Lu.* **Open** 9pm-2am Tue-Sun. **Admission** free. **No credit cards. Map** p246 A9.

Newcomer Shanghai Studio hadn't yet found its feet as we went to press, but it was showing promise. The entrance is grand – take the large red doorway at the back of the building and follow art-filled corridors until you reach the basement. With several darkish rooms leading off from the main bar, including a dancefloor, Shanghai Studio has something of a rabbit warren feel about it. While limiting ogling opportunities, the layout does set it apart from other bars on the scene, as does the refreshingly chilled house music played here in the early evening.

### Transit Lounge
*19G, No.2, 1950 Huaihai Zhong Lu, French Concession (1312 069 8426 mobile). Metro Hengshan Lu.* **Open** 8pm-2am daily. **Admission** free. **No credit cards. Map** p246 A9.
Housed in the same complex as Shanghai Studio, the Transit Lounge isn't so much a bar as manager Masa's front room. In fact, that's literally what it is. Knock at 19G and you'll be warmly welcomed into a cosy living room, with the barman (also Masa) operating from the kitchen. Attracting mainly Japanese, this is a new and totally different addition to what is becoming Shanghai's unofficial gay quarter.

## Saunas & massage

### Lianbang
*228 Zhizaoju Lu, by Xietu Lu, Xintiandi (6312 5567).* **Open** 24hrs daily. **Admission** RMB 40. **No credit cards. Map** p248 J10.
China has a tradition of public bathhouses but Lianbang goes well beyond the naked camaraderie of the average local scrubbing spot. Look for the red door, hidden down an alley that serves as entrance to a neighbouring hotel and massage complex. Pay the admission (RMB 40 gives you access to all floors) and switch your shoes for slippers, then you can explore the three floors of dingy corridors and rooms filled with languid pyjama-clad locals of all ages lounging, smoking, napping or getting it on. The sauna attracts few foreigners, so your every move will be scrutinised, and be mindful that you need to keep your jammies on once you're out of the bath.

### Mr Muscle Massage
*375 Xinfeng Lu, by Xikang Lu, Jingan (6227 7419/ salspash@yahoo.com.cn). Metro Jingan Temple.* **Open** noon-2am daily. **Treatments** *Oil massage* RMB 169/hr. **Credit** AmEx, DC, MC, V. **Map** p242 D2.
Just to remove any doubt that these boys are ripped, the comparatively stylish foyer includes weight-lifting equipment. Though the name suggests an oasis of Adonis-like masseurs, this isn't exactly Miami Beach – but the boys are certainly tall and strong. As well as the usual massages on offer, there are many beauty treatments on offer, including footbaths (RMB 50 for 1hr) and facials (RMB 99). Staff are professional and, though a bit further out of the centre of town, Mr Muscle Massage is much cleaner than the older and more established massage centres.

# Mind & Body

Luxe day spas are the current vogue, but Chinese medics have been massaging for millennia.

**Magpie**. See p175.

Shanghai's sumptuous spas and traditional therapies are the perfect antidote to the city's pollutants and partying ways. Right up there with streetside dumplings and tailor-made clothes, thorough and affordable massage is one of the great privileges of life in Shanghai. From the worn divans of the ubiquitous neighbourhood foot massage joints to decadent private suites in world-class urban day spas, there are treatments to suit all preferences and budgets. And with many places open until the early hours of the morning, it's very Shanghai to unwind on the massage table after a hectic day at work or even a night on the town.

The pampering scene may be taking off right now, but none of this is particularly new. Medical massage (*tuina*, meaning 'push' or 'grasp'), used in traditional medical practice for a range of ailments from chronic pain to allergies, has at least a 2,000-year history in China. *Tuina* works by addressing the *qi*, or internal energy, of the patient to balance their overall state of health.

The first of Shanghai's new wave of massage centres opened in the late 1990s, kicking off with reflexology studios and the ingenious concept of **blind massage** (*see p176*). Reflexology involves massaging specific regions of the feet that are believed to correspond to particular organs or body systems. Be warned: if you have a low pain threshold, you should make it abundantly clear.

For relaxation and fun, nothing beats the mid-market retreats, which still represent a bargain compared to what you could expect to pay for similar treatment in the West. These tranquil urban oases with exotic Asian design details, silk pyjamas and chill-out music usually provide a simple menu of massages, including Chinese massage, which focuses on rubbing and rolling hands over muscles from neck to toes and sometimes the scalp and face, and Japanese shiatsu, which is usually carried out on a floor mat with the emphasis on finger, palm and elbow pressure.

The latest boom in the spa market is in the ultra-chic, brand-name day spas, many of which are located in five-star hotels. International heavyweights like **Evian** (*see p176*), **L'Institut de Guerlain** (*see 177*) and **Banyan Tree** (*see p176*) have chosen Shanghai for their China flagships and offer the very best in holistic treatments and beauty care using high-tech equipment and products – at equally high-end prices.

*Tuina* is still actively practised in clinics and hospitals. Many places in Shanghai offer this kind of traditional treatment, as well as acupressure (*see p174* **Under pressure**), acupuncture, *qigong* (an ancient practice using movement, meditation and breathing to increase the flow of *qi* in the body) and other Chinese therapies.

## Chinese medicine

Traditional Chinese medicine (TCM) is rooted in ideas of balance and harmony. In Chinese cosmology, creation is thought to be born from the marriage of two polar principles: yin and yang. **Yang** represents active, hot and bright; **yin** represents things that are passive, cold or

# Under pressure

Needling, scraping, bear testicles – traditional Chinese medicine isn't for the faint-hearted. However, acupressure – one of its earliest forms – offers a relatively painless, non-invasive therapy with a 5,000-year track record. It is an ancient healing art based on the same principles as acupuncture. It involves applying physical pressure to key acupoints on the surface of the body. Stimulating these points along the body's energy channels (meridians) releases muscular tension and promotes the flow of healing energy (known as *qi*).

Acupressure can be effective in relieving headaches, eyestrain, sinus problems, muscle tension, insomnia, menstrual cramps, digestive disorders and anxiety. Self-acupressure has been a common part of everyday life in China for thousands of years and, even today, school students have scheduled breaks to run through a series of facial massaging exercises.

There are several kinds of acupressure massage techniques, all using the same trigger points. It is offered at local massage parlours either as Japanese shiatsu, a vigorous session administered on a bamboo mat with pressure applied to each point for only three to five seconds, or Chinese massage (*tuina*), incorporating pressing, kneading, rubbing and tapping

actions. Chinese medicine clinics also offer fire cupping, a method of applying acupressure by creating a vacuum next to the patient's skin using small cups. The cups stay on the skin for five to 15 minutes to draw out any 'stagnant' *qi*. The bruises clear up in a few days.

With the exception of cupping, patients are fully clothed throughout an acupressure treatment and loose-fitting pyjamas are generally provided. Try **Body & Soul – The TCM Clinic** (*see below*) or the **VIP Clinic of Shanghai Qigong Institute** (*see p175*) for acupressure therapies, **Green** (*see p175*) for body massage with cupping, or **Dragonfly** (*see p175*) and **CHI – The Spa** (*see p176*) for acupressure massage in a spa setting.

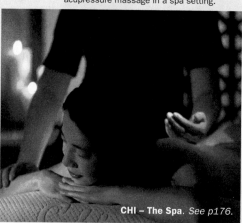

CHI – The Spa. *See p176.*

dim. The relationship between the two elements is fundamental to the traditional Chinese world outlook, and is seen to affect all aspects of life, from personal health to the state of the weather.

In TCM, yang represents the energy and movement of the body, while yin is the flesh, blood and bone. Harmony of this union means good health, while disharmony leads to disease; thus the strategy of TCM is to redress any imbalances. Diagnosis starts by assessing the pulse, face, tongue and body, and also takes the patient's medical history, living habits and emotional well-being into consideration.

Many Chinese believe that the strength of Western medicine is in its trauma-care and therapies for acute problems, while TCM excels in treating chronic problems and applying

preventive medicine. Western expats living in Shanghai seem to concur, and many visit TCM doctors for help with asthma, migraines, nicotine addiction and even losing weight.

Unfortunately, without a solid understanding of the philosophy or language, trotting off to the nearest Chinese medicine centre can be a thoroughly bewildering – and often painful – experience. For holistic healing in comfortable, English-speaking environs, try the following.

### Body & Soul – The TCM Clinic

*Suite 5, 14th floor, Anji Plaza, 760 Xizang Nan Lu, by Daji Lu, Old City (5101 9262/www.bodyand soul.com.cn).* **Open** 9am-6pm Mon, Wed, Fri; 9am-8pm Tue; 1-10pm Thur; 10am-3pm Sat. **Credit** AmEx, DC, MC, V. **Map** p248 L9.

German Doris Rathgeber trained in traditional Chinese medicine, in China, in Chinese. Her clinic offers TCM therapies, complemented with Western medical knowledge, in a comforting environment – not a pickled scorpion in sight. The 15 multilingual physicians specialise in acupuncture, internal medicine, gynaecology, *tuina*, physiotherapy and psychological consulting. They can concoct some special herbs for jet-lag sufferers too.

## VIP Clinic of Shanghai Qigong Institute

*3rd floor, 218 Nanchang Lu, by Sinan Lu, French Concession (5306 4832). Metro Shanxi Nan Lu.* **Open** 8am-4.30pm Mon-Sat. **No credit cards.** **Map** p247 G7.

A classic 1920s home located in one of Shanghai's most evocative neighbourhoods has been converted into a traditional Chinese hospital with a top-floor clinic catering specifically to expats. Acupuncture, Chinese massage therapy, Chinese medicine, scraping and cupping are offered by experienced practitioners. One speciality is a six-week acupuncture weight-loss treatment using dissolvable needles, which are inserted in the body and absorbed over two-week periods. Yikes. This is also the only official *qigong* institute in China.

# Massage

Beyond the street-corner blind massage parlours is a tier of mid-market body-rub joints. Perfumed sanctuaries of incense candles and Asian-inspired design, they generally offer a menu of Chinese-style foot and body massages, Japanese shiatsu and aromatherapy oil treatments.

## Dragonfly

*206 Xinle Lu, by Donghu Lu, French Concession (5403 9982/www.dragonfly.net.cn). Metro Shanxi Nan Lu.* **Open** 11am-2am daily. **Treatments** *Massage* RMB 120-200/hr. **Credit** AmEx, MC, V. **Map** p246 D7.

Having spawned ten Shanghai branches in three years, this enormously popular therapeutic retreat wins points for its affordability, stylish Zen ambience and simple menu of great massages. If walking into these candlelit, dark-wood and lemongrass-scented oases doesn't instantly relax you, the aromatherapy oil massage or deluxe hour-long foot massage on comfy recliners surely will. Most branches also boast a 'nail spa'. Couples should book the 'Love Nest', a VIP room on the top floor of the Xinle Lu flagship, with two antique beds and its own shower and spa. **Other locations**: throughout the city.

## Everlasting

*380 Shanxi Bei Lu, by Beijing Xi Lu, Jingan (6218 3079). Metro Shimen Yi Lu.* **Open** 10am-10pm daily. **Treatments** *Massage* RMB 98-280/hr. **Credit** AmEx, DC, MC, V. **Map** p243 E4.

The grand stone façade and friendly reception lead first-time visitors to expect something more than the

basic set-up of the treatment room, but there should be no complaints about the quality of the massage. Specialities include essential oil body massage, hot stone therapy, head yoga massage and facial treatments (not offered at every branch).

**Other locations**: 319 Shanxi Nan Lu, French Concession (6474 9188); 175 Xiangyang Nan Lu, by Nanchang Lu, French Concession (6415 9494); 2nd floor, Peace Square, 18 Shuicheng Lu, by Hongqiao Lu, Gubei (6208 2379); 807 Yuyuan Lu, by Jiangsu Lu, Changning (6252 9102); 706A-B, 168 Lujiazui Xi Lu, Lujiazui (5047 1336).

## Green

*58 Taicang Lu, by Songshan Lu, Xintiandi (5386 0222/www.greenmassage.com.cn).* *Metro Huangpi Nan Lu.* **Open** 10.30am-2am daily. **Treatments** *Massage* RMB 90-238/hr. **Credit** MC, V. **Map** p248 J7.

Conveniently situated beside Xintiandi, Green was one of Shanghai's first posh massage parlours. The simple communal rooms with semi-enclosed bamboo screens hardly rate as such today, but this affordable neighbourhood joint – boasting some of the most consistent, no-nonsense masseurs in town – continues to be extremely popular with locals and foreigners. Try the speciality aromatic ear massage using a lit candle, or the oil foot massage with milk. Across the road, the upscale Lotos Spa (2F, West Tower Somerset Grand Hotel, 8 Jinan Lu, by Shunchang, 3308 0088) – which shares its owner with Green – is a little-known gem with ten Balinese-style treatment rooms.

## Magpie

*685 Julu Lu, by Shanxi Nan Lu, French Concession (5403 3867). Metro Shanxi Nan Lu.* **Open** noon-2am daily; house calls noon-midnight. **Treatments** *Massage* RMB 128-188/hr. **Credit** AmEx, DC, MC, V. **Map** p243 F6.

In contrast to the minimalist calm of other massage parlours, Magpie is positively kitsch – stuffed with antique Chinese furniture amassed by its owner. Rooms are large and can hold several massage beds, so there's not much in the way of privacy. Still, the place offers a divine oil massage: the secret is in the combination of oil and the application of a steam machine. The purifying lymph gland massage is thought to work against body toxins. **Photo** *p173*.

## Ming

*298 Wulumuqi Nan Lu, by Jianguo Xi Lu, French Concession (5465 2501). Metro Hengshan Lu.* **Open** 11am-2am daily. **Treatments** *Massage* RMB 88-248/hr. **Credit** AmEx, DC, MC, V. **Map** p246 C10.

The design is striking: you enter across a small bridge over running water into Japanese-style treatment rooms with whitewashed walls, black beams and pale wood floors. The setting is classy – if a little cramped – and the towels are, hands down, the softest in town. Slip into pyjamas (provided) to receive treatment from highly professional masseurs. Between 11am and 4pm each day women receive a 20% discount. The full body massage has to be one of the best in town.

# Blind massage

One of the perks of being in Shanghai is that almost every street has a massage centre, where you can get a traditional foot and body rub for about the price of a Starbucks coffee. What's most intriguing about the experience is that your masseur will probably be blind.

Massage is one of the few professions open to the blind in China and businesses employing the visually impaired get tax breaks. As a result you pay a lot less than you would at any 'sighted' establishment. Effective pressure point massages are not impeded by lack of sight either. But the parameters of vision are often stretched. Some 'blind' therapists have an uncanny knack of recognising that you're foreign before you've spoken. The only visual impairment seems to be tinted sunglasses.

Levels of cleanliness and service vary too. The standard blindman massage hall has dimmed lights and rows of massage tables with recliners for the footwork. Your feet will be soaked in hot water, dried, wrapped in towels, then massaged. For a standard Chinese body massage, the therapist will put a clean sheet over your (clothed) body – sometimes there will be a curtain for privacy, but usually not. And there's some lingo you should memorise before you go: '*qing/zhong yi dian*' (a little lighter/harder).

## Ease Massage Centre

*89 Fahuazhen Lu, by Xinfu Lu, Xujiahui (6281 1081). Metro Xujiahui.* **Open** noon-midnight daily. **Treatments** *Body or foot massage* RMB 95/100mins; RMB 35/50mins. **No credit cards. Map** p246 A9.

## Funing Blind Massage Centre

*597 Fuxing Zhong Lu, by Maoming Nan Lu, French Concession (6437 8378). Metro Shanxi Nan Lu.* **Open** 10am-2am daily. **Treatments** *Body or foot massage* RMB 60/hr. **No credit cards. Map** p247 F9.

## Jingbin Blindman Massage

*New Building, Jingan Hotel, 370 Huashan Lu, by Wulumuqi Bei Lu, French Concession (6248 1888 ext 6660). Metro Changshu Lu.* **Open** noon-2am daily. **Treatments** *Body or foot massage* RMB 68/hr. **No credit cards. Map** p242 C6.

## No.1 Comfort Club

*277 Xingguo Lu, by Wukang Lu, French Concession (6431 8281). Metro Changshu Lu.* **Open** noon-2am daily. **Treatments** *Massage* RMB 68-180/hr. **No credit cards. Map** p246 B9.

# Spas

At the high end of the pampering spectrum are Shanghai's clutch of ultra-luxe spas, which feature international-standard attention to detail, a full menu of beauty and therapeutic treatments, and some truly stunning interiors.

## Banyan Tree

*3rd floor, Westin Hotel, 88 Henan Zhong Lu, by Guangdong Lu, the Bund (6335 1888/www. banyantreespa.com/shanghai). Metro Henan Lu.* **Open** 10am-midnight daily. **Treatments** *Facial & body packages* from RMB 1,000. *Massage* from RMB 780. **Credit** AmEx, DC, MC, V. **Map** p244 L5.
Originating from Phuket, the Banyan Tree spas are an Asian success story founded on opulent treatment rooms, and a holistic approach to healing and rejuvenation drawing on ancient Asian remedies. Rooms are richly decorated in themes of earth, gold, water, wood and fire, which correspond with treatments including facials, scrubs and Balinese, Hawaiian, Swedish and Thai massage (many of Banyan's experienced therapists are Thai). Come to be pampered like royalty – and expect to pay royal prices.

## CHI – The Spa

*6th floor, Tower 2, Pudong Shangri-La, 33 Fucheng Lu, by Yincheng Dong Lu, Pudong (6882 8888 ext 460/www.shangri-la.com). Metro Lujiazui.* **Open** 10am-midnight daily. **Treatments** *Facials* from RMB 730. *Massages* from RMB 650. **Credit** AmEx, DC, MC, V. **Map** p245 O5.
An entire floor of the hotel is devoted to this Tibetan temple of tranquillity. Inspired by the legend of Shangri-La, the chain's new spa concept draws on the mystical aura and ancient healing rituals of the Himalayan region, with 37 body, water, massage and facial therapies designed around the five Chinese elements. A reverent atmosphere pervades the soaring space, awash in rich ochre hues, moody candlelight and traditional Tibetan accents. Signature therapies include the mountain *tsampa* rub, aquamarine energising facial using crystal wands, and massage with healing stones. Just as heavenly are the soft chenille robes, cinnamon and mulberry organic teas, and post-treatment ting of tiny Tibetan cymbals gently coaxing you back to the real world.

## David's Camp Men's SPA & Skin Care Centre

*2nd floor, 200 Yanan Xi Lu, by Wulumuqi Bei Lu, French Concession (6247 3602/www.davids campspa.com). Metro Jingan Temple.* **Open** 9am-midnight daily. **Treatments** *Facials* from RMB 260. *Massage* from RMB 150/30mins. **Credit** AmEx, DC, MC, V. **Map** p242 C6.
Expensive treatments for *Vogue Hommes* types in a modern Asian setting. Ascend the sweeping marble staircase for Japanese shiatsu (the most popular treatment) and thorough facials using Swiss products. The Chinese staff have limited English, but deliver treatments with a delicate touch. Women can accompany their man for couple treatments in the VIP room.

## Evian Spa

*2nd floor, Three on the Bund, 3 Zhongshan Dong Yi Lu, by Guangdong Lu, the Bund (6321 6622/www. threeonthebund.com). Metro Henan Lu.* **Open** 10am-10pm daily. **Treatments** *Facials* from RMB 520. *Massages* from RMB 480/hr. **Credit** AmEx, DC, MC, V. **Map** p245 M5.

Mandara Spa.

Evian's sparkling women-only day spa at Three on the Bund has a 35m-high (115-ft) atrium, 14 individually designed treatment rooms, indoor streams filled with Evian mineral water, and a deluxe menu of French beauty treatments (using Sothys and Darphin products), Eastern holistic therapies, hairdressing and new-age colour and hydro therapies. When you think you've plumbed the depths of indulgence, you are lead to the post-treatment recovery area where you can chill out on white lounge chairs with a hot herbal neck pillow and a pot of hibiscus tea. An Express Beauty treatment menu allows you to have a quick wash and blow-dry (in your own private cubicle with TV and DVD player), pre-dinner manicure or half-hour quick-fix facial.

### L'Institut de Guerlain

*26th floor, Regent Shanghai, 1116 Yanan Xi Lu, by Panyu Lu, Changning (6115 9607/www.spa chakra.com). Metro Jiangsu Lu.* **Open** 6am-10pm daily. **Treatments** *Facials* from RMB 770. *Massages* RMB 770/hr. *Full-day packages* from RMB 4,220. **Credit** AmEx, DC, MC, V. **Map** p240 C4.

The first L'Institut de Guerlain in China has adopted 'European clinical' over 'Asian exotic' and is all filmy white decor, blond woods, high-tech equipment and cuddly Frette bathrobes. Each treatment – from an express facial to a full-day package – begins with a foot bath and massage, during which you complete a questionnaire to evaluate skin, nutrition, environment and lifestyle focus. Treatments, products and advice by confident English-speaking therapists are then tailored accordingly, using pleasantly perfumed Guerlain crèmes and serums. Special treatments include a state-of-the-art Vichy rainshower body polish, hydrotherapy baths, medical pedicure and full-day experiences with spa cuisine.

### Mandara Spa

*6th floor, JW Marriott, Tomorrow Square, 399 Nanjing Xi Lu, People's Square (5359 4969 ext 6798/www.mandaraspa.com). Metro People's Square.* **Open** 10am-10pm daily. **Treatments** *Facial* RMB 500. *Massages* from RMB 860/90mins. **Credit** AmEx, DC, MC, V. **Map** p244 H5.

This is the first Chinese location of the Asian resort spa giant. Experienced massage therapists offer treatments in 'old Shanghai' themed rooms with traditional grey bricks, antique rosewood furniture and blue and white porcelain sinks. The exotic ambience and scents of sandalwood and lemongrass are a world away from the stark glass and marble hotel lobby outside, and the huge terrazzo bathtubs, soothing music and steam showers make for a thorough pampering. As well as luscious Eastern therapies like the Pearl of the Orient facial, à la Empress Dowager Cixi, there is a menu of short and effective treatments for men and women on the go, concentrating on specific areas of the body. **Photo** *above.*

## Yoga

Nothing at all to do with China – yoga has its roots in India, of course – but since the country opened up to the world at large, it has gained its fair share of followers here too. Specialist centres include **Breeze Yoga & Pilates Centre** (7th floor, 120 Xizang Zhong Lu, by Guangdong Lu, People's Square, 6350 1086, www.breezeyoga.com) and **+ Yoga Centre** (299 Fuxing Xi Lu, by Huashan Lu, French Concession, 6433 4330, www.yplus.cn). In addition, yoga and Pilates classes are offered at many gyms (*see p196*).

**Arts & Entertainment**

# Music

Shanghai's music scene is growing – it just isn't quite sure what it wants to grow into.

After a decade of labouring underground, playing only to those in the know, Shanghai's independent music scene has finally come out of the closet. There's been a proliferation of new music venues and several of Shanghai's art museums now offer conceptual music at weekends. Shanghai still has some way to go before it can call itself a music city – Filipino cover bands dominate the expat pubs and the substance-driven DJ scene dominates the evening offerings – but there is at least now a decent crop of alternatives.

Indeed, Shanghai rock, pop, metal and hip hop have been quietly blossoming since around 2000, when the city government removed a ban on the word 'rock' and on showing long-haired men in the media. There's now a decent stable of bands, although only a few manage to draw crowds. Independent Shanghai music is split into two amicable camps, one mainstream pop-rock, the other underground and more alternative. The former is mostly influenced by British groups such as Blur, Suede, the Clash, the Cure and U2, although they are also fiercely adoring of older Chinese and Taiwanese music. The resulting sound has been dubbed 'Shampoo' by one band, although the moniker is not widely used. The more prominent Shampoo groups include the heavy but melodic **Crystal Butterfly**, the ethereally gothic **Cold Fairyland**, the cheerfully poppy **Honeys**, the edgy **Terrified Bird** and rising punksters **Sonnet**. The underground camp ranges in style from grunge, punk and death metal to folk and electronica, and is represented by bands such as Shanghai's oldest extant band **Godot**, death metallers **Capitol Crime**, folk-sound set-up **Third Yellow Chicken**, and **Topfloor Circus**, performance artists with an eclectic musical repertoire.

Currently leading the live-music cavalry is **Yuyintang**, a concert organisation founded by Zhang Haisheng, sound engineer and former lead singer of the now disbanded Vicky's Area. Opening its own concert space in 2006, Yuyintang puts on weekly shows by a range of Shanghainese bands, along with a smattering of foreign groups and groups from around China. Otherwise, 'Shampoo' bands perform mostly at the state-of-the-art **Ark Live House** and campus concerts, reflecting their youthful audience. Underground bands play to crowds

of artists and young expats at galleries and museums, as well as at new venues like **Shuffle** and **021 Bar**.

Shanghai also has a growing Chinese folk scene, with some overlap with the rock scene. Cold Fairyland singer Lin Di has a solo career as a folk artist and has cut albums in Taiwan with singer Liu Xing. Their disks are available care of **Bandu Music**, an aspiring label and bar-café that hosts traditional Chinese music concerts every Saturday night.

Hip hop is gaining in popularity with young Shanghainese, but isn't quite what would be known as hip hop in the West (*see p180* **Hip hop hopes**). A separate scene of MCs (foreign and Chinese) exists on the nightlife circuit rapping at various nightclubs, particularly **Pegasus Club** (*see p185*).

## LABELS AND DISKS

Record stores are dominated by hits from Hong Kong and Taiwan, including popular favourites like Chinese band Yu Quan and Taiwanese boy band F4. **Fanyin** is Shanghai's sole major independent rock record label, although some Shanghai bands are signed to Beijing labels; bands often make their records or demos available at their gigs. Distribution woes largely keep local independent music out of most stores, but chain store **Maya** stocks some Chinese rock, particularly at larger outlets like the one in Xujiahui, and **WALL** (Changle Lu, French Concession) offers a selection of records and demos by Shanghai artists. **Bandu** (*see p179*) stocks local folk music.

The multinational recording giants have a presence in Shanghai, but have shown little interest in supporting local talent, preferring to promote their international stables. They do increasingly, however, lure international stars to the city, including in 2006 the Rolling Stones and the Black Eyed Peas.

## Major venues

An increasingly regular stream of famous Asian and Western performers packs out one or other of three large venues. The largest, **Shanghai Stadium** (1111 Caoxi Bei Lu, by Zhongshan Nan Er Lu, Xujiahui, 6438 5200, www.shanghai-stadium.online.sh.cn), has featured performers such as Mando-pop stars Faye Wang and Zheng Jun, as well as the Rolling Stones. It consists of the *tiyuchang* or Grand Stage, an 80,000-seat outdoor stadium built in 1997, and the *tiyuguan*, a smaller indoor arena; both are typically called Shanghai Stadium in English. Nora Jones and Deep People are among the acts to have played at the **Hongkou Stadium** (715 Dongtiyuhui Lu, by Zhongshan Beier Lu, Hongkou, 6540 0009), which was rebuilt in its current 35,000-seat incarnation in 1999. Concerts are also sometimes held at the **Changning Stadium** (777 Wuyi Lu, by Zhongshan Xi Lu, Jingan, 6228 9488) – also known as the Shanghai International Stadium. Tickets for the big stadiums vary from RMB 10 to RMB 10,000.

## Pop & rock

In Shanghai, the visual and the aural arts are beginning to rub shoulders to pleasing effect, with various galleries and art museums hosting regular concerts: **Shanghai Duolun MoMA** (*see p97*) features predominantly Beijing electronica artists; **Zendai MoMA** (*see p95*), which opened in 2005 with an 'Urban Folk' festival, has since hosted everything from Chinese rock to underground European punk groups; and the spacious **DDM warehouse** (*see p168*) regularly hosts cutting-edge gigs, as well as underground dance and theatre (the line-up is dominated by Beijing punks, but local musicians also feature). The **Zhu Qizhan Art Museum** (580 Ouyang Lu, Hongqiao, 5666 1967, www.zmuseum.org) holds events examining the artistic side of music, with presentations on such topics as sound art and the history of hip hop. Many of Shanghai's pro rockers and visiting musicians from across China hang out at the more traditionally grungy **Time Passage** (*see p131*); sometimes, due to beer and pressure from owner Ai Jun, they'll take the floor to jam.

### Ark Live House

*181 Taicang Lu, North Block, Lane 15, Xintiandi (6326 8008/www.ark-lh.com). Metro Huangpui Nan Lu.* **Open** 5.30pm-1am daily. **Admission** free. **Credit** AmEx, DC, MC, V. **Map** p248 H7.

Opened in 2001 and named after Japanese supergroup (believe us, they're big over this way) L'arc en Ciel, Ark is Shanghai's premier destination for non-covers live music. It boasts one of the best sound systems in China (so say the musicians) and an eclectic line-up. Most foreign acts are Japanese metal, punk and pop bands, joined by the occasional Western group. Ark also regularly showcases established and new Shanghai groups, and at least one Beijing or Guangzhou group passes through each month. Sporadic weekend afternoon concerts pull in mad throngs of student fans.

**Paramount Ballroom.**
*See p181.*

### Yuyintang

*1st floor, No.100, Lane 200, Longcao Lu, by Tiandong Lu, Xuhui (6436 0072/www.yuyintang. com). Metro Caobao Lu.* **Admission** RMB 30. **No credit cards.**

The city's premier concert promoter organises concerts at least weekly in its scuffed but authentic warehouse space in southern Shanghai, and also arrange shows elsewhere in town. The bilingual website has forthcoming gigs; admission prices vary depending on the popularity of the band playing.

### Bandu Music

*1st floor, Building 11, 50 Moganshan Lu, by Changhua Lu, Jingan (6276 8267/www.bandumusic. com). Metro Shanghai Railway Station.* **Admission** free. **No credit cards.** **Map** p242 D1.

Located in the Moganshan Lu arts district (*see p166*), Bandu Music is an unassuming coffeeshop and bar that organises weekly Chinese folk music concerts (8pm Sat). It also sells the best selection of Chinese music discs in Shanghai.

### Shuffle

*137 Xingfu Lu, by Fahuazhen, Changning (6283 2769/www.shufflebar.com). Metro Yanan Xi Lu.* **Admission** free. **No credit cards.**

This recently opened dive stages music concerts at least once a week. Most of its clientele is scruffy young expats and foreign students from nearby Jiaotong University, which makes for rowdy times.

# Hip hop hopes

Hip hop touched down in Shanghai in 1998 and now it's moonwalking all over the city, with hip hop classes at the dance studios, hip hop nights proliferating on the clubbing scene and funky Shanghai kids strutting their low-waisted baggy pants up and down Huaihai Lu. But it's not quite hip hop as it's known in the West. The genre arrived in Shanghai via Taiwan, Japan and, in particular, South Korea, mutating along the way into something considerably more clean-cut called 'chopstick hip hop'.

The scene in Shanghai is mostly about fashion, with the kids in their basketball jerseys totally into the attitude, dancing and lifestyle. But, when it comes to the music, they are getting hip over some decidedly mainstream hops. Tuned into MTV videos, they think Usher is hip hop, update their wardrobes at the local market and are 'lovin' it' that the hugely popular McDonald's hip hop theme tune features Taiwanese pop star Jay Chow.

There is, thankfully, a small pocket of dedicated hip hop followers on the quest for an authentic, indigenous style. The **Dragon Dance Studio** (4th floor, 1095 Wuding Lu, by Jiaozhou Lu, the Bund; 1338 177 7193 mobile) is a giant posse of Shanghai b-boys, dancers, MCs, DJs and graffiti artists, which organises a variety of hip hop-related events. Its huge success demonstrates how vital these sorts of semi-educational communities are for Shanghai, where youth culture is still in its early stages. But it's Shanghai, remember, not the Bronx. In Shanghai graffiti is displayed in art galleries – at **da>SPACE** (84 Fujian Nan Lu, by Guangdong Lu, the Bund, www.da-space.com), for example – and no one carries guns, nor do they rap about them. Instead, it's about good clean fun, with a healthy dose of frontman ego – something that Shanghai's only children have in plentiful supply.

Another person who is nurturing an independent hip hop scene is local hero **Gary Wang** (DJ V-Nutz), who launched DJ commune the **Lab** (5th floor, 343 Jiaozhou Lu, by Wuding Lu, Jingan, 5213 0877, www.the lab.cn) in May 2006. 'It's a space for DJs, MCs and live performers to come together, exchange ideas and make independent music,' he explains. The monthly old skool night 'Bring It Back to the Roots' is one way it provides some much-needed context to the scene and a refreshing alternative to Shanghai's bling-bling parties. Expect to see PAs from local stars MC Tang King (Pun Pun) and Webber (formerly Yin Tsang, who released the 2003 album For the People on the Scream label; pictured above), plus the Lab's own retinue of talented turntablists and performers. And rest assured that Jay Chow and his catchy McDonald's tune are well off the play list.

For more on the hip hop clubbing circuit, visit www.smartshanghai.com, and be sure to check out **Pegasus Club** (see p185), which figures large on the local hip hop scene.

Concerts are usually heavy metal, both local and foreign, but there are exceptions.

## 021 Bar

*2893 Yangshupu Lu, by Dinghai Lu, Hongkou (1391 801 5880 mobile/www.shrock.cn). Metro Hongkou Stadium.* **Open** 9pm-midnight daily. **Admission** RMB 15. **No credit cards.**
Another dive with heavy metal leanings and a student clientele, but situated near the more remote Fudan and Tongji Universities.

## Tang Hui

*85 Huating Lu, by Huaibai Zhong Lu, French Concession (5403 4408). Metro Changsu Lu.* **Open** 10am-2am daily. **Admission** free. **No credit cards. Map** p246 A9.
Like Time Passage (see p131), Tang Hui is about informal jams rather than proper concerts. Owner Zhang Du had his own band in the late 1990s, but now just ropes in friends to play – mainly clichéd cover versions. Tang Hui's previous location was

tiny, but the new venue is a slick, sprawling ode to local music on the first two floors, with the third and fourth floors devoted to eclectic electronic sets. Decor retains the bamboo matting, concrete and red paint of the original venue, and the ambience is very friendly. Expect cheap drinks and a diverse set of local hipsters and expats who wouldn't tread anywhere near the likes of image-conscious Bar Rouge (*see p123*).

## Jazz

Shanghai's jazz scene is almost an exact negative of the rock scene: it is bar-centred, dominated by expats and rarely original. Pretty much every four- or five-star hotel has a resident jazz act, but the bar at the **Portman Ritz-Carlton** (*see p37*) stands out: streamlined and elegant, with low-slung and comfortable chairs, it hosts excellent American jazzers, changing the roster every few months. The most (in)famous jazz venue in Shanghai is the bar of the historic **Peace Hotel** (*see p32*), but now six old-timers play retro jazz and big band favourites to a crowd made up exclusively of tourists.

Despite the city's healthy number of independent venues, Shanghainese jazz groups – even individual performers – are thin on the ground. Notable exceptions like the band **Five Guys on a Train** and flamboyant gay singer **Coco** (a semi-celeb in this defiantly straight city) stick strictly to the standards. The imported bands performing in the city's jazz bars are at least tight and professional, injecting verve into their covers and often wrapping up with an energised jam. The **Glamour Bar** (*see p125*) often hosts weekend gigs of a high quality, while Taiwanese-owned **CJW** (*see p105*) – Cigars, Jazz and Wine – approaches jazz as an upmarket lifestyle accessory, but does book competent foreign bands.

Many upper-income young Shanghainese are developing a serious appetite for jazz, in no small part because of its perceived associations with Western sophistication. The cultural bureau has responded by organising a number of jazz festivals, all theoretically annual but none yet reliably so. Jazz acts are also included in most general festivals; for more on festivals and events in Shanghai, *see pp152-156*. Between these and the independently organised events, Shanghai can now attract international jazz figures of the stature of Wynton Marsalis and Quincy Jones.

### Cotton Club
*1416 Huaihai Zhong Lu, by Fuxing Xi Lu, French Concession (6437 7110). Metro Changshu Lu.* **Open** 9.30pm-12.30am daily. **Admission** free. **Credit** AmEx, DC, MC, V. **Map** p246 C8.
No relation to the New York original, Shanghai's oldest outlet of jazz and blues is the closest thing in town to a sure bet for smooth sounds. A good crowd

of both Westerners and Chinese packs the small, smoky club for nightly sets. Compared to most clubs, which rotate bands every few months, consistency is key at the Cotton Club. The house band consists mostly of foreigners, some of whom have been playing there for years. A handful of semi-regulars join in and jam a couple of nights a week.

### Five
*Basement, 20 Guangdong Lu, by Zhongshan Dong Yi Lu, the Bund (6329 4558/www.numberfive.cn). Metro Henan Lu.* **Open** 10am-2am daily. **Credit** AmEx, DC, MC, V. **Admission** free. **Map** p245 M5.
Shanghai's most laid-back jazz house, Five is tucked away improbably at the bottom of the chic M on the Bund building, offering comfy leather chairs and cheap beer. The jazz, five nights a week from 9.30pm, is competent and the atmosphere sultry.

### House of Blues & Jazz
*158 Maoming Nan Lu, by Fuxing Zhong Lu, French Concession (6437 5280). Metro Shanxi Nan Lu.* **Open** 7pm-2am Tue-Sun. **Admission** free. **Credit** AmEx, DC, MC, V. **Map** p247 F8.
Brainchild of radio and TV personality Lin Dongfu, the House has existed in various incarnations around Shanghai since the mid 1990s. The current format has proved the most successful. Being a bit of an Old Shanghai buff, Dongfu has outfitted the club in deco style, with an impressive collection of antique furniture and lamps. The music is more modern, a mixture of blues and jazz fusion delivered by top-notch foreign bands.

### JZ Club
*46 Fuxing Xi Lu, near Wulumuqi Zhong Lu, French Concession (6415 0269). Metro Changshu Lu.* **Open** 9pm-3am daily. **Admission** free. **Credit** AmEx, DC, MC, V. **Map** p247 C8.
Opened in late 2003 by a local jazz enthusiast who studied music overseas, JZ has already established itself as one of Shanghai's leading jazz dives. Its unpretentious but stylish atmosphere and use of young, Chinese musicians makes it more accessible to young Shanghainese jazz aficionados than most of its competitors. Nor is JZ a place for Billie Holiday covers: the three nightly sets focus on contemporary jazz and fusion, often evolving into a rousing jam.

### Paramount Ballroom
*218 Yuyuan Lu, by Wanhangdu Lu, Jingan (6249 8866). Metro Jingan Temple.* **Open** 8.30pm-12.30am Mon-Thur, Sun; 8.30pm-1am Fri, Sat. **Admission** RMB 200. **Credit** AmEx, DC, MC, V. **Map** p242 C5.
Back in the 1930s the dizzyingly deco Paramount was once Shanghai's chicest dance hall; it reopened in 2001. On a stage overlooking the main second-floor dance hall, girls with a big band backing belt out swinging nostalgic renditions of pop songs, mostly pre-1950s but with a few reinvented revolutionary songs and modern tunes – think *Titanic* theme meets Richard Clayderman. The more mellow fourth-floor dance hall features a singer and a smaller band that is more exclusively preoccupied with jazz. **Photo** *p179*.

**Arts & Entertainment**

# Nightlife

Enjoy living up to Shanghai's reputation for debauchery.

Shanghai's nightlife scene has come a long way since the last edition of this guide, and even further over the past decade. Ten years ago all that was on offer to the intrepid traveller was a couple of fledgling expat bars offering weak beer, sticky floors and eager hostesses.

The infamous melange of sing-song girls, horny sailors and pockmarked gangsters was snuffed out under Communism, but when President Deng Xiaoping opened the city up to economic reform in 1992 the corks began popping again. A partying vanguard of foreign businessmen sought their pleasures in the hotel bars and embassy staff were out on the razzle each Friday night; decadent mass dance orgies and gleeful drug abuse were, however, still some way off.

Further relaxation of government restrictions on nightlife in the late 1990s coincided with the arrival of Chinese returnees from the West and curious foreign-language students. Shanghai had its first club-savvy crowd, and venues started to appear.

Thanks to the bloody-minded determination of the party organisers and a new generation of teens flirting with such music subcultures as chopstick hip hop (see p180), the scene is alive, kicking and maturing at a frantic pace. Every weekend the French Concession throbs with Shanghainese wide boys and girlies in counterfeit couture – not to mention drug dealers making a fast buck off Ecstasy-seekers (local clubbers have dubbed Ecstasy *yaotouwan*, or the 'head-shaking pill').

## THE CLUBBING SCENE

Shanghai has now played host to just about every one of the world's top 100 DJs. China's battle of the spirit giants, in particular Chivas and Smirnoff, makes sponsorship for these DJs and live acts easy to come by. With a great drinks promotion and a live act often costing no more than RMB 100 each weekend, the real winner is the globe-trotting clubber, whose only problem is being spoilt for choice.

The city is nonetheless home to an increasingly impressive roster of home-grown talent and foreign residents, providing a decent range of dance music. Local DJs still have a huge problem accessing the very heart of their trade: vinyl. Records are exotic fruit, something that locals can only lay their hands on abroad, mainly in Hong Kong, but – with the proliferation of download sites – access to the latest sounds is becoming easier. You'll now find everything from hip hop to electro-pop being mixed throughout the week, with a common complaint from the new wave of professional DJs not being empty or unresponsive dancefloors but rather the lack of repeat bookings – it seems Shanghai's lust for the new and innovative is never sated.

Because of this exploratory mentality, new venues spring up each weekend – and sometimes disappear just as quickly. 2005 saw the opening and prompt closure of Ibizan superclub Space. A mixture of a dreadful location and fickleness among clubbers resulted in empty dancefloors and it only lasted a month or so of trading. Rumour has it that Ministry of Sound has now been denied a licence – not once, but twice. Of the large international clubbing brands, only Godskitchen, with such events as the excellent **Bonbon** (see p183), and **Renaissance** (whose parties are usually at **Park 97**, see p184 **California Club/Lux**) has really hit the right buttons.

To the club-scene trio of dancing, drinking and drugging, Shanghai adds drunken drawling – otherwise known as karaoke. Shanghai is lousy with karaoke joints. Many are abysmal, but even the worst should not be confused with KTV bars, which are nothing short of brothels. And the best are a uniquely Chinese add-on to the clubbing scene, in which

## Top five Clubs

### For a big night out
**Rojam**. See p185.

### For the best sound in town
**Minx**. See p184.

### For China's take on hip hop
**Pegasus Club**. See p185.

### For a contradiction in terms
Stylish karaoke at **Partyworld**. See p185.

### For happy house
House nights at **Mint**. See p184.

Bonbon.

## Cabaret

### La Maison
*Unit 1, House 23, North Block, Lane 181 Taicang Lu, Xintiandi (5306 1856/www.lamaison.sh.cn). Metro Huangpi Nan Lu.* **Open** 11.30am-2.30pm, 6pm-midnight daily. **Show times** 8pm, 10pm daily. **Credit** AmEx, DC, MC, V. **Map** p248 H7.
A bit of Moulin Rouge in Shanghai, La Maison hosts cabaret shows with lots of feathers, leg and cleavage. Unfortunately, the price you pay for the show is that you are obliged to eat; the food is generally a poor attempt at French cuisine and, with main courses starting at around RMB 130, doesn't come cheap.

## Clubs

As in many cities these days, the membrane that separates club from bar can be pretty porous: the Tongren Lu **Blue Frog** (*see p128*) and upstairs at **Barbarossa** (*see p125*) are cases in point.

### Babyface 2
*Unit 101, Shanghai Square, 138 Huaihai Zhong Lu, by Puan Lu, French Concession (6375 6667/ www.babyface.com.cn). Metro Huangpi Nan Lu.* **Open** 9pm-2am daily. **Admission** RMB 60 Fri, Sat. **Credit** AmEx, MC, V. **Map** p248 J7.
Babyface is one of the biggest clubbing brands in China, with venues across the country. Its wealth of experience and pull among a mainly local crowd won it Tiesto's Asia tour in 2006, with every weekend seeing a big name at the helm (Judge Jules, Deep Fish, the Stanton Warriers). The new venue is bigger (capacity in the region of 2,000) and brighter than its predecessor on Maoming Lu, with a huge neon wall backing the DJ booth. The club is busy and booming every night of the week, so book tables in advance. However, Babyface is the mean bitch of the Shanghai club scene, sexy but with a sting. Westerners are always complaining about rude staff, lack of service, steep prices… problems the locals seem not to suffer. Resident DJs play a mix of house through to progressive and breaks, and international names are picked for their dancefloor-filling track selections.

### Bonbon
*2F, Yunhai Plaza, 1331 Huaihai Zhong Lu, by Baoqing Lu, French Concession (1332 193 9299 mobile/www.clubbonbon.com). Metro Changshu Lu.* **Open** 8.30pm-3am Tue, Wed; 8.30pm-5am Thur-Sat. **Admission** RMB 40-100 weekends. **Credit** AmEx, MC, V. **Map** p246 D8.
In 2006 Bonbon burst on to the scene care of promoter and global clubbing giant Godskitchen, which hosts a monthly event of its own, as well as supplying the regular flow of international talent. International quality doesn't stop with the DJs – it's evident in everything from the sound system to the drinks you can sip in a maze of private booths.

dancefloors are supplemented by warrens of karaoke boxes. Punters use them like chill-out rooms. At the same time, stylish karaoke complexes have been set up within stumbling distance of the hippest clubs – glitzy, Taiwanese-owned **Partyworld** (*see p185*) is a popular example, just across the park from Park 97 in Fuxing Park.

### PRACTICALITIES
The clubbing action starts on Wednesday with a 'Ladies Night' in most of the top venues, while Thursday is fast becoming hip hop night. Over the weekend you'll be spoilt for choice: international and local talent play every style imaginable. Pick up the city's free listings magazines to get the low-down – the best are *that's Shanghai, SH* magazine or www.smartshanghai.com; the former are distributed in hotels, bars and restaurants. But whichever style of club you're interested in, such is the fluidity of Shanghai that it always pays to check ahead that your chosen venue is indeed still functioning.

**Arts & Entertainment**

Weekends are consistently busy, with Saturday @ Bonbon often the biggest night in town. Thursday is hip hop night and, while the DJs aren't breaking down doors to grab awards, it is very popular with the teenage crowd. **Photo *p183*.**

### California Club/Lux

*Park 97, 2 Gaolan Lu, within Fuxing Park, French Concession (5383 2328/www.lankwaifong.com). Metro Shanxi Nan Lu.* **Open** 9pm-2am Mon-Thur, Sun; 9pm-late Fri, Sat. **Admission** varies. **Credit** AmEx, DC, MC, V. **Map** p247 G8.

A hedonistic entertainment complex, Park 97 has two floors of restaurants and bars, and is hugely popular with expats, locals and HK sophisticates. The newly renovated lower floor boasts a new addition to the Park 97 complex: **Lux**. An R&B club during the week, it puts on sexy house at the weekends, courtesy of a range of local and international guests. **California Club** plays a good mix of hard house and breaks from resident DJs Steve Bamford, Matt Kitshon and guests, while live acts entertain the upper floor. By 2am on a weekend, Park 97 becomes one large party space, with clubbers spilling out into the open air of Fuxing Park.

### DKD

*438 Huaihai Zhong Lu, by Chongqing Nan Lu, French Concession (6473 9449/www.clubdkd.com). Metro Huangpi Nan Lu.* **Open** 9pm-late daily. **Admission** RMB 40-50. **Credit** MC, V. **Map** p247 H7.

Originally a much smaller venue on Maoming Lu, DKD opened up this impressive basement club in 2005. The dark and intimate design attracts a fiercely loyal crowd. The club is regularly packed with clubbers hungry for the sounds of trance and deep house. Carl Cox, Paul Van Dyke and Miss Kitten are the pick of international stars to have played here of late. The residents include DJ Calvin – one of the most popular, and best, Chinese DJs in Shanghai.

### Fabrique

*8-10 Jianguo Zhong Lu, by Sinan Lu, French Concession (6415 0700/www.fabrique.com.cn).* **Open** 9pm-late Tue-Sat. **Admission** free Tue-Thur; RMB 60 Fri, Sat (incl 1 drink). **No credit cards**. **Map** p247 G9.

After a rocky start, Fabrique – part of the Bridge 8 'lifestyle' development – seems to have managed to establish a following among fashionable types. We have to admit that the club has seen some great nights (Crystal Method and DJ Frank Müller come to mind) but things seemed to have gone rather quiet as we went to press. Commercial house is the mainstay during the week, and R&B takes over at the weekend, plus there are regular – often less-than-classy – promotions such as 'Is your miniskirt this short?' to get the girls free drinks. The decor is industrial chic with high ceilings, a huge dancefloor, spacious seating upstairs and excellent visuals. No one can say Fabrique doesn't try but, despite all of this, the club has yet to hit the high notes.

Mint.

### Mint

*2F, 333 Tongren Lu, by Beijing Lu, Jingan (6247 9666). Metro Jingan Temple.* **Open** 6pm-2am Mon-Thur; 9pm-2am Fri, Sat. **Admission** RMB 50 Fri, Sat. **Credit** AmEx, MC, V. **Map** p242 D5.

Mint is now one of the hottest venues in town. This intimate club, set in a converted greenhouse, hosts a hugely popular ladies' night on Wednesdays, 'No Man's Land', with the boys locked out until 10.30pm; Fridays and Saturdays are also packed. Local residents Danny Rockwell and Marius keep the (largely expat) crowds dancing into the early hours, playing their mix of happy and vocal house music, perfect for the summer nights. Look out for the group's new project Pier One (*see below* **Minx/Monsoon Lounge**). **Photo** *above*.

### Minx/Monsoon Lounge

*Pier One, 82 Yichang Lu, by Jiangning Lu, Putuo (5155 8310/www.pierone.cn). Metro Zhongtan Lu.* **Open** *Minx Nightclub* 9pm-late daily. *Monsoon Lounge* 7pm-2am daily. **Admission** varies. **Credit** AmEx, MC, V. **Map** p242 C1.

Pier One's in-house club, Minx, boasts an extra-large DJ booth, flown in from NYC; a jaw-dropping speaker system, also custom-built in the Big Apple; and a spacious dancefloor. The kicking sound set-up was created by Gary Stewart Audio and makes Minx the city's undisputed aural champion. Still, Monsoon – the lounge bar on the beautiful roof terrace – manages to out-Minx Minx. Climb the stairs to the tinkling sounds of a waterfall and settle into Suzhou Creek's first oasis, a rooftop space complete with daybeds, a hot tub, bar and resident DJs. With a drinks list designed by Grey Goose mixologist Tom Warden, this is the perfect spot to unwind.

### Pegasus Club

*2nd floor, Golden Bell Plaza, 98 Huaihai Zhong Lu, by Longmen Lu, French Concession (5385 8189). Metro Huangpi Nan Lu.* **Open** 9pm-3am Thur-Sat. **Admission** RMB 30 Thur; RMB 50/100 men/women Fri; RMB 50 Sat. **Credit** AmEx, DC, MC, V. **Map** p248 J7.

Pegasus's Thursday night hip hop parties, hosted by DJ V-Nutz (China's 2002 DMC Champion), are legendary around these parts; otherwise, the club is a bit hit and miss. The increase in competition on the growing hip hop scene, largely confined to Thursday nights, hasn't affected this urban pioneer. Manager Paul Grey remains a solid supporter of local hip hop, and occasionally books quality international talents. Ice-T rapped up a storm in 2005, cementing Pegasus's image as the original and still the best.

### Rojam

*4th floor, Hong Kong Plaza, 283 Huaihai Zhong Lu, by Songshan Lu, French Concession (6390 7181/ www.rojam.com). Metro Huangpi Nan Lu.* **Open** 8.30pm-2am daily. **Admission** RMB 40-50. **Credit** V. **Map** p248 J7.

Rojam has a colossal main dancefloor-cum-bar area, where heaving crowds are strafed by a strobing light show and bombarded by atom-splitting techno and trance. There's some respite in two chill-out/VIP areas, karaoke rooms out the back (minimum food and drink spend RMB 360, rising to RMB 540 at weekends) and a laid-back top floor. The venue has recently hosted residencies from Corvin Darlek, the purveyor of his own new 'wet and hard' sound. An excellent venue for Shanghai clubbers in search of the bigger beat.

### Studio 78

*2F, 78-80 Tongren Lu, by Yanan Xi Lu, Jingan (6289 5117/www.studio78.com.cn). Metro Jingan Temple.* **Open** 6pm-2am Mon-Thur; 6pm-3am Fri, Sat. **Admission** free. **Credit** AmEx, MC, V. **Map** p242 D6.

An oasis on Tongren Lu's patchy bar strip, Studio 78 let off a disco bomb and the bar is now decked out like Huggy Bear's bedroom. An excellent crew of barstaff will prepare the Martinis while you relax under the light of a nearby lava lamp. The fish tank in the corner really is made out of a TV and the sounds are pure funk and disco from the 1970s to now. The management is always plotting a different event or theme to keep you amused, which makes this a great place to start your weekend.

### VIP Room

*459 Wulumuqi Bei Lu, by Yanan Xi Lu, Jingan (6248 8898/www.shanghaiviproom.com). Metro Jingan Temple.* **Open** 9pm-late daily. **Admission** average RMB 100. **Credit** AmEx, DC, MC, V. **Map** p242 C6.

With a list of investors that includes the legendary singer Faye Wong, it is no surprise that this huge club, the cavernous space of an old cinema, is so popular. With a musical focus on breaks and hard house, Gil (the manager and sometime resident DJ) is under no illusions about the tastes of his target market. The club is packed with the rich Shanghainese, Hong Kong and Taiwanese party set for most of the week, many opting to pay for the glass VIP rooms on the upper level. While a central bar dominates the ground floor, there's also a large dancefloor fronting the DJ booth where HK Top 100 DJ Rickie Stone can often be found.

## Karaoke

Such is the popularity of karaoke that the local pop industry is awash with tunes created specifically to be sung across Asia by millions of kara-cuties – girls with terrible voices who look so good that the men present cheer wildly regardless. However, the traveller looking for something more like Whitney Houston than Faye Wong needn't worry: most karaoke boxes have extensive English song lists. In any case, when lubed up on *baijiu* (*see p128* **Baijiu**), it hardly matters what's playing.

A new law demands that microphones be switched off at 2am, so lock-ins are becoming widespread for those in the know.

The following are a few of the better karaoke venues – although the karaoke rooms at **Rojam** (*see above*) are also well worth checking out.

### Langsha KTV

*6/F, 2018 Huashan Lu, by Guangyuan Xi Lu, Xujiahui (5407 0300/www.langshaktv.com).* **Open** 10am-2am daily. **Credit** AmEx, MC, V. **Admission** RMB 22-45 per room per hr (no min spend). **Map** p246 A10.

### Gold Glorious

*4th & 5th floors, Golden Bell Plaza, 98 Huaihai Zhong Lu, by Longmen Lu, Xintiandi (5385 8608). Metro Huangpi Nan Lu.* **Open** 8pm-2am daily. **Admission** min spend on food & drink RMB 980 in room for 6. **Credit** MC, V. **Map** p248 J7.

### Partyworld (Cashbox)

*109 Yandang Lu, within Fuxing Park, French Concession (6374 1111/www.cashboxpartuy.com). Metro Huangpi Nan Lu.* **Open** 8am-2am daily. **Admission** varies; average RMB 160/hr in room for 4. **Credit** MC, V. **Map** p247 G8.

**Other locations:** 68 Zhejiang Nan Lu, by Ninghai Dong Lu, Huangpu (6374 9909); 457 Wulumuqi Bei Lu, by Yanan Zhong Lu, Jingan (6249 0300).

### Pu-J's Podium

*Level 3, Jinmao Building, 88 Shiji Dadao, Pudong (5049 1234 ext 8732). Metro Lujiazui.* **Open** 7pm-1am Mon-Thur; 7pm-2am Fri, Sat. **Admission** min spend on food & drink RMB 1,200 in room for 4. **Credit** MC, V. **Map** p245 O5.

# Performing Arts

A city of extraordinary venues but lacking just that little bit of stage presence.

Though Shanghai boasts a number of spectacular theatres – including the new Shanghai Oriental Art Centre (SOAC) and the Shanghai Grand Theatre – the architecture rather too often surpasses the art. These striking venues tend to cater to a rather non-committal crowd, offering a commercially driven blend of ballet (*The Nutcracker, Swan Lake* et al), hit musicals (*The Phantom of the Opera, The Lion King*) and some big-name international classical music acts (Pavarotti, Carreras).

Shanghai may still play second fiddle to Beijing, but the city's art scene has developed substantially in recent years. The former cultural wasteland of Pudong welcomed the high-profile Shanghai Oriental Art Centre in 2004, an extraordinary building by Paul Andreu, which is crafted in the shape of a blossoming butterfly orchid.

A slew of new festivals has also broadened horizons; in 2005 Shanghai held its first **Asian Contemporary Theatre Festival** and **Shakespeare Festival**; 2006 saw the first instalment of the **Beckett Festival** and the city's first contemporary dance festival, **Shanghai Dance** (Jin Xing Dance Theatre, www.shanghai-dance.com). And in any given month you can catch a dozen worthwhile performances, including dance, English-language or -subtitled drama, Chinese drama and sketch comedy, dance, acrobatics (*see p188* **Turning tricks**) and Shanghai's most prominent theatrical form, opera. Not a bad show for a developing – albeit a very fast-developing – country.

Shanghai has an enviably rich seam of traditional dance, but hasn't had the momentum to move beyond the traditional and test the boundaries. There are few contemporary dance troupes and only a few players of any real significance; chief among them is Shanghai-based dancer/choreographer Jin Xing, who single-handedly funded and organised Shanghai's first dance festival in 2006 and now runs the successful **Jin Xing Modern Dance Company** (*see p189*).

Although the language is a barrier to the majority of visitors, Shanghai's local theatres stage some interesting fare. Look out for the Chinese classics (*Dream of the Red Chamber, Teahouse*); Shanghainese classics (*Song of Everlasting Sorrow, Love in a Fallen City*), based on novels by Eileen Zhang; and more modern fare, such as plays drawn from internet novels or 'white collar theatre' focusing on the trials and tribulations of Shanghai's 'chuppies' (Chinese + yuppy). Still deeper dramas take place in the murky depths of **Downstream Garage** (3rd floor, No.100, Lane 200, Longcao Lu, Hongqiao, 5448 3368, www.downstreamgarage.com), a free rehearsal space where students, amateurs and professionals mingle, performing works (in Chinese) that wouldn't make it to a main stage. Shanghai's performing arts scene is beginning to ferment, no doubt about it, but the wine won't be ready for pouring for another decade.

## TICKETS AND INFORMATION

The easiest way to get tickets is to buy them at the venue just before the show starts; for big hits (such as the musicals at the Shanghai Grand Theatre), advance booking is essential. If the box office is sold out, the *huangniu* ('yellow cows', or touts) will be happy sell you tickets at inflated prices. Tickets can also be bought through **China Ticket Online** (800 810 3721, 6374 8445, http://shdx.piao.com.cn/en_piao) or the **Shanghai Cultural Information and Booking Centre** (6217 2426/3055, www.culture.sh.cn).

For information about what's on, check listings in the local free press, particularly *that's Shanghai* (www.thatssh.com).

## Major venues

### Lyceum Theatre

*57 Maoming Nan Lu, by Changle Lu, French Concession (6256 5544). Metro Shanxi Nan Lu.* **Open** *Box office* 9am-7pm daily. **Tickets** RMB 100-580. **No credit cards. Map** p247 F7.
The Lyceum was built in 1931. Several redecorations later it still, thankfully, boasts stunning art deco architecture. The programme focuses mostly on traditional Chinese performing arts and children's dramas, such as *Thumbelina* and *The Ugly Duckling*, along with local productions of Shaolin Monks, Beijing and Yue opera, and *pingtan* (a unique Suzhounese form of storytelling involving songs, jokes and various Chinese instruments). **Photo** *p187*.

### Majestic Theatre

*66 Jiangning Lu, by Nanjing Xi Lu, Jingan (6217 4409). Metro Shimen Yi Lu.* **Open** *Box office* 10am-7.30pm daily. **Tickets** RMB 20-4,000. **No credit cards. Map** p243 E5.

*Arts & Entertainment*

When it went up in 1941, the dome-shaped Majestic was considered one of the best theatres in Asia and hosted performances with Beijing opera superstars. Nowadays the focus is on local farces, Eileen Zhang dramas, dance – both ballet (*Swan Lake*) and modern (*STOMP*, the Cloudgate Dance Theatre from Taiwan) – and musicals (*Mamma Mia!*), plus some English-language drama (*Last of the Red Hot Lovers*), folk music, opera and *pingtan*.

### Shanghai Centre Theatre

*1376 Nanjing Xi Lu, by Xikang Lu, Jingan (6279 8663/acrobatics 6279 8948/www.shanghaicentre. com). Metro Jingan Temple.* **Open** *Box office* 9am-7.30pm daily. **Tickets** RMB 100-200. **No credit cards. Map** p243 E5.
Part of the same complex as the Portman Ritz-Carlton (*see p37*), the Shanghai Centre has an electric programme of modern dance and ballet, mime and various foreign musical performances. The regular default performance (7.30pm daily) is a popular acrobatic show from Shanghai Acrobats (www.shanghaiacrobats.com).

### Shanghai Circus World

*2266 Gonghe Xin Lu, by Guangzhong Lu, Zhabei (6652 7750/6630 0000/www.era-shanghai.com). Metro Shanghai Circus World.* **Open** *Box office* 9am-8pm daily. **Tickets** RMB 80-580. **No credit cards. Map** p240 D1.
At Shanghai Circus World, which looks like a giant golden golf ball half-embedded in the ground, audiences are treated to a fantastic display of 'new circus' acrobatics. *ERA: Intersection of Time* (7.30pm daily), choreographed by Canadian Eric Villeneuve, has a distinct foreigner-awed-by-Shanghai flavour, but is no less spectacular for it. It combines graceful moves with slick multimedia touches – and enough death-defying moves to keep the adrenalin pumping all around the arena. *ERA* is set to run until mid 2008. *See also p188* **Turning tricks.**

### Shanghai Concert Hall

*523 Yanan Dong Lu, by Xizang Zhong Lu, People's Square (5386 6666/www.shanghaiconcerthall.org). Metro People's Square.* **Open** *Box office* 9am-7.30pm daily. **Tickets** RMB 20-1,500. **Credit** AmEx, DC, MC, V. **Map** p244 J6.
Formerly known as the Nanking Theatre, the Shanghai Concert Hall has come a long way – literally. The 74-year-old building was moved 66m (217ft) to the south-east in 2003 – at great cost – to reduce the noise from the Yanan elevated highway. It slid nicely into place above the People's Square metro station. The faint rumble of trains can only occasionally be heard and it's an attractive venue. It has become a top-notch classical music venue, hosting such acts as the Vienna Johann Strauss Capelle, Yo-Yo Ma, Regina Carter, various Western orchestras and themed children's concerts. **Photo** *p189.*

### Shanghai Grand Stage

*1111 Caoxi Bei Lu, Shanghai Stadium, Xujiahui (6438 5200). Metro Shanghai Stadium.* **Open**

**Lyceum Theatre.**
**See p186.**

*Box office* 9am-7pm daily. **Tickets** RMB 80-1,680. **No credit cards. Map** p240 C5.
The indoor stage of Shanghai Stadium is neither friendly nor cosy, but this is usually where the shows that are too big for the likes of the Shanghai Centre (*see p67*) end up. Expect the likes of the Backstreet Boys, Michael Bolton and a whole host of their Canto-pop counterparts.

### Shanghai Grand Theatre

*300 Renmin Dadao, by Huangpi Bei Lu, People's Square (6386 8686 ext 2116/www.shgtheatre.com). Metro People's Square.* **Open** *Box office* 9am-7.30pm daily. **Tickets** RMB 80-6,000. **Credit** AmEx, DC, MC, V. **Map** p244 H5.
This impressive modern theatre with a distinctive curved roof is Shanghai's premier venue for opera, classical music, ballet and drama, and home to the Shanghai Broadcasting Symphony Orchestra. The most popular billings are imported big-hit musicals – *Cats, The Phantom of the Opera, The Lion King* – which are performed in English, by foreign actors and producers; the theatre has also staged operas

# Turning tricks

Acrobatics in China has a long, rich history, dating back several thousand years to the Warring States Period (475-221 BC). Prior to 1949, it was frowned upon by the well-to-do, but in the 1950s the People's government recognised and developed it as a national art

form. China now has more than 120 national troupes with over 12,000 performers. The art has developed over the generations to incorporate everyday objects – saucers, chairs, jars, plates – and other traditions such as the Chinese martial art *wushu*.

The **Shanghai Acrobatic Troupe** is one of the most famous in China and tours internationally. The best place to see it perform is Shanghai Circus World (*see p187*), a futuristic globe in the north of the city with high-tech lighting, stereo sound and rotating stages. The current show, *ERA: Intersection of Time*, running until mid 2008, is a spectacular – and hugely popular – display of 'new acrobatics', incorporating dance, elaborate costumes, live music and dazzling lighting. It's all there: balancing acts, trapeze artists, magicians, human towers and the strong man who performs unbelievable feats with a giant porcelain pot.

For more traditional acrobatics, visit the **Shanghai Centre Theatre** (*see p187*) for balancing acts performed with barrels, parasols and bowls.

such as *The Barber of Seville*, and *Swan Lake* is performed every few months, along with other classics such as *The Nutcracker* and *Giselle*, often by the Shanghai Ballet. A steady stream of Yue and Kun opera is complemented by the occasional visit by an international star of classical music.

## Shanghai Oriental Art Centre

*425 Dingxiang Lu, by Shiji Dadao, Pudong (6854 7757/www.shoac.com.cn). Metro Science & Technology Museum.* **Open** *Box office* 10am-8pm daily. **Tickets** RMB 100-1,800. **No credit cards.** **Map** p241 G4.

Completed for a whopping US$120 million at the end of 2004, the high-profile SOAC has been touted as the jewel of Pudong or, as its French architect Paul Andreu explains, 'a light in the darkness'. There can be no doubt that it shines, with a glass façade that's simultaneously reflective and transparent, though wood panelling on the inside makes it warmer than you might expect. Inside the petals of the orchid-shaped building are three halls (a 2,000-seat orchestra hall, a 1,000-seat lyric theatre and a 330-seat chamber music hall) equipped with state-of-the-art sound and lighting systems and the largest pipe organ in China. SOAC is typical of the Shanghai attitude towards culture – if you build it, they will come – and programming has so far struggled to find a purpose. With the Shanghai Grand Theatre (*see p187*) the premier venue for musicals and the

Shanghai Concert Hall (*see p187*) the leading classical venue, SOAC has to rely on local residents to fill its seats. The bill mixes ballet, Chinese drama and classical music, with the 2005/6 season welcoming the Russian Ballet, José Carreras and the titled 'God Bless China' vocalist concert.

## Yi Fu Theatre

*701 Fuzhou Lu, by Yunnan Zhong Lu, People's Square (6322 5294/www.tianchan.com). Metro People's Square.* **Open** *Box office* 9.30am-7.30pm daily. **Tickets** RMB 30-500. **No credit cards.** **Map** p244 J5.

Around since 1921, but massively revamped in the early 1990s, Yi Fu is the main venue for grand Chinese operas, particularly the Beijing variety – as indicated by the huge Beijing opera mask that dominates the entrance. It also stages Yue and Kun opera performances. Regular weekly performances on weekends at 1.30pm and 7.15pm.

## Other venues & companies

The quality of Shanghai's smaller venues is variable, but the occasional interesting show does emerge.

## Shanghai Art Theatre (Yihai Theatre)

*466 Jiangning Lu, by Wuding Lu, Jingan (6256 8282). Metro Shimen Yi Lu, then taxi or 15min walk.*

Open 10am-8pm daily. Tickets RMB 30-280.
No credit cards. Map p243 E3.
The Art Theatre is used mainly for classical music, plus occasional productions of Yue and Yang opera, dance and sizzling revolutionary shows.

## Shanghai Theatre Academy

*630 Huashan Lu, by Zhenning Lu, French Concession (6248 8103/www.sta.edu.cn). Metro Jingan Temple.* Open *Box office* 8.30am-4.30pm daily. Tickets RMB 20-80. No credit cards. Map p246 B7.
Budding thesps from the Academy periodically stage interesting drama and dance shows at the school's theatre, including experimental numbers.

# Classical music

Shanghai's classical music scene suffers from a shortage of talent, but things are looking up. There are over 20 million young pianists in China and foreign masters, such as Michael Tilson Thomas (San Francisco Symphony) and Liszt master Leslie Howard, have been providing masterclasses and workshops. In the meantime, big international acts make frequent appearances in the city.

Two major new music venues – **Shanghai Concert Hall** (*see p187*) and **Shanghai Oriental Art Centre** (*see p188*) – have injected some life into the scene. Although the appetite for classical music among locals and expats remains small, the city hosts a dozen major performances a month by local and international performers. In addition to big venues, some hotels have regular recitals: the **Jinjiang Hotel** (*see p41*) has concerts the first Sunday of each month, starting at 7pm (RMB 50), and the **InterContinental Hotel Pudong** (777 Zhangyang Lu, Pudong, 6248 1888 ext 3894) hosts concerts on the third Sunday of every month, starting at 2pm (RMB 80). Students of the **Conservatory of Music** (20 Fenyang Lu, 6431 0334) regularly host 7pm weekend concerts at their auditorium. Perhaps most surprisingly, the **Glamour Bar** (*see p125*) hosts international pianists and cellists.

## Shanghai Broadcasting Symphony Orchestra

*Office: 1498 Wuding Xi Lu, by Jiangsu Lu, Jingan (6252 3277/fax 6252 3267).*
Despite its youth (established in 1996), the SBSO has already notched up high-profile collaborations with artists including Placido Domingo, Pavarotti, Isaac Stern and Lang Lang. Under the direction of Chen Zuohang, it is the resident orchestra at the Shanghai Grand Theatre (*see p187*).

## Shanghai Symphony Orchestra

*www.sh-symphony.com*
Asia's oldest orchestra, the SSO began in 1879 as the Shanghai Public Band and was expanded into the Shanghai Municipal Council Symphony Orchestra under the baton of Italian pianist Mario Paci in 1922; its first Chinese director took over – surprise, surprise – in 1949. Current director Chen Xieyi has built himself a reputation through collaborations with the likes of John Nelson, Gil Shaham, Yo-Yo Ma, José Carreras and Placido Domingo.

# Dance

## Jin Xing Modern Dance Company

*Office: Room 601, 128 Weihai Lu, by Huangpi Bei Lu, People's Square (6327 0040).*
Though her name Jin Xing (Gold Star) is a tad kitsch, no one can dispute the fact that she's earned it. The opinionated choreographer and dancer – formerly a male army colonel – founded her own dance company in 1999, making it China's first privately funded contemporary dance company, and has put endless hours and huge amounts of money into supporting the local dance scene in her role as director of the Shanghai Dance festival. Her most interesting work was *Shanghai Beauty*, a meditation on different concepts of beauty across various cultures, which mixes modern with various forms of Chinese folk dance. The combination upset the purists at home but garnered considerable praise abroad.

## Shanghai Oriental Youth Dance Troupe

*Office: 1674 Hongqiao Nan Lu, by Shuicheng Lu, Hongqiao (6270 6586/fax 6270 6586).*
One of the city's most innovative dance companies, although to call it 'experimental' would perhaps be an exaggeration. Successful shows have included *Wild Zebra, Farewell My Concubine* and, most

**Shanghai Concert Hall.** See p187.

recently, *Guardian of the Red Cloud*. The 30-strong troupe has an average age of 20 and frequently tours internationally.

## Shanghai Song & Dance Ensemble

*Office: 1650 Hongqiao Lu, by Shuicheng Nan Lu, Hongqiao (6219 5181/fax 6275 9642/www. 52921234.com/gewutuan).*
The city's most high-profile troupe focuses on ethnic dance, large-scale opera and ballet. Established in the late 1970s, the ensemble is currently blessed with the 28-year-old principal dancer and choreographer Huang Doudou. As a boy, Huang Doudou says his father hung him from the rafters in order to increase his height; today he aims to stretch the boundaries of traditional Chinese dance. Using the influences of Chinese opera and acrobatics, he has created the intriguing shows *Zen Shaolin* and *Drunken Drum*. His crowning moment was a piece by composer Tan Dun, performed for the opening ceremony of the 2004 Olympic Games in Athens.

# English-language theatre

English-language theatre is on the increase, performed both by local groups and by foreign drama troupes on tour; musicals at the **Shanghai Grand Theatre** are also performed in English. For cabaret, *see pp182-185* **Nightlife**.

## Shanghai Dramatic Arts Centre (SDAC)

*288 Anfu Lu, by Wukang Lu, French Concession (6473 4567/www.china-drama.com). Metro Changshu Lu.* **Open** *Box office* 10am-7pm daily. **Admission** RMB 80-800. **No credit cards. Map** p246 C7.
SDAC established itself as a high-calibre venue that wasn't afraid to push the boundaries in 2003, when it premièred taboo-breaking AIDS melodrama *The Dying Kiss*. This is also where Eve Ensler's rabble-rousing *Vagina Monologues* was intended to run in late 2004, before it was stopped by the authorities. Classics such as *Endgame* play alongside Chinese opera versions of *Waiting for Godot*. It's common to find Chinese adaptations (subtitled in English) of Western plays, such as *Noises Off*, *Closer* and *Jane Eyre*, along with festivals focusing on Shakespeare, Beckett or contemporary Asian theatre.

# Chinese opera

Chinese opera is wrought from monotone music, simple props and minimalist staging. To express an action such as opening a door or riding a horse, only dance-like movements are used. It's fascinating but often impossible to understand, with costumes, make-up and movements carrying specific motifs as well as denoting the age, status and personality of a character. The plot fodder is more familiar: heroes battle foes, good faces evil, lovers escape from unjust parents. To get a basic grasp of the

story, you need to be aware of the four standard roles: *sheng* (male role), *dan* (female role), *jing* (painted face) and *chou* (clown).

Adding to the confusion are the many varieties of Chinese opera – estimates range from 300 to thousands of different types. Generally, these are distinguished by their use of local dialects and distinct 'melodies'.

Beijing opera (also called Peking opera) is considered the most refined – and, despite initiatives that strive to bring Beijing opera to a younger crowd, the faithful fans are nearly always from an ageing generation. Weaving together elements of mime, dance, swordplay, song and acrobatics, it is a combination of operatics, drama and sketches. Add high-pitched voices accompanied by loud gongs, crashing cymbals and droning strings and you have a performance art that is compelling for some, torture for others.

Huju, or Shenju, is Shanghainese opera, but Yueju, the style from nearby Shaoxing, is better known and more melodic, usually focusing on love stories. The older Kunju opera, established in the 16th century, originates from the Kunshan region in nearby Jiangsu province.

In order to seduce the young ones, opera troupes have been putting on Chinese opera versions of Western dramas including *Hamlet*, *Peer Gynt* and *Waiting for Godot*. We couldn't really think of a worse combination than the latter, but crowds apparently loved it.

# Festivals & events

Shanghai's governing bodies see festivals as a good way of raising the city's arts profile, but the festivals are often poorly organised, with shoddy publicity and shoddier talent. The last **Shanghai International Arts Festival** in October (*see p156*), for example, managed to attract a handful of big musical names, but had precious little dance or drama. Conversely, privately organised festivals such as the **Asian Contemporary Theatre Festival** and May's **Shanghai Dance** (www.shanghai-dance.com), both held at the **SDAC** (*see above*), have proved the city can host successful and challenging festivals. For Shanghai Dance 2007, Jin Xing (*see p189*) hopes to bring in Pina Bausch, DV8 and the Peeping Toms.

Other fests include the **Shanghai International Spring Music Festival** (May), a cornucopia of international and local musicians playing everything from classical to jazz; the **Shanghai International Tourist Festival** (Sept), which features open-air concerts and a large, tacky float parade; and the biennial **Shanghai International Ballet Competition** (June/July 2007).

# Sport & Fitness

Big-bucks sports events belie apathy at the grassroots.

The extraordinary form of the **Qi Zhong Tennis Stadium.** *See p193.*

Michael Schumacher, Tiger Woods and Roger Federer are just a few of the sports superstars who now visit Shanghai on a regular basis. They might appease the press by saying it's because they love Chinese food, but there may be another incentive: Woods, for example, was offered $3 million to attend the HSBC Champions Golf Tournament in 2005, for which the prize money of $5 million was higher than any other tournament in Asia.

Figures like this on the professional scene certainly place Shanghai on a par with other sporting cities. But it's the futuristic facilities that really tickle us amateurs. If you're in town during a tennis tournament, consider a trip out to the new $200 million **Qi Zhong Tennis Stadium**. The retractable roof opens like a giant magnolia flower coming into bloom and you get the feeling that you might just spot James Bond in the crowd. No wonder Shanghai

gets to host the Tennis Masters Cup through to 2009. For those who prefer their sport steered not served, the **Shanghai International Circuit** is just as mind-boggling.

And we very much doubt it will stop there. International sporting event rights holders can't get enough of Shanghai – and Shanghai is pretty keen on them as well. What better way is there to project your city into living rooms around the world? The events themselves make huge losses, but the municipal government earns it all back through inward investment. Tiger Woods is actually one of Shanghai's brand ambassadors.

But, more crucially, who's looking out for sports at the grassroots level (*see p195* **Sporting future**)? Hosting such top-league events won't necessarily boost the domestic scene. And no one's dribbling that ball of investment down to the locals' end of the pitch.

# Spectator sports

Sports fans are largely content to follow the action from the city's sports bars, notably **Malone's** (*see p127*), **O'Malley's** (*see p129*), the **Long Bar** (1376 Nanjing Xi Lu, by Shanxi Nan Lu, 6279 8268) and the self-explanatory **British Bulldog** (1 Wulumuqi Nan Lu, by Dongping Lu, Xuhui, 6466 7878). To follow local sports check **www.s2mgroup.com.cn**, which carries an events calendar plus news.

## Athletics

In 2005 Shanghai won the right to host the world's top athletics competition, the **IAAF Grand Prix** (www.iaaf.org), for the following five years. The event is sure to draw big names, especially in 2009, when it counts as one of the crucial Golden League meetings. It takes place in September at the Shanghai Stadium.

### Shanghai Stadium

*1111 Caoxi Bei Lu, by Zhongshan Nan Er Lu, Xuhui (6438 5200/www.shanghai-stadium.online.sh.cn). Metro Shanghai Stadium.* **Map** p240 C5.

## Football

Having not qualified for the 2006 World Cup, Chinese football's head hangs low. The few Chinese players that have been signed overseas aren't helping either. National captain Du Wei had the greatest chance, but only lasted four months at Celtic. He played just 45 minutes in his one game against Clyde before he was packed off. But you can now join the local fans and cheer him back on his home turf, turning out for Shanghai Shenhua FC. Even if you're not gripped by stunning play, you will be entertained by the pitch etiquette (or lack of it) and the small but animated crowd. Matches take place most Sundays at the Hongkou Stadium; tickets start at around RMB 50 and can be bought on site just before the game. Call 5696 7633 for match times.

### Hongkou Stadium

*444 Dongjiangwan Lu, by Sichuan Bei Lu, Hongkou (6540 0009/www.51fb.com). Metro Hongkou Stadium.* **Map** p241 E1.

## Motor sports

The new **Shanghai International Circuit** is the pride of auto fans nationwide. Its shape emulates the Chinese character *shang*, meaning 'to grow', and symbolises money, money and more money. If you miss the annual **Formula 1** race (held in October; *see p156*), there are still the Motor GP (motorcycle), Formula 3, BMW, Renault, Formula 3000 and new A1 competitions. To get hold of cut-price tickets, try the touts at the Shanghai Stadium shuttle bus stop or at the circuit itself; RMB 2,000 F1 tickets go for as little as RMB 200.

### Shanghai International Circuit

*2000 Yining Lu, by Jiajin Highway, Anting, Jiading (9682 6999/www.icsh.sh.cn). Shuttle bus from Shanghai Stadium.* **No credit cards**.

## Table tennis

What better place to soak up some of the local culture than by watching the country's most famous sport? Local and national tournaments take place regularly across the city. Check http://tabletennis.sport.org.cn (in Chinese) for forthcoming events; otherwise, call the venues below. Tickets vary in price but the cheaper seats, where you are elevated above the play, are actually better for watching the game. Try the **Hongkou Stadium** (*see above*) or the **Yuan Shen Sports Centre**.

### Yuan Shen Sports Centre
*655 Yuan Shen Lu, by Zhangyang Lu, Pudong (5821 4336). Metro Dongfang Lu, then taxi.* **Open** 1-10pm Mon-Fri; 9am-10pm Sat, Sun. **Admission** RMB 20 1-6pm Mon-Fri, 9am-noon Sat, Sun; RMB 25 6-10pm Mon-Fri, noon-10pm Sat, Sun. **No credit cards.**

## Tennis

Shanghai has secured the **Tennis Masters Cup** (www.masters-cup.com) until 2009, possibly because of the stunning tennis stadium. Every November eight of the biggest stars in men's tennis descend on the city to battle it out for the title. Tickets cost between RMB 280 and RMB 4,800.

### Qi Zhong Tennis Stadium
*3028 Kunyang Bei Lu, Minhang (tickets 6384 9622). Shuttle bus from Metro Xinzhuang.*

## Participation sports

Some of the free city magazines, especially *that's Shanghai* (www.thatssh.com), detail a huge variety of sports from scuba diving in the local aquarium to kite-surfing on the Huangpu River. Also visit the online sports community **Active Sports Active Social** (www.asas.com.cn) to find out more about local sports leagues.

## Basketball

Most universities have games in the evening; strictly speaking they are for students, but you may be able to join in. For casual games try **Xujiahui Park** (between Zhoujiabang Lu and Hengshan Lu, 7.30am-9pm daily). Teams are mixed and the play is friendly. Participation is free and there is no official organiser – you just have to turn up.

### ASAS basketball
*Luwan Sports Centre, 135 Jianguo Xi Lu, by Shanxi Nan Lu, French Concession (contact Tom Zheng 1391 731 6770 mobile/Stephen Lee 1381 862 2562 mobile/services@asas.com.cn).* Attend weekly informal Wednesday-night get-togethers (8.30-10.30pm, RMB 400/2 mths; RMB 75/ session) or instead join one of 50 teams in the ASAS basketball league. A payment of roughly RMB 350 per person will cover gym rental, referee and team strip. Women are welcome.

### Girls Basketball
*Xujiahui Park basketball court, Wanping Lu, near Zhaojiabang Lu, Xujiahui (contact virginia_tan@126.com).* Half-court pick-up games take place every Thursday night 7-9pm (unless it rains). This is the sole women-only session in town.

## Dragon boat racing

This is a traditional Chinese form of rowing, using long, narrow, painted boats that sit around 20 between dragon head and tail. Rowers are kept to their stroke by the beat of a drum. It's very demanding, but if you're going to row in China, this is how.

### Shanglong Dragon Boat Club
*Contact dragonboatsh@yahoo.com.* **Meetings** 8am Sun at Gubei Starbucks, 20 Shuicheng Nan Lu, for onward travel to Dianshan Lake (45mins away). **Fee** RMB 50/wk.
This club, formed in 1999, has been dubbed the 'United Nations Dragon Boat Team' thanks to its mix of nationalities. Practice sessions involve more than one boat, so beginners are welcome. Remember to bring a change of clothes (this is obligatory – everything gets wet).

## Football

Shanghai's international league is the most competitive amateur league in China, with 13 teams competing weekly. They are sponsored by different bars around the city, who offer pitch rent, team strip, transport and a good chance of a free beer at the end of the match. Top of the league are the Shanghai Shooters, who take the game extremely seriously. For slightly more informal play talk to the teams at **O'Malley's** (*see p129*), **Big Bamboo** (132 Nanyang Lu, by Xikang Lu, Jingan, 6256 2265) or **Long Bar** (1376 Nanjing Xi Lu, by Shanxi Nan Lu, 6279 8268).

### Shanghai International Football League
*Tianma Golf & Country Club, 3958 Zhaokun Lu, Tianma Town, Songjiang (5766 1666/www.eteams.com/sifl).* **Meetings** 11am Sat. **Admission** free. Matches take place at the club's two pitches.

## Golf

Check the local magazines for golf leagues. Local bar **Sasha's** (*see p130*) runs a corporate league; for up-to-date times and prices, call the manager Daniel on 6474 6628.

### Binhai Golf Club
*Binhai Resort, Baiyulan Dadao, Pudong (5805 8888/ www.binhaigolf.com).* **Rates** *Non-members* RMB 780 Mon-Fri; RMB 1,480 Sat, Sun. **Credit** MC. V.
Designed by five-times British Open Champion Peter Thomson, Binhai is a course packed with bunkers.

### Lujiazui Golf Club
*501 Yindheng Zhong Lu, Pudong (5878 3844/ www.lujiazui-golf.com). Metro Lujiazui.* **Admission** RMB 60/hr 6.30am-1pm; RMB 120 1pm-midnight

Mon-Fri; RMB 100/hr 6.30-10am, 9pm-midnight; RMB 120 10am-9pm Sat, Sun. **Credit** MC, V.
A 229m (751ft) driving range in the Lujiazui business district, with 98 bays.

### Sheshan International Golf Club
*Lane 288, Linyin Xin Lu, Shanghai Sheshan National Holiday Zone (5765 5765/www.sheshan golf.com).* **Members only.**
Designed by Nelson & Haworth and only 35mins out of Shanghai, this course came under the spotlight as the host of the 2005 HSBC Champions Tournament. See if you can do better than Tiger Woods, who walked away without the title – if you can afford annual membership of RMB 1,280,000, that is, or know someone who can (non-members can visit as guests of members).

## Horse riding

Horse riding is growing in popularity in Shanghai. Most schools, including **Huijhang Riding Ranch** (517 Xinhua Lu, Pudong, 5084 8898) and **Jialiang Equestrian Club** (1858 Sanlu Lu, Pudong, 3411 0089, www. horsechina.com) still use retired racehorses, but the family-run **Meadow Brook** breeds its own horses and gets the best reviews.

### Meadow Brook
*3088 Shenzhuan Highway, Qingpu (6983 0055/ www.meadowbrookshanghai.com).* **Open** 9am-5.30pm daily. **Rates** *Without instructor* RMB 210/45mins Mon-Fri; RMB 260/45mins Sat, Sun. *With local instructor* RMB 130/lesson. *With foreign instructor* RMB 260/lesson. **No credit cards.**
Recently awarded a three-star rating by the UK's Hartpury College ('leader in land-based studies and sport'), this facility is by far the most professional stables in town (or, more accurately, an hour out of town). Beginners enjoy sand tracks, while more advanced riders can take on the grass courses.

## Ice skating

### Hongkou Swimming Pool Leisure Rink
*500 Dongjiangwan Lu, by Dongtiyuhui Lu, next to Hongkou Stadium, Hongkou (5671 5265). Metro Hongkou Stadium.* **Open** 10am-5pm Mon-Fri; 5-9pm Mon-Fri, Sat, Sun. **Rates** RMB 35-40/2hrs. **Map** p241 E1.
This outdoor pool is transformed into a partially outdoor ice rink in winter. The sport is new here, so there's no need to worry about your skill level.

## Racquet sports

Tennis and squash courts increase in number with the arrival of each new upmarket residence or hotel. Court rental costs around RMB 50 per hour. Badminton is a popular sport in China,

and locals can often be seen starting up casual games in parks. For badminton or squash, try **Shanghai Stadium** (*see p192*). Or take the one-hour shuttle bus out of town to the peaceful **Shanghai Racket Club**.

### Shanghai Racket Club
*555 Jinfeng Lu, Huacao Town, Minhang (2201 0088/www.src.com.cn). Shuttle bus (journey time 1hr) leaves from Portman Ritz-Carlton (see p37) every hr.* **Open** 5.30am-10pm daily. **Members only.**
Only make the trip out here if you plan to spend some serious time at the club. The facilities – indoor and outdoor pools, indoor and outdoor tennis courts, squash courts, table tennis, a gym, a children's play area and three restaurants – make that quite easy to do. It's members only but if you book yourself into one of the guestrooms (RMB 568 double) then you have access to all the fantastic facilities.

## Rugby

### Shanghai Rugby Football Club
*Biyun Lu, by Lanan Lu, Pudong (5030 3886/ www.shanghaifootballclub.com).* **Open** 9.30am-4.30pm Sat, Sun.
A proper centre for the sport in Shanghai and its expat fans, equipped with large playing fields and a clubhouse for refreshments. Check the website for details of multiple-team leagues and tournaments, and for the many other sports hosted here (Aussie rules and Gaelic football, netball, cricket, Ultimate frisbee and so on).

## Sailing

### Shanghai Boat & Yacht Club
*Shanghai Water Sports Centre, 289 Yingzhu Lu, Qingpu (www.shanghaibyc.org).* **Membership** RMB 2,000/yr, plus joining fee RMB 500.
Meet on Sundays before 10am at Oscar's (1377 Fuxing Zhong Lu, by Baoqing Lu, French Concession, 6431 6528) for onward travel to the centre. Help is offered to beginners, although this is not an instructing club. Monthly socials take place at Oscar's on the last Thursday of the month.

## Skiing & snowboarding

### Shanghai Yinqixing Indoor Skiing
*1835 Qixing Lu, by Gudai Lu, Minhang (6478 8666/www.yinqixing.com). Free shuttle bus from Xinzhuang metro station every 30mins.* **Open** 9.30am-10.30pm Mon-Thur; 9.30am-1am Fri, Sat. **Admission** RMB 98/hr Mon-Thur; RMB 118/hr Fri, Sat. **Credit** AmEx, MC, V.
The second-biggest indoor slope in the world holds more novelty value than serious skiing action, but the new on-site Mellowpark snowboard park is causing quite a stir with its boxes, rail and kicker. For up-to-date information on snowboarding events, visit www.mellowparks.cn.

# Sporting future?

While school kids in most countries are kicking around footballs or writing love letters to their heart-throbs, Chinese kids seem focused on one thing: their future. Academic achievement reigns supreme in a country whose university applications far outweigh the number of places available. In some provinces the university acceptance rate is as little as four per cent of those who sit the entrance exam.

'It's not just pressure from your parents or the teachers,' explains one 24-year-old, looking back over her school days, 'the whole of society is telling you that there's only one way to have a better life, and that's by going to university.' So from primary school onwards the education system is focused on passing tests. And physical education gets knocked out of the ring of examined subjects in the first round, with sport relegated to the sidelines with a couple of 40-minute lessons per week.

Even extra-curricular sporting activity is frowned upon: your average Chinese kid leaves school around 5.30pm and will work until midnight with a short break for dinner. This isn't only a questionable way of maturing a healthy child, it's an absolute catastrophe for sports marketing. As Mark Thomas, who has been tackling this problem with his Shanghai-based events company S2M, notes: 'Without widespread participation in sports, there is no grassroots sports network,

and that is what fuels the business of sport.' In other words, there's no passion, which means no fans and – ultimately – no money.

Go to a football match in Shanghai and you'll see the evidence. Locals can watch top-class footie played by the teams in the China Super League, but stadiums are lucky to get 10,000 people in. Granted, Chinese football is a badly administered sport, but the fundamental problem is the lack of following. The Chinese haven't grown up playing the sport or following a team, so there's no lifetime bond.

The same goes for basketball, which has seen a recent explosion in popularity. Even though kids look passionate about it, they don't actually care about the China Basketball League. Ask a real Chinese basketball fan which league he follows and it will most likely be America's NBA. So you might wonder where prodigies such as cash-rich Chinese basketball hero Yao Ming slam-dunked from. China tends to reserve all its sport coaching for a chosen few who are sent to elite sports schools from a young age.

The good news is that the Chinese government is working (slowly, mind) to introduce more sport at school and to provide better sporting facilities. Things are already a lot rosier than they were a few years ago, but it will be some time yet before high-school kids trade their after-school study for interschool sports leagues.

## Swimming

Shanghai's hotels and fancy apartment complexes usually have pools and most of them allow visitors in for around RMB 100 per session. For something in the lower price range, you can visit the pool at **Shanghai Stadium** (*see p192*) or the outdoor pool on the **East China Normal University** campus. Swimming hats are obligatory but they can usually be purchased on site.

### Dino Beach

*78 Xinzhen Lu, Minhang (6478 3333/www.6478 3333.com). Metro Xinzhuang, then bus 763 for 4 stops.* **Open** *Late June-early Sept* 9am-9pm daily. **Admission** RMB 120/day (RMB 60/day children) Mon-Fri; RMB 150/day (RMB 75/day children) Sat, Sun; free children under 0.8m. **No credit cards**.
A popular water amusement park with an artificial beach and the world's biggest wave pool.

### East China Normal University

*3683 Zhongshan Bei Lu, by Jinshajiang Lu, Putuo (6223 2954).* **Open** 3-9pm daily. **Admission** RMB 10. **No credit cards**.
One of the city's few public outdoor pools. It's quite busy and a decent size, but don't expect any frills.

### Mandarin City

*788 Hongxu Lu, by Shuicheng Nan Lu, Changning (6405 0404 ext 8612). Bus 69, get off at Guyang Lu stop.* **Open** 7.30am-9pm Mon, Wed, Fri-Sun; 1-9pm Thur. **Admission** RMB 60/day; RMB 40 children. **No credit cards**.
An open-air pool inside a residential compound.

## Martial arts

Would-be Bruce Lees looking to learn their craft in Shanghai can sign up for karate, tae kwon do, viet vo dao and judo; check the local magazines and gyms (*see p196*) for further details of courses and classes.

**Arts & Entertainment**

## Kung fu

Most schools teach modern kung fu, which only covers the basics of the original form. Learning traditional kung fu takes a lifetime's commitment and most Masters have been practising since childhood. The instructors below teach the traditional form and expect extreme dedication from pupils. Foreigners are humoured because they pay money.

### Long Wu International Kung Fu Centre

*1 Maoming Nan Lu, by Julu Lu, French Concession (5465 0042/www.shanghaiwushu.com). Metro Shanxi Nan Lu.* **Times** 7-9pm daily. **Rates** RMB 1,500/3mths. **No credit cards. Map** p243 F6.
This is the most popular location for group classes, with many different teachers available.

### Wang Xiao Peng

*Zongteng3@yahoo.com.cn/1350 173 0640.*
Wang (aka Darren) is a sixth-generation member of the Heart and Soul 6 Harmony Boxing Kung Fu family. He teaches tai chi and kung fu motivational training for corporate executives. If the harmony of business and kung fu principles doesn't turn you off, you can also find Wang instructing classes at Tongji University. Private classes cost around RMB 200. This is a good option for those who don't speak Chinese and aren't short of cash.

## Tai chi

Tai chi practice in the early mornings remains one of the most magical aspects of Shanghai. Groups start at 4.30am in winter and 5am in summer, continuing until around 9.30am. You should ask the Master's permission to join in with a particular group and offer payment, although usually it is free. If he sees you are committed, he will guide you, but it may be months before this happens. **Fuxing Park**, **Renmin Park** and **Liuxun Park** (next to Hongkou Stadium, *see p192*) are the most popular locations.

## Fitness

For yoga studios and classes, *see p177*.

## Dance

### Jazz du Funk

*6th floor, Building 2, 412 Weihai Lu, by Shimen Yi Lu, French Concession (6253 3410/www.jazzdufunk. com). Metro Shimen Yi Lu.* **Rates** (20 classes) RMB 1,500. **No credit cards. Map** p243 F5.
Beginner, intermediate and advanced belly dancing, hip hop, tango, jazz, street jazz, jazz ballet, ballet, flamenco, tap and salsa. Dancewear available.

### Shanghai Swings

*No.5, basement floor, 20 Guangdong Lu, by Zhongshan Dong Yi Lu, the Bund (contact Jimbo 1316 625 5905 mobile/www.chinaswings.com).* **Admission** RMB 80/lesson (incl 1 soft drink). **Map** p245 M5.
Remember the swinging '20s every Wednesday night on the Bund. Beginners welcome from 8.30pm to get in some practice before the swing band starts at 9.30pm. Sunday lessons also take place, check the website for exact location.

## Gyms

Prices average RMB 1,500 per month for the luxury of a swimming pool; standard gym facilities cost around RMB 600 per month. Check with your hotel concierge or consult the full listings in *that's Shanghai*. Customer service, however, is something no amount of money can buy, with staff often too busy with their own workouts to bother with the customers.

### Fitness First

*Plaza 66, 1266 Nanjing Xi Lu, by Tongren Lu, Jingan (6288 0152). Metro Jingan Temple.* **Open** 6.30am-11pm Mon-Thur; 6.30am-10pm Fri; 8am-10pm Sat, Sun. **Membership** RMB 2,100/3mths (min). **Credit** AmEx, DC, MC, V. **Map** p243 E5.
Down in the basement of a plush shopping centre, FF is spacious, with rows of high-tech equipment, nationally certified trainers and a particularly well-organised free weights area. There's also a solarium.

### Kerry Centre Gym

*2nd floor, Kerry Centre, 1515 Nanjing Xi Lu, by Tongren Lu, Jingan (6279 4625). Metro Jingan Temple.* **Open** 6am-11pm daily. **Membership** RMB 13,000/yr. **Credit** AmEx, DC, MC, V. **Map** p242 D5.
Small but perfectly formed. Membership is limited, so the place never gets crowded. The facilities include a swimming pool, jacuzzi, steam room, sauna, solarium and outdoor tennis courts.

### Physical

*5th floor, Metro City, 1111 Zhaojiabang Lu, by Hengshan Lu, Xujiahui (6426 8282). Metro Xujiahui.* **Open** 7am-10pm daily. **Membership** RMB 500/mth. **Credit** AmEx, MC, V. **Map** p246 A11
A large basic gym with swimming pool, sauna and aerobics studio in the middle of shopping-mall land.

### Total Fitness

*6th floor, 819 Nanjing Xi Lu, by Shimen Yi Lu, Jingan (6255 3535/www.totalfitness.com.cn). Metro Shimen Yi Lu.* **Open** 7.30am-10.30pm Mon-Fri; 8am-10pm Sat, Sun. **Membership** RMB 688/mth; day pass RMB 150. **Credit** MC, V. **Map** p243 F5.
Total has no swimming pool, but there is exercise machinery aplenty, plus a sauna and a solarium. Plus, for those who care, this is the only gym in Shanghai to boast a boxing ring.

**Arts & Entertainment**

# Trips Out of Town

**Tongli**. *See p202.*

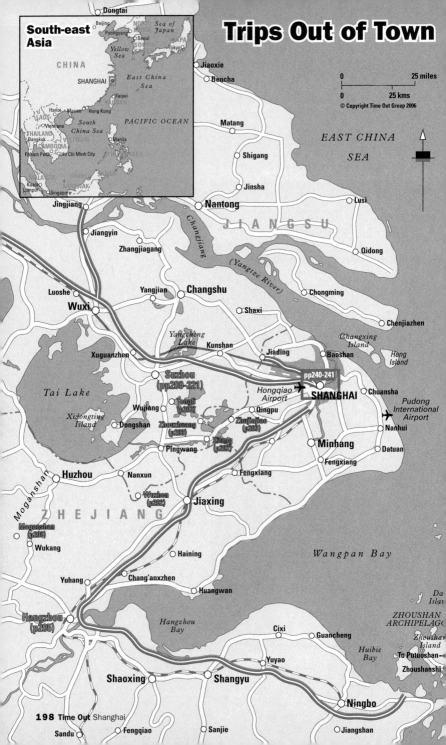

# Trips Out of Town

## South-east Asia

0 — 25 miles
0 — 25 kms
© Copyright Time Out Group 2006

EAST CHINA SEA

PACIFIC OCEAN

**JIANGSU**

Dongtai

Jiaoxie

Bencha

Matang

Shigang

Jinsha

Lusi

Jingjiang

**Nantong**

Qidong

Jiangyin

Zhangjiagang

Changjiang (Yangtze River)

Luoshe

Yangjian

**Changshu**

Shaxi

Chongming

**Wuxi**

Yangcheng Lake

Kunshan

Jiading

Baoshan

Changxing Island

Heng Island

Chenjiazhen

Xuguanzhen

**Suzhou** (pp209-221)

Jiading

Baoshan

pp240-241

**SHANGHAI**

Chuansha

Tai Lake

Tongli (p224)

Wujiang

Zhouzhuang (p223)

Zhujiajiao (p225)

Hongqiao Airport

Qingpu

Pudong International Airport

Xidongting Island

Dongshan

Xitang (p222)

Pingwang

Nanhui

Datuan

**Minhang**

Moganshan

**Huzhou**

Nanxun

Wuzhen (p222)

Fengxiang

Fengxiang

**Moganshan** (p208)

**ZHEJIANG**

**Jiaxing**

Wangpan Bay

Wukang

Haining

Yuhang

Chang'anzhen

Huangwan

Da Islan

ZHOUSHAN ARCHIPELAGO

**Hangzhou** (p205)

Hangzhou Bay

Cixi

Guancheng

Zhoushan Island

Huibie Bay

To Putuoshan

Yuyao

Zhoushanshi

**Shaoxing**

**Shangyu**

**198** Time Out Shanghai

Sandu

Fengqiao

Sanjie

**Ningbo**

Jiangshan

# Getting Started

It's easy to get shot of town, less easy to leave the crowds behind.

The canals of **Zhouzhuang**. *See p203.*

Shanghai is a good starting point for exploring the Yangtze River delta, meaning **Jiangsu** and **Zhejiang** provinces. These are two of the most prosperous provinces in China, which means that they are quite heavily urbanised. Tourist hotspots can get claustrophobically crowded on weekends and at peak seasons, so it may be necessary to travel quite far if you're looking for tranquillity and scenes of unspoilt Chinese countryside.

Water is a big feature of the landscape – lakes, canals and rivers are among the most famous attractions – and a disconcertingly large number of towns claim to be 'the Venice of the East'. Don't be fooled: the only real similarity is likely to be criss-crossing canals. Several **canal towns** (*see p201*) – which once served as trade hubs, shipping cargo along the waterways – now see duty as film sets and as backdrops of ye olde China for snap-happy visitors. Tourist interest inspired the authorities to clean up the waterways, but rising popularity has meant bigger and bigger crowds.

As the old Chinese saying goes, 'In heaven there is paradise, on earth there are Suzhou and Hangzhou.' **Suzhou** (*see p209*), to the west of

Shanghai, is famed for its ornamental gardens. Once China's cultural capital, it is now a hub for high-tech manufacturing – a fact that seems a little incongruous when you're enthralled by the cunning landscaping in one of the gardens.

**Hangzhou** (*see p205*) is the capital of Zhejiang province, to the south of Shanghai, and access point to the most famous lake in China: Xihu (West Lake). Nearby **Moganshan** (*see p208*), once a summer getaway for the harried denizens of Shanghai, is regaining its popularity as a destination for those needing to get away from the hype and buzz of the city. The lush rolling hills and mountains of Zhejiang also encompass the Zhoushan archipelago, of which the Buddhist holy island **Putuoshan** (*see p212*) is a part.

Hangzhou, Moganshan and Putuoshan are best visited over a couple of days; for the latter two especially, journey times make a day-trip too much of a rush. The other destinations described can all be reached in less than half a day, making them more suitable for day-trippers.

As a general rule, the further you get from Shanghai, the less likely you are to find English speakers, swanky facilities and Western luxuries. Accommodation in the canal towns, for example, can be quite basic (despite the fact that some of these towns are turning into tourist traps). But wandering off the well-trodden path and putting up with a lower glitz factor can be the only way to enjoy stunning views and meet friendly folk.

## TOURIST INFORMATION

Official tourist information and service centres may be hard to find outside Shanghai – some places have a China International Travel Service (CITS), but they aren't always much help. Travel agents within Shanghai are usually able to provide better information, and there are some good websites: try www.travelchinaguide.com, www.chinatravel.com or www.chinatripadvisor.com. For hotel reservations and discounts, try www.ctrip.com. Some destinations also have dedicated websites with photos and information.

## BASICS

Hotel prices given are the rack rate. Off-peak discounts of up to 40 per cent can often be negotiated, especially on winter weekdays. For Spring Festival, the May and October holidays, and the summer season (about mid July to mid September) prices may rise much higher.

# Getting around

## By bus

Local buses run to all the destinations covered in this chapter except Moganshan. Special sightseeing buses also run from a few venues around town. The buses are used largely by domestic day-trippers and typically leave from 8am onwards and return before dark.

For information (in Chinese) call 6426 5555 or go to www.chinassbc.com. The main terminal is at **Shanghai Stadium** (666 Tianyaoqiao Lu, by Zhongshan Nan Er Lu, Xuhui, 6426 5555). Buses also depart from **Hongkou Stadium** (444 Dongjiawan Lu, by Sichuan Bei Lu, Hongkou, 5696 3248), **Shanghai Circus World** (2266 Gonghe Xin Lu, Zhabei, 5665 9121), **Yangpu Stadium** (640 Longchang Lu, 6580 3210) and **Huangpu Station** (at Nanpu Bridge, 1588 Waima Lu, 6378 5559).

## The best Trips

### For sunbathing on the beach
**Putuoshan** isn't just for pilgrims seeking blessings from Guanyin. The fine sand beaches are also ideal for worshippers of the sun. See p212.

### For garden-hopping
Chinese ornamental gardens are quite different from the European variety. **Suzhou** is where to go to be captivated by each little fengshui'd detail. See p209.

### For romantic walks in the country
Stroll amid forests of lush green bamboo and look up to the misty mountain tops of **Moganshan**. See p208.

### For walks under moonlight
**Xihu** (the West Lake), endlessly praised by China's greatest poets, is at its most spectacular under the light of the moon. See p205.

### For living out a Ming Dynasty fantasy
In **Xitang** you can drink Chinese wine by the water, bathed by the light of red lanterns, then retire for the night to Ming Dynasty-style digs at the inn. Silk robes optional. See p202.

## By rail

Rail travel offers a more communal experience and (sometimes) better views. Choose 'hard seat' or 'soft seat', with the option of a hard seat definitely not one for the faint-hearted. Trains run to Hangzhou, Suzhou and Wuzhen. Tickets can be bought on the day of travel at the train station, where the 'English-speaking' window, rather conveniently, usually has the shortest queue. Tickets are also available through **China Youth Travel Service** (see p217). A partial timetable can be found online at **www.china-train-ticket.com**. During the Spring Festival and the May and October holidays, train stations get very crowded and a certain ruthlessness can be required if you want to get tickets.

## By car

Except for Putuoshan, the places listed in this chapter are all accessible by car and roads are generally in quite good condition – until you take off down the country lanes. There is usually a car park near the entrance of each of the canal towns, which are all small enough to explore on foot; the sights of Suzhou are all within town, so a car might not be necessary at all. It is, however, especially useful to have a car for exploring Hangzhou and Moganshan, as you can stop at will to explore the surrounding countryside.

## By boat

Fast ferries to Putuoshan leave from **Luchaogang Dock** (timetables 5828 2201) in the Nanhui disctrict (to the south of Shanghai); slow ferries leave from **Wusong Dock** (timetables 5657 5500), situated where the Huangpu River flows into the sea. Both fast and slow ferry tickets are available from 59 Jinling Dong Lu (no phone), which also sells tickets to other domestic destinations. Go in person to buy the tickets, preferably a few days in advance. For more details about ferries to Putuoshan, see p214.

## By bicycle

Weekly cycle trips out of the city offer an interesting way to see the places in this chapter. **Shanghai Bike Club** (5266 9013, www.bohdi.com.cn, neril@bohdi.com.cn) offers rental and repair services, and organises trips. **Cycle China** (139 1707 1775 mobile, www.cyclechina.com, shanghai@cyclechina.com) can arrange private bike tours too.

# The Canal Towns

A charming sojourn in ye olde China.

Tongli. *See p202.*

If you're hankering after postcard-perfect scenes of old China, the canal towns should be your excursion of choice. They have served as backdrop for many a Chinese drama series and even the odd Hollywood flick (Xitang has a supporting role in *Mission: Impossible III*). All the towns offer similar attractions: a cluster of old buildings (some dating back to the 1600s and the Ming Dynasty), bridges and criss-crossing canals, costumed gondoliers, numerous teahouses and souvenir shops, and an entry price of around RMB 60. While the canal towns vary in size and each claims to offer unique attractions, not many visitors will have either the time or the inclination to see them all. Of the many towns you could visit, we've picked out the most scenic and accessible ones.

All the canal towns line the banks of the Grand Canal system. It's the world's longest and oldest man-made waterway, first burrowed across the mighty Yangtze River delta in 486 BC. When completed in AD 610 during the Tang Dynasty, it stretched almost 1,800 kilometres (1,120 miles) from Hangzhou all

the way to Beijing, and is considered one of China's greatest feats of engineering. In recent years the government has realised that it might have something worth preserving here, and made it a 'key state-level cultural relic' in 2006. Meanwhile, the canal towns have been slugging it out for ever bigger pieces of the tourist pie – each claiming to boast more culture, more history and more speciality cuisine.

They are mostly charming places, and some offer lodgings that extend the illusion of being in old China. Most places to stay, though, remain quite basic. Back in Shanghai, **Jinjiang Tours** (191 Changle Lu, 6289 7830) can help with reservations; when you plan your visit, consider going during the week – towns are less busy and many hotels offer discounts. Another option is to stay in **Suzhou** (*see p209*) or **Hangzhou** (*see p205*) and make day trips from there – Tongli, for example, is two-and-a-half hours from Shanghai but just 18 kilometres (11 miles) from Suzhou. It's worth noting that, as with most day-trip destinations, the canal towns offer a very different (and much calmer) atmosphere at night.

# Tongli

## Sightseeing

Tongli (**photo** *p201*) is one of the larger canal towns. Tourist buggies ply between the attractions, but it's small enough to cover on foot. All signposts are in both English and Chinese. Besides the expected bridges, canals and pretty old buildings, Tongli boasts the **China Sex Museum** (*see below*). Originally on Shanghai's bustling Nanjing Road, the museum moved to various city spots – each one more secluded than the last – before being offered a home in Tongli. It's now just behind Tongli's pride and joy: the UNESCO World Heritage site **Tuisi Garden**. One of the region's finest examples of a Ming Dynasty garden – comparable even to the finest in Suzhou (*see pp210-211*) – Tuisi was built between 1885 and 1887 by a retired government official. Several halls and adjoining corridors were built to create the illusion that they float on water, and the pavilions, rockeries and winding corridors are beautifully conducive to contemplation (*tuisi* means 'retreat and meditate') when hordes of tourists aren't thronging the grounds. A **boat service** (0512 6063 1987, RMB 180 one-way), departing from the town's entrance, will take you to Zhouzhuang (*see p203*).

### China Sex Museum

*Wu Jiang (0512 6332 2973/www.chinasexmuseum. com). Open 7.45am-5.30pm daily. Admission RMB 20 (over-18s only).*

Housed in what used to be a girls' school back in the Qing Dynasty are more than 4,000 items of erotica, representing over 5,000 years of Chinese sexual history. You can admire double-headed dildos, brush-paintings of alfresco orgies, sex chairs and tiles that depict a couple enjoying themselves with a variety of animals. Far less amusing but no less interesting are the saddles with wooden erections used to 'ruin' adulterous women and foot-binding equipment. There's also an outpost of the museum at the exit to the Bund Tourist Tunnel (*see p92*).

## Where to eat & stay

There are many canalside eateries at Shangyuan Jie, all of which offer similar fare (tea and regional snacks) – and menus in English. **Nanyuan Teahouse** (0512 6332 2677), built in the Qing Dynasty, is a pleasant century-old spot to stop for a cuppa.

Basic accommodation is readily available in Tongli's guesthouses, which are typically above restaurants along the canals, from RMB 80 a night for a standard room. There is a tourist information centre and booking office for accommodation in the town square.

# Xitang

## Sightseeing

Xitang used to be more low-key than Tongli and Zhouzhuang, being further from Shanghai and, by extension, having relatively fewer tourists. That all changed with the filming here of 2006 Hollywood blockbuster *Mission: Impossible III*. Still, Xitang remains smaller, quieter and, some would say, prettier than its rivals, and its residents are more laid-back, mostly going about their own business rather then trying to hawk souvenirs. One of Xitang's designated attractions is the **Pearl Button Museum**, where you can watch buttons being made by hand; further down the cobbled lane is the **Fan Museum**. Unlike other canal towns, many of Xitang's narrow alleys are roofed. At dusk, red lanterns are hung along the length of the 1,300-metre (4,290-foot) main alley – it's a beautiful sight.

## Where to stay

There are several Ming Dynasty residences that have been converted into guesthouses, complete with antique furniture and – making summer nights uncomfortable – no air-conditioning. Lodgings with air-conditioning are also available, of course, but do cost slightly more. Especially charming Ming-style digs can be found at **Jing Yi Xuan** (8 Shipi Long, 0573 456 5264, RMB 80 Mon-Fri, RMB 100 Sat, Sun).

# Wuzhen

## Sightseeing

This is another canal town (**photo** *p203*) that escapes being overrun by tourists by virtue of its distance from Shanghai. It's about three-and-a-half hours from Shanghai, but just an hour from Hangzhou (*see p205*). Local specialities are rattan baskets and cloth shoes, examples of which are widely available in tourist-tat versions from little alley shops. Wuzhen was once the refuge of rich people fleeing the turbulence of the Ming and Qing Dynasties; part of the attraction was doubtless the place's relative inaccessibility. Many of the residences they built remain well preserved – two examples are the **Zhu Family Hall** and the **Xu Family Hall**. Shadow puppet shows featuring intricately sewn leather puppets and depicting ancient legends are put on at the **Shadow Puppet Play House**, one of the few places where you can still see this dying art being performed. Get a taste of local rice wine, *sanbai* ('thrice white'), at the end of a visit to the **rice wine distillery**.

## Where to stay

For accommodation, try the **Guangye Hotel** (Ziye Lu, 0573 871 8988, double RMB 260), which has clean rooms.

## Zhouzhuang

### Sightseeing

This is the largest and most famous of the canal towns (**photo** *p204*), as well as the most expensive – admission is RMB 100 compared to around RMB 60 for the rest. The picturesque bridges and well-preserved buildings featured in a series of watercolours by the late Chen Yifei, one of China's best-known contemporary artists, and exhibited in New York. His painting of the Twin Bridges was sold to a petroleum bigwig who then presented it to Deng Xiaoping. Suddenly, Zhouzhuang's stock went through the roof. Over 60 per cent of the buildings in the town centre date back to the Ming and Qing Dynasties or even earlier. Tourists flock to experience the town officially identified as 'Number One Water Town' and among the 'Top 50 Destinations for Foreigners', braving the almost constant calls of souvenir touts.

In addition to the famous bridges, other attractions include **Shen's Residence**, built in 1742, a rambling residence of 100 rooms surrounding a central courtyard. Down the same lane, **Zhang's Residence** is even older, though smaller.

### Where to eat & stay

Finding somewhere to eat in Zhouzhuang is easy: restaurants and teahouses line the banks of the canal near the town square. A speciality here is *wansanti* – pig trotters stewed in brown sauce. On Zhenfeng Jie, a Western-style café serves up freshly brewed coffee and ice-cream.

The three-star **Zhouzhuang Hotel** (103 Quanfu Lu, 0512 5721 6666, doubles RMB 480) is the biggest hotel in town.

## Zhujiajiao

### Sightseeing

This is the smallest of the canal towns mentioned here – and the closest to Shanghai, requiring only a 50-minute bus ride – which is a formula for claustrophobia, especially at the weekend. Hordes of tourists throng the **Setting Fish Free Bridge**, where they can toss goldfish into the murky water to chalk up karma points. There are a total of 36 stone bridges – but it's impossible to keep count as

Wuzhen.
*See p202.*

you canter along the labyrinthine cobbled lanes. Zhujiajiao was a bustling commercial centre in the Song and Yuan Dynasties, and a hub in the Ming and Qing Dynasties. These days it's frequented by TV crews from Shanghai.

## Getting there & around

### By taxi
Most of the four- and five-star hotels in Shanghai can arrange taxis or minivans that will ferry their guests to the canal towns.

### By bus
All the canal towns enjoy regular bus connections to Shanghai with **Shanghai City Sightseeing Buses** (Shanghai Stadium, Gate 5, 666 Tianyao Qiao Lu, 6426 5555), leaving daily. The buses for Tongli depart at 9.30am and return at 4.30pm. Those for Wuzhen depart at 9.30am and return at 6pm. Xitang tours leave at 8.45am; they include a morning at the nearby town of Jiaxing. Zhouzhuang buses depart at 7am, 8.30am, 9.05am, 9.45am and return at 2.30pm or 4pm. Zhujiajiao tours depart every half hour from 7.30am to 11am and return half-hourly until 4pm. Ticket prices range from RMB 70 to RMB 160, depending on whether lunch and guides are included in the fare.

### By train
Visiting the canal towns by train is more complicated than by bus. The best option is to take a train to either Jiaxing or Suzhou and travel onwards to the canal towns from there. Almost every train that heads south, including those to Hangzhou, stops at Jiaxing. Regular services to Jiaxing depart hourly from 7am to noon from the Shanghai Railway Station

(*see p217*). From Jiaxing train station there are minibuses to Xitang (RMB 5) and Wuzhen (RMB 12), or you can take a taxi.

### Guided tours
**Jin Jiang Optional Tours** (191 Changle Lu, 6445 9525) offers a convenient one-day group tour with an English-speaking guide. It also tailors individual tours with drivers and guides. Prices start at RMB 580 per person (depending on destination), with lunch.

## Tourist information

The entrance ticket booths of the canal towns double as tourist information centres. The ticket price usually includes an English-language map of each town; ask for one if it is not provided. In Tongli, English-speaking guides are available for hire at RMB 160 per person. Each town has a website that provides background information, enabling you to get an overall feel for the place before you arrive.

### Tongli
*www.china-tongli.com*

### Xitang
*www.xitang.com.cn*

### Wuzhen
*www.wuzhen.com.cn*

### Zhouzhuang
*www.zhouzhuang.net*

### Zhujiajiao
*http://lyw.sh.gov.cn/en/scenic_spot/zhujiajiao.aspx*

Zhouzhuang.
See p203.

# Hangzhou & Moganshan

Long a tourist paradise, Zhejiang's lake city is gentrifying into a commercial and cultural hotbed – with nearby Moganshan a welcome hilly retreat.

## Hangzhou

Hangzhou is much hyped as the 'tourist capital of China', which is nothing new: Marco Polo – who stopped here in the 13th century – described it as one of the world's most splendid cities. Its appeal is the gorgeous, island-dotted **Xihu** (West Lake), which stretches three kilometres (two miles) and is surrounded by rolling hills and lush green forests scattered with pagodas and temples. For thousands of years the views have inspired Chinese poets and writers; now they appeal to newly-weds posing in bridal finery against the backdrop of so many ancient Chinese love stories.

Hangzhou is also the capital of one of China's richest provinces, and has the encroaching development to show for it. While the suburbs suffer the same ugly sprawl as the rest of China, downtown has gentrified into a sparkling centre of luxury consumption. Beemers and Bentleys crowd the narrow streets, and the likes of Louis Vuitton, Dolce & Gabbana and Giorgio Armani peddle their pricey wares in Wulin Square and from the lakefront Eurostreet development. Yet the city also retains a countercultural edge, thanks to the **China Academy of Art** (218 Nanshan Lu), the nation's second-most-important art institute. Specialising in new media, it attracts creatives from around China, many of whom stay on after graduation. Hangzhou's heady student environment nourishes a small but strong music scene, with regular concerts, a handful of excellent bands and even some independent music labels.

### HISTORY

The setting of the modern town of Hangzhou was formed in the first century BC, when river currents flowing into the sea threw up enough silt to form a lake. The Grand Canal was then built at the end of the sixth century AD, making Hangzhou the centre of trade between the north and the south. In the Tang era the city continued to thrive, and during the Song Dynasty – when the Tartars invaded the north – the imperial family relocated to Hangzhou (from 1138 to 1279), making it the country's imperial city. When the Song Dynasty was overthrown by the Mongols, Hangzhou remained an important commercial centre, revered for the beauty of its gardens. Ming rulers later deepened the Grand Canal, increasing trade opportunities by allowing boats laden with goods to sail up to Beijing. Two Qing emperors also favoured Hangzhou as a place of rest, and added to its architecture. However, the Taiping Rebellion in the mid 19th century (*see p11*) destroyed much of the city, which was later rebuilt.

## Sightseeing

Although a Shanghai–Hangzhou Maglev is in the offing, in the meantime most visitors arrive by normal train (*see p207*), usually terminating at the swanky new station to the east of the lake. (The slow, local trains, however, arrive and depart from an older and more remote station in the eastern part of town.) From here you can walk to the centre (it's a couple of kilometres or about a mile); head north, then take a left along Jiefang Lu.

First stop for most is **Xihu**, the lake. To escape the shores, there are two causeways – the Baidi, running across the north side, and the Sudi, running from north to south. It's on these paths in the early evening, meandering through the willows with fish leaping out between the lily pads and an orange moon rising above the water, that the enchanting power of the lake begins to make itself felt – in spite of the crowds. Baidi runs on to **Gushan** (Solitary Hill), the lake's biggest island. Formed by a volcanic explosion, it now has a more sedentary character, including a hillside park dotted with small wooden studios where you can watch members of the Xiling Yinshe (Xiling Seal Engravers' Society) at work. Xiling has historically been a centre of innovation in traditional Chinese art, and in the mid 1800s produced artists like Wu Changshuo, father of the modern Haipai, or Shanghai Style, of brush painting. There is also a small museum of seal carving here, beside Xiling Bridge (0571 8781

5910, admission free). It's possible to rent boats (prices vary, peaking at sunset), which are paddled out into the lake from the south end of the Baidi, or to join the outings aboard a mock dragon boat for an hour-long tour of the lake's islands (RMB 45, tickets from the pine stands around the lake).

For lake views head off Beishan Lu, up one of many hidden footpaths, through the moist woodlands to **Qixiashan** (which means 'the Mountain Where Rosy Clouds Linger'). The stone path meanders past hawkers (woodland dwellers living in tumble-down cottages), **Baochu pagoda** (a 1933 reconstruction of a Song Dynasty tower) and, more interestingly, a **Baopu Daoist Compound** – home to an elegant group of both male and female followers of the Taoist religion who can often be heard, or seen, performing their traditional ceremonies, especially in the late afternoon.

In the city itself, the main street of interest to travellers is the **Qinghefang Lu** tourist street, a tastefully reconstructed historical street with views of the lake's misty blue mountains in the background. The shops and cafés sell Chinese medicine, folk art, the area's renowned Longjing tea, woodcarvings and stinky tofu. To escape the smell, there are two nearby sights of interest, both lodged in restored Qing Dynasty houses: the **Guanfu Classic Art Museum** (131 Hefang Jie Lu, 0571 8781 8181, RMB 15) is a fine furniture museum, tracing the social history of furniture in China from straw mats to opium beds, while the **Hu Qing Yu Museum of Traditional Chinese Medicine** (95 Dajingxiang Lu, off Hefang Jie Lu, 0571 8702 7507 ext 8620, RMB 10) is exactly what it says on the plaque.

### Excursions

West of the city is **Feilai Feng** (meaning 'the Hill that Flew Here'; RMB 15), which people visit to see the Buddhist sculptures. Also in the area is the **Lingyin Si** (1 Fayun Nong, 0571 8796 8665, RMB 30), one of the biggest temple complexes in China and one of the few that managed to survive the Cultural Revolution intact. It's fully functioning, with daily services. Further afield is the village of **Longjing**, set amid lovely emerald-green tea plantations. Just south is the **Hupaomeng Quan** park, where a natural spring issues forth the only water serious tea-suppers would consider using to boil their brew. If you want to test your water is the real thing, Hupao spring water is supposed to have a surface tension so strong that a cup can be filled three millimetres too high and still won't spill.

Those who like to watch others get wet can head up to the **Liuhe pagoda** (House 8, 147 Nanshan Lu, 0571 8659 1401, RMB 20), situated on a stunning site over the Qiantang River. It was originally built to appease the Dragon King, who was thought to be responsible for the floods that routinely wrecked farmers' crops. Now, ironically, it has become the favoured spot from which to watch the – as yet unsurfed – tidal bore that's at its height every autumn equinox.

## Where to eat & drink

To entice more tourists to visit Hangzhou, RMB 1 billion has been invested in the first phase of **Xihutiandi** ('West Lake Heaven and Earth'), Hangzhou's version of Shanghai's sleek Xintiandi entertainment complex. **Jamaica Coffee** (12 Xihutiandi, 0571 8701 2861) is a good spot for a coffee and a pastry and **Butterfly Laguna** (House E, 147 Nanshan Lu, 0571 8702 7711) specialises in South-east Asian cuisine.

For Hangzhou cuisine, don't miss **Zhang Sheng Ji** (77 Shaunglin Lu, 0571 8602 6666), which serves the most famous rendition of local speciality 'beggar's chicken' (a whole chicken cooked inside a ball of mud). Simple but tasty Western food can be had at lakeside **Paradise Restaurant** (36 Hubin Lu, 0571 8706 2888), from a balcony overlooking the lake. By far the best upmarket restaurant in town is **Peppino** (Shangri-la Hotel, 78 Beishan Lu, 0571 8797 7951 ext 23), which serves Italian food and fine wines. A duo of art professors designed and now run the quirky but swanky **Yee Chino** (Yulinglong, 171 Zhongshan Bei Lu, 0571 8707 0777) and **Gold Chino** (4th floor, 149 Qingchun Lu, 0571 8721 0777), which serve mid-priced Chinese fusion dishes in gorgeous settings.

**Wushan Lu** is great for local snacks and own-made specialities, but its night market – selling an array of goods from *qipaos* and wooden sandals to kitsch Maoist memorabilia and 'antiques' – has moved to **Jiefang Lu**.

For nightlife, Hangzhou's professional – not student, in other words – art and design types congregate in the mellow, eclectically designed **Common's Place** (1 Wanshouting Jie, 0571 8506 2166), near Wuling Square. **Kana's Pub** (152 Nanshan Lu, 0571 8706 3228) is one of Hangzhou's original foreign-run bars, renowned for its cocktails and live music.

For cheap alcohol, thumping tunes and a young crowd, the collection on bars opposite the China Academy of Art on Nanshan Lu is where it's at. These include **JZ Club** (6 Liuying Lu, 0571 8702 8298), an old villa with nightly jazz sessions; **Night & Day** (240 Nanshan Lu, 0571 8777 0275), which has a Latin-tinged live music and dancing; and **1828 Bar & Grill** (262 Nanshan Lu, 0571 8791 9020), which serves ownmade beer (24RMB/pint) and bar snacks.

**Xihu** lake. *See p205.*

By far the busiest bar street in town is Shuguang Lu, where you'll find **Traveller Bar** (No.176, 0571 8796 8846), which has live jazz daily; **Reggae Bar** (No.95, 0571 8796 1587), which does a mean pizza and pulls in a student crowd; and **You To Bar** (85 Shuguang Lu, 0571 8797 6788), which rocks with live music and rowdy local beer-swillers. **Maya Bar** (94 Baisha Quan, 0571 8799 7628) serves good burritos and some of the strongest long drinks in town.

For clubbing, check out **SOS** (3/F Huanglong Hengli Mansion, 5 Huanglong Lu, 0571 5683 6688), with international DJs and dancers. For a more unusual spot, seek out the **In** (Building 3, 23 Yanggong Di, 0571 8763 4380); it's small but hugely popular at weekends. Elsewhere, there's **G Plus** (6th floor, 169 Qingchun Lu, 0571 8703 0077), which has welcomed turntable luminaries such as James Lavelle from UNKLE and Howie B, and, more recently, house supremos Eddie Halliwell and Randall Jones. **Babyface** (12 Hubin Lu, 0571 8779 1168) is situated underground next to Eurostreet, and features a similiar mix of DJs and pretty people to its Shanghai branch.

Pick up a copy of listings magazine *MORE Hangzhou* for details of what's on.

## Where to stay

**Shangri-La** (78 Beishan Lu, 0571 8797 7951, www.shangri-la.com, doubles from RMB 1,600) is a safe bet for those who want to go five-star – but be sure to stay in the west wing for views of Xihu. The new **Hyatt Regency** (28 Hubin Lu, 0571 8779 1234, www.hyatt.com, doubles RMB 1,700) opened in 2005 and is conveniently situated smack in the middle of the new lakefront development. The **New Hotel** (58 Beishan Lu, 0571 8766 0000, doubles RMB 780) is a 1920s building with an ugly but

unobtrusive add-on. Another mid-range option is the **Elan Holiday Hotel** (218-215 Nanshan Lu, 0517 8716 4788, rooms from RMB 500), a cute boutique hotel by the art academy.

For cheap and friendly, plus a site next to the lake with a pleasant outdoor eating area, head for the **Hangzhou International Youth Hostel** (101 Nanshan Lu, 0571 8791 8948, www.yhachina.com, dormitory bed from RMB 45, doubles from RMB 200).

## Getting around

The bus network covers most destinations but taxi rides within Hangzhou should not cost much more than RMB 15. Most places round the lake can be reached on foot, and touring by bike isn't a bad idea; these can be hired from several hotels, including the **Radisson Plaza** (333 Tiyuchang Lu, 0571 8518 8888, RMB 20/hr). Taxi and minibus drivers will approach tourists to offer a variety of excursions, at set day rates; bargain hard.

## Getting there

Hangzhou is 170 kilometres (105 miles) southwest of Shanghai. At least five trains per day leave for Hangzhou from Shanghai Railway Station (RMB 25-47, soft-seat), with the first departure at 7.38am. The journey takes between two and three hours. Alternatively, another six trains per day leave from the Shanghai South Railway Station, for a shorter journey of about 90 minutes. When the recently approved new Maglev is complete, the journey will take less than half an hour – but you'll have to wait until at least 2010 to enjoy zipping here from Shanghai at speeds of up to 430kph (270mph). By bus, take a **Shanghai City Sightseeing Bus** (line 20, RMB 218, daily 8.30am) from Shanghai Stadium (666 Tianyaoqiao Lu, Xujiahui, 6426 5555).

# Moganshan

The village of Moganshan – up in the cool, green hills of north Zhejiang – originally came to life as a heat retreat for Shanghai's foreign residents and for missionaries from the interior. In 1898 they claimed the peak as their exclusive summer playground, leap-frogging up the slopes past the mountain springs where Song Dynasty emperors once gambolled in the shade of the bamboo. The foreigners rode up on sedan chairs carried by porters, as there were no roads at the time. Well-to-do Chinese soon followed, and so did the infamous Shanghai gang leader Du Yuesheng. Chiang Kaishek honeymooned here briefly. The original international inhabitants built European-style villas and ran the village like the city concessions they were escaping from, forming an association to decide who was allowed to join their elite community. In 1949 the Communist government turned the village into a retreat for deserving cadres and a state sanatorium.

Now the party may be starting again, with a handful of city folk renting and restoring some of the village's ageing villas. The winter of 2005/6 also saw a frenzy of restoration by the local hotels, and the opening of the village's first ever coffeeshop (*see below*).

## Sightseeing

On entering Moganshan visitors pay RMB 80 (plus RMB 10 per car) to access 'the sights', which don't add up to much. There are a couple of waterfalls, the house where Chiang Kaishek stayed – an empty shell with a few pieces of furniture – and the place where Chairman Mao had an afternoon nap – another empty shell with one metal framed bed. You can play at being decadent with a sedan chair ride, offered by villagers for a fee. The real joy, however, is in wandering off the tourist path and up towards the back of the village. Here you'll find a disused school, a church and chapel built by the original missionaries, and an ageing municipal, spring-fed swimming pool. There is also a market in the middle of the village, selling wild tea and mushrooms picked in the forests.

Other distractions include a meander to an outlying pagoda; follow the road out of the village in a north-westerly direction, past some villas, until the road forks three ways. Take the paved path in the middle to Guai Shi Jiao (Weird Stone Corner). Maps are available in the village, but they're in Chinese. However, a walk off the mountain in any direction will take you through the bamboo forests into the valley below, where you'll encounter plenty of farmers and, eventually, an isolated Buddhist temple.

## Where to eat & drink

Eating and drinking can be done at any of the small restaurants on **Yin Shan Jie**, the main street. Local specialities are bamboo shoots, as well as wild celery and wild partridge. **Moganshan Lodge** (0572 803 3011, www.moganshanlodge.com, lunch/dinner RMB 60-95) offers good, straightforward Western food. It also serves good coffee and has a comfy bar.

## Where to stay

The Radisson hotel group manages two villas on the mountain: the luxuriant country pad once belonging to **Du Yuesheng** and the **Priest Villa** (for both: 0572 303 3601, rooms from RMB 1,100). Cheaper and simpler rooms can be had at any one of the many hotels, some in old villas, all over the mountaintop. Prices range from RMB 150 up to RMB 1,000 or more for a suite.

## Getting there

Moganshan is some 60 kilometres (about 40 miles) north of Hangzhou; from there it's a one-hour taxi journey (RMB 200). Alternatively, you can catch a bus (RMB 12) from Hangzhou North Station (758 Moganshan Lu, 0571 8809 7761) to Wukang, which is at the foot of the mountain. From Wukang a minibus will take you to the top.

In the cool of the mountains: **Moganshan**.

# Suzhou

Even Marco Polo was charmed by this watery beauty.

Back when Shanghai was no more than a little fishing village, ancient Suzhou was a cultural and fashion leader. Hailed as one of the most beautiful places in the Middle Kingdom, it attracted the political and cultural elite in droves during the 14th century. Many of the ornamental gardens and elaborate residences they built to amuse themselves remain here, remarkably well preserved, and have endured as one of China's favourite tourist attractions.

With a history spanning 2,500 years, Suzhou is one of the oldest cities in China. Built by Emperor Helu back in 514 BC, it was also definitely one of the most prosperous at its peak. Blessed with fertile land, Suzhou is also dotted with lakes linked by a criss-crossing network of canals. The completion in AD 600 of the Grand Canal, a trading artery that linked Suzhou to the capital Beijing, turned the city into a major commercial hub. The Grand Canal was an important waterway that linked the city to the capital. As the story goes, Marco Polo was so impressed he was moved to proclaim it the 'Venice of the East'.

The old town reached its present dimensions in the 12th century, and remnants of the city wall that enclosed it can still be seen. Once renowned for its silk industry, the scenic canal town is now the world's top producer of notebook computers and digital cameras – a fact that's hard to credit while you amble across another quaint antique bridge. Just take a ten-minute taxi ride from downtown, though, and you'll see Suzhou's other face: the Suzhou Industrial Park. Only 3.5 kilometres (two miles) from the old town, it seems like another world, a place devoid of any trace of the old town or the famously idyllic ornamental gardens – it is this high-tech side of Suzhou, however, that keeps the city one of China's most prosperous.

As a major tourist stop, Suzhou has a well-developed infrastructure. Streets are well laid out and there is easy access to accommodation, transport, entertainment and the tourist sites.

## Sightseeing

Suzhou's classical gardens, which date to the Ming Dynasty (1368-1644), and its canals are the city's chief attractions. But you shouldn't be so intent on garden-hopping (*see p210*) that you ignore the city's other diversions.

A good way to experience Suzhou's charm is to board a **sightseeing boat**. Tours (0512 6752 6931) depart from a landing on the large canal directly across the road from the railway station at the northern end of town. The boats go to four different destinations: Tiger Hill (Huqiu;

in the far north-western end of town), Coiled Gate (Pan Men; in the south-western corner), West Garden (Xi Yuan; the western part of town) and Cold Mountain Temple (Hanshan Si; near West Garden). The longest trip – to Hanshan Si – takes about 40 minutes, whereas it takes only ten minutes for visitors to get to the Pan Men Scenic Area.

**Pan Men**, or Coiled Gate (2 Dongda Jie, 0512 6526 0004, www.szpmjq.com, 7.30am-5.30pm daily, RMB 25; **photo** *p209*), is a good place to disembark for a walk along the old city wall to the top of the original city gate, and to take in **Ruiguang Pagoda**, reputedly the oldest in Jiangsu province. From Pan Men, it is a short walk north-east to the lovely **Blue Wave Pavilion** (Canglang Ting, *see p211*); this garden's sprawling grounds make some of the others feel decidedly claustrophobic.

Renmin Lu is the main road running north–south across town. At its northern end, near the railway station, is the **Suzhou Silk Museum** (2001 Renmin Lu, 0512 6753 6538, open daily, RMB 15). This overview of the city's 4,000-year-old silk industry comes to life with the displays of antique looms and silk embroidery, and especially the reproduction of a 13th-century silk farm, complete with real worms. Silk products are sold at the badly lit museum shop, but a better place to buy them is the **Suzhou Embroidery Factory** (262

Jingde Lu, 0512 6522 2403, www.szseri.com, open daily). Directly across the road from the Silk Museum, the **North Temple Pagoda** (Beisi Ta; 652 Renmin Lu, RMB 25; **photo** *below*) affords a panoramic view of the city and the outskirts from the grand height of nine storeys. The pagoda, which is in the grounds of a temple complex dating back to the 17th century, has been rebuilt several times over its 750-year history.

Further out of town, **Tiger Hill** (Huqiu; 0512 6532 3488, RMB 60) is the final resting place of the Emperor Helu, founder of Suzhou, and a popular spot for tourists. The man-made hillock got its name, according to local legend, from a white tiger that came to guard the king's tomb. Helu had a keen interest in swords, which explains why he was buried with 3,000 of them. On top of the little hill is the 1,500-year-old **Yunyan Pagoda**, propped up by concrete struts. Tiger Hill is four kilometres (2.5 miles) north-west of the city centre and can be reached by tourist buses 1 and 2, or by taxi.

Located in the heart of Suzhou's bustling downtown, on the Guangqian Jie thoroughfare, is the Taoist **Temple of Mystery** (Xuan Miao Guan). There's nary a hint of mystery about it but the grounds are pleasant and the huge temple hall (Sanqing Dian) is worth a look, as is the busy bazaar that also occupies the square.

North Temple Pagoda.

## The gardens of Suzhou

The famous Suzhou gardens were intended by their creators to contain all the elements of the universe in miniature, manifesting the harmonious principles of Taoism, the ancient Chinese philosophy. The gardens once numbered over 200, but only 69 remain well preserved. The attention to detail is staggering, with nothing – neither pebble nor plant – left to chance.

Weekends see crowds thronging Suzhou's top attractions, and it may be necessary to queue and wait your turn to cross a bridge – admittedly, this isn't terribly conducive to experiencing the meditative calm these gardens are meant to instill. If you don't want to spend an entire afternoon moving from garden to garden, the **Garden for Lingering** and the **Humble Administrator's Garden** are generally the best to visit, although the **Garden of the Master of Nets** is perhaps the most beautiful if you can bear the crowds. For more information, visit the **Suzhou Municipal Administrative Bureau of Gardens** website or call the tourist information line (www.szgarden. sz.js.cn, 0512 6520 3131).

## Blue Wave Pavilion

*3 Canglangting Jie, by Renmin Lu (0512 6519 4375/www.szwsy.com/clt).* **Open** 7.30am-5pm daily. **Admission** RMB 20.

Originally built for a prince around AD 950, this is one of the older and bigger gardens. The design is less formal than that of other Suzhou gardens, with wilderness areas and winding, pond-lined corridors replacing the usual fussy pavilions. The carved lattice windows are considered to be among Suzhou's finest and the garden is home to some rare bamboos.

## Garden for Lingering

*338 Liuyuan Lu (0512 6557 9466/www.gardenly. com).* **Open** 7.30am-5.30pm daily. **Admission** RMB 40.

One of the largest of the gardens, with an impressive collection of bonsai and a wilderness area. Fans of traditional horticulture will enjoy the Crown of Clouds Peak, a 6m (18ft) chunk of rock from nearby Taihu Lake. In an attempt to give a sense of the garden being lived in rather than just looked at, women decked out in full Ming Dynasty regalia play instruments and sing in pavilions and walled recesses.

## Garden of the Master of Nets

*11 Kuojiatao Xiang, down an alley off Shiquan Jie (0512 6529 6567/www.szwsy.com).* **Open** 7.30am-5.30pm daily. **Admission** RMB 30.

Tiny and charming, this garden is everybody's favourite – which means it tends to be the most crowded. It's home to a group of wood-block painters who sell their work in one of the pavilions. Each night the garden hosts a popular traditional dance and music performance that moves from pavilion to pavilion.

## Humble Administrator's Garden

*178 Dongbei Jie (0512 6751 0286/www.szzzy.cn).* **Open** 7.30am-5.30pm daily. **Admission** RMB 70.

Ming Dynasty courtier Wang Xianchen built this garden around 1513 when he retired. The most talked-about feature is the interconnected, bamboo-covered islands and waterfront pavilions. It is widely considered one of the most beautiful gardens, second only to the Garden of the Master of Nets (*see above*).

## Lion Grove Garden

*23 Yuanlin Lu, by Lindun Lu (0512 6777 3263/ www.szszl.com).* **Open** 7.30am-5.30pm daily. **Admission** RMB 30.

The Buddhist monk Tianru built this garden in memory of his master Zhong Feng in 1342. It changed hands a number of times and suffered many centuries of neglect. The current name comes from its labyrinthine limestone rockery, for which stones from Taihu Lake were arranged in the shape of lions playing, roaring, fighting and sleeping.

## Where to eat & drink

The area around the Temple of Mystery (Xuanmiao Guan) on Guanqian Jie bustles with a number of eateries, all claiming to serve authentic Suzhou bites. The city's native Wu cuisine is known to be soft in texture and sweet in taste; the **Suzhou Snack Restaurant** (19 Taijian Nong, Guanqian Jie, 0512 6523 7603, RMB 2-85) musters a good rendition. For a fuller meal, try **Songhelou Caiguan** (72 Taijian Nong, Guanqian Jie, 0512 6770 0688, RMB 10-138), said to be the oldest restaurant in town, its history stretching back over 2,000 years. The house specialities are marinated duck (*gusu laya*) and 'squirrel Mandarin fish' (*songsu guiyu*). **Caizhizhai** (91 Guanqian Jie, 0512 6727 6198, RMB 6-100 per box) has been in business since the 19th century and sells Suzhou-style cakes and sweets. For Western food, try local expat hangout **Sicily Pub & Restaurant** (1 Shaomozhen Xiang, Guanqian Jie, 0512 6523 2393, RMB 20-50).

## Where to stay

The **Sheraton** (259 Xinshi Lu, 0512 6510 3388, www.sheraton-suzhou.com, doubles RMB 1,000-1,650) is the city's best five-star option. It's in a replica of a traditional Chinese house and garden. The **Bamboo Grove Hotel** (168 Zhuhui Lu, 0512 6520 5601, www.bg-hotel.com, doubles RMB 998) was about the smartest lodging in town before Sheraton arrived. It's still pretty nice: three interconnected, low-rise buildings overlook an inner garden courtyard. As we went to press the **Nanyuan Guesthouse** (249 Shiquan Jie, 0512 6519 7661, doubles RMB 480) was due to reopen as a five-star after a series of renovations. Expect prices to have risen, but the location inside a walled garden compound near the Humble Administrator's Garden, with lovely secluded grounds, remains.

## Getting there

Suzhou is 88 kilometres (55 miles) west of Shanghai. **Trains** from the Shanghai Railway Station take an hour and cost RMB 13-20; the best option is the Nanjing express service, which departs hourly from 5.33am and costs RMB 25 one-way. Going by **coach** takes about 90 minutes and costs RMB 30. Coaches leave hourly between 7.20am and 5.30pm from the Shanghai Southern bus station (399 Laohumin Lu) or half-hourly from 7.10am to 8pm from the Hengfeng bus station (next to the railway station at 70 Hengfeng Lu). Sightseeing **buses** depart daily at 8.30am from Shanghai Stadium (666 Tianyaoqiao Lu) and cost RMB 168, including bus fare, admission and a guide. A return trip from Shanghai to Suzhou by **taxi** should cost around RMB 500; ask your hotel to make the arrangements.

**Trips Out of Town**

# Putuoshan

An island of Buddhist worship and tourist mayhem.

Chinese characters are marked on rocks across **Putuoshan**. *See p213.*

Putuoshan, one of the 1,000 islands of the Zhoushan Archipelago in the East China Sea, appeals both to pilgrims and to tourists. Its greenery and golden sand beaches are as much of a draw as the temples that dot the island. This is one of the four holy Buddhist mountains in China, and devotees come to worship Guanyin, goddess of mercy (*see p213*

Mercy me!). Unfortunately, it's more Buddhist theme park than holy ground when the summer peak season arrives. Between the tour groups thronging the grounds of the temples, the piped music in designated 'scenic areas' and the hawkers of Buddhist paraphernalia, nirvana couldn't be further away. Visiting off-season should mean you can find yourself cheaper accommodation – there will certainly be a calmer atmosphere, much more conducive to appreciating the island's many charms.

## HISTORY

The Boddhisattva Guanyin was enshrined on the island in AD 916. As the legend has it, a Japanese monk was travelling with a statue of Guanyin when a storm stranded him on the island. The goddess appeared to him in a vision and promised to return him home safely if he left the statue behind. He did, and she hasn't left the island since. Guanyin literally means 'observing the sounds' and in Chinese Buddhism the name is taken to mean 'the one who hears the cries of the world'. She is revered for her compassion, as well as for her supposed ability to grant male children.

Pilgrimage site it may be, but Putuoshan has also been ravaged by fighting and destruction. The island received imperial patronage and for centuries enjoyed the attention and favour of rich devotees. At its peak, it was home to hundreds of temples and thousands of monks. But Japanese pirates and Dutch traders stopped by to plunder and pillage periodically in the 16th and 17th centuries. Until 1949 around 2,000 monks and nuns lived on the island, but the Cultural Revolution further decimated the temples: today only three main temples and some 30 nunneries remain. Continuing the theme of conflict, the island is now home to a naval base – be careful what you photograph.

## Sightseeing

The three biggest temples on the island are Puji Temple, Fayu Temple and Huiji Temple. The main area of worship is **Puji Temple**, which houses a handsome bronze statue of Guanyin. Old cobblestone streets lead to Haiyin Pool in front of the temple, where pilgrims set turtles free as a gesture to gain karmic merit. Before sunrise, visitors can join the monks and nuns in early morning chanting to the deities. Around the main temple are smaller shrines and pagodas, as well as stalls selling Buddhist trappings, souvenirs and dried seafood – an island speciality. The area can get crowded but it is at least smoke-free: burning incense has largely been banned in all the temples.

**Fayu Temple**, the second-largest, is two kilometres (1.2 miles) north of Puji Temple. It's arranged into six ascending tiers up a hill, beginning from the stone gateway. About a kilometre (half a mile) north of Fayu is **Huiji Temple**, built in the Ming Dynasty. It sits on top of Foding Hill which, at 300 metres (1,000 feet) above sea level, is the highest peak on the island. Visitors who choose to proceed on foot

will be rewarded with the sight of small shrines and, more rarely, pilgrims prostrating themselves on each of the 1,000 steps. For those who find the climb too strenuous, a cable car offers views of a new pagoda and temple that are under construction at the northern end of the island.

A giant **statue of Guanyin** looking out to sea at the southern tip of the island has become an iconic Putuoshan sight. The 33-metre (108-foot) statue in bronze and gold was built in 1997 and depicts the goddess holding a ship's wheel, supposedly watching out for seafarers and fishermen. Her four grizzly faced protectors are the Buddhist guardians of the world, each of whom leads an army of supernatural creatures to keep evil at bay.

Around the island are various 'rock stars' – rocks with special markings (*pictured p212*) that can be easily identified by the crowds of tourists wanting to be photographed beside them. One such rock, which has the Chinese character for 'heart' engraved on it, is about 500 metres (1,640 feet) west of Puji Temple. Supposedly, 100 people can stand on it at the same time.

Near the oversized Guanyin statue is Chao Yin Dong, or the **Cave of Tidal Sounds**. Guanyin is said to have appeared here to visitors throughout the ages. These visions eventually led to a cult of suicide after a monk burnt his fingers in offering to the goddess, who then appeared before him. Following his example, dozens of believers in the Ming Dynasty flocked to the site and threw

# Mercy me!

For casual visitors, it is wise to avoid jostling with the pilgrims who flock to Putuoshan from all over China and Asia to celebrate Guanyin's birthday.

Guanyin – the goddess of mercy, who is also known as Avalokitesvara – is remembered on three special days. They are the 29th of the second month in the lunar calendar, the 19th of the sixth month, and the 19th of the ninth month. These days mark her birth, the commencement of her Buddhist studies and the day she became a nun.

The grandest ceremonies are held at **Puji Temple**, but expect other temples to be packed as well, with all-night ceremonies and chanting. Hotels and ferries are fully booked on these dates and prices will also reach their peak.

themselves on to the rocks below in hope of attaining nirvana. Suicides at this spot are now expressly forbidden – by a sign on the rock. On the easternmost part of the island a small temple sits wedged in a gully between two cliff-faces at **Fan Yin Dong**, which means 'Sanskrit Sound Cave'.

Sun worshippers can get their fix at **Hundred Step Beach** or the **Thousand Sand Beach**, which lie next to each other. The Hundred is a hive of activity in summer, with water sports equipment available for rental, and sand sculptures (of Buddhist symbols, naturally) adding to the festive atmosphere. Both beaches have an entrance fee of RMB 23; go in the evening or during the colder seasons to avoid the charges. The pleasant Golden Sand Beach in the south of the island is smaller, quieter and free.

## Where to eat & drink

Seafood is an island speciality. Simple dishes prepared in the Chinese style – complete with bones and shells – can be had at any one of the numerous small restaurants on the island. Clusters of restaurants can be found near the harbour along the road at **Xishan** new village (near the naval base) or **Longwan village** (near Golden Sand Beach). The buildings themselves are rather ugly and the food is served on rough-shod outdoor tables, but the fresh seafood and seasonal vegetables are delicious.

Near Puji Temple, the **Putuoshan Teahouse** (6 Xianghua Jie, 0580 609 1208) provides traditional vegetarian Buddhist options as well as Shanghai cuisine. Note that hotel food has a bad reputation in Putuoshan.

## Where to stay

There are currently two Chinese four-star hotels on the island: the **Putuoshan Hotel** (93 Meicen Lu, 0580 609 2828, www.putuoshan hotel.com, doubles RMB 1,188) and **Xilei Xiao Zhuang** (1 Xianghua Jie, 0580 609 1505, doubles RMB 1,280). Both are very near Puji Temple and the Hundred Step Beach. For something with more character, **Xilin Hotel** (next to Xilei Xiao Zhuang, 0580 609 1119, doubles RMB 688) is converted from a small monastery. Failing these, hotel touts at the harbour hawk double rooms from RMB 200 in two-star establishments; bargaining is expected. Many restaurant operators also offer accommodation, but the condition of the rooms and legality of their offers are uncertain. It is advisable to book ahead during peak season, but at other times hotels are mostly empty. Note that prices vary greatly according to the season.

## Getting around

Putuoshan is only 12 square kilometres (4.5 square miles) long, making exploration on foot easy and pleasant. Air-conditioned minibuses pick up and drop off passengers at all the attractions; fares range from RMB 2 to RMB 10. The cable car to Foding Hill costs RMB 40 return or RMB 25 one-way.

## Getting there

### By air

Flights from Shanghai's Hongqiao Airport to Putuoshan Airport (which is actually on nearby Zhujiajian Island) are operated by China Eastern (95108, www.ce-air.com); the journey takes roughly 30 minutes. From the airport, take a taxi to Wugongzhi Dock before zipping across the ocean on a five-minute speedboat trip to Putuoshan.

### By sea

**Slow ferries** leave from Wusong Dock (251 Songbao Lu, timetables 021 5657 5500), situated where the Huangpu River flows into the sea. (The easiest way to get to the dock is by taxi but you can also take buses Nos.51, 116, 522 or 728.) The slow ferries leave Shanghai at 8pm daily and arrive in Putuoshan at 7.30am the next morning; they return at 4.30pm daily and arrive in Shanghai at 6.20am the next morning. One-way tickets are RMB 99 to RMB 462, depending on the class of travel.

**Fast ferries** leave from Luchaogang Dock (timetables 021 5828 2201) in the Nanhui district (to the south of Shanghai). A bus service runs to the dock (8am, 8.15am, 2pm daily) from 1588 Waima Lu (near Nanpu Bridge, just out of central Shanghai). The ferry crossing takes four or four-and-a-half hours; tickets are RMB 221. The ferry leaves at 9.30am, 10am and 3.30pm, and the price includes both the bus and the ferry legs of the journey. There is a return ferry from Putoshan at 4.30pm daily.

Both fast and slow ferry tickets are available from the Wusong dock ticket office at 59 Jinling Dong Lu. Go in person to buy the tickets, preferably a few days in advance.

An alternative 15-minute ferry goes from Shenjiamen Dock in Zhoushan. Bus tickets to Shenjiamen Dock are available at the Shanghai Stadium for RMB 138; departures are hourly from between 8.25am and 5.25pm every day, journey time roughly six hours. The ferry, costing RMB 18, leaves for Putuoshan every ten minutes from 6.30am to 5.30pm. For the return leg, bus tickets from Shenjiamen to Shanghai can be bought from ticket offices at Putuoshan harbour.

## Tourist information

Entrance to Putuoshan Island is currently RMB 115 (including RMB 5 for insurance), which is paid on arrival. Each site visited within the island costs an additional fee, ranging from RMB 5 to RMB 47.

# Directory

# Directory

## Getting Around

### By air

Shanghai has two airports:
all international and some
domestic flights go through
the newer **Pudong**, while
**Hongqiao** handles domestic
flights only. Shuttle buses
(6834 6189) run between the
two every 20 to 30 minutes
(Hongqiao 6am-9pm; Pudong
7am-last flight; RMB 30).

#### Pudong International Airport

*9608 1388/www.shairport.com/*
Pudong International Airport is
30km (18 miles) from the city
proper and 40km (25 miles) from
Hongqiao Airport. A **taxi** to
downtown Shanghai will cost
around RMB 160 and take about
45-60mins. To downtown Pudong
it's around RMB 130 and will take
roughly 30mins. Avoid the touts:
they charge four times the rate.

The bullet-quick **Maglev** train
connects the airport with Longyang
Lu metro station on the outskirts of
Pudong. The journey only takes
seven minutes, but on arrival you
are still a half-hour taxi or metro
ride from downtown Shanghai –
and the metro from Longyang Lu
is inconvenient with heavy
luggage. Tickets are available at
the entrance gates to the Maglev
(with same-day plane ticket single
RMB40, otherwise single/return
RMB 50/80; VIP single/return
RMB 100/160). The service runs
every 20mins, 7am-9pm.

Public **airport shuttle buses**
(6834 1000) depart from outside
the baggage claim to different
locations around the city. Useful
lines include Bus No.5 (6834
6830), which departs to Shanghai
Railway Station every 30 minutes
(5am-9pm, RMB 18) and stops
at People's Square. Bus No.2
(6834 6612) goes to Jingan Temple
and leaves every 20 minutes

(7.20am-9.30pm, RMB 19). These
shuttle buses are much cheaper
than taxis. Many hotels also offer
shuttle bus services.

**Left-luggage facilities** are
situated in the domestic arrivals
hall (6834 6324), domestic
departures hall (6834 5201),
international arrivals hall (6834
6078) and international departures
hall (6834 5035). Rates are low,
and depend on the size of the piece
of luggage. The service is open
from 6am until last flight.

**Lost property** is located
between the 8th and 9th door of the
domestic arrivals hall (6834 6324).

There is a reliable HSBC
**ATM** near the visa section
in international arrivals.

China Telecom has a **cybercafé/
business centre** (6834 6519,
open 7am-9pm) in the international
terminal; business-class passengers
can use machines in the lounges.

#### Hongqiao Airport

*6268 8918 ext 2/
www.shairport.com*
Hongqiao is the closest airport to
downtown Shanghai, with most
central destinations ten to 15km
(six to nine miles) away. A **taxi**
should cost no more than RMB 45
and will take around half an hour.
Hongqiao also has many public
**buses** (5114 6532), which depart
from in front of the arrivals hall.
Useful lines include the Special
Line, a direct service to Jingan
Temple (every 15mins, 6am-
9.30pm, RMB 4), Bus No.938
leaves for Pudong (10-15mins,
6am-9.30pm, RMB 2-4) and Bus
No.925 for People's Square (10-15
mins, 6am-9pm, RMB 2-4).

The **left-luggage facility** is in
the domestic arrivals hall (5114
4520). Rates depend on bag size.

**ATMs** are located in the arrivals
hall, near the customs office, and
in the departure hall, near the
airport tax booth; the Bank of
China ATM is the most reliable.

For domestic travellers, Shanghai
Airlines offers a **downtown
check-in facility** (1600 Nanjing

Xi Lu, 3214 4600), which only
operates if your scheduled
departure is after 11am. Check
your luggage in two and a half
hours before departure, get your
boarding pass, then hop on the
direct airport bus (RMB 19).

#### AIRLINES

Major airlines currently flying
to Shanghai include:

**Air Canada** *Room 3901, United
Plaza, 1468 Nanjing Xi Lu, Jingan
(6279 2999/www.aircanada.ca).*
**Air China** *600 Huashan Lu,
by Wulumuqi Bei Lu, French
Concession (5239 7227/www.
airchina.com.cn).*
**American Airlines**
*Room 702, Central Plaza, 227
Huangpi Bei Lu, People's Square
(6375 8686/www.aa.com).*
**British Airways** *Suite 703,
Central Plaza, 227 Huangpi Bei
Lu, People's Square (6375 8385/
www.ba.com).*
**Northwest Airlines**
*Room 207, East Tower, Shanghai
Centre, 1376 Nanjing Xi Lu, by
Xikang Lu, Jingan (6884 6884/
www.nwa.com).*
**Shanghai Airlines**
*212 Jiangning Lu, by Beijing
Xi Lu, Jingan (6255 0550/www.
shanghai-air.com).*
**United Airlines** *Room 3301-
3317, 31F, Shanghai Central
Plaza, 381 Huaihai Zhong Lu
(3311 4567/www.united.com).*
**Virgin Atlantic Airways**
*Suite 221, 12 Zhongshan Dong
Yi Lu, by Fuzhou Lu, the Bund
(5353 4600/www.virgin.com/
atlantic).*

### By rail

Rail services are generally used
for short-distance travel within
China. In Shanghai, trains run
from either the **Shanghai
Railway Station**, in the north
of the city, or **Shanghai South**
or **West Railway Stations**.
For more info on travel by

train, visit **www.rail.sh.cn**.
Buying tickets at the Shanghai
Train Station requires patience
and persistence. Try the
English-language counters
or better still one of the
conveniently located ticket
offices around town, such
as the ones on **Nanjing Lu**
(108 Nanjing Xi Lu, by Xizang
Lu, Jingan, 6327 8430) or
**Fuzhou Lu** (431 Fuzhou
Lu, by Fujian Lu, the Bund,
6326 0303 ext 3109).

### Shanghai Railway Station

*385 Meiyuan Lu, Zhabei
(6317 9090/6354 5358).
Metro Shanghai Railway
Station.* **Map** p243 F1.
For Beijing, Hong Kong and
Suzhou. Beware of pickpockets.

### Shanghai South Railway Station

*200 Zhaofeng Lu, Xinlonghua
(6317 9090/5125 5114). Metro
Shanghai South Railway Station.*
**Map** p240 B6.
Trains for Hangzhou.

### Shanghai West Railway Station

*22 Taopu Lu, by Caoyang Lu,
Putuo (6317 9090). Metro
Caoyang Lu.* **Map** p240 B2.
Alternative station on the same
line as Shanghai Railway Station.

## By sea

Located at the mouth of the
Huangpu River, Shanghai
is in an excellent position if
you want to cruise down the
coastline of China and beyond.
Most domestic ships/ferries
dock at the **Qiandao Wusong
Passenger Terminal** (100
Songpu Lu, Hongkou, 5667
1207), 1.5km north-east of the
Bund. Overseas ships dock at
the **International Passenger
Terminal** (1 Waihongqiao Lu,
6595 9529), also 1.5km north-
east of the Bund.

### TICKETS

Tickets can be booked directly
at the ferry offices or through
one of the following agencies:

**China International Travel
Service (CITS)** *2 Jinling Dong
Lu, by Zhongshan Dongyi Lu, the
Bund (6323 8770).* **Map** p245 M6.
**China Youth Travel
Service/STA Travel**
*2 Hengshan Lu, by Dongping Lu,
French Concession (6474 1523).*
**Map** p246 C9.

## Public transport

Shanghai's public transport
system is near unfathomable
without some fluency in
Chinese. Buses are plentiful, but
lack of English signage – not to
mention overcrowding – makes
using them a headache. The
metro is an exception: efficient
and with some English signs
(for a metro map, *see p256*).
Again, though, it suffers from
too many bodies in too little
space. It's best for longer
journeys, such as to Pudong.
For convenience and minimal
stress, taxis are usually best.

## Fares & tickets

Visitors planning to use public
transport fairly frequently over
a week or more can buy a
**stored-value card** (*jiaotong
ka*). Available at metro stations,
they are valid for the metro,
buses and even taxis, and cost
RMB 100 – the stored value is
RMB 70, with RMB 30 a
deposit refundable when the
card is returned. The card
deducts a fee when scanned
by the reader above the metro
turnstile, or by scanners on
bus and taxi dashboards. There
is no expiry date on the credit.
Note that on Shanghai's
public transport discount
tickets for children, students
and the elderly are only valid
for Chinese nationals.

## Metro

Metro stations are identifiable
by their red-on-white 'M' signs.
Not always easy to spot, signs
in English are present in
stations; announcements
are also bilingual.

There are currently five
metro lines. **Line 1** runs south
from Baoshan, through the
Shanghai Railway Station
down through People's Square,
the French Concession and
Xujiahui to Xinzhuang in the
southern suburbs. **Line 2** runs
west from Zhangjiang (which is
out beyond Pudong) via the
Bund area, People's Square
(where it connects with Line 1)
and Jingan to terminate at
Zhongshan Park (an extension
out to Hongqiao Airport is
due to be completed in 2007 –
mind you, it was due for late
2004 when we published the
last edition). The partially
elevated **Lines 3** and **4** loop
out around the city centre; with
the exception of the extension
north of Shanghai Railway
Station, which runs via East
Baoxing Lu (for Duolun Lu)
and Hongkou Stadium, they're
little use to visitors. As we went
to press the southern section of
Line 3 from Damuqiao Lu to
Lancun Lu was closed,
scheduled to reopen in mid
2007. Likewise, **Line 5** is a
suburban line running from
the western terminus of Line 1
into Minghang district.
The metro runs from
5-5.30am to 10.20-11.30pm
and trains are very frequent.
Note that Lines 3, 4 and 5
start later (6-7am) and close
earlier (9.30-10.30pm). Ticket
machines or staff at the metro
stations sell single-journey
metro tickets costing RMB 3-7,
depending on the distance
travelled. Keep your ticket
until you exit.

## Buses

There are over 1,000 bus lines
in Shanghai. Prepare to hit a
major language barrier when
using them – the destinations
are listed only in Chinese and
there is no English-language
phone line. Chinese-speakers
can contact the **Shanghai
Urban Transportation
Bureau** (6317 6355).

**Directory**

Don't expect peaceful rides – buses are crowded, unbearably so during rush hour. Air-conditioned buses have a clever snowflake symbol by the bus number. There is also the added stress of potential pickpocketing. Buy tickets from the on-board conductor (RMB 2-3) or use a stored-value card (*jiaotong ka, see p217*).

## Taxis

Travelling by taxi is not an extravagance. Fares are cheap and taxis plentiful; the only noticeable shortages are during rush hour or in rain. If you're having trouble finding a taxi, head to a five-star hotel and you should find plenty waiting at the forecourt taxi rank.

Taxis are metered and, in our experience, drivers are scrupulously honest about observing them. Fares are set at RMB 11 for the first two kilometres (1.2 miles) and then RMB 2 for every additional kilometre. Fares rise after 11pm.

Tipping is not expected. Cash or stored-value cards (*jiaotong ka, see p217*) are accepted forms of payment.

Most drivers have only limited English, so you must get your destination written in Chinese – most hotels supply cards with the addresses of major sites in both English and Chinese. Failing that, ask the concierge to write it out for you. Keep hold of business cards for places to which you might return.

The driver will supply you with a receipt (*fapiao*). This shows the taxi number and the company telephone number – useful if you discover you've left something in the cab.

The phone number for complaints is 962000.

Those with mobile phones can take advantage of the **Guanxi** SMS service to access bilingual addresses. Simply type in the name of the

restaurant, hotel or bar and text it to 885074. Seconds later you receive a message asking you to chose a location; press C for addresses in Chinese.

### TAXI COMPANIES
**Bashi Taxi** *6431 2788*.
**Dazhong Taxi** *96822*.
**Jinjiang Taxi** *6464 7777*.
**Qiangsheng** *6258 0000*.

## Cycling

Cycling is a popular way to get around the city. Cyclists should, however, be cautious of Shanghai's aggressive drivers and its dangerously ill-kept roads. Bikes should be registered at a police station, but bike shops can offer this service. The **Captain Hostel** (*see p35*) offers bike rental and tours.

### Giant Bicycle Store
*743 Jianguo Xi Lu, by Yueyang Lu, Xujiahui (6437 5041). Metro Hengshan Lu.* **Open** 9am-8pm daily. **No credit cards**. **Map** p246 D10.
Can provide everything from top-of-the-line mountain bikes and flash racing machines to inexpensive city pushbikes.

## Driving

Tourists are not forbidden from taking to Shanghai's roads, but there is plenty of red tape to deter them.

## Licences

Most expats apply for Chinese licences at the **Shanghai Vehicle Management Bureau** (1101 Zhongshan Bei Yi Lu, 6498 7070). To do this you will need your passport, residence permit, health certificate and a driving licence held for over three years, plus an official translation of that driving licence. You will also have to undergo a short written driving test and a medical examination. The total cost of the application is RMB 210.

Drivers with less than three years' experience are also required to take a road test.

Travellers without a tourist visa who intend to rent a car can get a temporary licence at the **Pudong Airport Public Security Bureau** (open 9am-4pm Mon-Thur), a short drive from the main terminal. You'll need the papers mentioned above, plus an international driving licence. Again, you will undergo a written test and a medical. The length of licence issued depends on your residence permit.

If you do not have a foreign driving licence, you will be required to attend driving lessons for 70 hours at the **Shanghai Traffic Rules Education** school (2175 Pudong Dadao, 5631 7000).

## Vehicle hire

Those visiting Shanghai on tourist L-visas are unable to drive rental cars, but they can hire a car with a driver. Average daily rental costs are about RMB 600-800.

### Car rental companies
**Dazhong** *100 Guohuo Lu, by Zhongshan Nan Lu, Old City (6318 5666)*. **Map** p249 M10.
**Hertz Car Rental** *Suite 306, Chengfeng Centre, 1088 Yanan Xi Lu, Hongqiao (6252 2200)*. Also at Pudong International Airport.
**Shanghai Anji Car Rental** *Hongqiao Airport, 81 Huanbing Lu, Hongqiao (6268 0862)*. **Map** p240 A4. Avis partner in China.

## Walking

Distances are such that the city centre is easily navigated on foot. But beware: pavements double as express lanes for bicycles and scooters, but at least they are well maintained. Crossing can be a challenge – look left, then right, then left again and be careful not to step into Shanghai's busy bike lanes.

# Resources A-Z

## Addresses

All street signs are written in both Chinese and Pinyin (romanised Chinese) but, in a recent fit of Anglicisation, the authorities have erased certain useful Pinyin bits. Thus 'Xizang Nan Lu' is rendered as 'Tibet Road, South'. It may be intellectually stimulating to know this is the meaning, but nary a taxi driver will understand the English. Thus, keep in mind these simple pieces of Chinese: *lu* means street or road; the prefix *bei* is north, *dong* is east, *nan* means south, *xi* is west. When getting around it is common to give the cross street of the address, for example Nanjing Xi Lu, by Jiangning Bei Lu; 'by' is *kaojin*.

## Age restrictions

The legal age for marriage (implying consensual sex) is 22 for men and 20 for women; there's no age of consent for homosexuals as gay sex is not officially recognised. Under-18s are still considered minors and are not allowed to smoke, but there's no legal drinking age.

## Attitude & etiquette

*See p224* **Attitude problems**.

## Business

First, visit the business site of the Shanghai government: **www.investment.gov.cn**.

## Business cards

Business cards are offered or accepted with both hands. Cards can be printed at **Copy General** (Kerry Centre, 1515 Nanjing Xi Lu, by Tongren Lu, Jingan, 6279 4207). *See also p224* **Attitude problems**.

## Chambers of Commerce

**American Chamber of Commerce** *Portman Ritz-Carlton, 1376 Nanjing Xi Lu, Jingan (6279 7119/www.amchamshanghai.org).* **Map** p242 D5.

**Australian Chamber of Commerce** *1440 Yanan Zhong Lu, Jingan (6248 8301/ www.austchamshanghai.com).* **Map** p242 C6.

**British Chamber of Commerce** *17th floor, Westgate Tower, 1038 Nanjing Xi Lu, Jingan (6218 5022/www.sha.britcham.org).* **Map** p243 F5.

**Canada China Business Council** *Hong Kong Plaza, 283 Huaihai Zhong Lu, by Songshan Lu, Xintiandi (6390 6001/www.ccbc.com).* **Map** p248 J7.

## Convention centres

These are the major conference and convention venues:

**Shanghai Everbright Convention & Exhibition Centre** *66 Caobao Lu, by Caoxi Lu, Xujiahui (6484 2500/www.secec.com).* **Map** p240 C5.

**Shanghai International Convention Centre** *2727 Riverside Avenue, by Lujiazui Lu, Pudong (5037 0000/www.shicc.net).* **Map** p245 N5.

**Shanghai Mart** *2299 Yanan Xi Lu, by Gubei Lu, Hongqiao (6236 6888/www.shanghaimart.com.cn).* **Map** p240 A4.

**Shanghai New International Expo Centre** *2345 Longyang Lu, by Hunangong Lu, Pudong (2890 6666/www.sniec.net).* **Map** p241 G4.

## Couriers

**DHL** *Sinotrans, Shanghai International Trade Centre, 2200 Yanan Lu, by Loushanguan Lu, Hongqiao (6275 3543/www.dhl.com).* **Open** 8.30am-6pm Mon-Fri; 8.30am-4pm Sat. **No credit cards. Map** p240 B4.

**FedEx** *10th floor, Aetna Building, 107 Zunyi Lu, by Xianxia Lu, Hongqiao (6275 0808/www.fedex.com).* **Open** 8.30am-6pm Mon-Fri; 8.30am-3pm Sat. **No credit cards. Map** p240 B4.

**UPS** *Suite 23, 166 Lujiazui Dong Lu, Pudong (3896 5599/www.ups.com). Metro Lujiazui.* **Open** 8.30am-6.30pm Mon-Fri; 9am-2pm Sat. **No credit cards. Map** p245 O5.

## Office hire & business centres

Most major four- and five-star hotels (*see pp30-44* **Where to Stay**) offer business services, but you'll pay premium rates.

# Travel advice

For up-to-date information when travelling to a specific country – including the latest news on safety and security, health issues, local laws and customs – contact the department of foreign affairs of your home country government. Most have websites packed with useful advice for would-be travellers.

**Australia**
www.smartraveller.gov.au

**Canada**
www.voyage.gc.ca

**New Zealand**
www.safetravel.govt.nz

**Republic of Ireland**
http://foreignaffairs.gov.ie

**UK**
www.fco.gov.uk/travel

**USA**
http://travel.state.gov

**Directory**

### Executive Centre

*3501 CITIC Square, 1168 Nanjing Xi Lu, by Shanxi Bei Lu, Jingan (5292 5223/www.executive centre.com).* **Map** p243 E5. Full-service office rental with complete secretarial support.

## Translators

### Shanghai Interpreters Association *Room 702, 66 Nanjing Dong Lu, by Henan Zhong Lu, the Bund (6323 3608). Metro Henan Lu.* **Open** 9.30am-4pm Mon-Fri. **No credit cards.** **Map** p244 L4.

**Speed Shanghai** *Ziyuan Mansion, Guangyuan Lu, by Huashan Lu, Xujiahui (6447 4184/www.speed-asia.com). Metro Xujiahui.* **Open** 8.30am-5.30pm Mon-Sat. **No credit cards.** **Map** p246 A10.

## Consumer

Buyer beware. Returning faulty products is a trial, even with a receipt or guarantee. Consumers can file an online complaint with the **Shanghai Bureau of Quality & Technical Supervison** at www.sbts.sh.cn (or call 6275 8710) but it's in Chinese only.

## Customs

Visitors can bring in 400 cigarettes and two 0.75-litre bottles of alcohol, plus one each of the following items: camera, portable tape-recorder, portable cine-camera, portable video-camera and portable computer. There are no restrictions on the amount of foreign currency.

It's forbidden to take out of China any antiques over 200 years old. Check with the shop when you make your purchase, and keep the receipt and the shop's business card to present to customs if necessary.

## Disabled

Shanghai poses problems for disabled travellers. Wheelchair access is provided at airports,

metro and train stations, and at a handful of the international five-star hotels, but nowhere else. Pavements on major streets have raised strips for the visually impaired to follow. But the amount and quality of special-needs facilities should improve shortly, given that Shanghai is to host the 2007 Special Olympics.

**Shanghai Disabled Persons' Federation** *189 Longyang Lu, Pudong (5873 3212/fax 3889 0002/shdisabled@online.sh.cn).*

## Drugs

Street drugs are becoming more readily available, especially in nightclubs, but the punishments for drug-use remain harsh. Consulates can offer only very limited legal assistance to those caught with illegal drugs.

## Electricity

China runs on 220 volts. The most common type of plug is the dual prong, either parallel or at a 45° angle, as in Australia. 110-volt appliances may be redundant – adaptors have been known to overheat.

## Embassies & consulates

All foreign embassies are located in Beijing, but many countries also maintain a consulate in Shanghai.

### Australian Consulate *22nd floor, CITIC Square, 1168 Nanjing Xi Lu, by Shanxi Bei Lu, Jingan (5292 5500/ www.shanghai.china.embassy. gov.au).* **Open** 8.30am-5pm Mon-Fri. **Map** p243 E5.

**British Consulate** *Room 301, Shanghai Centre, 1376 Nanjing Xi Lu, by Tongren Lu, Jingan (6279 7650/www.uk.cn/bj/index. asp?city=4).* **Open** 8.30am-4.30pm Mon-Fri. **Map** p243 E5.

**Canadian Consulate** *Room 668, Shanghai Centre, 1376 Nanjing Xi Lu, by Tongren Lu,*

*Jingan (6279 8400/www.shanghai. gc.ca).* **Open** 8.30am-5pm Mon-Fri. **Map** p243 E5.

**Irish Consulate** *Room 700A, Shanghai Centre, 1376 Nanjing Xi Lu, by Tongren Lu, Jingan (6279 8729).* **Open** 9.30am-5.30pm Mon-Fri. **Map** p243 E5.

**New Zealand Consulate** *15th floor, Qihua Tower, 1375 Huaihai Zhong Lu, by Fuxing Lu, French Concession (6471 1108/ www.nzembassy.com).* **Open** 8.30am-5.30pm Mon-Fri. **Map** p246 C8.

**South African Consulate** *Room 2706, 222 Yanan Xi Lu, by Loushanguan Lu, Hongqiao (5359 4977/sacgpolitical@yahoo.com).* **Open** 8am-4.30pm daily. **Map** p240 B4.

**US Consulate** *1469 Huaihai Zhong Lu, by Wulumuqi Nan Lu, French Concession (6433 6880/ http://shanghai.usembassy-china. org.cn).* **Open** 8am-5pm Mon-Fri. **Map** p248 C6.

## Emergencies

For more useful numbers, *see below* **Health**; *p222* **Helplines**; and *p225* **Police.**

### Useful numbers

**Ambulance** *120.*
**Directory assistance** *114.*
**Police** *110.*
**Fire service** *119.*
**IDD code enquiry** *114 or 10000.*
**Operator-assisted Yellow Pages** *96886.*
**Time** *117.*
**Weather forecast** *121.*

## Gay & lesbian

*See pp169-72* **Gay & Lesbian.**

## Health

China does not have reciprocal healthcare agreements with other countries, so it is advisable to take out private insurance. However, some clinics do accept private international insurance such as BUPA or TIECARE. Check with your insurance provider before departure.

Vaccinations against Hepatitis A and B, polio, tetanus, flu, chickenpox, typhoid, tetanus-diphtheria, Japanese encephalitis (if travel plans include rural areas) and rabies are the most commonly recommended; there are major problems with tuberculosis and hepatitis A here, so be sure to get those shots before travel. Some travellers may complain of stomach upsets due to the change in diet. Tap water should be avoided in the city, not so much because of bacteria but due to potential heavy metal content. The bottled water sold everywhere is fine, and ice made from purified water is common.

## Hospitals

Shanghai has some good public hospitals and private international clinics. The main public hospitals (*yiyuan*) will treat visitors on an outpatient or emergency basis, often in a special foreigner ward. For international and local clinics you will need to bring your passport and cash for the consultation fees, which vary wildly (RMB 100-500).

Be aware that Chinese hospitals often prescribe antibiotics and drips regardless of whether the cause of illness merits such action. The tendency to overprescribe is exacerbated because hospitals in China also act as general pharmacies, and upwards of 60 per cent of their income is made from drug sales. Make sure you're clear about the necessity of any medication prescribed.

The following hospitals provide comprehensive medical care. Levels of hygiene are well maintained and staff are knowledgeable, but comfort and privacy may be lacking. Both Chinese- and Western-style treatment is available at these hospitals.

In an emergency, dial 120.

### Huashan Hospital Foreigners' Clinic

*19th floor, 12 Wulumuqi Zhong Lu, by Huashan Lu, French Concession (6248 9999 ext 2500). Metro Changshu Lu or Jingan Temple.* **Open** *Clinic* 7am-5pm Mon-Fri. *Emergencies* 24hrs daily. **Credit** AmEx, DC, MC, V. **Map** p246 C8.
Part of one of Shanghai's largest hospitals, with modern facilities. Staff outside the Foreigners' Clinic may only have limited English.

### Ruijin Hospital

*197 Ruijin Er Lu, by Yongjia Lu, French Concession (6466 4483). Metro Shanxi Nan Lu.* **Open** 24hrs daily. **Credit** AmEx, DC, MC, V. **Map** p247 F9.
The full range of medical facilities; some English is spoken.

## Private clinics/ doctors

### International Medical Care Centre of Shanghai

*People's Hospital No.1, Wujing Lu, by Wusong Lu, Hongkou (6324 3852).* **Open** 24hrs daily. **Credit** AmEx, DC, MC, V. **Map** p245 M1.
This private health centre, attached to a teaching hospital, offers all medical services, including dentistry. The standard of care in the Medical Centre is higher than in other departments.

### Shanghai East International Medical Centre

*551 Pudong Nan Lu, by Pudong Dadao, Pudong (5879 9999/ www.seimc.com.cn). Metro Dongchang Lu.* **Open** *Clinic* 8am-9pm Mon-Fri; 9am-2pm Sat; 9am-1pm Sun. *Emergencies* 24hrs daily. **Credit** AmEx, DC, MC, V. **Map** p241 F3.
Joint-venture clinic run by Shanghai East Hospital and a US healthcare group. Expat doctors and English-speaking nurses provide experienced, world-class family healthcare.

### World Link

*Suite 203, Shanghai Centre, 1376 Nanjing Xi Lu, by Tongren Lu, Jingan (6279 7688/www.world* *link-shanghai.com). Metro Jingan Temple.* **Open** 9am-7pm Mon-Fri; 9am-4pm Sat; 9am-3pm Sun. **Credit** AmEx, DC, MC, V. **Map** p243 E5.
One of several World Link clinics in Shanghai. Doctors are from the US, UK, Canada and Japan, and assistance is available in English, Japanese and Chinese. Clinics offer a complete range of services from walk-in treatment for minor ailments to internal medicine. Dental treatment is also available.

## Contraception & abortion

Due to its one-child policy China has some of the most affordable, modern and accessible contraceptive and abortion facilities in the world. Contraceptives are available over the counter at pharmacies throughout the city. Abortions are available at the hospitals listed above. For help, contact the **American Sino OB-GYN Clinic** (6210 3246).

## Dentists

The following services are all English-speaking.

### Arrail Dental

*Unit 204, Lippo Plaza, 222 Huaihai Zhong Lu, Xintiandi (5396 6538/www.arrail-dental. com). Metro Huangpi Nan Lu.* **Open** 9am-8pm Mon-Thur; 9.30am-6.30pm Fri-Sun. **Credit** AmEx, DC, MC, V. **Map** p248 H7.
Dental treatment by American-trained staff, with strict CDC/ADA infection control protocols. Popular with US Consulate staff.

### DDS Dental Care

*1325 Huaihai Zhong Lu, French Concession (6466 0928). Metro Changshu Lu.* **Open** 9am-5pm Mon-Sat. **Credit** AmEx, DC, MC, V. **Map** p246 C8.
Affordable and complete dental treatment. The Western-trained Chinese staff speak English.

### Dr Harriet Jin's Dental Surgery

*Room 1904, Hui Yin Plaza, 2088 Huashan Lu, by Hengshan Lu, Xujiahui (6448 0882). Metro*

*Xujiahui.* **Open** 9am-6pm Mon-Fri; 9am-1pm Sat. **Credit** AmEx, DC, MC, V. **Map** p246 A11.
A small clinic with a big following among expats – Dr Jin used to work in the UK.

## Opticians

Most optical shops will grind lenses (after an on-site eye exam or to a prescription) within a few hours and at a reasonable price. Opticians can be found on Nanjing Xi Lu in Jingan and Huaihai Nan Lu in the French Concession.

Try **Shanghai Sanye Wholesale Eyeglasses Market** (515 Shenjiazai Lu, by Shanghai Train Station North Square, Zhabei, 5632 1259) for great deals. Prices start as low as RMB 90.

## Pharmacies & prescriptions

All medication is available over the counter, although certain antibiotics require a prescription. It is always advisable to purchase medicine at larger pharmacies to avoid the risk of counterfeit drugs.

**Huaihai Pharmacist** *528 Huaihai Zhong Lu, by Chongqing Nan Lu, French Concession (5383 2101). Metro Huangpi Nan Lu.* **Open** 24hrs daily. **Credit** MC, V. **Map** p247 H7.

**Huashi Pharmacist** *910 Hengshan Lu, by Tianping Lu, French Concession (6407 8985). Metro Xujiahui.* **Open** 24hrs daily. **No credit cards.** **Map** p246 B10.

**No.1 Pharmacy** *616 Nanjing Dong Lu, by Zhejiang Lu, People's Square (6322 4567). Metro Henan Lu.* **Open** 9am-10pm daily. **Credit** AmEx, DC, MC, V. **Map** p244 K4.

## STDs, HIV & AIDS

For hospitals, *see p221;* World Link's service is very discreet.

**AIDS Information & Counselling** *1380 Zhongshan Xi Lu, Hongqiao Lu, Hongqiao (6437*

*0055). Metro Hongqiao Lu.* **Open** 8.30am-5pm Mon-Fri. **No credit cards.**

**Shanghai Venereal Disease Association** *196 Wuyi Lu, Changning (6251 1807). Metro Zhongshan Park.* **Open** 7.45am-7pm Mon-Fri; 7.45am-4.45pm Sat; 7.45-11am Sun. **No credit cards.**

## Traditional Chinese medicine (TCM)

*See pp173-7* **Mind & Body**.

## Helplines

### Lifeline Shanghai

*6279 8990/www.lifelineshanghai. com.* **Open** noon-8pm daily.
English-speakers are almost always available.

## ID

Chinese citizens are expected to carry photo ID at all times. Foreigners should carry their passport or a photocopy of its information page and the page with the China visa.

## Insurance

China has no reciprocal agreements with other countries: be sure to take out adequate health and travel insurance before you arrive.

## Internet

Most hotels offer internet services for a fee. Top-end joints usually offer free broadband to anyone with a laptop (as do **Arch**, *see p128*, and **KABB**, *see p109*). Otherwise, there are **internet cafés** on every corner, most of them (especially 24-hour ones) gaming dens. An hour's surfing in such places can be as cheap as RMB 2; take ID with you. Wireless connections have begun to catch on in the city, so travellers with laptops can access the net at locations such as **Xintiandi** (*see pp77-9*) and **Element Fresh** (*see p105*).

### Cyber Bar & Café

*77 Jiangning Lu, by Nanjing Xi Lu, Jingan (6217 3321). Metro Shimen Yi Lu.* **Open** 24hrs daily. **Rates** RMB 5/hr. **No credit cards.** **Map** p243 F5.
An all-night bang-bang arcade. Very loud – notwithstanding the noise-reducing computer headsets.

### O'Richard's Bar & Restaurant

*2nd floor, Pujiang Hotel, 15 Huangpu Lu, by Garden Bridge, the Bund (6324 6388 ext 175). Metro Henan Lu.* **Open** 7am-2am daily. **Rates** RMB 15/hr. **No credit cards.** **Map** p245 N3.
Get some Qingdao beer and noodles while you surf.

### Shanghai Library

*1555 Huaihai Zhong Lu, by Gaoan Lu, French Concession (6445 5555). Metro Hengshan Lu.* **Open** 9am-8.30pm daily. **Rates** RMB 4/hr. **No credit cards.** **Map** p246 C8/9.
Here you'll catch the silver surfers getting online. No smoking or drinks, and you must show a passport or library card to use one of the 24 terminals. Some sites (e.g. hotmail) are periodically blocked.

## Language

Chinese has many dialects (Hong Kong people speak Cantonese, people in Shanghai they speak Shanghainese), but standard Chinese is called Mandarin or Putongua. For those who do not read Chinese characters there is a romanised alphabet called Pinyin.

English is not widely understood outside the top hotels and businesses, so get a copy of the address you're heading to written in Chinese and show it to the driver. Most business cards have Chinese and English addresses listed on them, making them a valuable tool for getting around. Listings magazines such as *that's Shanghai* and **City Weekend** have Chinese addresses for popular venues, and the Guanxi SMS-based directory (*see p218*) is good. *See also p231* **Vocabulary**.

## Left luggage

Luggage can be left at Pudong
International Airport and
Hongqiao Airport (for both,
see p216). Shanghai Railway
Station (6354 3193) and
Shanghai South Railway
Station (5122 5114) also have
left-luggage services (RMB
20/4hrs, RMB 80/day). Many
of the better hotels can arrange
long-term luggage storage for
their guests.

## Legal help

For help finding a lawyer and
basic information on Chinese
law, call the **Jun He** law firm
(Suite 2501, Shanghai Kerry
Centre, 1515 Nanjing Xi Lu, by
Tongren Lu, Jingan, 5298 5488,
junhesh@junhe.com). For more
information, see also p220
**Embassies & consulates**.

## Libraries

**Shanghai Library**
*1555 Huaihai Zhong Lu, by
Gaoan Lu, French Concession
(6445 5555). Metro Hengshan
Lu.* **Open** 8.30am-8.30pm daily.
**Map** p246 C8/9.
The Shanghai Library is the
largest of its kind in China.
It has an outstanding collection
of Chinese books, both antique
and modern, but the range of
foreign-language books is limited.
The library also houses an art
gallery and an internet café
(see p222).

## Lost property

To report a crime contact the
police hotline (110). For items
left in taxis, look at the receipt
and use the contact number on
the back to trace the vehicle.
Hotel concierges can also
assist in tracking down lost
things. If a passport is lost,
contact the relevant consulate
immediately (see p220).
   For Pudong International
Airport lost property, call 6834
6324; for Hongqiao Airport,
call 6268 8899 ext 42071.

## Media

### Magazines

Shanghai has a multitude
of free English-language
magazines with listings. The
most popular are *City Weekend*
(www.cityweekend.com.cn)
and *that's Shanghai* (www.
thatssh.com), both monthlies.
Other titles include *Shanghai
Talk* and *Metrozine*. Pick them
up free at cafés, restaurants
and bars around town.

### Newspapers

Newsstands offer two main
English-language newspapers,
the locally produced *Shanghai
Daily* (www.shanghaidaily.
com) and the Beijing-printed
*China Daily* (www.chinadaily.
com.cn). The *Shanghai Star*
(www.shanghai-star.com.cn),
which comes out on Tuesday
and Friday. The Chinese-
language *People's Daily*
can be read in English at
http://english.peopledaily.com.
cn. The *Oriental Morning Post*
includes an English-language
supplement on Friday.
   Newspaper editorial is
scrutinised by the government,
necessitating self-censorship.
   It is very difficult to get hold
of international newspapers
in Shanghai, but the Portman
Ritz-Carlton should be able to
provide a copy of *The Times*
or the *Financial Times* – at a
price. For more on where to
buy international newspapers
and magazines, see p137.

### Radio

The **BBC World Service**
can be picked up at 17760,
15278, 21660, 12010 and 9740
kHz. The **Voice of America
(VOA)** is at 17820, 15425,
21840, 15250, 9760, 5880
and 6125 kHz. For tuning
information click on 'Radio
Schedules' at www.bbc.co.uk/
worldservice or on 'Radio:
Frequencies' at www.voa.gov.

## Television

News in English is shown
at 10pm Mon-Sat on the
Shanghai Broadcast Network
(SBN). A cultural magazine in
English, Citybeat, airs at 10pm
on Sunday. English-language
news is also shown on CCTV 9
at 4pm, 7pm and 11pm on
weekdays and at noon on
weekends. Most top-end
hotels have at least BBC, CNN,
ESPN, HBO and Star World.

## Money

The monetary unit in China
is the **RMB** (*renminbi*), also
known as the *yuan* (written)
or *kuai* (spoken). Bills come in
denominations of RMB 100, 50,
20, 10, 5, 2 and 1, coins include
1 *yuan*, 5 and 1 *jiao* pieces (10
*jiao* equals RMB 1).
   The exchange rate is usually
in the region of RMB 8 to the
dollar, RMB 15 to the pound.
   Note that few countries
outside Asia recognise RMB,
so change any leftover cash
at the airport as you leave.
Bring receipts to prove that
the amount you want to change
back is less than the amount
first changed into RMB. ATM
receipts don't count; you'll need
official receipts from exchange
counters or bank tellers.

### ATMs

ATMs are widely available
but they may not accept
foreign cards even if they
display the Interact logo.
HSBC provides some of the
more reliable ATMs, including
at the following locations:

**HSBC the Bund** *15A Zhongshan
Dongyi Lu, by Jiujiang Lu, the
Bund.* **Map** p245 M4.
**HSBC Hong Kong Plaza**
*Hong Kong Plaza, 282 Huaihai
Zhong Lu, by Huangpi Nan Lu,
Xintiandi.* **Map** p248 H7.
**HSBC Shanghai Centre**
*Shanghai Centre, 1376 Nanjing
Xi Lu, by Tongren Lu, Jingan.*
**Map** p243 E5.

**Directory**

# Attitude problems

The intricacies of Chinese etiquette mean that it's all too easy for beginners to feel lost or embarrassed. The pitfalls are many.

## Face off

You've enjoyed a feast in a restaurant with your local host and the bill arrives. Your host reaches for his credit card. 'No,' you say, 'I'll pay.' A to-and-froing ensues and, to end the discussion, you grab the bill and pay, anxious to show your generosity. You've just committed a serious faux pas. Your host has lost 'face' and that's the cardinal sin in Shanghai.

Face is a peculiar Chinese concept and its importance can never be underestimated. Some folk go to great lengths to acquire it by displays of wealth or generosity.

Complimenting someone on their appearance or business acumen – especially in front of their pals or colleagues – is a sure-fire winner. Confrontation and criticism are guaranteed face-destroyers. When in doubt, be lavish with those compliments.

## Greetings

Chinese people have a family name, followed by a first name – Chen Wu, for example. To address someone, use their family name together with their professional title or 'Mr', 'Madam' or 'Miss', plus the family name – eg Mr Chen. Only family members or close friends use first names. Always acknowledge the most senior person first.

The Chinese will nod or bow slightly as an initial greeting. Handshakes are also popular, but wait for your Chinese counterpart to initiate the gesture.

## Public behaviour

Avoid expansive gestures, unusual facial expressions and sarcasm as these can generate confused reactions. The Chinese do not use their hands when speaking, and will become annoyed with a speaker who does.

The Chinese, especially those who are older and in positions of authority, dislike being touched by strangers. Conversely, the Chinese generally stand closer to each other than Europeans and North Americans.

Do not put your hands in your mouth – it's considered vulgar. Hence nail-biting, flossing and similar practices are also no-nos. Post-dinner tooth picking is acceptable with one hand covering the mouth. Members of the same sex often hold hands in public.

## Conversation

Negative replies are considered impolite. Instead of saying 'no', answer 'Maybe', 'I'll think about it' or 'We'll see.'

Questions about your age, income and marital status are common. If you don't want to reveal this information, remain unspecific.

In Chinese culture, the question 'Have you eaten?' is the equivalent to 'How are you?' in Western culture; it's a superficial inquiry that does not require a literal answer.

Do not be surprised if there are periods of silence during business or dinner. It is a sign of politeness and of thought. Do not try to fill the silence with words.

## Gestures

Shanghainese body language has several gestures that appear strange. These include touching one's own face several times quickly in a similar manner to scratching, but with the forefinger straight. This means 'Shame on you!'. It is a semi-joking gesture.

Pointing to the tip of one's nose with raised forefinger means 'It's me' or 'I'm the one'.

Using both hands in offering something to a visitor or another person equals respect. For example, when one's tea cup is being refilled by the host or hostess, putting one or both hands upright, palm open, beside the cup means 'Thank you'.

## Gifts

Official policy in Chinese business culture forbids giving gifts, though enforcement of this policy is rather sporadic; the practice is seen as akin to bribery. Consequently, your gift may be declined. In many organisations, however, attitudes towards gifts are beginning to relax. Discretion is still important, and if you wish to give a gift to an individual, you must do it privately, in the context of friendship, not business. The Chinese will sometimes decline a gift three times before finally accepting, so as not to appear greedy.

## Numbers

Eight is considered one of the luckiest numbers in Chinese culture. If you receive eight of any item, consider it a gesture of good will. But avoid four of any item – in Mandarin, the word 'four' sounds similar to 'death'. Scissors, knives or other sharp objects can be interpreted as the severing of a friendship or other bond.

**HSBC Tower** *101 Yincheng Dong Lu, by Pudong Dadao, Pudong.* **Map** p245 P5.

## Banks

**ABN AMRO** *28th floor, Jinmao Tower, 88 Shiji Dadao, Pudong (800 820 2877). Metro Lujiazui.* **Open** 10am-noon, 2-5pm Mon-Fri. **Map** p245 O5.
**Bank of China** *200 Yincheng Zhong Lu, by Lujiazui Lu, Pudong (3883 4588). Metro Lujiazui.* **Open** 24hrs Mon-Fri. **Map** p245 O5.
**China Construction Bank** *1632 Yincheng Dong Lu, by Lujiazui Lu, Pudong (5888 0000). Metro Lujiazui.* **Open** 9am-5pm Mon-Fri. **Map** p245 O5.
**CitiBank** *20th floor, Marine Tower, 1 Pudong Dadao, by Shiji Dadao, Pudong (5879 1200). Metro Lujiazui.* **Open** 9am-5pm daily. **Map** p245 O5.
**HSBC** *101 Yincheng Dong Lu, by Pudong Dadao, Pudong (6841 1888). Metro Lujiazui.* **Open** 9am-5pm daily. **Map** p245 P5.

## Bureaux de change

If you want to change cash or travellers' cheques, there are two desks just beyond customs at the airports. In the city itself only certain banks, including those above, offer this service. Hotel guests can usually change money their reception desk.

Black-market money changers are often found on the Bund or outside banks. Some established money changers even do business inside bank premises, next to official exchange counters. Black-market traders offer slightly better rates, but there's no receipt and no comeback if you're shortchanged or slipped bogus notes (common in RMB 100 and 50 denominations).

## Credit cards

China has limited infrastructure in place for use of credit cards. They are most commonly accepted at four- and five-star hotels and high-end restaurants. Be warned,

though: an extra four per cent handling fee is usually charged on all credit card transactions. Visa and MasterCard are the most widely accepted; American Express and Diners Club are also recognised, but less commonly so.

### Lost/stolen credit cards
**AmEx** *6279 8082.*
**Mastercard** *10 800 110 7309.*
**Visa** *6323 6656.*

## Tax

A 15 per cent surcharge is added to bills at high-end hotels, but there is no departure tax levied at the airport.

## Natural hazards

There are limited natural hazards in Shanghai. The occasional typhoon has swept through the city causing minor floods and wind damage. Warnings will appear in the Chinese media. At present there is no English-language warning system, but the English-language **weather forecast** hotline is 12121.

Air pollution varies depending on location. For details of **air quality** ring 969221. Mosquitoes are an annoyance during the summer months, but repellent is widely available.

## Opening hours

Opening hours are as in the West; museums are usually open seven days a week.

**Banks** 9am-5pm Mon-Fri. (Some banks open seven days a week.)
**Bars** 11am/noon-2am daily.
**Businesses** 9am-6pm Mon-Fri.
**Municipal offices** 8am-5pm Mon-Fri. (Some offices may close for one hour at lunchtime.)
**Post offices** 9am-6pm daily.

## Police

Police stations can be identified by a red light and a sign that says 'Jingcha'. Police

wear a dark navy uniform. There are numerous private security guards throughout the city who do not enforce the law but wear a similar uniform to local police. Traffic crossing guards armed with shrill whistles are also prominent at every major road junction in Shanghai; disobey them at your peril – jaywalking can be punished with a RMB 50 fine.

## Police stations

**Hangpu Police Sub-bureau** *174 Jinling Dong Lu, by Henan Nan Lu, Old City (5358 0089). Metro Henan Lu.* **Map** p244 L6.
**People's Square Policemen Admin** *499 Nanjing Xi Lu, by Chengdu Lu, People's Square (6386 2999). Metro People's Park or Square.* **Map** p244 H5.

## Postal services

The Chinese mail service is reliable and its staff honest, if slightly surly. International mail is processed promptly, but domestic mail can be slow. Postcards to any destination around the world cost RMB 4.50. Letters under 20 grams to Europe, Australia and North America cost RMB 6. Letters over 20 grams are charged an additional RMB 1.80 per 10 grams. Packages cost RMB 18 for 100 grams, then RMB 15 for every additional 100 grams. It's best to write the address in both English and Chinese.

There is a post office in every district – either call 11185 or 6325 2070, or go to www.chinapost.gov.cn to find local addresses. The main post office (*see p226*) is north of Suzhou Creek and as such is not particularly convenient for most visitors. More useful branch offices include one at the **Shanghai Centre** (1376 Nanjing Xi Lu, by Tongren Lu, Jingan) and one at **Xintiandi** shopping plaza. Both have English-speaking staff. *See also p219* **Couriers.**

**Directory**

### Main post office

*276 Bei Suzhou Lu, by Sichuan Bei Lu, Hongkou (6393 6666). Metro Henan Lu.* **Open** 7am-10pm daily. **Map** p245 M3.

## Property

### Finding a home

The number of agencies targeting foreign clients in Shanghai has ballooned in recent years. Most are legit, but there are lots of unlicensed agencies; exercise caution.

The only legislative requirement of the Shanghai Municipal Government is that foreigners register at the relevant Foreign Affairs Police station (*see below*) within 72 hours of signing a lease on any property.

**Changning** *1171 Yuyuan Lu (6251 1688).*
**Haungpu** *Jinling Lu (6328 0123).*
**Hongkou** *Minhang Lu (6324 2200).*
**Jingan** *Nanjing Xi Lu (6247 1600).*
**Jinshan** *135 Zhujing Lu (5731 7301).*
**Luwan** *Jianguo Zhong Lu (6473 5330).*
**Pudong** *1500 Yangao Lu (5061 4567).*

### Real-estate agents

#### Phoenix Property Agency

*Yujia Building, 1336 Huashan Lu, by Pingwu Lu, French Concession (6240 4052/www. shanghai-realty.net).* **Open** 9am-6pm Mon-Fri. **Map** p246 A8. Established in 1999 and noted for its nose for unique properties. The website has extensive listings.

#### Space

*Suite 204, 30 Donghu Lu, by Xinle Lu, French Concession (5404 2199/www.space.sh.cn). Metro Changshu Lu.* **Open** 9am-5pm Mon-Fri. **Map** p246 D7. Space specialises in high-end residential property. The firm's up-to-date online property search engine is useful for finding properties for a variety of budgets and locations.

### Types of housing

#### Old flats

Generally apartment buildings with individually owned flats (or flats granted to a family by the government). They are largely tenanted by local Chinese families due to convenient central locations and reasonable prices. If you can manage to rent one, expect prices in the order of $500 to $2,000 per month.

#### New flats

High-rise developments with Western standards and amenities. Dependent on layout, size and location, prices range from $500 to $4,500 per month, with the top end running to penthouses, roof gardens, multiple bedrooms and the like.

#### Serviced apartments

These often offer concierge services and/or hotel-quality facilities and are generally the only places available for short-term lease. Apartments range from studios to six-bedroom affairs, with city-centre prices per month ranging from $2,500 to $15,000.

#### Old houses

The city's old (Concession era) terraced and fully detached houses are, of course, over-subscribed. It you can find one, it'll cost $3,000 to $7,000 per month, depending on location, state of renovation and whether it has a garden.

#### Villas

Sterile, gated communities located on the outskirts of town in such districts as Hongqiao, Xuhui and Pudong. Expect gardens, service-oriented management, security and a high standard of facilities – and prices in the order of $7,000 to $20,000 per month.

### Precautions

A few things to be aware of:

● Any property that has a management company will have a monthly management fee. Check with your agent to see if this is a separate payment or whether it is included in the negotiated rent.
● Test to see that you can run your air-conditioners at the same time as the microwave and other appliances. If in doubt, insist on an opt-out clause in your lease.
● Determine which parts of the house being shown to you are for private and which parts are for common use.

## Religion

Religion is still a sensitive topic. While long-established religions such as Christianity, Islam, Buddhism and Taoism are recognised (Judaism seems a border-line case), the primacy of the Communist Party must always be acknowledged. Steer clear of sensitive topics such as Falun Gong or religious freedom in Tibet.

### Buddhist
#### Jingan Temple
*1686 Nanjing Xi Lu, by Wanghangdu Lu, Jingan (6256 6366/www.shjas.com). Metro Jingan Temple.* **Map** p242 C5.
#### Longhua Temple
*Lane 2853, Longhua Lu, Longhua (6457 6327). Metro Longcao Lu.* **Map** p240 C5.
#### Temple of the City God
*249 Fangbang Zhong Lu, by Anren Jie, Old City.* **Map** p249 M7.

### Catholic
#### All Saints' Church
*425 Fuxing Zhong Lu, by Danshui Lu (6385 0906). Metro Huangpi Lu.* **Services** 7.30am, 9.30am, 7pm Sun. **Map** p247 H8.
#### Dongjiadu Lu Catholic Church
*185 Dongjiadu Lu, by Wanyu Jie, Old City (6378 7214).* **Services** 7am Mon-Sat; 6.30am, 8.30am Sun. **Map** p249 O9.
#### Moore Memorial Church
*316 Xizang Zhong Lu, Jiujiang Lu, People's Square (6322 5029). Metro People's Park or Square.* **Services** 7am, 9am, 2pm, 7pm daily. **Map** p244 J5.

**Shanghai Grace Church**
*375 Shanxi Bei Lu, by Weihai Lu, Jingan (6253 9394). Metro Shimen Yi Lu.* **Services** 7.30pm Mon-Fri; 9am Sat; 9am, 7pm Sun. **Map** p243 F6.

**St Joseph's Church**
*36 Sichuan Nan Lu, by Jinling Dong Lu, Old City (6336 5537).* **Services** 7am Mon-Sat; 6am, 7.30am Sun. **Map** p245 M6.

**St Ignatius Cathedral**
*158 Puxi Lu, by Caoxi Bei Lu, Xujiahui (6438 2595). Metro Xujiahui.* **Services** 6.15am Mon-Fri; 6.15am, 6pm Sat; 6.15am, 10am, 6pm Sun. **Map** p246 A11.

**St Peter's Church**
*270 Chongqing Nan Lu, by Fuxing Zhong Lu, Xintiandi (6467 8080). Metro Huangpi Nan Lu.* **Services** 5pm Sat; 10.30am Sun. **Map** p247 H8.

## Jewish
**Jewish Community of Shanghai** *62 Changyang Lu, by Zhoushan Lu, Hongkou (6512 0229). Bus 22, 37.*

## Muslim
**Jinxing Mosque**
*No.117, Lane 77, Fulu Lu, Pinliang, Yangpu (6541 3199).*

## Protestant
**Hengshan Community Church**
*53 Hengshan Lu, by Wulumuqi Lu, French Concession (6437 6576). Metro Hengshan Lu.* **Services** 4pm Sun. **Map** p246 C9.

## Safety

Shanghai is remarkably safe. Crime against foreigners is negligible and what little occurs tends to be limited to pickpocketing. Women usually get about independently without harassment.

## Smoking & spitting

Shanghai is a smoker's paradise. Cigarettes are inexpensive and smoked by all. Feel free to light up anytime, anywhere: enquiries after non-smoking areas in a bar or restaurant will be met with much amusement.

Spitting is the most beloved non-spectator sport in town. From a mild spittle to a full-on, lung-rattling, expectorant cough, it is a prevalent and revolting habit. The belief that it is healthy to expel noxious fluids from the body may have something to do with spitting's popularity. The habit was actively discouraged during the SARS outbreak of 2003 and gobbing was on the wane for a time, but it since seems to have made a tremendous comeback.

## Study

### Chinese-language schools

#### Creative Methodology
*8C Xinan Building, 200 Zhenning Lu, by Yuyuan Lu, Jingan (6289 4299/www.talkingchina.com). Metro Jinagsu Lu.* **Rates** RMB 50-70/hr for small classes (up to 10 students); RMB 135/hr for individual classes. **No credit cards. Map** p242 B6.
The centre offers eight different levels of classes in addition to business Chinese, Shanghai dialect and Mandarin for Cantonese speakers. Tutoring is by bilingual teachers from a variety of respected Shanghai universities.

#### Ease Mandarin
*Room 101, No.2, Lane 25, Wuxing Lu, by Kangping Lu, French Concession (5465 6999/ www.easemandarin.com). Metro Hengshan Lu.* **Rates** RMB 2,900/3 months of twice weekly classes. **No credit cards. Map** p246 B9.
One of the most popular schools for expats wanting to study Mandarin. Friendly, helpful and dedicated teachers make the programme effective and engaging. Classes incorporate work on speaking, writing and reading.

#### Learning Mandarin Centre
*Room 6012, 887 Huaihai Zhong Lu, by Ruijin Er Lu, French Concession (6431 6104/www. l-e-c.net). Metro Shanxi Nan Lu.* **Rates** RMB 110/hr. **Credit** MC, V. **Map** p247 F7.

In a convenient central downtown location, this school focuses on teaching English to Mandarin speakers but also offers classes for students of Mandarin.

#### Mandarin Center
*16 Songyuan Lu, by Hongqiao Lu, Hongqiao (6270 7668/www. mandarin-center.com). Metro Hongqiao.* **Rates** 50/hr for small classes (up to 10 students); 125/hr for individual lessons; RMB 2,500-11,000/2- to 5-month term. **Credit** AmEx, MC, V. **Map** p240 B4.
Offers morning, afternoon and evening classes in a popular location for expats. Classes range from two- and five-month programmes. Instructors follow a traditional approach to teaching Chinese, as the centre is affiliated with Fudan University.

## Telephones

### Dialling & codes
The country code for China is 86 and the city code for Shanghai is 021. Drop the prefix zero when dialling from overseas. Domestic calls require the city code but they are not necessary within Shanghai.

For outgoing international calls, dial the international access code, 00, followed by the country code, the area code and the local telephone number. The US and Canada country code is 1; the UK 44; Australia 61; and for New Zealand 64.

**USEFUL CITY CODES**
**Hangzhou** *0571.*
**Moganshan** *0572.*
**Nanjing** *025.*
**Putuoshan** *0580.*
**Suzhou** *0512.*

### Public phones
Chinese public phones take prepaid phone cards (IC Cards), available for RMB 20, RMB 30, RMB 50 and RMB 100. Users of public phones can make domestic and international calls. The latter can be pricey – over RMB 10 a minute. Rates for domestic

**Directory**

long-distance calls are RMB 0.20 for three minutes, with calls longer than three minutes charged at RMB 0.10 for every further six seconds.

## Operator services

**Local directory assistance** *114*.

For international enquiries and reverse-charge/collect calls, try phoning one of these numbers:

**AT&T** *6391 0391*.
**Global One** *10817/6279 8538*.
**MCI** *10817*.
**Sprint** *2890 9887*.

## Telephone directories

To order a copy of the *Yellow Pages*, call 5385 4017.

**Operator Assisted Yellow Pages** *96886*.

## Phonecards

Internet calling cards (or 'IP' cards), widely available in Shanghai, are an economical option for overseas calls. The access codes for US phone card users are: Sprint (10813); MCI (10812); and AT&T (10811).

## Mobile phones

The two mobile phone providers in Shanghai are China Mobile and China Unicom. Both use the GSM system. China Mobile uses GPRS phones and China Unicom uses CDMA phones. China Mobile is the larger of the two, but Unicom has lower rates. Mobile-users from Japan and North America should check that their roaming service will operate in China.

Both providers offer pre-pay and billed services. With the pre-pay system users can purchase a SIM card, put it into any GSM phone and add value to the account with a prepaid card. The billed system requires Chinese ID or a Chinese guarantor.

Local prepaid phone cards and SIM cards can cut the cost of mobile use in Shanghai. They are priced at RMB 100 and are sold at newsstands and convenience stores (try Parkson Department Store, 918 Hauihai Zhong Lu, by Ruijin Er Lu, French Concession). Incoming and outgoing calls are charged by the minute.

## Faxes

Most hotels are willing to accept incoming faxes for guests. Faxes can be sent from hotel business centres or the front desk and are charged at around RMB 10 per page.

## Time

China is eight hours ahead of GMT. The country does not operate daylight-saving time.

## Tipping

Hotel restaurants and other high-end, foreigner-aimed places usually add a 15 per cent surcharge to the bill. Everything else is at your discretion. Tour guides usually expect to be tipped.

## Toilets

Public toilets are available throughout the city but standards vary tremendously. They charge a marginal fee and also sell tissues, feminine hygiene products and cosmetic items. The squat toilet is most common, but some facilities have Western-style commodes. Hotels, bars and restaurants have Western-style toilets.

## Tourist information

The **main tourist office** is Shanghai Tourist Information Service Centre (303 Moling Lu, south exit of Shanghai Railway Station, 6353 9920, http://lyw.

sh.gov.cn/en/). A **tourist helpline** (6252 0000, open 10am-9pm daily) has some English-speaking operators. The tourist offices themselves offer a limited selection of free information in English – the services tend to be geared toward local Chinese rather than international travellers. Concierges at top hotels offer a much higher standard of customer service.

There is a tourist bureau in every district. These are the best (which isn't saying much):

**Jingan District Tourist Information & Service Centre** *1699 Nanjing Xi Lu, by Wulumuqi Bei Lu, Jingan (3214 0042). Metro Jingan Temple.* **Open** 9am-5.30pm daily. **Map** p242 C6.
**Luwan District Tourist Information & Service Centre** *127 Chengdu Nan Lu, by Huaihai Zhong Lu, French Concession (5382 7330). Metro Huangpi Nan Lu.* **Open** 9am-9pm daily. **Map** p247 G7.
**Pudong New Area Tourist Information & Service Centre** *168 Lujiazui Lu, by Yincheng Lu, Pudong (6875 0593). Metro Lujiazui.* **Open** 9am-6pm daily. **Map** p245 O5.
**Yuyuan Tourist Information & Service Centre** *Yu Bazaar, 159 Jiujiaochang Lu (6355 5032).* **Open** 9am-8pm daily. **Map** p249 M7.

## Visas & immigration

All visitors to China require a visa. These are obtained through a Chinese embassy or consulate. Most tourists are issued with a single-entry visa, valid for entry within three months of issue and good for a 30-day stay. Processing times and fees vary. In the UK the cost is £30 and you need to allow three working days for processing. Two passport photos are required for the application. A next-day express service is available for twice the standard fee.

Business visas are usually multiple entry and valid for three to six months from the date of issue. They allow the visitor to stay for the full specified period. These require a letter of invitation from the host business or corporation and in some cases a copy of the business licence.

For more information on current visa regulations and application procedures check the following websites:

**UK citizens**
*www.chinese-embassy.org.uk.*
**US citizens**
*www.china-embassy.org.*
**Canadian citizens**
*www.chinaembassycanada.org.*

Visa extensions of 30 days are easy to get. They take three days to process and cost RMB 160 for Britons and RMB 125 for Americans. Extensions are available from the Public Security Bureau (PSB) just north of the Bund:

**PSB** *1500 Minsheng Lu, near Yinchun Lu, Pudong (2895 1900). Metro Science & Technology Museum.* **Open** 9am-5pm Mon-Sat. **Map** p241 G4.

## Long-term residence

Long-term residency requires a 'green card' or residence permit. The paperwork for a green card requires at least ten passport photos – one to go with each of the ten completed forms necessary for the application. It's a five-step process beginning with the acquisition of your initial **tourist visa** (*see p228*). Beyond this you need a certificate of health, an employment visa, your company's business licence and a work permit: only then can you apply for the green card. Employers will need to help you with the process.

For the **health certificate**, the required examinations and tests can be done in your home country, but it's much easier to do it in Shanghai. There is a

new, efficient and clean testing facility (1701 Hami Lu, Hongqiao, 6268 6171, open 8.30am-11am, 1.30-3pm Mon-Sat). Get there early (by 8am) and you should be out within the hour. To take a 'health exam' you'll need a copy of your passport plus a copy of the photo and China visa pages; two passport photos; and RMB 700. The exam includes tests for STDs, chest X-rays, a sonogram, a vision test and general health queries.

For the **employment visa** you need an invitation letter from your company, your company employment licence and your newly obtained health certificate.

For the **work permit** (or 'red book') you'll need your employment application letter and CV, the contract you've signed with your company, your health certificate, your passport (plus photocopies of the photo page) and three passport photos.

Finally, for the **residence permit** ('green card') you will need the completed application form, the original and a photocopy of your entire (!) passport, two passport photos, your health certificate, your work permit (the original and a photocopy) and a copy of your company's business licence. The green card is valid for 12 months.

## Water

Don't drink tap water – bottled water is widely available.

## Weights & measures

China uses the metric system for measurements.

1 kilometre = 0.62 miles
1 metre = 1.09 yards
1 centimetre = 0.39 inches
1 kilogram = 2.20 pounds
1 gram = 0.035 ounces
1 litre = 1.76 pints
0° Celsius = 32° Fahrenheit

## What to take

Everything you are likely to need can be found in Shanghai, although it may take some finding. Prices may be slightly more expensive for foreign or imported goods. Although most medications, from aspirin to Zoloft, are available in China, it's wise to bring all essentials with you – important medication may not be available here, and foreign prescriptions will not be accepted at pharmacies unless endorsed by a certified local practitioner.

## When to go

### Climate

The weather is a major factor in planning a visit to Shanghai. There are times of the year when the city's high humidity can be seriously debilitating, making a visit to the city distinctly uncomfortable. A summary of what to expect during the year follows, but bear in mind that Shanghai's weather can be very unpredictable.

**Spring** (March to mid May) is often pleasant and is one of the best times to visit weather-wise, although some of the heaviest rainfall is recorded during this time. Bring a medium-weight jacket or sweaters for the evenings, which can be cool. Spring is also the time of fresh blooms, so it's great for visits to the Yu Gardens (*see p70*) and the gardens of Suzhou (*see p210*).

**Summer** (late May to mid September) is hot, hot, hot and stiflingly humid. Ironically, you'll probably still need to bring an extra layer for when you're indoors, as shops, restaurants, bars and hotels tend to crank up the air-conditioning to icy levels. Also be aware that in the month from mid June –

**Directory**

Mei-Yu Season – the city receives perhaps a quarter of its annual rainfall. Summer is also prime festival time.

**Autumn** (late September to early December), along with spring, is generally the best time to visit Shanghai; temperatures are comfortably warm, and humidity drops to a bearable level. Sunny days and clear skies are quite common.

**Winter** (mid December to February) gets chilly, windy and cloudy, so you need to bring extra layers of clothing. Although the temperature rarely drops below zero, it seems much colder due to the humidity – this is really not a good time to be around Shanghai, although the New Year festivities bring a little colour and warmth.

### Public holidays

Many Shanghai public holidays are festival days dependent on the lunar calendar, so each year the dates change.

**New Year's Day** *1 January*
**Chinese Lunar New Year** *3-7 days in January/February*
**Labour Week May Holiday** *1-5 May*
**Mid Autumn Festival** *August or September – no bank holiday*
**National Week** *1-5 October*

## Women

Shanghai is a very safe city for women. There is minimal harassment and crime rates are low. Women can travel independently at night, but it's still sensible to be cautious.

Some useful women's groups in Shanghai include:

**American Women's Club** *6415 9801*.
**Australian Women's Social Group** *6415 9475*.
**Brits Abroad** *6466 1948*.
**Expatriates Professional Women's Society** *epws2001@yahoo.com*.

## Working in Shanghai

Expect to spend about two months searching for a job; www.chinahr.com and www.competencechina.com are good starting points.

Many temporary jobs in China for English-speakers pay quite well. Typically, these jobs include voice recording, writing, teaching English or even modelling. Wages generally start at RMB 100/hr and are paid in cash. Contracts for this type of work are uncommon. Although it is illegal, some foreigners work on this basis until getting a full-time job. The police rarely monitor this type of activity but significant fines can be levied on anyone who is caught out.

Internships are a good way into the system if you have limited China-based work experience. Many consulates, US or European companies offer internships. These positions can and do often turn into paid employment on completion.

### Work visas

For a work visa you need:

● A passport with at least six months' validity and at least one blank page.
● One completed visa application form with one additional passport photo.
● A visa notification issued by the authorised Chinese unit.
● Your company's business licence.
● Either a work permit issued by the Chinese Labour Ministry or a Foreign Expert's Licence issued by the Chinese Foreign Expert Bureau.
● A visa notification issued by the authorised Chinese unit or proof of kinship is required for spouse or accompanying family members.

Allow three to four days for processing the documents.

For more information, go to www.molss.gov.cn.

# Average climate

| | Temp (°C) | Temp (°F) | Humidity (%) | Rainfall (mm) | Sunshine (hrs) |
|---|---|---|---|---|---|
| **January** | 7-9 | 45-48 | 18 | 45-50 | 131 |
| **February** | 8-10 | 46-50 | 22 | 60-65 | 158 |
| **March** | 12-14 | 54-58 | 27 | 80-85 | 58 |
| **April** | 18-20 | 65-68 | 48 | 90-95 | 159 |
| **May** | 23-25 | 74-78 | 54 | 110-115 | 180 |
| **June** | 27-29 | 80-84 | 73 | 160-165 | 103 |
| **July** | 31-33 | 88-92 | 76 | 140-145 | 96 |
| **August** | 31-33 | 88-92 | 75.5 | 140-145 | 99 |
| **September** | 27-29 | 81-84 | 73 | 136-141 | 145 |
| **October** | 22-24 | 72-76 | 52 | 55-60 | 104 |
| **November** | 16-18 | 61-65 | 45 | 50-55 | 112 |
| **December** | 10-12 | 50-54 | 25.5 | 40-45 | 186 |

# Vocabulary

In Shanghai people speak Shanghainese (*see p222* **Language**). It's substantially different in pronunciation from Mandarin and Cantonese, with several sounds that are not found in any other Chinese dialect. The bulk of the vocabulary is the same, but there are lots of variations and unique words and phrases. It's considered a coarse and uncultured dialect, unsuited to formal occasions. In such cases, people typically switch to Mandarin, which is the city's second language.

Grammatically, Chinese is easier than many languages. There are no tenses – Chinese words have only one form. Suffixes are used instead to denote tenses. There are no comparative adjectives. The most challenging part of learning Chinese is often the tones, as each sound has four different inflections, each of which can change the meaning of a word. Even for the Chinese, the various tones only avoid confusion up to a certain point: complete understanding is gained from the context.

In the written language, characters take the place of an alphabet. A character can be a word or part of a word, but normally a word consists of two or more characters. There are about 20,000 characters in a normal Chinese word processor. For those who do not read characters there is a romanised alphabet called Pinyin. However Chinese rarely understand it when spoken by non natives. Note that not all consonants in Pinyin are pronounced as in English:

| | |
|---|---|
| c | like the 'ts' in 'hits' |
| q | like the 'ch' in 'chase' |
| r | like the 's' in 'measure' |
| x | like the 'sh' in 'shop' |
| z | like the 'dz' in 'duds' |

## Phrases

| | |
|---|---|
| my name is... | *wo jiao...* |
| my last name is... | *wo xing...* |
| I am | *wo shi* |
| American | *meiguo ren* |
| British | *yingguo ren* |
| Australian | *aodaliya ren* |
| European | *ouzhou ren* |
| hello | *nihao* |
| goodbye | *zaijian* |
| thanks | *xiexie* |
| how are you? | *ni zenmeyang* |
| you're welcome | *bu keqi* |
| sorry | *duibuqi* |
| correct/right | *dui* |
| incorrect/wrong | *bu dui* |
| don't want | *bu yao* |
| don't have | *meiyou* |
| I don't know | *wo bu zhi dao* |
| I don't understand | *wo bu mingbai* |
| please speak more slowly | *qing shuo de man yidian* |

## Getting around

| | |
|---|---|
| Is this taxi free? | *zhei che you ren ma?* |
| turn left | *zuo guai* |
| turn right | *you guai* |
| go straight | *yizhi zou* |
| stop the vehicle | *ting che* |
| I want to go to | *wo yao qu* |
| hotel | *da jiu dian* |
| airport | *feijichang* |
| train station | *huochezhan* |
| metro | *ditiezhan* |
| this place (point) | *zhe ge difang* |
| I want to return home | *wo yao hui jia* |

## Shopping

| | |
|---|---|
| how much is it? | *duoshao qian?* |
| too expensive | *tai gui le* |
| cheaper? | *pianyi dian?* |
| too big | *tai da* |
| too small | *tai xiao* |
| please give me a receipt | *qing gei wo fapiao* |

## Eating & drinking

| | |
|---|---|
| beer | *pijiu* |
| water | *shui* |
| English tea | *yinguo cha* |
| the bill please | *mai dan* |
| telephone | *dianhua* |
| bar | *jiuba* |
| pub | *jiuguan* |
| café | *kafeiguan* |
| restaurant | *fandian/canguan* |

## Dates & times

| | |
|---|---|
| Monday | *xingqiyi* |
| Tuesday | *xingqier* |
| Wednesday | *xingqisan* |
| Thursday | *xingqisi* |
| Friday | *xingqiwu* |
| Saturday | *xingqiliu* |
| Sunday | *xingqitian* |
| morning | *zaoshang/shangwu* |
| afternoon | *xiawu* |
| evening | *wanshang* |
| today | *jintian* |
| tomorrow | *mingtian* |
| yesterday | *zuotian* |
| day after tomorrow | *houtian* |
| day before yesterday | *qiantian* |

## Numbers

| | |
|---|---|
| zero | *ling* |
| one | *yi* |
| two | *er* |
| three | *san* |
| four | *si* |
| five | *wu* |
| six | *liu* |
| seven | *qi* |
| eight | *ba* |
| nine | *jiu* |
| ten | *shi* |

## Emergency phrases

| | |
|---|---|
| There's an emergency! | *zheshi jinji qingkuang* |
| Please can you help me? | *ni neng bu neng bang wo ge mang* |
| I lost my passport | *wo de huzhao diu le* |
| I need to see a doctor | *wo yao kan bing* |
| Call an ambulance! | *qing jiao jingcha jiuhuche* |
| Fire! | *zhao huo le!* |
| Police! | *jingcha!* |

## Mobile phones

| | |
|---|---|
| I'd like to buy a mobile charge card | *wo xiang mai chongzhe ka* |
| I'd like to buy a SIM card | |
| phone charger | *dianhua chongdianqi* |
| mobile phone for hire | *zuyong yidong dianhua* |
| prepaid mobile | *yufu yidong dianhua* |

# Further Reference

## Books

### Memoirs

**Jung Chang** *Wild Swans* (1992) A moving memoir that spans three turbulent generations of women in China, from the death throes of Imperial China to Tiananmen Square.
**Nien Cheng** *Life and Death in Shanghai* (1987) Cheng, accused of being a British spy, was put under house arrest in 1966 and jailed. On release she was told her daughter had committed suicide; in reality she was beaten to death by Red Guards.

### Non-fiction

**Jung Chang & Jon Halliday** *Mao: The Unknown Story* (2005). New biography of Mao Zedong, controversial enough to have been banned in China.
**Christian Datz & Christof Kullmann** *Shanghai: Architecture & Design* (2005) A CD-sized primer to Shanghai's fabulous modern buildings, lavishly illustrated.
**Edward Denison & Guang Yu Ren** *Building Shanghai: The Story of China's Gateway* (2006) Terrific book about Shanghai's rapid growth and troubling lack of coherent planning.
**Stella Dong** *Shanghai: The Rise and Fall of a Decadent City* (2000) The tabloid version of high-jinks and low life as played out in the Shanghai of the 1920s and '30s.
**Lynn Pan** *In Search of Old Shanghai* (1982) Waxes historical on Shanghai's glory days. The text is by area, not chronological, but is undermined by the lack of an index.
**Harriet Sergeant** *Shanghai* (1991) Vivid portrait of life with the 'whore of the orient' in the 1920s and '30s, compiled from first-hand interviews.

### Fiction

**JG Ballard** *Empire of the Sun* (1984) Part fiction, part autobiography, the story of a young boy separated from his parents in wartime Shanghai and interned by the Japanese. A chilling meditation on mind, body and the things people do to survive.
**Tom Bradby** *The Master of Rain* (2002) A young Englishman battles Chinese gangsters, distracted by a Russian whore, in this 1920s thriller.
**Bo Caldwell** *The Distant Land of My Father* (2001) Young girl leaves millionaire dad behind in Shanghai. Dad interned by Japanese, loses all, travels to America, reunion. Aww.

**Kazuo Ishiguro** *When We Were Orphans* (2000) An Englishman raised in Shanghai returns to find the dark truth about the deaths of his parents. No happy endings.
**André Malraux** *Man's Fate* (1933) Malraux's characters pierce the quandaries of ideology and loyalty posed by the early days of the Cultural Revolution.
**Mian Mian** *Candy* (2003) Semi-autobiographical tale of a Shanghai 'bad' girl. Sex, drugs and brand names are mixed with unconvincing literary references.
**Anchee Min** *Becoming Madame Mao* (2000) Patchy but brave attempt to get inside the mind of China's very own Lady Macbeth.
**Wei Hui** *Shanghai Baby* (2002) Semi-autobiographical tale of the other Shanghai 'bad' girl. More sex, drugs and brand names, mixed with more unconvincing literary references.

## Film

**Code 46** (Michael Winterbottom, 2003) Moody sci-fi thriller in which Shanghai stars as a Brave New World, a job it performs matchlessly without recourse to any CGI trickery.
**The Empire of the Sun** (Steven Spielberg, 1987) Terrific adaptation of JG Ballard's extraordinary story, demonstrating that old Shanghai wasn't all glamour.
**The Goddess** (Wu Yonggang, 1934) Ruan Lingyu ('the Greta Garbo of China') as a single mother trying to pay for her son's education – but there's only way to earn the money.
**Jasmine Women** (Hou Yong, 2004) Visually stunning tale about three generations of Shanghai women, superbly acted by Zhang Ziyi and Joan Chen.
**The Lady from Shanghai** (Orson Welles, 1947) Nothing to do with Shanghai at all; the closest it gets is Rita Hayworth talking Mandarin in San Francisco's Chinatown. A wonderful film all the same.
**Mission: Impossible III** (JJ Abrams, 2006) Tom Cruise swings from the city's skyscrapers and drops in on canal town Xitang in the franchise's palatable third portion.
**Pavilion of Women** (Ho Yim, 2001) Melodramatic US-Chinese co-production concerning interracial love during wartime. It stars Willem Dafoe but still plays like a bad soap.
**Shanghai Express** (Josef von Sternberg, 1932) Kidnapped foreigners on the Beijing-Shanghai line. None of it was shot in China but it's Dietrich at her best and still outshone by Anna May Wong.

**Suzhou River** (Lou Ye, 2000) Surreal tale of lost love and betrayal set on the industrial banks of Shanghai's murky creek. Modern film noir, Chinese style.
**Shanghai Story** (Peng Xiaolian, 2004) Wonderfully subtle film about a group of feuding siblings brought back together around their ailing grandmother. Won China's equivalent of the Oscar.
**Shanghai Triad** (Zhang Yimou, 1995) Classic gangster pic set in 1930s Shanghai, considered China's answer to *The Godfather*.
**The White Countess** (James Ivory, 2005) A leaden script and performances from the leads that would shame a plank are almost redeemed by Chris Doyle's cinematography. But not really.

## Music

**Assorted artists** *Fanyin Music Box* (2003) Twelve tracks by nine Shanghai bands showcase everything from pop to rock to metal to grunge.
**Crystal Butterfly** *Mystical Journey* (2005) Debut by one of Shanghai's oldest and most famous bands. Filed somewhere between U2 and the Cure, with a Shanghainese twist.
**The Honeys** *On the Street* (2002) Debut album of long-time local pop-rock favourites runs the gamut from fast, catchy tunes to soaring ballads.
**Night Bus** *Night Bus* (2004) Perky pop-rock with jazzy influences.
**Chen Lirong** *Old Shanghai Gramophone* There are loads of remakes of Old Shanghai classics, mostly with bombastic martial music and Cultural Revolutionary Opera vocal trills. This one takes a more '80s/'90s tack, reimagining the old jazz favourites with heavily synthesised oompah beats.
**Li Xianglan** *Fragrance of Night* (2003) One of Shanghai's most enduring anthems from its 1930s heyday. Combines the original version with 16 other tracks.
**Ian Widgery** *The Original Shanghai Divas Collection* (2003) The top Chinese pop stars from the '20s and '30s, remixed with uptempo grooves and laid-back break beats for one of the hippest CDs in town.
**Various** *Shanghai Jazz: Musical Seductions from China's Age of Decadence* (2004) Jazz musos currently working in Shanghai contribute to a lively collection of jazz faves from Old Shanghai.
**Xiao Yao** *Lost Topic* (2004) Singer-songwriter Xiao mixes hard beats and electronica into surprisingly pleasant melodies.

# Index

Note: page numbers in **bold** indicate section(s) giving key information on topic; *italics* indicate photos.

**Index**

# Advertisers' Index

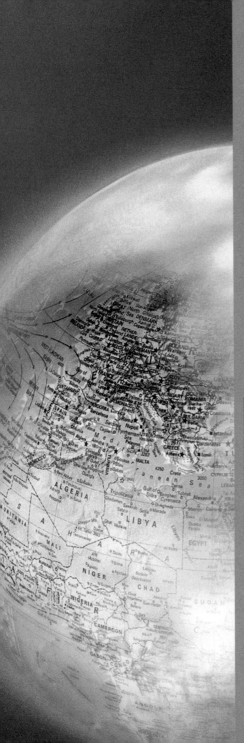

| | |
|---|---|
| Place of interest and/or entertainment . . . . . . . . . . | |
| Railway station . . . . . . . . . . . . . . . . . . . . . . . . . . . . . | |
| Park . . . . . . . . . . . . . . . . . . . . . . . . . . . . . . . . . . . . . . | |
| Hospitals/universities . . . . . . . . . . . . . . . . . . . . . . | |
| Hotels . . . . . . . . . . . . . . . . . . . . . . . . . . . . . . . . . . . . | |
| Area name . . . . . . . . . . . . . . . . . . . . . . . . . . . JINGAN | |
| Metro station . . . . . . . . . . . . . . . . . . . . . . . . . . . . . . | Ⓢ |
| Motorway . . . . . . . . . . . . . . . . . . . . . . . . . . . . . . . . . | |
| Raised highway . . . . . . . . . . . . . . . . . . . . . . . . . . . . | |

# Maps

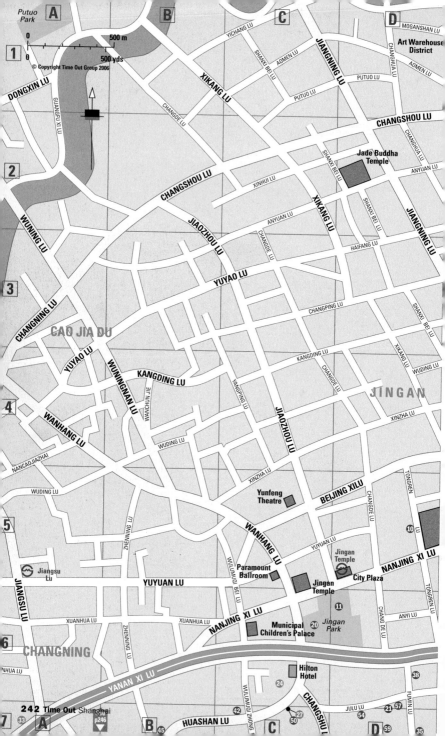

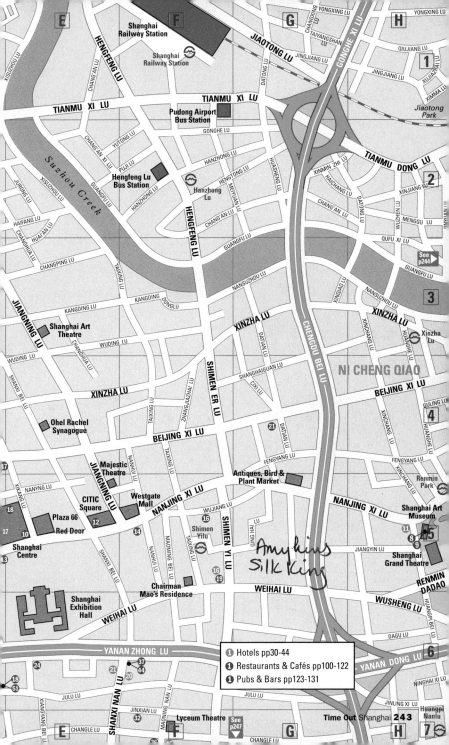

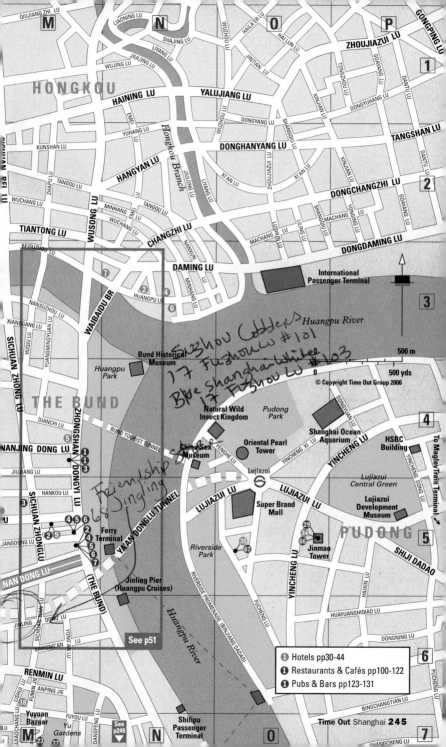

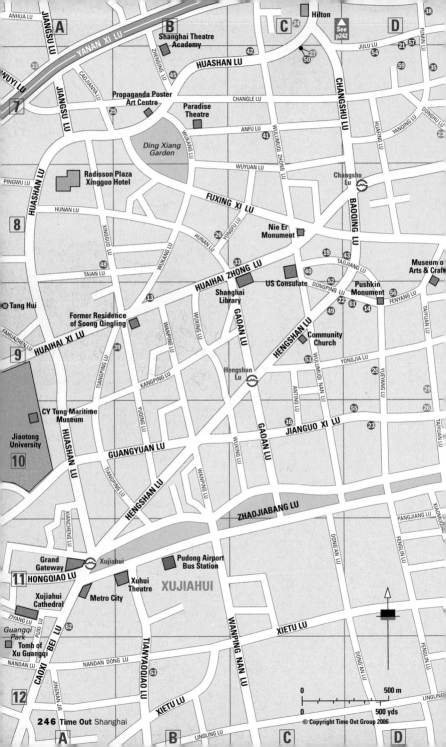

© Copyright Time Out Group 2006

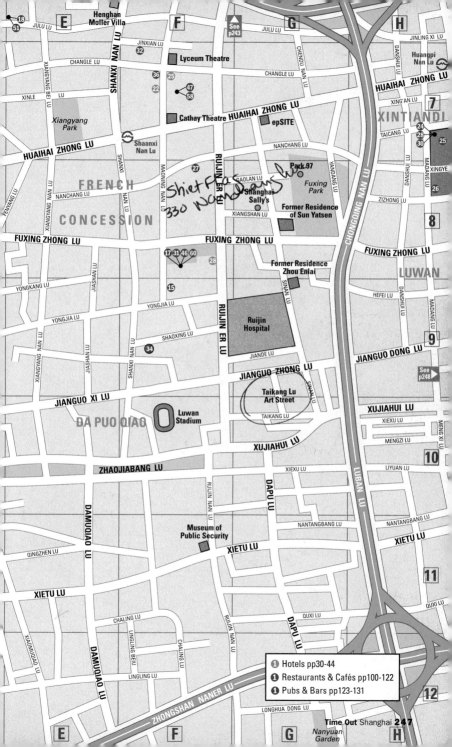

JINLING XI LU
DANSHUI LU
Huangpi Nanlu
XING'AN LU
HUAIHAI ZHONG LU
JINLING ZHONG LU
SONGSHAN LU
LONGMEN LU
See p244
XIZANG NAN LU
YUNNAN NAN LU
RENMIN LU
FUYOU LU
L
Fuyou Lu Mosque
HENAN NAN LU
CHENXIANGGE
ZIHUA LU
JIUCANG JIE
CHANGSHENG

Dajing Lu Market

OLD
SHANGHAI
XUELONGDI JIE

XINTIANDI

Huaihai Park

TAICANG LU
24
28
30
25  19
11  12
Xintiandi
29
XINGYE LU
27
26
UME Cineplex

ZIZHONG LU

8

FUXING ZHONG LU

LUWAN

HEFEI LU

9

JIANGUO DONG LU

See p247

XUJIAHUI LU

XIEXU LU
MENGZI LU

10

LIYUAN LU

NANTANGBANG LU

XIETU LU

11

12

248 Time Out Shanghai

Dongtai Lu Antiques Market

Flower & Bird Market

FUXING ZHONG LU

FUXING DONG LU

Confucius Temple

LAO XI MEN

Hunan Stadium

LUJIABANG LU

Peach Garden Mosque

Penglai Park

Shanghai Museum of Folk Collectibles

People's Hospital Shanghai No.9

ZHONGSHAN NAN LU

ZHONGSHAN NANYI LU

GAOXIONG LU

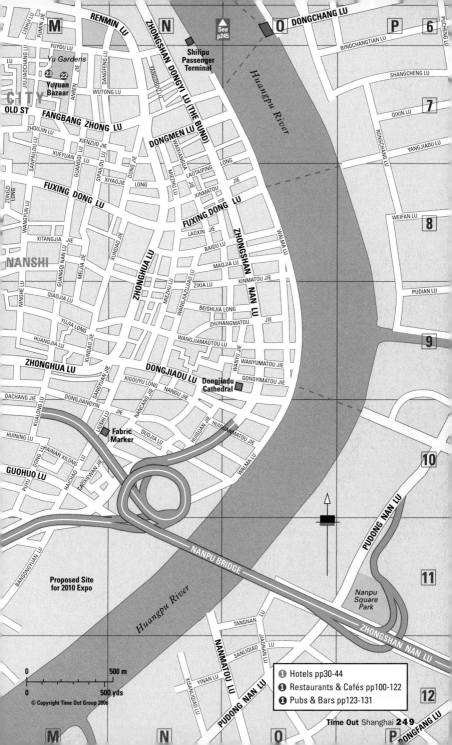

# Street Index

# Chinese Translations

**THE BUND** ........................................ **外滩**
Bund Centre ...................................... 外滩商贸
Bund Historical Museum ................... 外滩历史博物馆
Bund Museum ................................... 外滩博物馆
Bund Tourist Tunnel ........................ 外滩人行观光隧道
Chinese Post Office ......................... 邮政局大楼
Garden Bridge (Waibaidu Qiao) ........ 公园桥(外白渡)
Huangpu Park ................................... 黄浦公园
M on the Bund ................................. 米氏餐厅
Metropole Hotel ............................... 新城饭店
Natural History Museum ................... 自然博物馆
Shanghai Friendship Store ............... 上海友谊商店
Shanghai Mansions .......................... 上海大厦
Suzhou Creek ................................... 苏州河
Three on the Bund ........................... 外滩三号
**Streets** ........................................ **街道**
Beijing Dong Lu ............................... 北京东路
Jiulong Lu ........................................ 九龙路
Nanjing Dong Lu .............................. 南京东路
Yanan Dong Lu ................................ 延安东路
Zhapu Lu ......................................... 乍浦路

**PEOPLE'S SQUARE &**
**NANJING DONG LU** ....................... **人民广场和南京东路**
City Hall .......................................... 大会堂
Great World ..................................... 大世界
Hong Kong Shopping Centre (D Mall) ... 香港购物中心
Moore Memorial Church ................... 沐恩堂
Shanghai Art Museum ...................... 上海美术馆
Shanghai Concert Hall ..................... 上海音乐院
Shanghai Grand Theatre ................... 上海大舞台
Shanghai Museum ............................ 上海博物馆
Shanghai No.1 Department Store ...... 上海第一百货公司
Tomorrow Square ............................. 明天广场
Urban Planning Centre ..................... 城市规划中心
Yi Fu Theatre ................................... 逸夫舞台
**Streets** ........................................ **街道**
Huanghe Lu ..................................... 黄河路
Fuzhou Lu ........................................ 福州路
Guangdong Lu .................................. 广东路
Renmin Dadao .................................. 人民大道
Xizang Zhong Lu .............................. 西藏中路

| | |
|---|---|
| Yanan Dong Lu | 延安东路 |
| Yunnan Nan Lu | 云南南路 |

**JINGAN** 静安
| | |
|---|---|
| Antiques, Bird and Plant Market | 古玩、花鸟市场 |
| Chairman Mao's Residence | 毛泽东故居 |
| Children's Palace | 上海市少年宫 |
| CITIC Square | 中伥泰富广场 |
| Jade Buddha Temple | 玉佛寺 |
| Jingan Park | 静安公园 |
| Jingan Temple | 静安寺 |
| Ohel Rachel Synagogue | 摩西会堂 |
| Plaza 66 | 恒隆广场 |
| Shanghai Centre | 上海商城 |
| Shanghai Centre Theatre | 上海商城剧院 |
| Shanghai Exhibition Centre | 上海展览中心 |
| Westgate Mall | 梅龙镇广场 |
| **Streets** | 街道 |
| Maoming Bei Lu | 茂名北路 |
| Moganshan Lu | 莫干山路 |
| Nanjing Xi Lu | 南京西路 |
| Weihai Lu | 威海路 |
| Wujiang Lu | 吴江路 |

**OLD CITY** 老城
| | |
|---|---|
| Chenxiangge Nunnery | 沉香阁 |
| Cixiu Nunnery | 慈修庵 |
| Confucius Temple | 孔庙 |
| Dajing Pavilion | 大镜亭 |
| Dongjiadu Cathedral | 董家渡天主堂 |
| Fabric Market | 布料批发市场 |
| Fuyou Lu Market | 福佑路市场 |
| Fuyou Lu Mosque | 福佑路清真寺 |
| Hua Bao Building | 华宝楼 |
| Kuixing Pavilion | 魁星楼 |
| Nanpu Bridge | 南浦桥 |
| Peach Garden Mosque | 小桃园清真寺 |
| Shanghai Museum of Folk Collectibles | 上海民间收藏陈列馆 |
| Temple of the City God | 城皇庙 |
| White Cloud Taoist Temple | 白云寺 |
| Yu Gardens | 豫园 |
| Yuyuan Bazaar | 豫园小商品市场 |
| **Streets** | 街道 |
| Anren Lu | 安仁路 |
| Dongjiadu Lu | 董家渡路 |
| Fangbang Zhong Lu | 方浜中路 |
| Fuyou Lu | 福佑路 |
| Henan Nan Lu | 河南南路 |
| Jiujiaochang Lu | 旧校场路 |

| | |
|---|---|
| Longhua Martyrs Cemetery | 龙华烈士陵园 |
| Longhua Temple | 龙华寺 |
| Shanghai Botanical Garden | 上海植物园 |
| Shanghai Zoo | 上海动物园 |
| Soong Qingling Mausoleum | 宋庆龄陵墓 |
| St Ignatius cathedral | 圣依纳爵主教座堂 |
| **Streets** | **街道** |
| Hongqiao Lu | 虹桥路 |
| Zhongshan Xi Lu | 中山西路 |

| | |
|---|---|
| **PUDONG** | **浦东** |
| Bund Tourist Tunnel | 外滩人行观光隧道 |
| Century Park | 世纪公园 |
| Jinmao Tower | 金茂大厦 |
| Lujiazui Development Museum | 陆家嘴发展陈列馆 |
| Lujiazui Financial and Trade Zone | 陆家嘴金融贸易区 |
| Natural Wild Insect Kingdom | 上海自然野生昆虫馆 |
| Oriental Pearl Tower | 东方明珠电视塔 |
| Pudong International Airport | 浦东国际机场 |
| Science & Technology Museum | 上海科学馆 |
| Shanghai History Museum | 上海历史博物馆 |
| Shanghai Ocean Aquarium | 海洋馆 |
| **Streets** | **街道** |
| Lujiazui Lu | 陆家嘴 |
| Shiji Dadao (Century Boulevard) | 世纪大道 |

| | |
|---|---|
| **HONGKOU** | **虹口** |
| Doland: Shanghai Duolun Modern Art Museum | 多伦现代美术馆 |
| Former Residence of Lu Xun | 鲁迅故居 |
| Huoshan Park | 霍山公园 |
| Jewish Refugee Museum | 犹太难民博物馆 |
| Lu Xun Memorial Hall | 鲁迅纪念馆 |
| Lu Xun Park | 鲁迅公园 |
| Ohel Moshe Synagogue | 摩西会堂 |
| **Streets** | **街道** |
| Dongdaming Lu | 东大名路 |
| Duolun Lu | 舵轮路 |
| Huoshan Lu | 霍山路 |

| | |
|---|---|
| **TRIPS OUT OF TOWN** | **周边地区** |
| Hangzhou | 杭州 |
| Moganshan | 莫干山 |
| Putuoshan | 普陀山 |
| Suzhou | 苏州 |
| Tongli | 同里 |
| Wuzhen | 乌镇 |
| Xitang | 西塘 |
| Zhouzhuang | 周庄 |
| Zhujiajiao | 朱家角 |

# Shanghai

**All Time Out Guides are written by a team of local experts, with a unique insider perspective. They contain comprehensive arts and cultural coverage, along with hundreds of independent reviews. For every destination, our critics identify the best, the worst, the most fashionable and the most overrated. All hotels, restaurants, bars and sights now marked on maps.**

**Time Out Shanghai** plunges deep into the economic powerhouse of 21st-century China, sizing up the shiny malls and the cut-price markets, the hippest restaurants and the best dumplings joints, the luxe spas and the no-frills massage parlours – and everything in between. It also guides you to nearby canal towns, pristine gardens and misty islands.

'The most thorough entry into the heart of China's new revolution'
The Sunday Times

'Honest, authoritative, encyclopaedic, incisive and, most importantly, always written by locals… these are definitely the best, most comprehensive city guides in print today'
The Independent

'These books are the most hip and culturally savvy I've used'
The New York Times

'Fantastic, au courant listings of hotels and restaurants'
Food & Wine

Selected as best Shanghai guidebook by The Sunday Times.

Cover photography
Grand Hyatt
zefa/J.Raga